母亲身份研究读本

A Theoretical Reader in Motherhood

刘 岩 编著

WUHAN UNIVERSITY PRESS

武汉大学出版社

图书在版编目(CIP)数据

母亲身份研究读本/刘岩编著. —武汉:武汉大学出版社,2007.7
 ISBN 978-7-307-05528-5

 Ⅰ.母…　Ⅱ.刘…　Ⅲ.母亲—角色理论—文集　Ⅳ.C913.11-53

中国版本图书馆 CIP 数据核字(2007)第 052110 号

责任编辑:谢群英　　　责任校对:王　建　　　版式设计:詹锦玲

出版发行:**武汉大学出版社**　(430072　武昌　珞珈山)
　　　　　(电子邮件:wdp4@whu.edu.cn　网址:www.wdp.com.cn)
印刷:湖北恒泰印务有限公司
开本:720×1000　1/16　印张:27　字数:454 千字　插页:2
版次:2007 年 7 月第 1 版　　2007 年 7 月第 1 次印刷
ISBN 978-7-307-05528-5/C · 180　　　定价:34.00 元

目　录
A Table of Contents

第二篇 边缘、消音与癫狂
——女性主义框架中的母亲

Part 2 Marginalization, Silencing and Madness
— *Mothers in Feminist Theories*

第三篇 科技、解构与后现代
——后现代语境下的母亲身份

Part 3 Technology, Deconstruction and Postmodernity
— *Motherhood in Postmodern Context*

写在前面
Foreword

我们都是由母亲生育的。

这一事实使得母亲身份问题成为女性主义理论家关注的焦点。母亲身份问题在两性关系以及性别差异问题上占据着举足轻重的地位。

首先,母亲被认为是父权社会所有女性的最终归宿。法国哲学家德·波伏娃曾经指出,"只有通过获得身为母亲的经验,女性才能实现身体的命运;这是她的自然'召唤',因为她整个的有机结构是为繁衍种族而设计的。"[①]美国社会学家、心理学家南茜·乔德罗也认为,"女性拥有广泛意义的、甚至几乎具有排他性的母亲角色,这是对她们生育孩子和哺养孩子能力的一种社会和文化层面上的解读。"[②]德·波伏娃和乔德罗似乎都认为,女性的生理和身体特点经过文化和社会性的诠释之后就确定了女性必然充当母亲的角色。事实上,"女性承担的母亲角色是社会分工中具有普遍性和持久意义的少数要素之一。"[③]既然母亲角色是社会分工,女性似乎就没有太多理由拒绝这一角色。如果一个女性拒绝这一角色,她甚至会面临不被社会接受的窘境。因此,在传统观念下成长起来的许多女性,如果一生中未能生儿育女便会感到自己的生活是彻底失败的[④]。

法国女性主义理论家伊里加蕾指出,母亲身份被认为是父权制度下"女性惟一有价值的命运",它"通常意味着为丈夫、为国家、为男性的文化权力生育子

---

① Simone de Beauvoir, *The Second Sex*, trans., H. M. Parshley (Harmondsworth: Penguin Books Ltd., 1972), p.501.

② Nancy Chodorow, *The Reproduction of Mothering: Psychoanalysis and the Sociology of Gender* (Berkeley, CA: University of California Press, 1978), p.30.

③ Ibid., p.3.

④ 参见 Toril Moi, *What Is a Woman? And Other Essays* (New York: Oxford University Press, 1999), pp.40-41。

女从而延续父系传宗接代的线索。"①母亲身份是女性的命运,这反映出在传统父权价值体系下男性对女性的期待。女性的生育能力是保证男性世系延续的一个很重要的途径,因而也保证了整个父权体制的延续。因此,女人必须做母亲,必须能够生养子女,这对于男人来说至关重要。亚德里安·里奇敏锐地观察到,"女性的'不孕'……(对男人来说)是诅咒",因为"男人需要孩子以巩固他在社会的地位"。从这个意义上说,耶和华那句"生育并繁殖吧"就成为发布给所有女性的一个纯粹父权主义的命令②。里奇在同一本书中还简明地得出结论认为:"没有母亲身份和制度化的异性性行为,父权制就不能延续。"③因此,女性 = 母亲 = 子宫,这个等式就成为最自然、也最有意义的。评论家林恩·哈弗也得出同样的结论,她说:"在父权体制下,做女人就意味着做母亲。"④由于许多女性迟早要做母亲,母亲身份已经成为女性身份的一个极端而终极的代表。

第二,母亲在西方文明中是一个重要的文化象征,"一个强有力的象征,甚至形成了西方思想的主体结构。"⑤在诸多同母亲形象相联系的意义中,最突出的莫过于母亲代表了生命起源这一说法。母亲把生命赋予孩子,通过把孩子带到这个世界中来,母亲给予孩子以生命。事实上,她不仅给予孩子以生命而且还承担大部分养育孩子的责任,尤其是当孩子们年幼的时候。从这个意义上说,母亲代表了生命的开端、人类历史的开端甚至其它所有事情的开端。母亲生育孩子,这一事实更加强了母亲这一称呼所蕴含的生命象征。具悖论性的是,母亲不仅是生命的象征,同时又代表了死亡。由于妇产科学技术的局限,在 20 世纪许多年间,生孩子在很多国家要冒生命的危险。因此,"做母亲是生死攸关的大事。"⑥从另一个角度说,在赋予孩子以生命的同时,母亲也同时决定了他们最终

---

① Luce Irigaray, *Thinking the Difference*, trans., Karin Montin (London: The Athlone Press, 1994), p. 99.

② Adrienne Rich, *Of Woman Born: Motherhood as Experience and Institution* (New York: W. W. Norton & Company Inc., 1976), p. 119.

③ Ibid., p. 43.

④ Lynne Huffer, *Maternal Pasts, Feminist Futures: Nostalgia, Ethics, and the Question of Difference* (Stanford, CA: Stanford University Press, 1998), p. 15.

⑤ Ibid., p. 7.

⑥ Nancy Chodorow, *Feminism and Psychoanalytic Theory* (New Haven, CT: Yale University Press, 1989), p. 86.

的死亡命运。无人能逃脱这一命运，每个人从一出生起就踏上了朝向同一目标的旅程。因此，母亲是源头，也是回归之所①。这样说来，母亲孕育了整个生命周期。在西方文化中，母亲的形象经常同丰饶、生产、起源以及死亡相关的事物联系在一起，或是与具有容器形状的事物联系在一起。常见的意象包括大海、水、地球、自然、夜晚、洞穴和地狱。

第三，对母亲身份的表现反映了精神分析理论和女性主义的根本分歧。在《图腾与禁忌》中，弗洛伊德提出了一个后来统治了整个西方思想理论体系的假说，即西方文明基于父亲的牺牲：图腾父亲被一群嫉妒的兄弟所杀，这些兄弟后来又平均瓜分了女人。弗洛伊德援引弗雷泽的神话叙述，把神话仪式和活动解释为男性世系的起源。他说："毫无疑问，在基督神话中，原罪是针对上帝这一圣父所犯下的。"②弗洛伊德对古典神话的诠释表明了他对人类文明的态度，这个文明显然是父权主义的③。伊里加蕾敏锐地意识到这一点恰恰是弗洛伊德理论的基础，因而直接反驳弗氏的这一假说。在1982年5月于蒙特利尔召开的以"女性与疯狂"为主题的研讨会上，伊里加蕾提出西方文明不是基于杀父，而是基于杀母。她说，"当弗洛伊德在《图腾与禁忌》一书中描述杀父是建构原始人群的理论的时候，他忽略了一个更为古老的谋杀，即杀母，这才是建构某种秩序的基础。"④在随后不久接受美国记者采访时，伊里加蕾又重申了她的主张。她说："整个西方文化基于杀母。"⑤谋杀母亲来维持男性秩序，这是西方文明的基础。伊里加蕾所说的谋杀不是消灭物质意义上的母亲，而是把母亲从权力中心驱除，使母亲的话语无法表达，母亲的欲望受到压制。

---

① Lynne Huffer, *Maternal Pasts, Feminist Futures: Nostalgia, Ethics, and the Question of Difference* (Stanford, CA: Stanford University Press, 1998), p.7.

② Sigmund Freud, *Totem and Taboo*, trans., James Strachey (London: Routledge & Kegan Paul, 1950), p.154.

③ Juliet Mitchell, *Psychoanalysis and Feminism: A Radical Reassessment of Freudian Psychoanalysis* (London: Penguin Books, 1974), p.366.

④ Luce Irigaray, "The Bodily Encounter with the Mother," trans., David Macey, *The Irigaray Reader*, ed., Margaret Whitford (Cambridge, Mass.: Blackwell Publishers, 1991), p.36.

⑤ Luce Irigaray, "Women-Mothers, the Silent Substratum of the Social Order," trans., David Macey, *The Irigaray Reader*, ed., Margaret Whitford (Cambridge, Mass.: Blackwell Publishers, 1991), p.47.

性别差异可以追溯到母亲在男性和女性话语中的不同表现,对母亲的表现导致了一系列其它相关问题,如:如何看待女性的生育能力,男孩和女孩如何以自己的方式看待母亲,母亲是否以同样的态度对待男孩和女孩,以及同一个母亲关照下成长的不同性别的孩子如何获得自己不同的性别身份等等。因此,讨论母亲身份成为处理性别关系问题的立足点。

由于母亲的生活是一种特殊形式的女性生活,母亲所面临的问题是许多女性将要以不同方式面对的。从这个意义上说,理解母亲就是理解女性。①

本书选取了20篇西方学界关于母亲身份的研究文章或著作节选,按照内容分为三篇排列。

第一篇,"自然召唤与家庭化——西方文明中的母性传统"。本篇选取的6篇文章或著作节选聚焦父权体制对女性承担母亲这一社会角色的期待,在传统父权社会,女性作为母亲成为一种自然的召唤,女性因而被禁锢在家庭。

第二篇,"边缘、消音与癫狂——女性主义框架中的母亲"。本篇选取的9篇文章或著作节选从女性主义立场出发展现母亲身份如何把女性从父权秩序中边缘化,母亲的话语如何被压抑,母亲形象如何被塑造成疯狂的异类。

第三篇,"科技、解构与后现代——后现代语境下的母亲身份"。本篇选取的5篇文章或著作节选从多元视角探讨后现代背景下母亲身份的解构以及生育技术对传统母亲身份、家庭结构、两性关系构成的挑战。

每一篇中的文章或著作节选按照发表的时间顺序排列,以方便读者了解西方理论家在母亲身份问题上所持主要观点的发展和演变历程。第二篇中法国女性主义理论著作排列在美国女性主义理论著作之前,以方便读者观照这两组理论内部的相似和之间的差异。

选文末的注释均为原作者/编者所加。

---

① 关于母亲在西方文明中的象征意义以及母亲身份在性别关系中的核心作用,参阅刘岩著,《西方现代戏剧中的母亲身份研究》(中国书籍出版社,2004年),第3~39页。

第一篇
Part 1

自然召唤与家庭化
——西方文明中的母性传统

Natural Calling and Domestication
— The Maternal Tradition in Western Civilization

本篇收入的6部著作节选从不同侧面描述母亲在传统父权体制中所处的地位、应该承担的责任以及男性视野中的母性、母职与母道。6位作者或者从自身的女性经验和母亲经历出发,或者借用其他女性作家对女性经验的描述,对男性给予女性的期待进行了剖析和批判。她们认为,在西方文明传统中,女性做母亲被视为女性独特的生理机制向她们发出的"自然召唤",生理性别决定了男女两性的所有差异。这样的性别劳动分工不仅把女性/母亲束缚在了家庭范畴,而且也促使女性/母亲不得不背负着养育孩子方面的不利指责。

波伏娃的"母亲"选自她的压卷之作《第二性》,作者描述女性在怀孕过程中经历的心理和生理变化,解释男孩和女孩对母亲生活的不同意义,认为在做母亲的过程中,女人完成了上天赋予她的自然使命。亚德里安·里奇同样认为母性是对女性发出的神圣召唤(选自《生于女性》中的"神圣的召唤"),然而,制度化的母性束缚了女性的发展潜

力,母性经历被男性利用为父权制度服务。在从同一部书中节选的
"母性的家庭化"中,里奇通过追溯人类历史论述了母亲形象蕴含的
神性逐渐消失、母亲被局限在家庭的过程。南茜·乔德罗的"女性为
什么做母亲"选自她的代表著作《母性角色的再生》,该文指出,女性
注定要承担母亲角色,这是性别劳动分工中最为普遍的要素之一。在
与苏珊·康特拉托合著的"完美母亲的幻想"(选自《女性主义与精神
分析理论》)中,作者阐明父权体制下的母亲常常被妖魔化或被理想
化。林恩·哈弗所著《母性的过去,女性主义的未来》中节选的"母性
的过去"集中讨论了母亲在西方文明中具有的象征意义。

1 西蒙·德·波伏娃,"母亲"
Simone de Beauvoir,"Mother"

西蒙·德·波伏娃(Simone de Beauvoir)于 1949 年发表的《第二性》(*Le deuxième sexe*;*The Second Sex*,英译者 H. M. Parshley,1953 年)问世距今已有半个多世纪。毫不夸张地说,这本书是 20 世纪最有影响的著作之一。它从根本上改变了女性对自身的认识,对男性的认识以及对自己所处的社会关系的认识。它唤醒了无数女性长期沉睡的自主意识,成为一部里程碑式的作品。"没有一本书如此深刻地影响了全世界妇女的处境和地位。"①更令世人瞩目的是,波伏娃的一生都在亲身实践着自己的理论和主张。

1908 年 1 月 9 日,波伏娃出生在巴黎一个中产阶级家庭,她的全名是西蒙·欧内斯廷·露西·玛丽·伯兰特·德·波伏娃。波伏娃曾这样解释自己的名字:"西蒙"的意思是漂亮,"欧内斯廷"是为了纪念祖父,"露西"是外祖母的名字,"玛丽"是为了歌颂圣母玛丽亚,而"伯兰特"则是她的姓氏②。波伏娃的父亲是一位律师,但一直倾心戏剧。母亲是一位虔诚的天主教徒。在这样一个信仰和观念发生严重冲突的家庭中成长起来的波伏娃从小就表示不再信仰上帝而要自己驾驭人生。她在晚年更是认为,宗教给人提供了逃避真理和逃避现实的借口③。她渐渐地喜欢独处,喜欢亲近大自然。既然人是不能永生的,那就更应该享受现世的快乐并在有限的范围内发挥自己的才能。

---

① 萨莉·J·肖尔茨著,龚晓京译,《波伏娃》,中华书局,汤姆森学习出版集团,2002 年,第 1 页。

② 同上,第 8 页。

③ http://www. webster. edu/~woolflm/women. html, n. p.

1926 年,波伏娃在索邦神学院(Sorbonne)学习文学和哲学,哲学家莫里斯·梅洛－庞蒂(Maurice Merleau-Ponty)和人类学家克劳德·莱维－斯特劳斯(Claud Lévi-Strauss)都曾是她的老师。她还结识了一些颇有个性但名声不佳的年轻人,这其中就包括后来成为波伏娃一生的挚友和知己的让－保罗·萨特(Jean-Paul Sartre)。波伏娃和萨特持续了一生的友谊,他们坦诚地对待自己和朋友,不隐瞒观点,相互尊敬,这样平等的爱情观被后人传为佳话。1931 年,波伏娃接受了马赛一家公立学校的教职,一边教书一边写作。1945 年,她同萨特、梅洛－庞蒂创办了《现代》(*Les Temps Moderns*)杂志。由于波伏娃在经济上是独立的,因而她同萨特以及其他异性朋友的关系非常平等。但由于害怕生活受到婚姻的局限,波伏娃拒绝了萨特的求婚。波伏娃不甘心囿于传统观念,这使她在保持同萨特亲密关系的同时又把自己的学生奥尔加·科萨基维克兹(Olga Kosakiewics)拉进了他们的关系之中。他们经常彻夜不眠探讨哲学问题。此后,波伏娃开始关注有关人类自由和世界和平的重大问题,并在 49 岁时完成了陆续写作了十几年的自传《一个规矩少女的回忆》(*Memoirs of a Dutiful Daughter*)。

此后,波伏娃到葡萄牙、突尼斯、意大利、瑞士、中国、前苏联、古巴、日本、巴西、美国、埃及、以色列等国游历和讲学,把自己的哲学思想和自由主张传播到世界各地,这使得她的著作在全世界拥有了广泛的读者。20 世纪 60 年代,波伏娃积极参与妇女解放运动,在堕胎和性暴力等敏感问题上维护女性权利。1980 年 4 月 15 日,萨特逝世。这对波伏娃是沉重的打击。她用《与萨特告别》(*Adieux: A Farewell to Sartre*)来表达对这位挚友的怀念。1986 年 4 月 14 日,波伏娃逝世。据说有近 5 000 人参加了她的葬礼,更有无数的人为她的辞世而哭泣①。

波伏娃重要的著作包括:《人总有一死》(*All Men Are Mortal*, 1946 年)、《建立一种模棱两可的伦理学》(*The Ethics of Ambiguity*, 1948 年)、《环境的压力》(*Force of Circumstances*, 1964 年)、《岁月将至》(*Coming of Age*, 1972

---

① 萨莉·J·肖尔茨著,龚晓京译,《波伏娃》,中华书局,汤姆森学习出版集团,2002年,第 24 页。

年)、《所说的和所做的》(*All Said and Done*, 1974 年)、《当灵魂首先到来》(*When Things of the Spirit Come First*, 1982 年)。

波伏娃是一位存在主义哲学家,她对萨特思想的影响恐怕很难过于夸大,因为萨特对她思想的启迪同样不能低估。存在主义不仅仅是一种哲学,更重要的,它还是一种世界观和人生态度。存在主义摈弃现有的制度,质疑其合法性和合理性,主张每一个个体主动地选择适合自己的价值体系。波伏娃把这种观念应用到自己生活的各个方面。身为女人,波伏娃更清楚、更真切地感受到社会对女性的歧视以及现有的制度对女性发展构成的局限。她在自传中这样说:"我确实不遗憾我是个女人;相反,这种性别给予我很大的满足感。我的成长经历使我确信,我的性别意味着智力低下,这是一个被许多女人承认的事实。……我认为我自己是'一颗女人的心和一个男人的头脑'的结合。我是独一无二的——惟一的一个。"

《第二性》的创作始于 1945 年,从构思到完稿经历了两年多的时间。1948 年 2 月,《第二性》的第一章《女人与神话》在《现代》杂志连载。1949 年 6 月,第一卷"事实与神话"由伽里马出版社出版。与此同时,《现代》杂志又开始连载第二卷的部分章节。1949 年 11 月,第二卷"当代女性"也由伽里马出版社出版。该书出版之初曾轰动一时,但很快被查禁。它对当时社会道德冲击之猛烈使它受到的批评、责难、曲解多于颂扬和赞誉①。该书于 1953 年被译成英语后,影响更为广泛,美国女权主义者甚至把它称为西方女性的《圣经》②。一些学者已经指出,H. M. Parshley 翻译的英译本有许多讹误和删节。但截至目前仍没有另一部更好的英译本问世③。在我国《第二性》中译本译者为陶铁柱,该书由中国

---

① 吴康如著,《〈第二性〉写作动机与出版始末》,载荒林主编《两性视野》,知识出版社,2003 年,第 97 页。

② 同上,第 99 页。

③ 关于学者对英译本的指责,参见陈欢著,《"正本清源"女性"圣经"》,载《中华读书报》,2004 年 8 月 4 日第 3 版。

书籍出版社于 1998 年出版①。

波伏娃在该书序言中说:"女人完全是男人所制定的那种人,所以她被称为'性',其含义是,她在男人面前主要是作为性存在的。对他来说她就是性——绝对是性,丝毫不差。……她是附属的人,是同主要者相对立的次要者。他是主体,是绝对,而她则是他者。"②这段话精彩地概括了波伏娃对男女两性存在状态的差异所做的观察。

《第二性》共分两卷。第一卷"事实与神话"从生物学、历史学和神话传说(文学)的角度分别追溯了女性被压迫的发展历程。第二卷"当代女性"则论述女性被压迫的现实已经衍变为一种体制。在这一卷中,波伏娃从女孩、少女、妻子、母亲、中老年妇女这几个女性经历的人生阶段剖析女性如何丧失了自我身份,而逐步屈从于男性为她们设定的社会角色中,使她们成为相对于男性而存在的"他者"(Other)。波伏娃还没有忘记讨论妓女、修女、情妇、同性恋女性这样一些特殊的女性人群。

波伏娃在第一卷中从生物学、精神分析学和历史唯物主义的角度对女性所处的第二性的社会地位进行追溯和分析。她认为,女人并不是天生就是女人的,而是通过不断按照社会对其性别的期望来塑造自己而逐渐成长为现在这个样子的。这一在当时看来非常激进的观点呼应着萨特的论断,人应该超越社会赋予我们的角色而深入观察我们的本质③。波伏娃主张,社会——父权社会——对女性的期望限制了女性的自由。曾经使许多女性引以为骄傲的母亲身份在波伏娃的著作中也受到质疑。"女人并不是生就的,而宁可说是逐渐形成的"。这一著名论断成为女性主义者反对以弗洛伊德为代表的本质主义者的口号。波伏娃还说:"并不是女性的低下地位造成了她们在历史上的微不足道,而是她们在历史上的微不足道导致了低下的地位。"她还指出,女

---

① 关于其它中译本以及即将出版的由波伏娃法语原著译出的中译本情况,参见陈欢著,《"正本清源"女性"圣经"》,载《中华读书报》,2004 年 8 月 4 日第 3 版。

② 西蒙·德·波伏娃著,《第二性》,陶铁柱译,中国书籍出版社,2004 年,第 4～5 页。

③ http://www.sonoma.edu/users/d/daniels/exphil/Simone_de_Beauvoir.html, n. p.

性和其它被压迫社会群体不同，她们从来没有强烈的团结意识，因为她们缺乏共同的居住地。这使得她们无法分享共同的文化或传统，虽然长期以来忍受压迫但却没有能够对此形成深刻的认识。

多数学者认为，《第二性》包含了波伏娃的存在主义思想，这尤其表现在她关于女性是他者的定位和描述。但也有学者通过研究波伏娃在 1927 年前后的日记说明波伏娃早在遇到萨特前就已经熟知哲学上自我与他者的二元对立关系，这一影响更多地来自哲学家柏格森（Henri Bergson）①。而波伏娃后来投身于女性的解放运动，其影响来自美国作家理查德・赖特（Richard Wright）②，后者作品中表现出的对受压迫黑人女性的同情为波伏娃提供了分析女性受压迫地位的活生生的样板③。

虽然《第二性》举世瞩目的地位不容动摇，但波伏娃自己却谦虚地说世界范围的女权运动并不是由这本书引发的④。她承认写作这本书使她认识了自己的生活，她的出身使她可以同男性平起平坐地讨论文学、艺术、哲学，而许多女性还没有这样的特权。女性作为一个阶层仍然处于受压迫的地位。虽然她知道在有生之年无法看到女性充分享有同男性的平等权利，但波伏娃对未来充满信心，因为"女性之间已经开始建立真正的友谊"，这种友谊基于姐妹之情，而不是一种同性恋友情。近年来虽然一些学者对波伏娃的理论假说——男性是规范，女性被父权体制定义为"非男"——提出质疑，但她观察到的文学作品中对女性形象的贬低却是有目共睹的事实。

本书选注的"母亲"出自《第二性》第二卷，是全书的第十七章，列在第五部"处境"之下。这是该书"最有争议性"的一章⑤。波伏娃开篇就说："女人是在

---

① 柏格森（1859～1941），法国哲学家。他对于时间的重新定义奠定了现代主义的重要理论基础。

② 赖特（1908～1960），美国黑人小说家，代表著作有《土生子》（*Native Son*，1940）。

③ 参见 Margaret A. Simons，"Is *The Second Sex* Beauvoir's Application of Sartrean Existentialism?" http://www.bu.edu/wcp/Papers/Gend/GendSimo.htm，n. p.。

④ Simone de Beauvoir，"Interview with Simone de Beauvoir"，Interviewed by John Gerassi，*Society*（Jan.-Feb.，1976），引自 http://www.marxists.org/reference/subject/philosophy/works/fr/debeauvoir-1976.htm，n. p. 本段观点均引自该访谈。

⑤ 萨莉・J・肖尔茨著，龚晓京译，《波伏娃》，中华书局，汤姆森学习出版集团，2002年，第87页。

做母亲时,实现她的生理命运的;这是她的自然'使命',因为她的整体机体结构,都是为了适应物种繁衍。"①波伏娃把母性看做一种社会结构化的体验,这种体验只有在女性地位发生变化时才能自由的实现②。根据内容这一章可以分为三个部分。

在第一部分,波伏娃主要讨论堕胎和避孕这两种人工阻止怀孕的手段。她指出,女性的生育功能并不是生物学上的偶然,而是人类社会长期选择的结果。女性的经济地位影响社会对其堕胎的看法,而从道德意义上讲,堕胎是对男性道德体系的挑战,因为女性可以在一定程度上决定自己是否怀孕:"避孕和合法堕胎使女性可以自由地选择怀孕与否(第550页)。"普遍来讲男性是禁止堕胎的,但他们却会把它视为解决麻烦的捷径(第549页)。

第二部分讲述女性在怀孕过程中经历的心理和生理变化。波伏娃指出,女性在不同成长阶段对怀孕所持观点也有所不同。对于小女孩来说,怀孕是一个奇迹或是一场游戏;对于青春期少女,怀孕则成为一种危险。一些女性对怀孕既渴望又焦虑,这种复杂的情感往往伴随女性一生(第550~551页)。波伏娃这样描述怀孕对女性的影响:

> 最为重要的是,怀孕是在女性身体内部上演的一出戏。她觉得这既是一种丰富又是一种伤害;胎儿是她身体的一部分,又是靠她的身体喂养的寄生物。她既占有他,又为他所占有。他象征未来,当怀着他时,她觉得自己和世界一样浩瀚。然而也正是这种富足消灭了她,她感觉自己现在什么也不是了。新的生命即将出现,并将证明他自己有权独立存在,她为此而自豪,但她也觉得自己被抛来抛去,成为某种黑暗力量的玩物。……孕妇成了大

---

① Simone de Beauvoir, *The Second Sex*, trans. H. M. Parshley (Alfred A. Knopf, Inc., 1952), p.550. 本节所引波伏娃观点除特别说明均出自 Parshley 所译《第二性》,以下只在正文标明页码,分号后第二个页码为引文在本书的页码。尽管有学者指出,Parshley"没有受过专业的哲学训练,缺乏对存在主义、女性主义和当时法国思潮的认识,把原著中的这部分内容简化甚至删掉了",但截至目前,Parshley 的译作仍然是波伏娃著作最为权威的英译本。参见陈欢著,《"正本清源"女性"圣经"》,载《中华读书报》,2004 年 8 月 4 日第 3 版。中译文参考了陶铁柱译本。

② 萨莉·J·肖尔茨著,龚晓京译,《波伏娃》,中华书局,汤姆森学习出版集团,2002年,第 6 页。

自然的俘虏，她是植物和动物，是储备着的胶质，是孵卵器，是卵子。（第553页）

紧接着，波伏娃详细分析了女性在怀孕不同阶段时的感受和态度。

第三部分讲述女性在完成生育孩子任务之后、在抚养孩子成长过程中的体验。一些女性认为生育孩子赋予她们创造力，她们感觉自己完成了一项自觉自愿的、富有创造性的任务。另一些女性则恰恰相反，她们感觉自己异常被动，受苦受难受尽折磨（第565~566页）。但不管怎样，每一位年轻母亲对出生的婴儿都怀有一种好奇，许多母亲对所承担的哺育婴儿的责任感到惊讶，一些人甚至认为自己同婴儿的关系是一种动物间的亲密关系。波伏娃认为，女性欣然地把婴儿视做阴茎的对等物，这一说法并不准确（第571页；第10页）。"对于女性来说，婴儿相当于她留给丈夫但丈夫却无法代表的情人。"这种描述虽然也并不能涵盖所有的情况，但一般来讲，母亲可以在婴儿身上得到一种肉体的富足感：不是屈从而是统治。"通过孩子，她得到了男人想从女人身上想得到的东西：他者。他集自然和理智于一身，他是猎物又是替身（第571页；第11页）。"随着孩子的成长，女性的心理也随之发生变化：

母子关系变得越来越复杂：孩子是替身，是第二自我［alter ego］。有时母亲很想把自己完全投射到他身上，但他却是一个独立的主体，因而难以驾驭。他如今无比真实，但在想象中他又是未来的少年和成人。他是财富和宝藏，但也是她的负担和暴君。母亲从他那儿得到的快活是一种慷慨，她必须通过为他服务、给予和使他幸福，才能得到自己的快活……。（第572页；第11~12页）

在谈到何谓母性（maternity）时，波伏娃这样说："母性通常是顾影自怜、无私利他、白日幻梦、真心诚意、信仰不坚、虔诚奉献和愤世嫉俗等品质的奇怪组合"（第573页；第12页）。波伏娃认为，女性对生活的不满促使她通过儿子寻求补偿，这样看来，母亲打孩子不仅仅是在打孩子，她是在对男人、对世界甚至对她自己实施报复（第573页；第13页）。一些母亲恰恰相反，她们把自己变成孩子的奴隶，以此填补空虚的心灵，惩罚自己未曾表露出的敌意（第574页；第13页）。

波伏娃清楚地区别儿子和女儿对母亲处境和心态产生的不同影响。她说，

许多女性都希望生一个儿子,因为

> 儿子可以成为男人中的领袖,成为士兵和创造者。他会让世界服从他的意志,而母亲也将分享这一不朽的英名。儿子将给母亲带来她未曾建造的房屋,未曾开垦的土地,未曾读过的书籍。通过他,母亲将拥有世界——惟一的条件是她拥有自己的儿子。(第576页;第16页)

于是,母亲对儿子怀有矛盾的心情:她希望儿子拥有无限的权力,但又希望他在自己的掌控之中,"统领世界却又匍匐在她脚下"(第577页;第16页)。而对于女儿,母亲则把自己身上的一切模糊不清的关系转嫁过去,"在女儿身上,母亲寻找一个复制品"(第577页;第17页)。因此,当女儿长大成人欲寻求独立的时候,母女之间的冲突便激化了。母亲会把女儿的行为视为对自己的背叛,她固执地阻止女儿逃离家庭,她无法容忍女儿成为"一个他者"(第579页;第17页)。通常情况下,受父亲宠爱的长女尤其成为母亲迫害的对象。母亲喜欢独立统治女性世界,无法容忍女儿真正成为自己的复制品。于是,随着女儿的长大,母女之间的冲突愈演愈烈,甚至会爆发公开的战争(第581页;第19页)。

在这一章的最后,波伏娃指出在母亲身份问题上人们通常持有两个错误观点。第一个错误观点认为,母性足以给女性的生活带上桂冠。但真实情况远非如此,母亲角色并不能赋予女性生活以真正意义。第二个错误观点认为,孩子在母亲怀抱里注定是幸福的。事实上,母爱不是天生的,父母双方童年时期的经历、父母之间的矛盾冲突都会给孩子的成长带来阴影。

这里选注的是《第二性》第二卷第十七章"母亲"一节的第571～577,579～581页,所选段落隶属该节第三部分。

The Mother

It has been asserted time and again that woman is pleased to acquire in the infant an equivalent of the penis, but this is by no means an exact statement. The fact is that the grown man no longer sees in his penis a wonderful toy as in childhood; the value it has for the adult lies in the desirable objects it enables him to possess. Similarly, the adult woman envies the male the prey he takes possession of, not the instrument by which he takes it. The infant satisfies that aggressive eroticism which is not fully satisfied in the male embrace; the infant corresponds, for the woman, to the mistress whom she leaves to the male and whom he does not represent for her. The correspondence is not exact, of course; every relation is *sui generis*, unique; but the mother finds in her infant—as does the lover in his beloved—a carnal plenitude, and this not in surrender but in domination; she obtains in her child what man seeks in woman; another combining nature and mind, who is to be both prey and *double*. The baby incarnates all nature. Colette Audry's heroine tells us that she found in her child "a skin for the touch of my fingers that fulfilled the promise of all kittens, all flowers." The infant's flesh has that softness, that warm elasticity, which the woman, when she was a little girl, coveted in her mother's flesh and, later, in things everywhere. The baby is plant and animal, in its eyes are rains and rivers, the azure of sea and sky; its fingernails are coral, its hair a silky growth; it is a living doll, a bird, a kitten; "my flower, my pearl, my chick, my lamb." The mother murmurs almost a lover's words, and like a lover she makes avid use of the possessive case; she employs the same gestures of possession; caresses, kisses; she hugs her child to her bosom, she keeps him warm in her arms and in her bed. Sometimes these relations are of a clearly sexual kind. In the confession already cited from Stekel, the mother says she felt ashamed because her nursing had a sexual tinge and her baby's touches made her shiver delightfully; when two years old he caressed her like a lover, almost irresistibly, and she had to fight the temptation to toy with his penis.

Maternity takes on a new aspect when the child grows older; at first it is only a baby like any other, it exists only in its generality, one example of a class; then little by little it takes on individuality. Women of very domineering or very sensual disposition then grow cool toward the child; and at this time, on the contrary, certain others—like Colette—begin to take a real interest in their offspring. The relation of mother to child becomes more and more complex: the child is a double, an *alter ego*, into whom the mother is sometimes tempted to project herself entirely, but he is an independent subject and therefore rebellious; he is intensely real today, but in imagination he is the adolescent and adult of the future. He is a rich possession, a treasure, but also a charge upon her, a tyrant. The mother's joy in him is one of generosity; she must find her pleasure in serving, giving, making him happy, like the mother described by Colette, Audry:

> *So he enjoyed a happy childhood, such as one reads of in books; but it was like the childhood of books as real roses resemble roses on postcards. And this happiness of his flowed from me as did the milk on which I had fed him.*

Like the woman in love, the mother is delighted to feel herself necessary; her existence is justified by the wants she supplies; but what gives mother love its difficulty and its grandeur is the fact that it implies no reciprocity; the mother has to do not with man, a hero, a demigod, but with a small, prattling soul, lost in a fragile and dependent body. The child is in possession of no values, he can bestow none, with him the woman remains alone; she expects no return for what she gives, it is for her to justify it herself. This generosity merits the laudation that men never tire of conferring upon her; but the distortion begins when the religion of Maternity proclaims that all mothers are saintly. For while maternal devotion may be perfectly genuine, this, in fact, is rarely the case. Maternity is usually a strange mixture of narcissism, altruism, idle daydreaming, sincerity, bad faith, devotion, and cynicism.

The great danger which threatens the infant in our culture lies in the fact that the mother to whom it is confided in all its helplessness is almost always a discontented woman: sexually she is frigid or unsatisfied; socially she feels herself inferior to man; she has no independent grasp on the world or on the future. She will seek to compensate for all these frustrations through her child. When it is realized how difficult woman's present situation makes her full self-realization, how many desires, rebellious feelings, just claims she nurses in secret, one is frightened at the thought that defenseless infants are abandoned to her care. Just as when she coddled and tortured her dolls by turns, her behavior is symbolic; but symbols become grim reality for her child. A mother who whips her child is not beating the child alone; in a sense she is not beating it at all: she is taking her vengeance on a man, on the world, or on herself. Such a mother is often remorseful and the child may not feel resentment, but it feels the blows.

This cruel aspect of maternity has always been known, but it has in the past been hypocritically attributed to the figure of the cruel stepmother, punishing the offspring of a "good" mother who is dead. In recent literature the "bad" mother has been frequently portrayed, and if such types seem somewhat exceptional, it is because most women have the morality and decency to repress their spontaneous impulses; nevertheless these impulses suddenly flash out at times in angry scenes, slaps, punishments, and the like. Along with the mothers who are frankly sadistic, there are many who are especially capricious and domineering; now they treat the child as a doll, now as an obedient little slave; if vain, they show it off; if jealous, they hide it away. Frequently they expect too much in the way of gratitude for their care. When Cornelia displayed her children and said "these are my jewels," she set an evil example for posterity; too many mothers hope to repeat this proud gesture and do not hesitate to sacrifice the ordinary little individual who is not fulfilling their hopes. They try to make him like, or unlike, their husbands, or they wish him to resemble other, admired relatives; they try to make him in the image of some hero. Such tyranny is harmful to the child and always disappointing to the mother. This educational obstinacy and the capricious sadism already referred to are often combined; the mother excuses her outbursts of anger by the pretext that she wants to "train" the child; and her lack of success in this enterprise increases her hostility.

Another common attitude, and one not less ruinous to the child, is masochistic devotion, in which the mother makes herself the slave of her offspring to compensate for the emptiness of her heart and to punish herself for her unavowed hostility. Such a mother is morbidly anxious, not allowing her child out of her sight; she gives up all diversion, all personal life, thus assuming the role of victim; and she derives from these sacrifices the right to deny her child all independence. This renunciation on the mother's part is easily reconciled with a tyrannical will to domination; the *mater dolorosa* forges from her sufferings a weapon that she uses sadistically; her displays of resignation give rise to guilt feelings in the child which often last a lifetime: they are still more harmful than her displays of aggression. Tossed this way and that, baffled, the child can find no defensive position: now blows, now tears, make him out a criminal.

The main excuse of the mother is that her child by no means provides that happy self-fulfillment which has been promised her since her own childhood; she blames him for the deception of which she has been the victim and which he innocently exposes. She did as she pleased with her dolls; when she helped a sister or a friend with a baby, the responsibility was not hers. But now society, her husband, her mother, and her own pride hold her to account for that little strange life, as if it were all her doing. Her husband, in particular, is irritated by the child's faults as he is by a spoiled dinner or the misconduct of his wife; his unreasonable demands often affect adversely the relation of mother to child. An independent woman—thanks to her solitary state, her freedom from care, or her authority in the house—will be much more serene in mind than one subject to domineering demands to which she must accede willy-nilly in forcing the child to accede.

For the great difficulty is to bring within preconceived patterns an existence as mysterious as that of an animal, as turbulent and disorderly as natural forces, and yet human. One can neither train a child without talking, as one trains a dog, nor make him listen to the reason through the use of adult words; and he takes advantage of this situation by answering words with animal-like sobs or tantrums and by opposing restraints with impertinent words.

The problem thus offered is certainly challenging, and the mother who has time for it enjoys her educational function: quietly settled in the park, she finds the child still as good an excuse for taking her ease as he was during pregnancy; often, being more or less infantile herself, she is very well pleased to be silly along with him, renewing the games and words, the interests and joys, of her own early days. But when the mother is busy with washing, cooking, nursing another baby, marketing, and entertaining guests, and particularly when she is occupied with her husband, the child is merely harassing and bothersome. She has no leisure for "training" him; the main thing is to prevent him from getting into trouble; he is always breaking or tearing or dirtying and is a constant danger to objects and to himself; he is on the go, he cries, he talks, he makes a noise. He is living his life on his own account, and this life of his disturbs that of his parents. Their interests and his do not mesh, and that causes all the trouble. Forever burdened with him, his parents constantly impose sacrifices he does not understand: he is sacrificed to their peace and quiet and also to his own future. Quite naturally he rebels. He does not comprehend the explanations his mother tries to give him, for she cannot penetrate into his consciousness; his dreams, his fears, his obsessions, his desires, make up a world into which she cannot see: the mother can only regulate from outside, blindly, an individual who finds her irrelevant rules an absurd imposition.

When the child grows older, this lack of comprehension remains: he enters a world of interests and values from which his mother is excluded; often enough he scorns her on that account. The boy especially, proud of his masculine prerogatives, laughs at orders from a woman: she insists on his attending to his duties, but she does not know how to solve his assigned problems or translate his Latin: she cannot keep up with him. The mother sometimes wears herself out to the point of tears in this thankless task. Its difficulty is seldom realized by her husband: it is the attempt to control a being with whom you are not in communication and who is none the less a human being, to obtrude yourself upon an independent stranger who is defined and affirmed only in revolting against you.

The situation varies according to the sex of the child; and though it is more difficult when a boy is concerned, the mother normally makes a better adjustment to it. Because of the prestige attributed to men by women, as well as the advantages they actually have, many women prefer to have sons. "How wonderful to bring a man into the world!" they say; we have seen that they dream of engendering a "hero," and the hero is obviously of the male sex. A son will be a leader of men, a soldier, a creator; he will bend the world to his will, and his mother will share his immortal fame; he will give her the houses she has not constructed, the lands she has not explored, the books she has not read. Through him she will possess the world—but only on condition that she possess her son. Thence comes the paradox of her attitude.

Freud holds that the relation between mother and son is the one of least ambivalence; but the fact is that in maternity, as in marriage and the love affair, woman takes an equivocal attitude toward masculine transcendence. If her experience in marriage or in love has made her hostile to man, it will give her satisfaction to domineer over the male reduced to his childish form; she will treat the arrogant sex in an ironical and unceremonious fashion. Sometimes, for example, she will frighten the child by threatening that the mark of his maleness will be cut off unless he behaves. Even if she is humbler, more gentle, and respects in her son the hero of the future, she is forced to reduce him to his present, immanent reality in order to make him really hers: just as she treats her husband as a child, so she treats her child as a baby. It is too rational, too simple, to believe that she would like to castrate her son; her dream is more contradictory: she would have him of unlimited power, yet held in the palm of her hand, dominating the world, yet on his knees before her. She encourages him to be soft, greedy, generous, timid, quiet, she forbids sport and playmates, she makes him lack self-confidence, because she intends to *have him* for herself; but she is disappointed if at the same time he fails to become an adventurer, a champion, a genius worthy of her pride. There is no doubt her influence is often injurious—as Montherlant and other writers have represented it to be. Fortunately for the boy, he can rather easily escape the toils: he is encouraged to do so by tradition and the social group. And the mother herself is resigned to it, for she knows very well that the struggle against man is an unequal one. She consoles herself by playing the part of *mater dolorosa* or by thinking how proud she is to have engendered one of her conquerors.

The little girl comes nearer to being wholly given over to her mother, and the claims of the latter are therefore increased. Their relations are much more dramatic. In her daughter the mother does not hail a member of the superior caste; in her she seeks a double. She projects upon her daughter all the ambiguity of her relation with herself; and when the otherness, the alterity, of this *alter ego* comes to be affirmed, the mother feels herself betrayed. It is between mother and daughter that the conflicts of which I have spoken take aggravated form.

[……]

Real conflicts arise when the girl grows older; as we have seen, she wishes to establish her independence from her mother. This seems to the mother a mark of hateful ingratitude; she tries obstinately to checkmate the girl's will to escape; she cannot bear to have her double become *an other*. The pleasure of feeling absolutely superior—which men feel in regard to women—can be enjoyed by woman only in regard to her children, especially her daughters; she feels frustrated if she has to renounce her privilege, her authority. Whether a loving or a hostile mother, the independence of her child dashes her hopes. She is doubly jealous: of the world, which takes her daughter from her, and of her laughter, who in conquering a part of the world robs her of it.

This jealousy is at first concerned with relations between the little girl and her father. Sometimes the mother makes use of the child to bind her husband to the home; if she fails she is naturally vexed, but if the scheme succeeds, she at once revives her childish complex in inverse form: that is, she is incensed against her daughter as she was formerly against her mother; she sulks, she feels abandoned and misunderstood. A Frenchwoman, married to a foreigner who dearly loved his daughters, one day cried angrily: "I have had enough of this living with aliens!"

Frequently the oldest girl, her father's favorite, is the special object of the mother's persecution. She loads her with disagreeable tasks, requires of her a sobriety beyond her age: since she is a rival, she will be treated as an adult; she, too, will have to learn that "life is no novel, no bed of roses; you can't do as you please, you are not on earth just to have a good time," and so on. Very often the mother slaps the child without rhyme or reason: "That will teach you." For one thing, she means to show that she still has the upper hand—for what is most vexatious is that the mother has no real superiority to oppose to a girl of eleven or twelve; the latter is already able to perform household tasks perfectly, she is "quite a little woman"; she even has a vivacity, a curiosity, and a clear-sightedness that make her in many ways superior to adult women. The mother likes to rule alone over her feminine universe; she wants to be unique, irreplaceable; and now she finds herself reduced by her young helper to the status of one among many who merely perform a general function. She scolds her daughter severely if, after two days' absence, she finds the house in disorder; but she is filled with anger and fear if she finds that the life of the family goes on perfectly well without her. She cannot bear to have her daughter become really her double, a substitute for herself.

It is even more intolerable, however, for her to have her daughter boldly assert herself as an *other*, an independent person. She systematically takes a dislike to the friends among whom her daughter seeks help against family oppression and who "work on her feelings"; she criticizes them, forbids her daughter to see them too often or even to be with them at all, on the pretext that they "have had a bad influence" on her. Any influence that is not hers is bad, but she feels a special animosity toward women of her own age— teachers, mothers of companions—with whom the little girl becomes affectionate; such feelings, she says, are ridiculous or morbid. Sometimes the child's gaiety, heedlessness, games, laughter, are enough to exasperate her. These things are more easily pardoned in boys, for they are enjoying their masculine privileges, as is natural; and she has long since given up a hopeless struggle. But why should her daughter, this other woman, enjoy advantages denied to her? Ensnared in "serious" matters herself, she is envious of all the occupations and amusements that take the girl out of the boredom of the home; this escape gives the lie to all the values to which she has sacrificed herself.

The older the child gets, the more does resentment gnaw at the mother's heart; each year brings her nearer her decline, but from year to year the young body develops and flourishes; it seems to the mother that she is robbed of this future which opens before her daughter. Here is the source of the irritation some women feel when their daughters first menstruate: they begrudge them their being henceforth real women. In contrast with the repetition and routine that are the lot of the older woman, this newcomer is offered possibilities that are still unlimited: it is these opportunities that the mother envies and hates; being unable to obtain them for herself, she often tries to decrease or abolish them. She keeps the girl in the house, watches her, tyrannizes over her; she purposely dresses her like a fright, gives her no leisure time, gets savagely angry if the girl uses make-up, if she "goes out"; all her resentment against life she turns against this young life which is springing toward a new future. She endeavors to humiliate the young girl, she ridicules her ventures, she nags her. Open war is often declared between them. Normally the younger wins, for time works with her; but her victory is tinged with wrongdoing. Her mother's attitude gives rise at the same time to revolt and remorse; the mere presence of her mother makes her a culprit. We have seen how heavily this feeling of guilt can burden her future. Willy-nilly, the mother accepts defeat in the end; when her daughter becomes an adult, a more or less uneasy friendship is established between them. But the one remains forever disappointed and frustrated; the other will often believe that she is under a curse.

2 亚德里安·里奇,"神圣的召唤"
Adrienne Rich, "The 'Sacred Calling'"

"地球上所有的人类生命都由女性孕育。"亚德里安·里奇(Adrienne Rich)在其《生于女性:经历与制度化的母性》(*Of Woman Born: Motherhood as Experience and Institution*)一书的前言有这样一句开场白。这本于 1976 年出版的论著使作者成为女性主义的主要代言人。该书叙述了作者身为女人、诗人、女性主义者和母亲的经历,这一经历由于母性的制度化而受到限制,作者个人的经历也因此具有了普遍意义。"几乎没有任何一部女性主义著作选集不收入她的作品或不讨论她的思想。"①

里奇于 1929 年 5 月 16 日出生于美国马里兰州巴尔的摩市一个中产阶级家庭,从小在父母教育下读书。父亲是约翰·霍普金斯大学的病理学教授,母亲是一位颇有才华的钢琴家、作曲家。童年时的里奇对父亲有更多的认同,敏感地处于父亲的犹太背景与母亲的南方新教主义思想的冲突之中。1951 年里奇从拉德克里夫女子学院(Radcliffe College)毕业,获荣誉毕业生称号。同年,她的第一部诗集《世界的改变》(*A Change of World*)出版并被著名诗人奥登(W. H. Auden)选作耶鲁青年诗人系列。奥登在序言中对里奇诗歌表现出的优雅的技巧和形式主义的风格给予了高度赞扬。20 世纪 50 年代里奇还创作了其它一些诗集,奠定了诗人的地位。1953 年,里奇同哈佛大学一位经济学家阿尔弗莱德·康拉德(Alfred Conrad)结婚,移居马萨诸塞州的剑桥

---

① Deborah Pope, "Adrienne Rich", *The Oxford Companion to Women's Writing in the United States* (Oxford University Press, 1995); http://www. english. uiuc. edu/maps/poets/m_r/rich/bio. htm, n. p.

市生活,并在随后的五年中生养了三个儿子。这五年是她情感经历最为复杂、艰难的时光,她在女性必须承担的家庭角色与自己的创造性艺术才华形成的矛盾中左右徘徊。50 年代的里奇并不能清楚地明白这些问题,因为社会文化大背景对此也没有深入的分析和认知①。

60 年代里奇积极投身于女权活动,对蔓延整个 60 年代的黑人民权运动、反越战运动以及女权运动给予了格外的关注和同情②。她先后创作出《儿媳快像》(*Snapshots of a Daughter-in-Law*, 1963 年)、《生活的必要》(*The Necessities of Life*,1966 年)和《一定要改变》(*The Will to Change*,1971 年)等作品,表达她对女性问题的关注。《儿媳快像》成为她创作生涯的分水岭,她开始用更自由、更独特的语言表现局限、对抗、逃离等人生主题。"走在屋顶的人"("The Roofwalker")中"我没有选择的生活/选择了我"表达出她对生活的无奈。1966 年,她随丈夫迁居纽约,为初到美国的穷人、黑人和第三世界的学生讲授英语课,在这期间,她再次对文化和民族的冲突感到震惊。她对詹姆斯·鲍德温③和西蒙·德·波伏娃的作品产生的共鸣使她更为关注黑人、女性等社会弱势群体。她决定"公开地作为一个女人来写作,创作出女人的身体和经验来"。她没有仅仅成为一个自白派,而是冷静地观察、记录并预言着女性面临的跨文化、跨历史、跨民族的普遍问题——话语优势、伴侣暴力以及同性恋身份④。里奇后来又在一些学院任教职。1976 年起与作家、编辑米歇尔·克里夫(Michelle Cliff)同居。1984 年后定居加利福尼亚。

里奇共创作了 19 部诗集、3 部文集——《论谎言、秘密与沉默》(*On Lies, Secrets and Silence*, 1979 年)、《血液、面包和诗歌》(*Blood, Bread and Poetry*, 1986 年)、《发现了什么:诗歌与政治笔记》(*What Is Found There:*

---

① Ibid., n. p.

② 关于里奇所受的政治影响,参见 Adrienne Rich, "The Possibilities of an Engaged Art: An Interview with Adrienne Rich," Interviewed by Ruth E. C. Prince, http://www. english. uiuc. edu/maps/poets/m_r/rich/onlineints. htm, n. p.。

③ 鲍德温(1924~1987),美国黑人小说家,代表作品有《去到山顶诉说》(*Go Tell It on the Mountain*, 1953 年)和《无人知道我的名字》(*Nobody Knows My Name*, 1961 年)。

④ Adrienne Rich, "The Possibilities of an Engaged Art: An Interview with Adrienne Rich," Interviewed by Ruth E. C. Prince, http://www. english. uiuc. edu/maps/poets/m_r/rich/onlineints. htm, n. p.

Notebooks on Poetry and Politics，1993 年）——以及 1 部论著。她的作品被译成德语、西班牙语、瑞典语、荷兰语、希伯来语、希腊语、日语、意大利语等多国文字。她荣获了许多基金和荣誉:1974 年荣获国家图书奖,两次荣获古根海姆基金,1999 年荣获莱南基金会终生成就奖,还荣获国家诗歌协会授予的杰出页献奖。

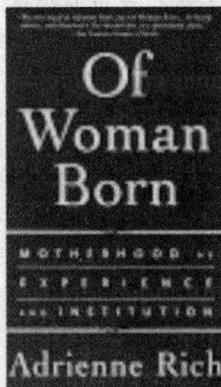

《生于女性:经历与制度化的母性》是里奇于 1976 年出版的一部专门讲述母亲身份的著作,由美国诺顿出版公司出版。这本书截至目前为止仍然是讲述母职(motherhood)、母道(mothering)的最有影响的一部女性主义著作。虽然该书大部分篇幅讲述的是里奇自己身为母亲的经历,但她从人类学、心理学、文学和女性主义视角对自己经历做出的分析使这部著作具有了指导、洞悉母性经历的普遍意义。

亚德里安·里奇在开篇这样说:"地球上所有的人类生命都由女性孕育"[1]。这样的开端奠定了女性母亲身份之独特性。她接着解释说,由于人类比其它哺乳类动物的哺育期长,也由于人类长期以来确立的劳动分工——女性不仅生育、哺乳子女而且还承担着养育子女的几乎全部责任——所以,人们首先是在女性身上认识了关爱与失望、力量与温柔这样一些情感(第 11 页)。

里奇接着描述了男性和女性对待"生于女性"这样一个事实所持的不同态度。首先,女性似乎很自然地接受了自己作为母亲的身份和命运,并把生育子女视为生活的主要内容和人生的基本责任。相比之下,男性却很难接受自己的生命依赖于女性这样的命运。作为父权文化的缔造者、命名者、表述者,男性的一生一直都在否定、弥补"生于女性"的事实(第 11 页)。第二,做父亲意味着提供卵子繁殖和滋养所需的精子,而做母亲却意味着一种持续的状态,至少是长达九个月的怀孕期,此间经历的身体、生理过程都不是天生具备的,而是后天学会并逐步获得的经历和体验(第 12 页)。第三,男人可以在强奸女人之后不负责任地一走了之,而女人却不得不面对流产、自杀、弃婴、杀子或独自养育非婚子女的

---

[1] Adrienne Rich, *Of Woman Born: Motherhood as Experience and Institution* (New York: W. W. Norton & Company Inc., 1976), p.11. 本节所引里奇观点除特别说明均出自此处,以下只在正文标明页码,分号后带二个页码为引文在本书的页码。

艰难选择,而无论女人做何选择,她的身体所经历的变化都是不可逆转的,她未来的生活被这一事件所彻底影响和改变(第12页)。

里奇还讲到她试图在该书中区别母性的两种意义:一种意义反映在任何一位女性具备的同生育能力和子女之间的潜在关系中;另一种意义表现在保证这样的潜在关系以及所有女性都处于男性控制之下的制度上。这两种意义相互影响,而后一种是大多数社会和政治体制的基石。虽然在某些文化传统中,女人的生育能力赋予了她们一种神秘的力量,让人们对女性产生敬畏和尊敬,甚至在社会生活中拥有表达意见的权利,但在有记录的大多数人类历史中,"制度化的母性束缚并贬低了女性的潜能"(第13页)。

里奇说,母亲的力量表现在两个方面:其一,母亲具有生育人类生命的生理潜能;其二,男性赋予母亲某种神秘力量,他们要么把女性当做女神一样崇拜,要么害怕被女性控制和湮没(第13页)。但事实上,女性的发展潜能在母亲身份上被扼杀了。历史上的许多女性并不是主动充当母亲的,甚至还有无数女性在生育孩子的过程中丧失了自己的生命。

该书共分十章,这里选注的"神圣的召唤"("The 'Sacred Calling'")是《生于女性》一书的第二章。该章共分四部分。

第一部分作者首先援引玛格丽特·桑格(Margaret Sanger)①所著《束缚中的母性》(*Motherhood in Bondage*,1928年)中一位女子寻求帮助的信以说明女性如何愿意完成母亲和妻子双重身份的角色要求。里奇指出,在父权社会,母性经历和性经历都被设计用来为男性利益服务,因此,诸如非法性关系、人工流产、女同性恋行为等对制度构成威胁的行为都被认为不轨或犯罪(第42页;第26页)。里奇还指出,制度化的性爱已经把女性定位为危险的、不贞洁的,是肉欲的象征(第42页;第26页)。"制度化的母性要求女性具有母亲的'本能'而不具有智慧,要求她们无私而不是自我实现,要求她们建立同他人的关系而不是创建自我"(第42页;第26页)。里奇还说,父权制度不仅要求女性承担延续种族所需要的痛苦和自我否定,而且还要求女性对自己的生存状况不加质疑。"没有制度化形式的母性和异性恋关系,父权制度就无法继续"(第43页;第27页)。

在第二部分,里奇开始追溯美国历史,追溯奴隶制下母亲身份的特点。她用

① 桑格(1879~1966)一生致力于控制女性非正常怀孕,她于1916年在美国创建第一家计划生育诊所,1927年在日内瓦组织召开第一届世界人口大会。

大量史实和历史文本说明在奴隶制下,美国妇女——无论是白人拓荒者母亲还是黑人女奴——每日都在全职履行经济生活中的生育功能(第44页;第28页),以至于在19世纪中叶,全职的、排他性的母性身份已经在人们思想中根深蒂固,"家庭"也成为一个具有宗教性的概念(第44页;第28页)。里奇继续用大量历史文本论证母亲如何服务于父权体制的利益。她说,母亲集宗教、社会良知和民族主义等诸多概念于一身。"体制化的母性激发并更新所有其它的体制"(第45页;第29~30页)。里奇还特别提到"家庭中的母亲"往往都有一些众所周知的坏性格,她自己的亲身经历表明,母亲发脾气会为孩子树立"坏榜样"。于是她得出结论说,"母爱被认为是持续的、无条件的。关爱和愤怒不能同时存在。女性的愤怒威胁着母性体制"(第46页;第31页)。

里奇在第三部分首先提出了一个问题:母亲被束缚在家庭、家庭与以挣钱、争斗、理想、挑战、力量为特征的男性世界的分离、家庭与公众的分离,这样一些人类历史发展后期才有的现象到底是从何时开始的呢? 又具有什么样的目的呢? 里奇通过回顾人类有定居生活的历史澄清说,家庭从来不是一个避难所,不是逃避外面残酷社会现实的休闲地,而是世界的中心、工作的中心,是维持生计的单位(第47页;第31页)。由于妇女和儿童是社会运作的有机部分,他们积极参与社会生产,所以此时的母性并不是女人的惟一职业。女性工资低廉,对男性工人构成威胁。于是,两种力量的结合——对儿童成长的人文关怀以及对父权价值观念的恐惧——导致控制妇女劳动时间的立法出现。从此,家庭成为女性真正的领域,男人和孩子的福利成为女性的真正义务和责任(第49页;第33页)。里奇用大量的史实和数据说明现实和理想之间的差距。虽然有无数妇女在外工作,但家庭中的母亲形象却已深入人心并发展成为一个危险的模式:"在日益残酷和冷漠的世界里,母亲是天使般关爱和宽容的源泉;女性是被男性逻辑和男性用所谓'客观'、'理性'的判断所统治的社会中富于协调(leavening)和感性的因素;在充满战争、残酷竞争和蔑视人类弱点的世界,母亲成为道德价值和温柔情感的象征与残留(residue)"(第52页;第36页)。

在第四部分的开头,里奇言简意赅地指出,"养育孩子给女性带来的身体和心理压力是迄今为止最为沉重的社会负担"(第52页;第36页)。男人可以用多种方法逃离工作压力,而女人如果未能完成好养育子女的责任,其品行则会受到质疑。里奇还进一步论述了工业化以及经济的进步如何把女性越来越严格地束缚在了家庭之中。更具悲剧性的是,父权体制已经对母性概念进行了改革,使得母亲不仅是孩子的生育者也是发展中经济所需要的全职劳动者(第54页)。由于女性成为计划生育新方法的实验对象,因此"女性的身体成为父权体制得以确立的土壤"(第55页)。

里奇在本章最后对中国情况的分析有明显的偏颇,她的依据主要是德耶拉希(Carl Djerassi)所著《对中国当代生育控制的几点观察》("Some Observations on Current Fertility Control in China"),该文载于《中国季刊》(*The China Quarterly*)1974年1~3月第57卷第40~60页。但从总体上看,里奇对母性这样一个对于女性发出的"神圣的召唤"所做的历史性追溯和分析仍然是独到并具先驱性的。母亲身份的制度化压抑了女性的发展潜能,把她们束缚在家庭并赋予她们一些具有模式化的品质特征,使女性不得不按照这样一些男性理想来塑造自己。

The "Sacred Calling"

1

One of the letters quoted in Margaret Sanger's *Motherhood in Bondage* (1928) comes from a woman seeking birth-control advice so that she can have intercourse with her husband without fear, and thus carry out her duties both as mother and wife: "I am not passionate," she writes, "but try to treat the sexual embrace the way I should, be natural and play the part, for you know, it's so different a life from what all girls expect. "[①] The history of institutionalized motherhood and of institutionalized heterosexual relations (in this case, marriage), converge in these words from an ordinary woman of half a century ago, who sought only to fulfill the requirements of both institutions, "be natural and play the part"—that impossible contradiction demanded of women. What strategy handed from ashamed mother to daughter, what fear of losing love, home, desirability as a woman, taught her—taught us all—to fake orgasm? "What all girls expect" —is that, was it for her, more than what the institution had promised her in the form of romance, of transcendent experience? Had she some knowledge of her own needs, for tenderness, perhaps, for being touched in certain ways, for being treated as more than a body for sex and procreation? What gave her the courage to write to Margaret Sanger, to try to get some modest control over the use of her body—The needs of her existing children? Her husband's demands? The dim, simmering voice of self? We may assume all three. For generations of women have asserted their courage on behalf of their own children and men, then on behalf of strangers, and finally for themselves.

The institution of motherhood is not identical with bearing and caring for children, any more than the institution of heterosexuality is identical with intimacy and sexual love. Both create the prescriptions and the conditions in which choices are made or blocked; they are not "reality" but they have shaped the circumstances of our lives. The new scholars of women's history have begun to discover that, in any case, the social institutions and prescriptions for behavior created by men have not necessarily accounted for the real lives of women. Yet any institution which expresses itself so universally ends by profoundly affecting our experience, even the language we use to describe it. The experience of maternity and the experience of sexuality have both been channeled to serve male interests; behavior which threatens the institutions, such as illegitimacy, abortion, lesbianism, is considered deviant or criminal.

Institutionalized heterosexuality told women for centuries that we were dangerous, unchaste, the embodiment of carnal lust; then that we were "not passionate", frigid, sexually passive; today it prescribes the "sensuous", "sexually liberated" woman in the West, the dedicated revolutionary ascetic in China; and everywhere it denies the reality of women's love for women. Institutionalized motherhood demands of women maternal "instinct" rather than intelligence, selflessness rather than self-realization, relation to others rather than the creation of self. Motherhood is "sacred" so long as its offspring are "legitimate"—that is, as long as the child bears the name of a father who legally controls the mother. It is "woman's highest and holiest mission," according to a socialist tract of 1914 ②; and a racist southern historian of 1910 tells us that "woman is the embodied home, and the home is the basis of all institutions, the buttress of society."③

A more recent version of the argument comes from the British critic Stuart Hampshire, who equates the "liberated woman" of today with Ibsen's panic-driven, suicidal heroine Hedda Gabler (who also refuses motherhood), in the following melancholy prophecy:

> *An entirely enlightened mind, just recently conscious of its strength and under-employed, finally corrodes and bleaches all the material of which respect is made—observances, memories of a shared past, moral resolutions for the future: no stain of weak and ordinary sentiment will remain, no differentiation of feeling and therefore no point of attachment. Why carry on the family, and therefore why carry on the race? Only a feminine skepticism, newly aroused, can be so totally subversive.* ④

Patriarchy would seem to require, not only that women shall assume the major burden of pain and self-denial for the furtherance of the species, but that a majority of that species—women—shall remain essentially unquestioning and unenlightened. On this "underemployment" of female consciousness depend the morality and the emotional life of the human family. Like his predecessors of fifty and a hundred and more years ago, Hampshire sees society as threatened when women begin to choose the terms of their lives. Patriarchy could not survive without motherhood and heterosexuality in their institutional forms; therefore they have to be treated as axioms, as "nature" itself, not open to question except where, from time to time and place to place, "alternate life-styles" for certain individuals are tolerated.

2

The "sacred calling" has had, of course, an altogether pragmatic reality. In the American colonies an ordinary family consisted of from twelve to twenty-five children. An "old maid," who might be all of twenty-five years of age, was treated with reproach if not derision; she had no way of surviving economically, and was usually compelled to board with her kin and help with the household and children. ⑤No other "calling" was open to her. An English working-woman whose childhood was lived in the 1850s and 1860s writes that "I was my mother's seventh child, and seven more were born after me—fourteen in all—which made my mother a perfect slave. Generally speaking, she was either expecting a baby to be born or had one at the breast. At the time there were eight of us the eldest was not big enough to get ready to go to school without help. "⑥ Under American slavery,

> ... it was common for planters to command women and girls to have children. On a Carolina plantation of about 100 slaves the owner threatened to flog all of the women because they did not breed. They told him they could not while they had to work in the rice ditches (in one or two feet of water). After swearing and threatening he told them to tell the overseer's wife when they got in that way and he would put them on the land to work. ⑦

Both the white pioneer mother and the black female slave, worked daily as a fully productive part of the economy. Black women often worked the fields with their children strapped to their backs. Historically, women have borne and raised children while doing their share of necessary productive labor, as a matter of course. Yet by the nineteenth century the voices rise against the idea of the "working mother," and in praise of "the mother at home." These voices reach a crescendo just as technology begins to reduce the sheer level of physical hardship in general, and as the size of families begins to decline. In the last century and a half, the idea of full-time, exclusive motherhood takes root, and the "home" becomes a religious obsession.

By the 1830s, in America, the male institutional voice (in this case that of the American Tract Society) was intoning:

Mothers have as powerful an influence over the welfare of future generations, as all other earthly causes combined.... When our land is filled with pious and patriotic mothers, then will it be filled with virtuous and patriotic men. The world's redeeming influence, under the blessing of the Holy Spirit, must come from a mother's lips. She who was first in the transgression, must yet be the principal earthly instrument in the restoration. It is maternal influence, after all, which must be the great agent in the hands of God, in bringing back our guilty race to duty and happiness. (Emphasis mine.)

The mother bears the weight of Eve's transgression (is, thus, the first offender, the polluted one, the polluter) yet precisely because of this she is expected to carry the burden of male salvation. Lest she fail, there are horrible examples to warn her:

It was the mother of Byron who laid the foundation of his preeminence in guilt.... If the crimes of the poet deserve the execration of the world, the world cannot forget that it was the mother who fostered in his youthful heart those passions which made the son a curse to his fellow-man. [8]

But female voices, also, swell the chorus. Maria McIntosh, in 1850, describes the ideal wife and mother:

Her husband cannot look on her ... without reading in the serene expression of her face, the Divine beatitude, "Blessed are the pure in heart". Her children revere her as the earthly type of perfect love. They learn even more from her example than from her precept, that they are to live, not in themselves, but to their fellow-creatures, and to the God in them.... She has taught them to love their country and devote themselves to its advancement .... [9]

Certainly the mother serves the interests of patriarchy: she exemplifies in one person religion, social conscience, and nationalism. Institutional motherhood revives and renews all other institutions.

The nineteenth-century "mother at home" seems, however, to have suffered from certain familiar evil traits, such as ill-temper.

> ... can a mother expect to govern her child when she cannot govern herself? .... She must learn to control herself, to subdue her own passions; she must set her children an example of meekness and of equanimity.... Let a mother feel grieved, and manifest her grief when her child does wrong; let her., with calmness and reflection, use the discipline which the case requires; but never let her manifest irritated feeling, or give utterance to an angry expression. ⑩

This from the male expert. *The Mother's Book* (1831), by Lydia Maria Child, advises:

> Do you say it is impossible always to govern one's feelings? There is one method, a never-failing one—prayer.... You will say, perhaps, that you have not leisure to pray every time your temper is provoked, or your heart is grieved. —It requires no time. —The inward ejaculation of "Lord, help me to overcome this temptation" may be made in any place and amid any employments; and, if uttered in humble sincerity, the voice that said to the raging waters, "Peace! Be still!" will restore quiet to your troubled soul. ⑪

Such advice to mothers gives us some sense of how female anger in general has been perceived. In *Little Women*, Marmee tells Jo, the daughter with an "Apollyon" of a "temper":

> I am angry nearly every day of my life, Jo; but I have learned not to show it; and I still hope to learn not to feel it, though it may take me another forty years to do so. ⑫

I recall similar indoctrination in my own girlhood: my "temper" was a dark, wicked blotch in me, not a response to events in the outer world. My childhood anger was often alluded to as a "tantrum", by which I understood the adult world to mean some kind of possession, as by a devil. Later, as a young mother, I remember feeling guilt that my explosions of anger were a "bad example" for my children, as if they, too, should be taught that "temper" is a defect of character, having nothing to do with what happens in the world outside one's flaming skin. Mother-love is supposed to be continuous, unconditional. Love and anger cannot coexist. Female anger threatens the institution of motherhood.

3

The nineteenth- and twentieth-century ideal of the mother and children immured together in the home, the specialization of motherhood for women, the separation of the home from the "man's world" of wage-earning, struggle, ambition, aggression, power of the "domestic" from the "public" or the "political" —all this is a late-arrived development in human history. But the force both of the ideal and of the reality is so great that, clearly, it serves no single, simple purpose.

How did this notion begin? And what purpose does it serve?

From earliest settled life until the growth of factories as centers of production, the home was not a refuge, a place for leisure and retreat from the cruelty of the "outside world"; it was a part of the world, a center of work, a subsistence unit. In it women, men, and children as early as they were able, carried on an endless, seasonal activity of raising, preparing, and processing food, processing skins, reeds, clay, dyes, fats, herbs, producing textiles and clothing, brewing, making soap and candles, doctoring and nursing, passing on these skills and crafts to younger people. A woman was rarely if ever alone with nothing but the needs of a child or children to see to. ⑬ Women and children were part of an actively busy social cluster. Work was hard, laborious, often physically exhausting, but it was diversified and usually communal. Mortality from childbirth and pregnancy and the loss of infant lives was extremely high, the life-span of women brief, and it would be naive to romanticize an existence constantly threatened by malnutrition, famine, and disease. But motherhood and the keeping of the home as a private refuge were not, could not be, the central occupation of women, nor were mother and child circumscribed into an isolated relationship.

On the Wisconsin frontier, pioneer mothers were innkeepers, schoolteachers, pharmacists, running a home as a subsistence unit with perhaps ten to fifteen children, taking in passing travelers and feeding and lodging them. The mother "collected wild plants, berries, barks, flowers and roots…. These she … dried and labeled … to be used upon short notice…. At times she was a surgeon … and fitted and bound together fingers, hanging on shreds; or removed a rusty spike from a foot, washed the wound … and saved the injured member." [14] The real, depleting burdens of motherhood were physical: the toll of continual pregnancies, the drain of constant childbearing and nursing.

The nineteenth century saw crucial changes in Western assumptions about the home, work, women, and women's relationship to productivity. The earliest factories were actually the homes of agricultural workers who began producing textiles, iron, glass, and other commodities for sale to a middleman, who might supply the raw materials as well as the market for the finished goods. [15] Women had worked alongside men even at the forges, had had almost a monopoly of the brewing trade, and the textile industry in particular had always depended on women; as early as the fourteenth century in England women had woven not only for the home but outside it.

Gradually those women who still worked at hand-spinning or weaving in the home were driven into the mills by the competition of power-spinning machines. There were no laws to limit the hours of labor; a woman worked for twelve hours, then returned to take up the burdens of her household. By 1844 a British factory inspector could report that "a vast majority of the persons employed at night and for long periods during the day are females; their labour is cheaper and they are more easily induced to undergo severe bodily fatigue than men. "⑯

These same women left children at home; sometimes in the care of a six- or seven-year-old daughter, a grandmother, or a neighbor's hired child. Sometimes an older woman would keep infants and young children in her house for a fee; instead of breast-milk the unweaned babies were fed watery gruel or "pap", or the mother, if she could afford it, was forced to buy cow's milk for her child. The children were dosed with laudanum to keep them quiet. The severance of the sphere of work from the sphere of child-raising thus immediately created disadvantage and hardship for both child and mother.

These women worked from necessity, to supplement a husband's inadequate or nonexistent wages; and because they were paid less, their employment was seen as threatening to male workers. Women's work was clearly subversive to "the home" and to patriarchal marriage; not only might a man find himself economically dependent on his wife's earnings, but it would conceivably even be possible for women to dispense with marriage from an economic point of view. ⑰ These two forces—the humanitarian concern for child welfare and the fear for patriarchal values—converged to provide pressure which led to legislation controlling children's and women's labor, and the assertion that "the home, its cares and employments, is the woman's true sphere".

The home thus defined had never before existed. It was a creation of the Industrial Revolution, an ideal invested with the power of something God-given, and its power *as an idea* remains unexpunged today. For the first time, the productivity of women (apart from reproductivity) was seen as "a waste of time, a waste of property, a waste of morals and a waste of health and life". Women were warned that their absence form home did not only mean the neglect of their children; if they failed to create the comforts of the nest, their men would be off to the alehouse. The welfare of men and children was the true mission of women. Since men had no mission to care for children or keep house, the solution was to get the women out of the factories.

As public opinion became aroused over the fate of children whose mothers worked in the mills, some efforts were made to set up nurseries; but in Victorian and Edwardian England, as in twentieth-century America, state-supported child-care was opposed on the grounds that it would violate "the sanctity of the domestic hearth and the decent seclusion of private life.... The family is the unit upon which a constitutional Government has been raised which is the admiration and envy of mankind. Hitherto, whatever the laws have touched, they have not dared invade this sacred precinct; and the husband and wife, however poor, returning home from whatsoever occupation or harassing engagements, have *there* found *their* dominion, *their* repose, *their* compensation for many a care". ⑱

In 1915 the Women's Cooperative Guild in Britain published a volume of letters written by the wives of manual laborers about their lives as mothers and workers in the home. These lives stood as far as possible in contradiction to the ideal of the home as a protected place apart from the brutal realities of work and struggle. The average woman had from five to eleven children with several miscarriages, most of them with no prenatal care and inadequate diet. "At the time when she ought to be well fed she stints herself in order to save; for in a working class home if there is saving to be done, it is not the husband and children, but the mother who makes her meal off the scraps which remain over, or 'plays with meatless bones.' " ⑲ The anxiety and physical depletion of incessant childbearing is a theme which runs throughout these letters. Many—against their principles, and often facing a husband's opposition—took drugs to bring on abortion, which were usually ineffective and on which the sickliness of the forthcoming child was blamed. But along with the ill-health, mental strain, and exhaustion of which the women write, go an extraordinary resiliency of spirit, the will to make do, and an active sense of the injustice of their situation.

In my early motherhood I took it for granted that women had to suffer at these times, and it was best to behave and not make a fuss…. I do not know which is the worst—childbearing with anxiety and strain of mind and body to make ends meet, with the thought of another one to share the already small allowance, or getting through the confinement fairly well, and getting about household duties too soon, and bringing on other ailments which make life and everything a burden. [20]

Many wrote of the damage done by ignorance, the young woman's total lack of preparation for marriage and pregnancy; and even more of the insensitivity of husbands demanding sex throughout pregnancy or immediately after delivery:

During the time of pregnancy, the male beast keeps entirely from the female: not so with the woman; she is the prey of a man just the same as though she was not pregnant…. If a woman does not feel well she must not say so, as a man has such a lot of ways of punishing a woman if she does not give in to him. [21]

I do not blame my husband for this birth. [The writer had had seven children and two miscarriages.] He had waited patiently for ten months because I was ill, and thinking the time was safe, I submitted as a duty, knowing there is much unfaithfulness on the part of the husband where families are limited…. It is quite time this question of maternity was taken up, and we must let the men know we are human beings with ideals, and aspire to something higher than to be mere objects on which they can satisfy themselves. [22]

The women were not only pregnant for much of their lives, but doing heavy labor: scrubbing floors, hauling basins of wash, ironing, cooking over coal and wood fires which had to be fed and tended. One woman, against her doctor's orders, did her ironing and kneading in bed while recovering from a miscarriage. [23] Despite their resentment of the husbands' sexual demands and opposition to abortion, the women tried to spare their men, who had worked hard all day, from further strain in the home:

I dare not let my husband in his precarious condition hear a cry of pain from me, and travail pain cannot always be stifled; and here again the doctor helped me by giving me a sleeping draught to administer him as soon as I felt the pangs of childbirth. Hence he slept in one room while I travailed in the other, and brought forth the liveliest boy that ever gladdened a mother's heart. ㉔

But there was no homecoming from work for the women.

Within the home or outside it, reality has always been at odds with the ideal. In 1860 in America a million women were employed; by the end of the Civil War there were 75,000 working-women in New York City alone. In 1973 the United States Census reported more than six million children under the age of six whose mothers worked full time outside the home. ㉕ Without free, universal, child-care, any woman who has ever had to contrive and improvise in order to leave her children daily and earn a living can imagine the weight of anxiety, guilt, uncertainty, the financial burden, the actual emergencies which these statistics imply. The image of the mother in the home, however unrealistic, has haunted and reproached the lives of wage-earning mothers. But it has also become, and for men as well as women, a dangerous archetype: the Mother, source of angelic love and forgiveness in a world increasingly ruthless and impersonal; the feminine, leavening, emotional element in a society ruled by male logic and male claims to "objective," "rational" judgment; the symbol and residue of moral values and tenderness in a world of wars, brutal competition, and contempt for human weakness.

4

The physical and psychic weight of responsibility on the woman with children is by far the heaviest of social burden. It cannot be compared with slavery or sweated labor because the emotional bonds between a woman and her children make her vulnerable in ways which the forced laborer does not know; he can hate and fear his boss or master, loathe the toil; dream of revolt or of becoming a boss; the woman with children is a prey to far more complicated, subversive feelings. Love and anger *can* exist concurrently; anger at the conditions of motherhood can become translated into anger at the child, along with the fear that we are not "loving"; grief at all we cannot do for our children in a society so inadequate to meet human needs becomes translated into guilt and self-laceration. This "powerless responsibility" as one group of women has termed it, is a heavier burden even than providing a living—which so many mothers have done, and do, simultaneously with mothering—because it is recognized in some quarters, at least, that economic forces, political oppression, lie behind poverty and unemployment; but the mother's very character, her status as a woman, are in question if she has "failed" her children.

Whatever the known facts [26], it is still assumed that the mother is "with the child". It is she, finally, who is held accountable for her children's health, the clothes they wear, their behavior at school, their intelligence and general development. Even when she is the sole provider for a fatherless family, she and no one else bears the guilt for a child who must spend the day in a shoddy nursery or an abusive school system. Even when she herself is trying to cope with an environment beyond her control—malnutrition, rats, lead-paint poisoning, the drug traffic, racism—in the eyes of society the mother *is* the child's environment. The worker can unionize, go out on strike; mothers are divided from each other in homes, tied to their children by compassionate bonds; our wildcat strikes have most often taken the form of physical or mental breakdown.

For mothers, the privatization of the home has meant not only an increase in powerlessness, but a desperate loneliness. A group of East London women talked with Hannah Gavron of the difference between trying to raise children in a street of row houses and in the new high-rise flats of postwar London: the loss of neighborhood, of stoop life, of a common pavement where children could be watched at play by many pairs of eyes. [27] In Cambridge, Massachusetts in the 1950s, some married graduate students lived in housing built on the plan of the "lane" or row-house street, where children played in a common court, a mother could deliver her child to a neighbor for an hour, children filtered in and out of each others' houses, and mothers, too, enjoyed a casual, unscheduled companionship with each other. With the next step upward in academic status, came the move to the suburbs, to the smaller, then the larger, private house, the isolation of "the home" from other homes increasing with the husband's material success. The working-class mothers in their new flats and the academic wives in their new affluence all lost something: they became, to a more extreme degree, house-bound, isolated women.

Lee Sanders Comer, a British Marxist-feminist, reiterates the classic Marxist critique of the nuclear family—the small, privatized unit of a woman, a man, and their children. In this division of labor the man is the chief or the sole wage-earner, and the woman's role is that of housewife, mother, consumer of goods, and emotional support of men and children. The "family" really means "the mother", who carries the major share of child-rearing, and who also absorbs the frustrations and rage her husband may bring home from work (often in the form of domestic violence). Her own anger becomes illegitimate, since her job is to provide him with the compassion and comfort he needs at home in order to return daily to the factory or the mine pit. Comer sees this division of labor as demanded by capitalism. But why should capitalism *in and of itself* require that women specialize in this role of emotional salvager, or that women and never men rear children and take care of the home? How much does this really have to do with capitalism, and how much with the system which, as Eli Zaretsky points out, predated capitalism and has survived under socialism— patriarchy? [28]

[...]

Notes:

① Margaret Sanger, *Motherhood in Bondage* (New York: Maxwell

Reprint, 1956), p. 234.

② John Spargo, *Socialism and Motherhood* (New York: 1914).

③ Benjamin F. Riley, *White Man's Burden* (Birmingham, Ala.: 1910), p. 131.

④ Stuart Hampshire, Review of Elizabeth Hardwick's *Seduction and Betrayal*, *New York Review of Books*, June 27, 1975, p. 21.

⑤ Arthur W. Calhoun, *A Social History of the American Family from Colonial Times to the Present* (Cleveland: 1917), I: 67, 87. Julia C. Spruill, *Women's Life and Work in the Southern Colonies* (New York: Norton, 1972), pp. 137-139; first published in 1938.

⑥ Margaret Llewelyn Davies, ed., *Life As We Have Known It* (New York: Norton: 1975), p. 1; first published in 1931 by the Hogarth Press, London.

⑦ Calhoun, *op. cit.*, II: 244.

⑧ Rev. John S. Abbott, *The Mother at Home, or The Principles of Maternal Duty* (New York: American Tract Society, 1833); this book was a best-seller in its time.

⑨ Maria J. McIntosh, *Woman in America: Her Work and Her Reward* (New York: Appleton, 1850).

⑩ Abbott, *op. cit.*, pp. 62-64.

⑪ Lydia Maria Child, *The Mother's Book* (Boston: 1831), p. 5.

⑫ Louisa May Alcott, *Little Women* (New York: A. L. Burt, 1911), p. 68.

⑬ Agnes Smedley, writing of her grandmother at the turn of the century, sketches a vigorous, powerful woman involved in productive work:

> She milked the cows each morning and night with the sweeping strength and movements of a man. She carried pails of skimmed milk and slopped the hogs; when she kneaded bread for baking it whistled and snapped under her hands, and her arms worked like steam pistons. She awoke the men at dawn and she told them when to go upstairs at night. She directed the picking of fruit—apples,

pears, peaches, berries of every kind, and she taught her girls how to can, preserve and dry them for the winter. In the autumn she directed the slaughtering of beef and pork, and then smoked the meat in the smokehouse. When the sugar cane ripened in the summer she saw it cut, and superintended the making of molasses in the long, low sugar cane mill at the foot of the hill.

This woman had five children of her own, and eight of her husband's from a prior marriage. (*Daughter of Earth* [Old Westbury, N. Y.: Feminist Press, 1973], pp. 18-19.)

⑭ Lillian Krueger, "Motherhood on the Wisconsin Frontier," *Wisconsin, A Magazine of History*, Vol. 29, No. 2, pp. 157-183; Vol. 29, No. 3, pp. 333-346.

⑮ Stella Davies, *Living Through the Industrial Revolution* (London: Routledge and Kegan, 1966).

⑯ Margaret Hewitt, *Wives and Mothers in Victorian Industry* (London: Rockliff, 1958), p. 22.

⑰ The social historian A. W. Calhoun suggests that in America the factory opened the way to a new economic independence for women which they had never had in the colonial period or the opening of the frontier. The need to keep the family patriarchal was at least one force behind the enactment of child-labor laws and of laws restricting the hours and conditions of work for women.

⑱ Hewitt, *Wives and Mothers in Victorian Industry*, pp. 153-154.

⑲ *Maternity: Letters from Working Women*, colleted by the Women's Cooperative Guild, with a preface by the Rt. Hon. Herbert Samuel, M. P. (London: G. Bell, 1915), p. 5.

⑳ Ibid., pp. 27-28.

㉑ Ibid., p. 49.

㉒ Ibid., pp. 67-68.

㉓ Ibid., p. 153.

㉔ Ibid., p. 47.

㉕ Calhoun, *op. cit.*, III: 86; Elinor C. Guggenheim, "The Battle for Day Care," *Nation*, May 7, 1973.

㉖ Twenty-six million children of wage-earning mothers, 8 million in female-headed households in the United States by the mid-1970s (Alice Rossi, "Children and Work in the Lives of Women," a paper delivered at the University of Arizona, February 7, 1976).

㉗ Hannah Gavron, *The Captive Wife: Conflicts of Housebound Mothers* (London: Routledge and Kegan, 1966), pp. 72-73, 80.

㉘ Lee Sanders Comer, "Functions of the Family under Capitalism," pamphlet reprinted by the New York Radical Feminists, 1974. Eli Zaretsky, "Capitalism, the Family, and Personal Life," *Socialist Revolution*, January-June 1973, p. 69.

3 亚德里安·里奇,"母性的家庭化"
Adrienne Rich, "The Domestication of Motherhood"

"母性的家庭化"是里奇所著《生于女性》一书的第五章。在本章中,里奇论述了在多民族神话中母亲的神性如何逐渐消失,母亲如何被束缚在家庭之中成为被男性控制的对象。本章共分五部分。

第一部分,里奇首先回顾了恩格斯(Frederick Engels)关于私有制和奴隶制起源的有关论述,她指出,对于恩格斯以及后来的马克思主义者来说,妇女的受压迫地位主要是经济方面的原因①。但像霍尼(Karen Horney)②这样的女性理论家却在自己的文章《两性之间的不信任》("The Distrust Between the Sexes")中谈及所有男性对女性怀有仇恨和焦虑情绪。根据这样的观点,里奇认为恩格斯对于私有制的论述虽然涉及男性购买者和女性被购买者之间的关系,但却忽视了母子、母女关系,这后一种关系实际上导致了男性占优越地位的性别政治。里奇接着援引另一位精神分析学家扎雷斯基(Eli Zaretsky)③的观点说,对于男性来说,女性既是某种特别需要的东西又是

---

① Adrienne Rich, *Of Woman Born: Motherhood as Experience and Institution* (New York: W. W. Norton & Company Inc. , 1976), p. 110. 本节所引里奇观点除特别说明均出自此处,以下只在正文标明页码,分号后第二个页码为引文在本书的页码。

② 霍尼(1885~1952),德国心理分析学家。她对精神分析理论做出的重要贡献在于她提出的个性理论、自我理论以及神经需要理论。

③ 扎雷斯基是纽约一所大学的历史学教授,他在家庭史、社会学史以及心理学史等领域都有著述发表。最新的一部著作是《灵魂的秘密:精神分析学的社会文化史》(*Secrets of the Soul: A Social and Cultural History of Psychoanalysis*,2004 年)。

某种特别可怕的东西:"她首先是母亲,必须被占有、被缩减、被控制,否则她就会把他重新吞入她那黑暗的洞穴或是把他凝视为石头"(第112页)。人类学家福克斯(Robin Fox)①也认为,母亲与子女的关系是人类纽带中最为基本的关系,也是所有社会纽带的基础(第113页)。虽然福克斯主张男人狩猎、攻敌、决策,但霍尼却强调作为社会基本力量的女性在男人眼中引起了焦虑,因为"女性是一个神秘的存在,可以同神灵沟通,因此具有某种可以用来伤害男性的魔力。因此男性必须通过让她处于屈服地位的方式来保护自己免受其魔力的伤害"(第114页)。

第二部分,里奇通过回顾人类历史集中论述男性心目中的女性形象。主要观点有这样几个:其一,虽然伟大女神(the Great Goddess)或伟大母亲(the Great Mother)的形象在史前就已经出现,但这一形象既蕴含善良、孕育生命的一面又包含黑暗的、否定的一面,因为死亡仅仅是生命周期的一个部分(第116页;第46页)。其二,女性的血同男性或其它动物的血有所不同,因为女性的血不仅同月经禁忌的诅咒和神秘相联系,而且也同失去童贞的魔力(mana of defloration)、生命的神秘转变过程以及同繁殖本身相联系(第117页;第47页)。其三,男性在其自我成长阶段把女性视为危险的因素,他一方面依赖女性得到情感上的支持,另一方面又害怕在她手中遭遇阉割和死亡(第118页;第48~49页)。

第三部分,里奇论述了母亲所具有的神性是如何逐渐消失的。她首先说明女性很早就把自己的身份定位于女儿和母亲,而男性却直到当上父亲才摆脱充当母亲儿子的被动身份(第118~119页;第48页~49页)。她接着指出,父权惟一神思想使男性需要子女——尤其是儿子——来巩固自己的地位,因此,耶和华的那句"生育并繁殖吧"完完全全是一句父权式的命令(第119页;第49页)。也正因为如此,女性的"不孕"——而不是男性的"不育"——通常被视为对女性不贞洁行为的惩罚。里奇运用大量神话传说描述母亲女神如何逐渐被贬值、被拒绝,她

① 福克斯(1934~)是新泽西州立大学人类学教授,这所大学的人类学系是他于1967年创办的。他的代表著作有《亲情与婚姻》(*Kinship and Marriage*,1967年)、《面对人类学》(*Encounter with Anthropology*,1973年)、《人类学的挑战》(*The Challenge of Anthropology*,1995年)等。

还援引斯雷特(*Philip Slater*)①的观点说,整个奥林匹亚神话都充溢着对成熟母性形象的恐惧(第 122 页;第 52 页),母亲常常过分地控制男孩子的行为,这反映出她对儿子的仇恨和嫉妒(第 123 页;第 52 页)。这在古代神话和古典戏剧中均有所表现。

里奇在第四部分集中讲述了太阳崇拜,她认为对太阳神的崇拜以及以太阳为中心的宗教的出现使母亲女神的作用逐渐削弱。她首先谈到埃及艺术和神话中太阳逐渐占据统治地位的过程,而后又谈到阿玛纳艺术②中著名的奈费尔提蒂(Nefertite)③雕像所展现的女性优雅,最后回到希腊神话中太阳神阿波罗如何吸收了伟大母亲诸多诱人的特征而成为"反母权制度的化身、天神的象征以及相对于地球神灵的斗士"(第 125 页;第 54 页)。月亮神允许相对立的因素共生共存,但太阳神却象征着分裂意识(第 125 页;第 55 页)。随着对太阳神崇拜的建立,母亲女神经历了性别的变化,女性也开始在男性神祇的律法统治下依据男性判断标准来规范自己的生活。

里奇在第五部分对本章的主要思想作了总结。她说,在前父权社会,幼年男子感到女性的生育能力是一种权威,感到自己是外来者;而在父权社会,男性在各种复杂的情感支配下创造出了一个有悖于女性有机本性的体系,从而扼杀了女性的进化过程。母亲于是成为男性猜忌、怀疑和厌恶的对象,女性的生育器官也因此成为父权技术的首要目标(第 127 页;第 57 页)。

本书收入的是第二、三、四、五几个部分。

---

① 斯雷特是美国社会学家,代表作有《追求孤独:冲突时期的美国文化》(*The Pursuit of Loneliness: American Culture at the Breaking Point*, 1970 年)。

② 古埃及第十八个王朝通常被历史学家称为"阿玛纳时期",关于这一时期艺术的特点,参见 http://www-scf. usc. edu/ ~ cipolla/virtour6. htm, n. p. 。

③ 奈费尔提蒂是公元前 14 世纪埃及王后,她支持国王进行宗教改革,她的半身彩色石灰石雕像流传后世。参见 http://www. akhet. co. uk/nefertit. htm, n. p. ; http://dsc. discovery. com/convergence/nefertiti/nefertiti. html, n. p. 。

The Domestication of Motherhood

[······]

2

Joseph Campbell, tracing the universality of the Great Goddess or Great Mother image from prehistory onward, asserts that "there can be no doubt that in the very earliest ages of human history the magical force and wonder of the female was no less a marvel than the universe itself; and this gave to woman a prodigious power, which it has been one of the chief concerns of the masculine part of the population to break, control and employ to its own ends."① He associates the glorification of hunting over agriculture, and the disappearance of female figurines at the end of the Aurignacian period (c. 30,000 B. C.), with the rise of this male self-assertion against the elemental power of woman. Female figurines were, he finds, "the first objects of worship by the species Homo sapiens. But there is a shift in the magic, ritual and imagery of Homo sapiens from the vagina to the phallus, and from an essentially plant-oriented to a purely animal-oriented mythology".

G. Rachel Levy offers a convincing and beautifully concrete recreation of Neolithic consciousness. She bases her conclusions, which are never dogmatic, on her actual explorations of Aurignacian caves, on a great variety of artifacts and wall-tracings, on the architecture of post-Neolithic cultures, and on studies of the prehistoric movements of wild herds and the distribution of wild grasses throughout Eastern and Western Europe. She suggests that a unified life-giving principle—the female principle embodied in the caves themselves and the goddess-cult figurines found within them— informed the existence of the hunting peoples. The beginnings of animal domestication and grazing, the development of agriculture, led, she feels, to the first consciousness of "movement in time"—i. e. , the seasons' cycles, the rotation of the stars, the gestation, birth, and death of animals and crops. This earliest sense of "movement in time" generated a sense of numerical relation, balance, cyclic symmetry which in turn made possible such advances as the development of pottery. ② But one essential by-product of this "mental revolution" was a growing consciousness of *duality*—a way of perceiving which, carried to its extreme and bifurcated, was later to become fundamental to patriarchal consciousness.

To acknowledge a cyclic change of aspects (that birth is followed by death, death by reincarnation; that tides ebb and flow, winter alternates with summer, the full moon with the dark of the moon) is to acknowledge that process and continuity embrace both positive and negative events—although, as parts of a process, events are less likely to become stamped as purely "positive" or "negative". Prepatriarchal consciousness, according to Levy, begins with an elemental unity which is sensed as female; and proceeds to an awareness of dynamics still presided over by a female presence: "In the growing consciousness of duality, the Mother retained her former abiding and fundamental status as the earth into which men return and out of which all birth emanates... no cult of a male divinity is discoverable in Neolithic archaeology... Female potency [was] the great subject of Aurignacian sculpture. "③

Even death was part of a movement in time, part of the cycle leading to reincarnation and rebirth. A "dark" or "negative" aspect of the Great Mother was thus already present from the beginning, inseparable from her benign, life-giving aspect. And, like death, violence, bloodshed, destructive power, were always there, the potentially "evil" half of the Mother's profile, which, once completely split off, would become separately personified as the fanged blood-goddess Kali, the killer-mother Medea, the lewd and malign witch, the "castrating" wife or mother. (As I was writing this, one of my sons showed me the cover of the current *National Geographic*—the photograph of a Peruvian Indian rowing a pure white llama to the annual ceremony on Titicaca Island where it would be sacrificed to the Earth Mother in exchange for a good harvest. This ceremony is performed by sorceresses

and the llama's blood sprinkled onto "Pacha Mama" [Mother Earth]. ④
Thus the bringing of life—i. e. , food—is associated, as in ancient times,
with bloodshed and killing, and both are associated with the Great Mother.
Such customs, if rare today, were once legion.)

Women's blood is different from the blood of men or animals. It is
associated not only with the "curse" and mysteries of the menstrual taboo,
but with the *mana* of defloration, the transformation mystery of birth, and
with fertility itself. There is thus a complex fusion of associations derived
from the several aspects of the female, which might be visualized as a cluster
like the one below:

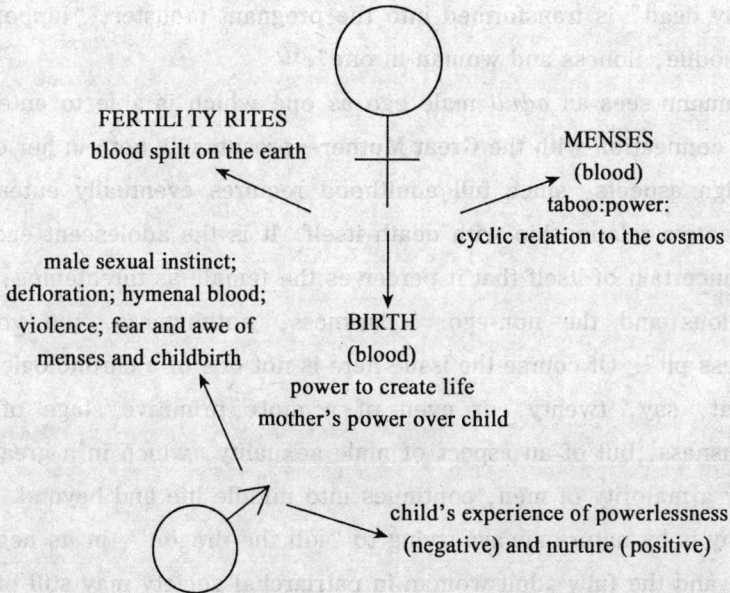

FERTILITY RITES
blood spilt on the earth

MENSES
(blood)
taboo:power:
cyclic relation to the cosmos

male sexual instinct;
defloration; hymenal blood;
violence; fear and awe of
menses and childbirth

BIRTH
(blood)
power to create life
mother's power over child

child's experience of powerlessness
(negative) and nurture (positive)

As Joseph Campbell acknowledges: "the natural mysteries of childbirth and
menstruation are as directly convincing as death itself, and remain to this day
what they must also have been in the beginning, primary sources of a
religious awe." ⑤

In the recurrent hero myth, the male infant grows up into the son/lover, who later undergoes *violence* (murder or castration) at his mother's hands. The myth of killing the dragon (another violence/blood myth) recounts the test by which the young man tries to surmount his dread of the Terrible Mother—his elemental fear of women. According to Mycenean myth, Apollo had to battle a female dragon before he could enter Delphi, which became his shrine. ⑥

The Neolithic triangle or the *yoni*—female genital symbols anciently inscribed at the entrance to a sacred area—become, in this struggle against female power, fanged Kali, or Medusa's face with its snarl of snaky hair. The beneficent "Cow Goddess beyond the grave" who "suckled the souls of the newly dead" is transformed into the pregnant monster, "hippopotamus and crocodile, lioness and woman in one". ⑦

Neumann sees an *adult* male ego as one which is able to enter into a creative connection with the Great Mother—presumably both in her dark and her benign aspects, since full adulthood requires eventually entering into some creative relationship with death itself. It is the adolescent ego that is still so uncertain of itself that it perceives the female as threatening; as "the unconscious and the non-ego... darkness, nothingness, the void, the bottomless pit". Of course the issue here is not one of a chronological phase ending at, say, twenty, or even of a more primitive stage of human consciousness, but of an aspect of male sexuality, which in a great many, probably a majority of men, continues into middle life and beyond. In fact, patriarchy is by nature always trying to "kill the dragon", in its negation of women; and the fully adult woman in patriarchal society may still often find only an adolescent son/lover, who wants her for his emotional sustenance even while somewhere within him he fears castration and death at her hands. This fear is the real dragon that has to be destroyed.

3

Woman has always known herself both as daughter and as potential mother, while in his dissociation from the process of conception man first experiences himself as son, and only much later as father. When he began to assert his paternity and to make certain claims to power over women and children on that basis, we begin to see emerging the process through which he compensated for—one could say, took revenge for—his previous condition as son-of-the-mother.

Patriarchal monotheism did not simply change the sex of the divine presence; it stripped the universe of female divinity, and permitted woman to be sanctified, as if by an unholy irony, only and exclusively as mother (without the extended *mana* that she possessed prepatriarchally)—or as the daughter of a divine father. She becomes the property of the husband-father, and must come to him *virgo intacta*, not as "second-hand goods"; or she must be ritually deflorated. If he is to know "his" children, he must have control over their reproduction, which means he must possess their mother exclusively. The question of "legitimacy" probably goes deeper than even the desire to hand on one's possessions to one's own blood-line; it cuts back to the male need to say: "I, too, have the power of procreation—these are *my* seed, *my* own begotten children, *my* proof of elemental power." In addition, of course, the children are the future receivers of the patrimony; by their prayers and sacrifices, they will ensure the father's spirit a safe passage after death; but they are also present assets, able bodies to work fields, fish, hunt, fight against hostile tribes. A wife's "barrenness" (until very recently it was the woman who was declared "barren" rather than the husband infertile) was a curse because she was, finally, the means of reproduction. A man needed children to enhance his position in the world, and especially, a man needed sons. The command of Yahweh: "Be fruitful and multiply,"[8] is an entirely patriarchal one; he is not invoking the Great Mother but bidding his sons beget still more sons. Thus, Engels is correct in his famous statement that in the patriarchal family the husband is the bourgeois and the wife and children the proletariat. But each is something more to each, something which both cements and can outlast economic bondage.

In the Middle East to this day, God is believed to strike a woman barren as punishment for some impiety (the woman is assumed to be the sinner, not her husband) and the production of daughters is a disaster, not simply for the mother, but for the daughters. The Hebrew scholar Raphael Patai says that "we know from historical documents relating to the Arab world from pre-historic times down to the 19th century that often a father decided to put to death a daughter either immediately upon her birth or at a later date. The usual method of putting a newborn daughter to death was to bury her in the sands of the desert". He quotes from the Koran the words of a father who asks himself, of his newborn daughter: "Shall he keep it in contempt, or bury it in the dust?" [9] The earlier background of female primacy I have described needs to be held in mind against the violence of this question— along with the fact that the Yahwists savagely repressed the cults of Astarte (originally Tanit, Asherah, or Ishtar) and denounced all worship of the Goddess as "an abomination". [10]

The Mother Goddess is gradually devalued and rejected; the human woman finds her scope and dignity increasingly reduced. Patriarchal man impregnates "his" wife and expects her to deliver "his" child; her elemental power is perceived more and more as a service she renders, a function she performs. In the *Eumenides* of Aeschylus, the Erinyes, representing mother-right, claim vengeance on Orestes for the crime of matricide. But Apollo declares that Orestes's murder of his mother was a just act because it avenged the death of his father Agamemnon; and he continues:

> *The mother is no parent of that which is called her child, but only nurse of the newplanted seed that grows. The parent is he who mounts.*

Athena, also a representative of father-right, denies having had any mother; she sprang from her father Zeus's brain and she acts like a true token woman, loyal only to "the man" as she does not hesitate to announce. [11]

And the medieval church held that a minuscule, fully formed *homunculus*, complete with soul, was deposited by the male in the female body, which simply acted as incubator. ⑫

The image of the divine family also changes. The Goddess, whether in Sumer, Minos, Mycenae, Phrygia, Knossos, or Syria, had often been represented with a young god, her son, servant, or consort, but always subsidiary to her. E. O. James perceives these young male images as the first sign of recognition of the male's part in fertilization. But for a long time the young god remained more son than husband, more consort than equal. Mellaart finds the role of the son of the goddess "strictly subordinate to hers"; of a male figure found in one of the Çatal Hüyük shrines, he says: "Presumably he represents an aspect of hunting, which alone was responsible for the presence of an independent male deity in the neolithic of Çatal Hüyük." ⑬ But in his earliest appearance he is a vegetation god, who must die and be reborn for the vegetative cycle to continue. In a sense, he is thus still annexed to the Mother of grains, fruits, and growing things. Later, the virgin-mother with her youthful child-mate is replaced by a father, his wife, and his children. In contrast to the "Divine Triad" of Mycenae cited by Leonard Palmer, which consists of two queens and a king, we find such images as the Egyptian Amarnan family, consisting of a father, his son, and his small grandson. ⑭ The mother is no longer virgin, "she-unto-herself"; she is "unto-the-husband," his unequal consort or his possession and subordinate, to be reckoned up with his cattle. ⑮

Devaluations of the Goddess are legion. Patai describes the struggle of Jewish patriarchal monotheism with the goddess-cults, of which the golden calf was one remnant (the horned bull or cow having been sacred to the Goddess throughout the world.) ⑯ He tells of women weaving "houses"— possibly garments—for Asherah in the temple at Jerusalem, and the baking of cakes for Astarte or Anath. Some remnant of female presence —heavily laden with what Jung would call anima-projection—survived in the concept of the Shekhina, "the loving, rejoicing, motherly, suffering, mourning and in general emotion-charged aspect of deity" (with what implications for centuries of Jewish mothers?). A female deity also reemerged in the Kabbalistic renascence of the thirteenth century, under the name Matronit, who, according to Patai is a distinct and often independent presence, but who seems to have left few ripples in the mainstream of Judaism. ⑰ The pig, declared an unclean animal in the Koran and the Old Testament, was a reiterative figure in goddess-religion; the sow was sacred in Crete, sometimes appeared as an embodiment of Isis, was sacrificed at the feast of Aphrodite, and was a symbol of the Eleusinian cult of Demeter. "Wherever the eating of pork is forbidden and the pig is held to be unclean, we can be sure of its originally sacred character. " ⑱

Jane Harrison describes the descent (in every sense) of the Hellenic figure of Pandora from the Cretan Earth-Mother, her conversion from the All-Giver to merely a beautiful girl dowered with gifts by all the Olympians and then sent as a temptress to man. Pandora's famous "box" which when opened released every kind of grief and trouble among men, was originally a *pithos* or *jar* in which the Earth-Mother stored all the goods of wine, grain, and fruits. Jane Harrison was struck by the "ugly and malicious theological animus" in Hesiod's telling of this tale: "he is all for the *Father* and the Father will have no great Earth-Goddess in his man-made Olympus. " ⑲

Slater sees the entire Olympian mythology as saturated with fear of the mature, maternal woman; the much-admired goddess, Athena, is born from her father Zeus's brain, is virginal, childless, and, as has been seen, affirms her loyalty to the male. Hera is a jealous, competitive consort, and destructive mothers like Gaea, Rhea, Medea, and Clytemnestra abound. He theorizes that this fear of the maternal woman derived from the sexual politics of fifth-century Greece, where women were ill-educated, were sold into marriage, and had no role except as producers of children, the sexual interest of men was homoerotic, and for intellectual friendships a man sought out hetaeras (usually foreign-born women) or other men. He assumes the mother to have been filled with resentment and envy of her sons, and, in her own frustration, excessively controlling of her male children in their earliest years. Her feelings would have been experienced by her sons as a potentially destructive hostility which is later embodied in mythology and classical drama. [20]

4

Sun-worship, which always postdates worship of a lunar deity (whether feminine or masculine) is another feature of patriarchal thought. The ancients saw the moon not as a reflector of solar light, but as independently glowing in the darkness of night; the sun was the inhabitant, rather than the source of daylight.

It is extraordinary to see concretely, as in Egyptian art of the Amarna period, the coming-into-dominance of the sun. Although a solar deity had long been central in Egyptian religion, there was still a strong goddess-cult embodied in the figures of Isis, Hathor, Nut, Nepthys. The fourteenth-century B. C. Pharaoh Akhenaton revolutionized Egyptian cosmology in setting up the Aten, or sun-disk, as the sole embodiment of a new religion. In his capital, the seat of the Aten at Tell-el-Amarna, he encouraged an art which over and over, in the sun-disk with its spreading rays, asserts the message of a monotheistic, heliocentric, and patriarchal universe.

When we think of Amarnan art we tend to think of the famous portrait bust of Nefertite. But her popularity in our times should not make us exaggerate her importance in her own. Amarnan art, in fact, reiterates images of woman and of the family which do not seem very different from contemporary stereotypes. In these incised or carven images, Akhenaton is already both patriarch and deity (Incarnation of the Aten). With him is his queen, Nefertite, of extraordinary bearing and elegance, who comes far closer to contemporary ideals of feminine, aristocratic beauty than do most prepatriarchal female images. But she is unmistakenly second; a consort, even a royal deity, depicted with dignity and pride, but essentially a token woman. In one *stele*, the royal family (Akhenaton, Nefertite, and three of their daughters) are represented in an informal, even intimate family scene showing a good deal of physical affection. But above them the Aten holds forth its rays, and *it* is the real center and keystone of the composition.

In establishing the worship of the Aten, Akhenaton not only ordered the destruction of many images of the earlier gods, and removed their names from monuments, but prohibited the plural form of the word "god". A reference in Cyril Aldred to the fact that "the words for 'mother' and 'truth' were cleansed of their old associations" is tantalizing, since the hieroglyph for "house" or "town" also symbolizes "mother," emphasizing the principle of collective as well as individual nurture. [21]

In the *Eumenides* of Aeschylus, Apollo, the Hellenic sun-god, becomes the spokesman for father-right, upheld by Athena, the goddess who denies her mother. Apollo is god of poetry and the lyre, twin brother of an independent sister, associated with light, with trees, with the art of healing. Jane Harrison notes that Apollo is derived from the god Paean, of the land where the styptic peony grows, and that this herb, which could stanch blood, was held in reverence throughout the East. But Artemis, his sister, is likewise associated with healing herbs, in her diminished state as goddess. Apollo's relationship to trees is interesting: The nymph Daphne, to escape rape by him, had herself turned into a laurel tree. This tree Apollo made his personal symbol; and it was with a laurel branch in his hand that he came to take over the oracular shrine of the earth-goddess, Themis, at Delphi [22] — killing, as we have seen, a female dragon on the way.

Thus Apollo assimilated a number of attractive aspects of the Great Mother—even to being paired with the moon. The Mother of Trees, of healing herbs and the preservation of life, becomes a male god; the lunar goddess becomes his sister. Slater calls him "the personification of anti-matriarchy, the epitome of the sky-god, a crusader against Earth-deities. He is all sunlight, Olympian, manifest, rational". [23] Now this of course is an extreme case of patriarchal "splitting"—in Jane Harrison's words, Greek orthodoxy would allow "no deed or dream of darkness" about Apollo. All was to be lucidity, radiant masculinity. Harding suggests that the worship of the moon embodies respect for the wisdom of instinct and natural law, and that sun-worship has to do with the idea of control of natural forces. [24] Indeed, Apollo is personified as driving the steeds of the sun. The "Apollonian" rational control of nature, as opposed to the instinctual excesses of the cult of Dionysus, the power of consciousness as opposed to the unconscious, the celebration of father-right over mother-right, come together in this mythology.

Why the sun should have come to embody a split consciousness, while the worship of the moon allowed for coexistent opposites, a holistic process, is an interesting question. The fact that the moon is itself continually changing, and is visible in so many forms, while the sun presents itself in one, single, unvarying form, may account for the kinds of human perceptions which would be powerfully drawn to one or the other. At all events, with the advent of solar religion, the Great Mother, in her manifold persons and expressions, begins to suffer reduction; parts of her are split off, some undergo a gender change, and henceforth woman herself will be living on patriarchal terms, under the laws of male divinities and in the light of male judgments.

5

There are really two modes in which man has related to woman-as-mother: the practical and the magical. He has, at one time, been utterly dependent on her. Predominantly, in all cultures, it is from women that both women and men have learned about caresses, about affectionate play, about the comfort of a need satisfied—and also about the anxiety and wretchedness of a need deferred.

Briffault was convinced that maternal sentiment far predated the mating instinct; the first love being the love of mother and child. He perceived tender feelings as a secondary female sexual characteristic, derived in the course of female evolution from the biological nature of the female organism.

It was the desire for that tenderness, which the male experienced from his mother, that originally induced him to modify his own sexual instinct in accordance with the mating, or stabilizing, impulse of woman. ㉕ According to Margaret Mead,

> The relationship in the male between his innate sexual impulses and reproduction seems to be a learned response.... Male sexuality seems originally focused to no goal beyond immediate discharge; it is society that provides the male with a desire for children, for patterned interpersonal relationships that order, control, and elaborate his original impulses. ㉖

Thus in prepatriarchal life the male child early perceived that the female power of procreation was charged with *mana*. The sacred, the potent, the creative were symbolized as female. When not absorbed in fending for existence, or ritually acknowledging the (female) powers ruling life and death, prepatriarchal man must have felt something of an outsider. As Mead remarks: "His equipment for love [sex] is manifest to the very small boy— but what is it to be a father? This is something that goes on outside one's own body, in the body of another." ㉗ The anthropologist Leo Frobenius gives us the words of an Abyssinian woman commenting on the richness and complexity of a woman's biological endowment as contrasted with a man's: "His life and body are always the same.... He knows nothing." ㉘

Patriarchal man created—out of a mixture of sexual and affective frustration, blind need, physical force, ignorance, and intelligence split from its emotional grounding, a system which turned against woman her own organic nature, the source of her awe and her original powers. In a sense, female evolution was mutilated, and we have no way now of imagining what its development hitherto might have been; we can only try, at last, to take it into female hands.

The mother-child relationship is the essential human relationship. In the creation of the patriarchal family, violence is done to this fundamental human unit. It is not simply that woman in her full meaning and capacity is domesticated and confined within strictly defined limits. Even safely caged in a single aspect of her being—the maternal—she remains an object of mistrust, suspicion, misogyny in both overt and insidious forms. And the female generative organs, the matrix of human life, have become a prime target of patriarchal technology.

Notes:

① Joseph Campbell, *The Masks of God: Primitive Mythology* (New York: Viking, 1972), pp. 315. ff. ; first published in 1959.

② G. Rachel Levy, *Religious Conceptions of the Stone Age* (New York: Harper Torchbooks, 1963), pp. 83-85.

③ Ibid. , pp. 27, 86-87, 100.

④ *National Geographic*, Vol. 144, No. 6 (December 1973).

⑤ Campbell, *op. cit.* , p. 372.

⑥ Leonard Palmer, *Mycenaeans and Minoans: Aegean Pre-History in the Light of the Linear B Tablets* (New York: Knopf, 1965), p. 347.

⑦ Levy, *op. cit.* , p. 120; Erich Neumann, *The Great Mother* (Princeton, N. J. : Princeton University Press, 1972), p. 153.

⑧ That imperative in Genesis is of course preceded by the myth of Adam, in which woman's procreative power is denied and *she* is taken out of the man's body. When Adam and Eve are cursed, Eve is told that "in sorrow [she] will bring forth children".

⑨ Raphael Patai, *Sex and Family in the Bible and the Middle East* (New York: Doubleday, 1959), p. 135.

⑩ Raphael Patai, *The Hebrew Goddess* (New York: Ktav, 1967), pp. 52, 97-98.

⑪ Aeschylus, *Oresteia*, trans. Richmond Lattimore (Chicago: University of Chicago Press, 1953), pp. 158, 161.

⑫ B. Ehrenreich and D. English, *Witches, Midwives and Nurses: A History of Women Healers* (Old Westbury, N. Y. : Feminist Press, 1973), pp.

8-9. Margaret Mead notes that it has always been more difficult to obscure the woman's role in procreation than the man's—yet she gives contemporary examples—the Rossel Islanders, the Montenegrins—of cultures in which the mother's role is held to be purely passive or is denied outright (*Male and Female* [New York: Morrow, 1975], pp. 59-60).

⑬ E. O. James, *The Cult of the Mother-Goddess* (New York: Praeger, 1959), pp. 47, 138; James Mellaart, *Çatal* Hüyük: *A Neolithic Town in Anatolia* (New York: McGraw-Hill, 1967), plate 84.

⑭ Palmer, *op. cit.*, p. 192; Cyril Aldred, *Akhenaton and Nefertite* (New York: Viking, 1973), p. 181.

⑮ In Judaism there is no divine family. Christianity's Holy Family— really the human family of Jesus—is distinct from the Trinity, or three-part Godhead of Father, Son, and Holy Spirit. Daly notes the ambiguity surrounding the Holy Spirit, which is invested with stereotypically "feminine" qualities but referred to by a masculine pronoun and supposed to have impregnated the Virgin Mary. As for the human family of Jesus, his words spoken to the Virgin Mary in the Gospels are suggestive: "Woman, what have I to do with thee?" The Virgin is, of course, *virgo intacta*, not *virgo* in the sense associated with the cult of Artemis.

⑯ In his *Ancient Judaism*, Max Weber hints at the rejection of "chthonic and vegetative" cults by the Hebrews; he is, of course, talking about cults of the Mother-Goddess. Another example of the method Daly has named "The Great Silence".

⑰ Patai, *The Hebrew Goddess*, pp. 26-27, 52, 97-98.

⑱ Erich Neumann, *The Origins and History of Consciousness* (Princeton, N.J.: Princeton University Press, 1971), p. 86.

⑲ Jane Harrison, *Mythology* (New York: Harcourt Brace, 1963), pp. 44. ff.

⑳ Philip Slater, *The Glory of Hera* (Boston: Beacon, 1968). Slater is another writer who comes close to a denunciation of patriarchy yet gets deflected. His thesis is that maternal overinvolvement with the son, deriving from the inferior and reduced status of women, results—in America as in fifth-century Greece—in a narcissistic male consciousness, given to "proving" itself through war, often through meaningless achievement and acquisitiveness, and through competition. He does not, like some writers, leave the problem at the mother's door; he is refreshingly aware that her relationship to her son occurs in a social context, the *reductio-ad-matrem* which gives no other opportunity for action, makes motherhood the definition of womanhood, and child-care (in the middle classes) a full-time, exclusively female occupation. Though many of Slater's observations are useful, his failure to connect the psychic pattern with the patriarchal context leaves his insights regrettably incomplete.

㉑ Aldred, *op. cit.*, pp. 11-12; Lewis Mumford, *The City in History* (New York: Harcourt, Brace and World, 1961), p. 13.

㉒ Jane Harrison, *op. cit.*, pp. 94-95.

㉓ Slater, *op. cit.*, pp. 137-141.

㉔ M. Esther Harding, *Woman's Mysteries* (New York: C. G. Jung Foundation, 1971), p. 31.

㉕ Robert Briffault, *The Mothers* (New York: Johnson Reprint, 1969), I: pp. 131-141.

㉖ Margaret Mead, *Male and Female: A Study of the Sexes in a Changing World* (New York: Morrow, 1975), p. 229; first published in 1949.

㉗ Ibid., p. 82.

㉘ Campbell, *op. cit.*, p. 451.

4 南茜·乔德罗，"女性为什么做母亲"
Nancy Chodorow, "Why Women Mother"

南茜·朱丽娅·乔德罗（Nancy Julia Chodorow）是一位深谙诸多学科的学者，她曾把自己描述为"一位自我定义的解读性或人本主义的心理分析社会学家和心理分析女性主义者"。这已经说明，她对社会学、心理学和女性主义都有所关注，并试图用跨学科的视角对心理分析学者和女性主义者共同关心的问题给予新的诠释和分析。

乔德罗于1944年1月20日出生在纽约城，父亲马文·乔德罗（Marvin Chodorow）是应用物理学教授，母亲名蕾·突瑞兹·乔德罗（Leah Turitz Chodorow）。乔德罗在著名的拉德克里夫女子学院（Radcliffe College）获得学士学位，曾跟随惠亭夫妇（Beatrice and John W. M. Whiting）学习人类学，在当时的岁月，突出文化和个性的人类学思想对性别问题相当敏感。1975年，乔德罗在布兰德斯大学（Brandeis University）荣获社会学专业哲学博士学位。在攻读博士学位期间，她师从菲利浦·斯雷特（Philip Slater）钻研心理分析社会学理论。斯雷特告诫乔德罗说，要充分理解个性就要研究无意识现象。惠亭和斯雷特的理论对乔德罗思想的形成产生了深远影响。与此同时，乔德罗还在旧金山精神分析研究所接受了心理分析培训。1973～1974年，乔德罗在韦尔兹利学院（Wellesley College）教授女性研究课程，1974～1986年她在加州大学圣克鲁兹分校（University of California, Santa Cruz）任社会学助理教授。在此期间的1977年，乔德罗同经济学教授麦克·雷奇（Michael Reich）结婚。他们有两个孩子,但很快便分道扬镳。乔德罗是美国国家人文科学基金会①成员,行为科学研究中心成员,美国社会学学会成员,全国女性研究学会成员。她还曾荣获斯坦福高级研究中心、古根海姆基金会、美国高级学会委员会等机构颁发的研究基金。2000 年她荣获美国心理学学会颁发的杰出贡献奖。乔德罗目前在加州大学洛杉矶分校教授社会学。

乔德罗在女性主义的第二次浪潮中表现特别积极,她在 20 世纪 80 年代初开始研究如何拯救曾在 20～40 年代接受训练的第二代女性心理分析学家,她的研究成果——《给三十年代女性提出的七十年代问题:早期女性心理分析学家的性属及断代研究》(Seventies Questions for Thirties Women: Gender and Generation in a Study of Early Women Psychoanalysts)——对女性主义研究方法做出了突出贡献,反映出 70 年代女性主义者日益增强的性别意识,也触及不同女性所处的迥异文化和心理背景。

乔德罗的主要论著还包括:

《母性角色的再生:精神分析与性别的社会学》(The Reproduction of Mothering: Psychoanalysis and the Sociology of Gender),加州大学出版社,1978 年。此书荣获杰希·伯纳德社会学家奖(Jessie Bernard Award for Sociologists);1990 年《当代社会学》杂志把它列为过去 25 年间最为重要的十部著作之一。

《女性主义与精神分析理论》(Feminism and Psychoanalytic Theory),耶鲁大学出版社,1989 年。

《女性气质、男性气质、性特征:弗洛伊德及其它》(Femininities, Masculinities, Sexualities: Freud and Beyond),肯塔基大学出版社,1994 年。

《情感的力量:精神分析、性别与文化中的个人意义》(The Power of Feelings: Personal Meaning in Psychoanalysis, Gender, and Culture),耶鲁大学出版社,1999 年。此书荣获心理人类学学会颁发的 L. 布莱斯·博厄奖(L. Bryce Boyer Prize)。

一些社会学家批评乔德罗的学说不是基于经验之上,理论上过于独树一帜,不理解社会决定论,低估了社会现实的力量。与此同时,心理女性主义者却又批

---

① 国家人文科学基金会(National Endowment for the Humanities)是美国政府一家独立的捐资机构,致力于对人文科学的研究、教育和保护。

评她太过经验主义,过于相信社会决定论,把无意识看做一种社会学现象而不是一个独特的存在①。乔德罗本人对此作过如下解释:

> 我同大多数美国精神分析学家不同,因为我依赖客体关系[object relations]理论,我一直把精神分析视为一种解读过程(而不是医学意义或者科学意义的)。我同许多人文主义学者的区别是,我把精神分析看做一种社会科学,这一科学虽然拥有坚实的理论基础但同时也是对人生的经验性研究。②

乔德罗把精神分析定义为"研究和理解人们如何产生并经历无意识幻想(形式心理、自我、身份)、如何在现在建构并重建人们感知的过去所运用的方法和理论"。她认为,精神分析学说并不能对心理发展提出普遍的解释,人们必须把现实的文化历史环境纳入考虑的范围。她指责弗洛伊德的著作仅仅对男人和女人"应该怎样"提出了未经支持的论断③。乔德罗把自己运用的方法称作多元的,她试图聚焦各种因素之间的关系,分析并批判男性统治,从而从女性主义角度定义性别和性属的意义④。

乔德罗最大的贡献是提出了关于性别体系的心理动态学必须有赖于历史的变化和发展⑤的观点。乔德罗在心理分析领域、尤其是女性心理领域做出的成就以及提出的学说使她当之无愧成为当今最为重要的女性主义理论家之一,她的著述被性别研究学者广泛引用。

乔德罗最为重要、最具影响的著作是 1978 年出版的《母性角色的再生》。该书共分三篇:"问题的提出:母性角色与性别的社会组织","心理分析讲述的

---

① http://www. webster. edu/ ~ woolflm/chodorow. html, n. p.

② Nancy Chodorow, *Feminism and Psychoanalytic Theory* (Yale University Press, 1989), p.18.

③ Jane Flax, *Disputed Subjects: Essays on Psychoanalysis, Politics, and Philosophy* (New York: Routledge, 1993), p.7.

④ http://www. webster. edu/ ~ woolflm/chodorow. html, n. p.

⑤ Deborah L. Rhode, *Theoretical Perspectives on Sexual Difference* (Binghampton: Vail-Ballou Press, 1990), p.2.

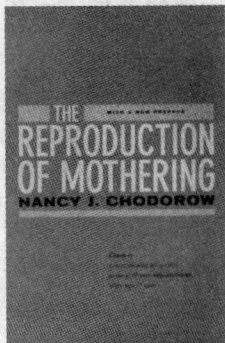

故事","性别个性与母性角色的再生。"乔德罗开宗明义地指出:"女性要做母亲"①。她说,在任何社会,养育孩子的责任首先都落在女性身上,如果孩子的生理母亲不在人世,继母、女性亲属或女性仆人则接替养育的任务(第3页)。这一普遍习俗或称社会结构对人类的内在精神结构和心理发展影响深刻。"女性充当母性角色,这是性别劳动分工中最为普遍、最为持久的少数要素之一"(第3页)。乔德罗指出,在过去的两个世纪中,社会生活发生了重大变化,妇女的社会地位也有所改变,但女性仍然承担着母亲的角色,担负着养育孩子的主要家庭责任(第5页),"生产的社会关系中发生的基本改变并不能保证在生产的家庭关系中也有相应的改变"(第6页)。母性是社会引发的心理过程的产物。一方面,它是"物质的",因为母性由于劳动分工而得以维系;另一方面,它又是"心理的",因为母性的再生是通过心理过程来实现的②。乔德罗使用"再生"一词以描述母性角色可以在下一代身上重复生成这一事实:劳动分工中受压抑的一方注定要在后代身上再生这一压抑的状态。

> 身为母亲的女性,培养了具有母性能力以及做母亲欲望的女儿,这样的能力和需要是建构并生发于母女关系本身的。相比之下,身为母亲的女性(以及不充当母亲角色的男性)培养出的儿子其养育能力与需要被系统地压制和剥夺。(第7页)

在这部书中,乔德罗大胆地对女性生理决定哺育婴儿的传统观念提出挑战。她认为,母性满足了女人对相互间亲密关系的心理需要③。乔德罗说,母亲同儿子的关系与同女儿的关系迥异,母亲同儿子的关系更为亲密一些,但她也清楚地知道儿子是与自己截然不同的存在,相比之下,母亲与女儿分享着某种意义上的

---

① Nancy Chodorow, *The Reproduction of Mothering*: *Psychoanalysis and the Sociology of Gender* (Berkeley: University of California Press, 1978), p. 3. 本节引用《母性角色的再生》均出自该书,以下只在正文注明页码,分号后第二个页码为引文在本页的页码。

② Kumiko Sato, http://www. personal. psu. edu/staff/k/x/kxs 334/academic/theory/chodorow_mothering. html, n. p.

③ http://www. webster. edu/~woolflm/women. html, n. p.

"同一性"("oneness")。大约三岁的时候孩子开始注意到性别的差异。女孩认为自己像母亲并对母亲的形象产生认同。母亲也对女儿有认同,并仿佛在女儿身上看到了自己的童年。这样,母女之间逐渐发展了一种亲密的、紧密的情感联系。女性的自我界线是有弹性的("flexible ego boundaries")。而男孩虽然认识到自己像父亲,但由于父亲总是工作在外,男孩无法把父亲的形象具体化,也无法同父亲建立紧密的纽带。结果,男孩强烈地意识到自己同其他人是多么的不同。同女性相比,男性的自我界限则是拘谨的("rigid ego boundaries")。在谈到儿童经历的俄狄浦斯阶段时,乔德罗说,女孩与母亲之间的前俄狄浦斯纽带在女孩对父亲产生迷恋之后仍然继续。在前俄狄浦斯阶段,婴孩首先经历对母亲的爱恋,孩子的需要与母亲满足这一需要的能力之间没有区别。逐渐地,孩子通过对自己身体自我的扩展意识开始建立一种真正的自我意识。

乔德罗认为,客体关系理论,即性别身份的形成,是家庭关系动态变化的结果。在接受保罗·E·林奇(Paul E. Lynch)采访时,乔德罗再次重申,男性并不是生来就具统治性的,男性的特征是在文化形成过程中、在家庭关系中人与人之间相互作用的结果。在男人/男孩、男人/女人这两组二元对立的关系中,男人自然成为更有力量、更有权力的一方①。乔德罗清楚地知道,心理学是由不同组织支持的社会体系。心理学和社会体系是相互支撑的。俄狄浦斯结构尤其支持着社会欲望体系②。性别身份尽管由社会引发,但却通过母子关系内化为人类心理状态。这种关系——在男孩看来母亲是客体,在女孩看来母亲是自我——将再生相同的母性体系。

在该书的前言,乔德罗对其接受的两个重要影响做出了明确说明。其一是盖尔·鲁宾(Gayle Rubin)③关于每一社会都由"性别/性属体系"所组织的理论。根据鲁宾的观点,把社会组织起来的"性别/性属体系"是一整套思想和学说,这些思想和学说使生理意义上的人类性别和生育活动受制于社会干预,于是,人们所知道的性别本身成为一个社会产品。鲁宾还指出,所有的社会"性

---

① http://www.cyberpsych.org/homophobia/noframes/chodorow.htm, n. p.

② Kumiko Sato, http://www.personal.psu.edu/staff/k/x/kxs334/academic/theory/chodorow_mothering.html, n. p.

③ 鲁宾,著名人类学家和女性主义理论家,代表著作有《女性交易:关于性别的"政治经济学"笔记》(*The Traffic in Women: Notes on the "Political Economy" of Sex*)和《思考性别》(*Thinking Sex*)等。

别/性属体系"都是以男性占主导地位的。其二是以米歇尔·罗萨尔多(Michelle Rosaldo)①和谢莉·奥特纳(Sherry Ortner)②为代表的女性主义者关于女性的母性角色是性别社会组织至关重要特征的观点。这些女性主义者认为,女性的首要位置是在家庭,男性的位置是在公共场所,这一分工决定了社会本身是男性的。社会给予男性创造的能力,给予男性维护社会机制的能力,这使得男性根据自己的意愿控制婚姻这一机制。乔德罗从这些观点中得到启示,发展了自己的学说,她说:"女性承担的母性角色决定女性的首要位置在家庭范畴,这为家庭与公众领域的结构划分奠定了基础"(第10页)。在西方社会,家庭与公众领域的区分由于工业资本主义的发展得以加强,家庭分工、女性的母性角色、母亲的特质以及异性婚姻持续不断地再生男性统治。

这里选注的是该书第一篇第二节:"女性为什么做母亲"。该节除引语外,分两部分:"自然论断"("The Argument from Nature")和"角色培养论断"("The Role-Training Argument")。在引语中,乔德罗陈述了本节主要观点:

> 女性承担的母性角色对性别劳动分工至关重要。女性承担的母性角色对女性的生活、对关于女性的认识、对男性意识和性别不平等的再生、对劳动力某种形式的再生等问题都具有深远影响。身为母亲的女性是社会再生领域的轴枢因素。(第11页;第68页)

乔德罗还指出,物质生产由原始社会的家族性转向现代社会的非家族性,随着生产的社会化,生产活动已经逐渐远离了家庭,然而,女性的生育活动和抚养孩子的活动仍然局限在家庭范围,家族纽带和亲情关系对女性来说仍然至关重要。"生育活动已经成为最直接定义和限制女性生活和女性自身的要素"(第13页;第69页)。

---

① 罗萨尔多(? ~1981),著名人类学家、女性主义理论家,曾创办斯坦福大学的女性研究专业,同蓝菲尔(Louise Lamphere)合作主编《女性、文化与社会》(Women, Culture, and Society,1974年)。

② 奥特纳(1941~),著名人类学家、女性主义理论家,代表著作是《女性与男性的关系如同自然与文化的关系吗?》(Is Female to Male As Nature Is to Culture? 1974年),与他人合编《文化/权力/历史:当代社会理论读本》(Culture/Power/History: A Reader in Contemporary Social Theory, 1994年)。

在第一部分"自然论断"中,乔德罗批判了关于女性承担母性角色的几种错误认识。第一种错误认识可以称为生理观。这种观点认为女性的生理特点——染色体和生殖器官——决定她注定要承担母亲角色。但是,乔德罗却论证说,染色体的差别和生殖器官的差别也并不完全是生理意义上的,况且,同性间的差别往往会比异性间的差别更大(第15页)。乔德罗指出,应该区分抚养孩子和生育孩子这两种行为,把养育视为人类活动(第16页)。第二种错误认识可以称为进化观。这种观点认为人类从狩猎时代起的进化过程决定了女性要做母亲,但乔德罗却坚信从进化和功能的角度不足以解释为什么女性要做母亲。第三种错误认识可以称为本能观。一些心理学家认为女性有做母亲的本能。但乔德罗却引用医学研究成果表明男人和女人面对孩子各种情感时的反应大同小异(第27页)。她总结说,"女性拥有广泛的、排他的母性角色,这是社会和文化对女性具有的生育和哺育孩子能力的一种解读"(第30页)。

在第二部分"角色培养论断"中,乔德罗提出了自己在这一问题上的认识,这一认识基于她对一些女性主义者观点的认同。乔德罗的观点可以归纳为以下几点:

第一,母亲身份的获得是女性角色培养和角色认同的结果(第31页;第70页)。女儿在成长过程中同自己的母亲产生认同,这种认同的结果便是女儿成长为母亲。

第二,母亲身份是性别劳动分工的基本构成要素(第32页;第71~72页)。作为性别分工的要素,母亲身份无论从结构上还是从因果关系上都同其它的机制内容相关,同时也再生性别的不平等。

第三,母亲身份不是一成不变的跨文化普遍规律(第32页;第72页)。母亲身份包含历史因素、心理因素、生理因素、社会因素、政治因素、经济因素等诸多相关内容。

乔德罗于是得出以下结论:

女人承担母亲角色,这是家庭生活和性别劳动分工的体制特点,这一现象是循环再生的。在此过程中,它导致成人生活的性别社会学中其它方面的再生,这些方面都与女人做母亲的事实相关。……多数对性别角色社会化的传统描述都依赖于个人意图和行为标准,这并不能充分解释女人的母亲身份。相比之下,精神分析却可以系统性地、结构性地解释社会化和社会再生。性别社会组织的主要特点通过家庭这一机制结构创造的个性特征传输给孩子,使他们成为具有不同性别身份的社会成员。(第38~39页;第80~81页)

这里节选的是本节引语以及第二部分"角色培养论断"。

Why Women Mother

It is woman's biological destiny to bear and deliver, to nurse and to rear children.

EDITH JACOBSON,

"Development of the Wish for a Child in Boys"

... the problem of maternity cannot be dismissed as a zoological fact... the theory of cultural motherhood should have been made the foundation of the general theory of kinship.

BRONISLAW MALINOWSKI,

"Parenthood, the Basis of Social Structure"

Mothers are women, of course, because a mother is a female parent, and a female who is a parent must be adult, hence must be a woman. Similarly, fathers are male parents, are men. But we mean something different when we say that someone mothered a child than when we say that someone fathered her or him. We can talk about a man "mothering" a child, if he is this child's primary nurturing figure, or is acting in a nurturant manner. But we would never talk about a woman "fathering" a child, even in the rare societies in which a high-ranking woman may take a wife and be the social father of her wife's children. In these cases we call her the child's social father, and do not say that she fathered her child. Being a mother, then, is not only bearing a child—it is being a person who socializes and nurtures. It is being a primary parent or caretaker. So we can ask, why are mothers women? Why is the person who routinely does all those activities that go into parenting not a man?

The question is important. Women's mothering is central to the sexual division of labor. Women's maternal role has profound effects on women's lives, on ideology about women, on the reproduction of masculinity and sexual inequality, and on the reproduction of particular forms of labor power. Women as mothers are pivotal actors in the sphere of social reproduction. As Engels and Marxist feminists, Lévi-Strauss and feminist anthropologists, Parsons and family theorists point out, women find their primary social location within this sphere.

Most sociological theorists have either ignored or taken as unproblematic this sphere of social reproduction, despite its importance and the recognition by some theorists, such as Engels, of its fundamental historical role. [1] As a consequence of ignoring this sphere, most sociological theorists have ignored women, who have been the central figures within it.

Engels helps us to understand this omission through his emphasis on the shift away from kinship-based forms of material production in modern societies. All societies contain both means of producing material subsistence and means of organizing procreation. Earlier societies (and contemporary "primitive" societies) were centered on kinship relations. Production and reproduction were organized according to the rules of kinship. This does not mean that the relations of production were based entirely on actual biological and affinal ties. In contemporary primitive societies, a kinship idiom can come to describe and incorporate whatever productive relations develop.

In modern societies, ties based on kinship no longer function as important links among people in the productive world, which becomes organized more and more in nonkinship market and class relations. Moreover, the relations of material production, and the extended public and political ties and associations—the state, finally—which these relations make possible, dominate and define family relations—the sphere of human reproduction. Many aspects of reproduction are taken over by extrafamilial institutions like schools. Kinship, then, is progressively stripped of its functions and its ability to organize the social world. ②

Because of their location within and concern with Western capitalist society, most major social theorists have made the recognition of this major historical transformation fundamental to their theories. They have, as a consequence, developed theories which focus on non-familial political, economic, and communal ties and have treated familial relations only to point out their declining importance. ③ This historical transformation also reinforces a tendency in everyday discourse. Social theorists, like societal members, tend to define a society and discuss its social organization in terms of what men do, and where men are located in that society.

It is apparent, however, that familial and kinship ties and family life remain crucial for women. The organization of these ties is certainly shaped in many ways by industrial capitalist development (though the family retains fundamental precapitalist, preindustrial features—that women mother, for instance). However, as production has moved out of the home, reproduction has become even more immediately defining and circumscribing of women's life activities and of women themselves.

Some theorists do investigate the family. Parsons's concern with the "problem of order" (what accounts for the persistence of social structures over time) and that of the Frankfurt Institute with the reproduction of capitalist relations of production and ideology have led both, in their attempts to understand social reproductive processes, to turn to the family as an area for sociological inquiry. ④ Feminist theorists, including Engels and Charlotte Perkins Gilman, ⑤ early recognized the family as a central agent of women's oppression as well as the major institution in women's lives. Anthropological theory also, in its concern with societies in which social ties for both men and women are largely defined through kinship, has developed an extensive and sophisticated analysis of kinship and the organization of gender—of rules of descent, marriage rules, residence arrangements, variations in household and family organization, and so forth. Consequently, anthropological theory has informed much family theory, including some feminist theories. ⑥

Most of these theories see women's mothering as central. While understanding the importance of this mothering for social reproduction, however, they do not take it as in need of explanation. They simply assume that it is socially, psychologically, and biologically natural and functional. They do not question and certainly do not explain the reproduction of mothering itself either cross-culturally or within modern societies. They understand how women as mothers currently produce men with particular personalities and orientations, and how women's social location and the sexual division of labor generate other features of the social and economic world and of ideology about women. But they do not inquire about how women themselves are produced, how women continue to find themselves in a particular social and economic location.

[……]

The Role-Training Argument

Nonfeminist theorists do not inquire about the reproduction of mothering or of the social relations of parenting, and seem to assume biological inevitability. This is true whether or not they recognize the sociological significance of the family and women's role in social reproduction. Feminist writers have alternate explanations, sometimes made explicit, sometimes assumed, each pointing to some elements in the process by which women come to mother. Moreover, they do so without relying on biological assumptions. At the same time, they are profoundly limited. ⑦

One important tendency in the feminist literature looks (along with social psychologists) at role training or cognitive role learning. It suggests that women's mothering, like other aspects of gender activity, is a product of feminine role training and role identification. Girls are taught to be mothers, trained for nurturance, and told that they ought to mother. They are wrapped in pink blankets, given dolls and have their brothers' trucks taken away, learn that being a girl is not as good as being a boy, are not allowed to get dirty, are discouraged from achieving in school, and therefore become mothers. They are barraged from early childhood well into adult life with books, magazines, ads, school courses, and television programs which put forth pronatalist and pro-maternal sex-stereotypes. They "identify" with their own mothers as they grow up, and this identification produces the girl as a mother. Alternately, as those following cognitive-psychological trends would have it, girls choose to do "girl-things" and, I suppose, eventually "woman-things," like mothering, as a result of learning that they are girls. In this view, girls identify with their mothers as a result of learning that they are girls and wanting to be girl-like. [8]

Margaret Polatnick presents a different view, in specific disagreement with socialization theories. She asks not how women come to mother, but why men do not. Her explanation is in terms of power differences and social control. She takes men's power and women's powerlessness as a given, and suggests that men use their power to enforce the perpetuation of women's mothering: "Men don't rear children because they don't *want* to rear children. (This implies, of course, that they're in a position to enforce their preferences)." [9] Her account goes on to show why people in our society who have power over others would choose not to parent. Parenting, as an unpaid occupation outside the world of public power, entails lower status, less power, and less control of resources than paid work. Women's mothering reinforces and perpetuates women's relative powerlessness.

All of these views share the assumption that women's mothering is a product of behavioral conformity and individual intention. An investigation of what mothering consists in helps to explain how it is perpetuated, and indicates the limitations of traditional socialization and social control explanations for the reproduction of mothering.

To begin with, women's mothering does not exist in isolation. It is a fundamental constituting feature of the sexual division of labor. As part of the sexual division of labor, it is structurally and causally related to other institutional arrangements and to ideological formulations which justify the sexual division of labor. Mothering also contributes to the reproduction of sexual inequality through its effects on masculine personality.

Women's mothering is not an unchanging transcultural universal. Although women, and not men, have primary responsibility for children, many features of this responsibility change. Family organization, child-care and child-rearing practices, and the relations between women's child care and other responsibilities change in response particularly to changes in the organization of production. Women's role as we know it is an historical product. The development of industrial capitalism in the West entailed that women's role in the family become increasingly concerned with personal relations and psychological stability. Mothering is most eminently a psychologically based role. It consists in psychological and personal experience of self in relationship to child or children.

As culture and personality research has demonstrated, an important element in the reproduction of social relations and social structure is the socialization of people with psychological capacities and commitments appropriate to participation in these relations and structures. In an industrial late-capitalist society, "socialization" is a particularly psychological affair, since it must lead to the assimilation and internal organization of generalized capacities for participation in a hierarchical and differentiated social world, rather than to training for a specific role. ⑩ Production, for instance, is more efficient and profitable when workers develop a willing and docile personality. In the last analysis, however, it is possible to extract labor by coercion (and it is certainly the case that there is some coercive element in needing to enter work relations in the first place).

The use of coercion is not possible in the case of mothering. Clinical research shows that behavioral conformity to the apparent specific physical requirements of infants—keeping them fed and clean—is not enough to enable physiological, let alone psychological, growth in an infant. ⑪ Studies of infants in understaffed institutions where perfunctory care is given, and of infants whose caretakers do not hold them or interact with them, show that these infants may become mildly depressed, generally withdrawn, psychotically unable to relate, totally apathetic and, in extreme cases, may die. Infants need affective bonds and a diffuse, multifaceted, ongoing personal relationship to caretakers for physical and psychological growth. ⑫

A concern with parenting, then, must direct attention beyond behavior. This is because parenting is not simply a set of behaviors, but participation in an interpersonal, diffuse, affective relationship. Parenting is an eminently psychological role in a way that many other roles and activities are not. "Good-enough mothering" ("good-enough" to socialize a nonpsychotic child) requires certain relational capacities which are embedded in personality and a sense of self-in-relationship.

Given these requirements, it is evident that the mothering that women do is not something that can be taught simply by giving a girl dolls or telling her that she ought to mother. It is not something that a girl can learn by behavioral imitation, or by deciding that she wants to do what girls do. Nor can men's power over women explain women's mothering. Whether or not men in particular or society at large—through media, income distribution, welfare policies, and schools—enforce women's mothering, and expect or require a woman to care for her child, they cannot require or force her to provide adequate parenting unless she, *to some degree* and *on some unconscious or conscious level*, has the capacity and sense of self as maternal to do so. ⑬

Role training, identification, and enforcement certainly have to do with the acquisition of an appropriate gender role. But the conventional feminist view, drawn from social or cognitive psychology, which understands feminine development as explicit ideological instruction or formal coercion, cannot in the case of mothering be sufficient. In addition, explanations relying on behavioral conformity do not account for the tenacity of self-definition, self-concept, and psychological need to maintain aspects of traditional roles which continue even in the face of ideological shifts, counter-instruction, and the lessening of masculine coercion which the women's movement has produced.

A second deficiency of role-learning and social control explanations for the reproduction of mothering is that they rely on individual intention—on the part of socializers, of girls who want to do girl-things or be like their mothers, and on the part of men who control women. There is certainly an intentional component to gender role socialization in the family, in schools, in the media. However, social reproduction comes to be independent of individual intention and is not caused by it. There are several aspects to social reproduction, all of which apply in the case of the reproduction of mothering.

Practices become institutionalized in regularized, nonarbitrary ways. Aspects of society—social and economic relations, institutions, values and ideology—develop their own logic and autonomy and come to mutually interact with and maintain one another. Aspects of society are not newly created every day, although they do develop historically through the intended activity of people. The conditions people live in are given as the historical outcome of previous human social activity, which itself has exhibited some regularity and consistency.

In the case of a mother-child relationship, there is an interactive base of expectations of continuity of relationship. This interactive base develops once a woman begins to care for a particular child, and usually includes gratification as well as frustration for both the child and the mother. More generally, women's mothering as an organization of parenting is embedded in and fundamental to the social organization of gender. In any historical period, women's mothering and the sexual division of labor are also structurally linked to other institutions and other aspects of social organization. In industrial capitalist societies, women's mothering is central to the links between the organization of gender—in particular the family system—and economic organization. ⑭ Sexual inequality is itself embedded in and perpetuated by the organization of these institutions, and is not reproduced according to or solely because of the will of individual actors.

Intentional socialization theories, just as they are generally not sufficient to explain social reproduction, are insufficient to explain the reproduction of the social organization of gender and its major features. The social organization of gender, in its relation to an economic context, has depended on the continuation of the social relations of parenting. The reproduction of these social relations of parenting is not reducible to individual intention but depends on all the arrangements which go into the organization of gender and the organization of the economy.

These institutions create and embody conditions that require people to engage in them. People's participation further guarantees social reproduction. Marx gives an example in the case of capitalism: "Capitalist production, therefore, of itself reproduces the separation between labour-power and the means of labour. It thereby perpetuates the condition for exploiting the labourer. It incessantly forces him to sell his labour-power in order to live, and enables the capitalist to purchase labour-power in order that he may enrich himself. It is no longer a mere accident, that capitalist and labourer confront each other in the market as buyer and seller." ⑮ Or, for instance, Lévi-Strauss describes a strongly enforced sexual division of labor as a condition for the reproduction of heterosexual marriage:

> Generally speaking it can be said that, among the so-called primitive tribes, there are no bachelors, simply for the reason that they could not survive. One of the strongest field recollections of this writer was his meeting, among the Bororo of central Brazil, a man about thirty years old: unclean, ill-fed, sad, and lonesome. When asked if the man were seriously ill, the natives' answer came as a shock: what was wrong with him? —nothing at all, he was just a bachelor. And true enough, in a society where labor is systematically shared between man and woman and where only the married status permits the man to benefit from the

fruits of woman's work, including delousing, body painting, and hair-plucking as well as vegetable food and cooked food (since the Bororo woman tills the soil and makes pots), a bachelor is really only half a human being.... ⑯

The sexual division of labor ... has been explained as a device to make the sexes mutually dependent on social and economic grounds, thus establishing clearly that marriage is better than celibacy... . The principle of sexual division of labor establishes a mutual dependency between the sexes, compelling them thereby to perpetuate themselves and found a family. ⑰

In the case of mothering, the economic system has depended for its reproduction on women's reproduction of particular forms of labor power in the family. At the same time, income inequality between men and women makes it more rational, and even necessary, in any individual conjugal family for fathers, rather than mothers, to be primary wage-earners. Therefore, mothers, rather than fathers, are the primary caretakers of children and the home.

Legitimating ideologies themselves, as well as institutions like schools, the media, and families which perpetuate ideologies, contribute to social reproduction. They create expectations in people about what is normal and appropriate and how they should act. Society's perpetuation requires that *someone* rear children, but our language, science, and popular culture all make it very difficult to separate the need for care from the question of who provides that care. It is hard to separate our parenting activities, usually performed by women and particularly by biological mothers, from women themselves.

Finally, people themselves need to be reproduced both daily and generationally. Most theoretical accounts agree that women as wives and mothers reproduce people—physically in their housework and child care, psychologically in their emotional support of husbands and their maternal relation to sons and daughters. If we accept this view, we have to ask who reproduces wives and mothers. What is hidden in most accounts of the family is that women reproduce *themselves* through their own daily housework. What is also often hidden, in generalizations about the family as an emotional refuge, is that in the family as it is currently constituted no one supports and reconstitutes women affectively and emotionally—either women working in the home or women working in the paid labor force. This was not always the case. In a previous period, and still in some stable working-class and ethnic communities, women did support themselves emotionally by supporting and reconstituting *one another*. [18] However, in the current period of high mobility and familial isolation, this support is largely removed, and there is little institutionalized daily emotional reconstitution of mothers. What there is depends on the accidents of a particular marriage, and not on the carrying out of an institutionalized support role. [19] There is a fundamental asymmetry in daily reproduction. Men are socially and psychologically reproduced by women, but women are reproduced (or not) largely by themselves.

We also need to understand the intergenerational reproduction of mothers. Parsons and theorists of the Frankfurt Institute have added significantly to our total picture of social reproduction by providing a model of the reproduction of social relations across generations. They argue that in industrial capitalist society, generational reproduction occurs through the creation in the family of men workers with particular personalities and orientations to authority. These social theorists have attempted to integrate a theory of large-scale social-cultural structure and its institutional and ideological reproduction with a theory of the way this structure reproduces itself through everyday interpersonal experiences and personality development in its members. These theorists of social reproduction describe how members of a society come to be (in Parsons's terminology) motivated to comply with role expectations. They describe how the structural organization of that institution in which people grow up, the family, entails that people develop personalities which tend to guarantee that they will get gratification or satisfaction from those activities which are necessary to the reproduction of the larger social structure. In Max Horkheimer's terms, "In so far as the continuance of all social forms goes, the dominant force is not insight but human patterns of reaction which have become stabilized in interaction with a system of cultural formations on the basis of the social life process."[20] And Parsons reiterates his claim: "The integration of a set of common value patterns with the internalized need-disposition structure of the constituent personalities is the core phenomenon of the dynamics of social systems."[21]

Parsons and Frankfurt theorists have investigated the family, and especially the organization of parenting. Furthermore, in their concern to develop a theory of socialization that relies on institutional and structural mechanisms, rather than on individual intention, they have turned to psychoanalysis "as a 'psychology of family' pure and simple"[22] for their method of inquiry. They have begun to develop a psychoanalytic sociology of social reproduction.

The empirical efforts of Parsons and the Frankfurt theorists, however, have been directed toward the reproduction of relations of production, and to men as workers. They, as well as Freudian social theorists[23] and Marxist feminists[24] after them, have been concerned with the way the family and women socialize *men* into capitalist society.[25] They have developed an extensive and important analysis of the relation of masculine psychological development to capitalist achievement or properly submissive or bureaucratized work behavior, as well as to the relation of masculine attitudes to women and femininity.[26] But they have not discussed feminine development at all.

The account which follows takes these theories as methodological models and extends their psychoanalytic sociology. I do not mean to deny the basic differences between the theories of Parsons and critical theorists such as Horkheimer. These differences are both methodological and political—but it is their political differences which have often obscured the similarities of their descriptions and their similar use of psychoanalysis. Empirically, both accounts describe how the development of industrial capitalism has affected family structure and personality. This is phrased in critical theory in terms of the decline of paternal authority and the father's role in the home, in Parsons's case in terms of the overwhelming importance of the mother. These changes have in turn affected masculine development: Men's orientation to authority and malleability as labor power have shifted.

Politically, Parsons is basically uncritical of the society he describes. Parsons focuses on the problem of order—so do critical theorists, but in Parsons's case, it always sounds as though he wants to understand order to contribute toward its maintenance. For the critical theorists, the problem of order is posed as the problem of understanding historically specific forms of domination. Parsons's theory, while treating culture, social organization, personality, and biology, tends to define society in terms of its value system, or culture. Critical theorists generally accord primary significance to the social organization of production, and relate values and particular forms of domination to this organization.

Finally, critical theorists like Horkheimer focus on disruptive elements which undermine the smooth reproduction of functional relationships. For Parsons, the family reproduces social and economic organization. For critical theorists, it both reproduces and undermines these forms. While Parsons makes a major contribution to our understanding of social reproduction, and especially to the part played by personality, it is evident that there are contradictions in the contemporary organization of gender and the family— ways in which expectations created in the family cannot be fulfilled, strains in women's and men's and parents' and children's roles and relationships, incompatible needs for women as child-rearers and workers in the labor force.

In the account which follows, I show how the structure of parenting reproduces itself. Like the psychoanalytic sociologists I discuss, I rely on psychoanalytic theory as an analysis of family structure and social reproduction. Psychoanalysis shows us how the family division of labor in which women mother gives socially and historically specific meaning to gender itself. This engendering of men and women with particular personalities, needs, defenses, and capacities creates the condition for and contributes to the reproduction of this same division of labor. The sexual division of labor both produces gender differences and is in turn reproduced by them.

The psychoanalytic account shows not only how men come to grow away from their families and to participate in the public sphere. It shows also how women grow up to have both the generalized relational capacities and needs and how women and men come to create the kinds of interpersonal relationships which make it likely that women will remain in the domestic sphere—in the sphere of reproduction—and will in turn mother the next generation. Women's mothering as an institutionalized feature of family life and of the sexual division of labor reproduces itself cyclically. In the process, it contributes to the reproduction of those aspects of the sexual sociology of adult life which grow out of and relate to the fact that women mother.

I suggested earlier that women's mothering was reproduced on a number of different levels. Because of the requirements of parenting, and particularly because of its contemporary largely psychological form, the genesis of psychological mothering capacities and orientations in women is fundamental and conditional to all of these. The capacities and orientations I describe must be built into personality; they are not behavioral acquisitions. Women's capacities for mothering and abilities to get gratification from it are strongly internalized and psychologically enforced, and are built developmentally into the feminine psychic structure. Women are prepared psychologically for mothering through the developmental situation in which they grow up, and in which women have mothered them.

Most conventional accounts of gender-role socialization rely on individual intention and behavioral criteria, which do not adequately explain women's mothering. Psychoanalysis, by contrast, provides a systemic, structural account of socialization and social reproduction. It suggests that major features of the social organization of gender are transmitted in and through those personalities produced by the structure of the institution—the family— in which children become gendered members of society.

Notes:

① See Robert V. Wells, 1971, "Demographic Change and the Life Cycle of American Families," *Journal of Interdisciplinary History*, 2, #2, pp. 273-282.

② See, for example, Alice Clark, 1919. *The Working Life of Women in the Seventeenth Century*, and Robert S. Lynd and Helen Merrell Lynd, 1929, *Middletown*.

③ Thus, Durkheim describes the shift from mechanical to organic solidarity. Tönnies distinguishes *gemeinschaft* and *gesellchaft* societies. Weber discusses increasing rationalization and the rise of bureaucracy and market relations. Parsons distinguishes particularistic, ascribed, affective role relationships from those based on universalistic, achieved, and nonaffective criteria. Marx gives an account of the way capitalist market relations increasingly dominate all social life.

④ See, for example, Talcott Parsons, 1942, "Age and Sex in the Social Structure of the United States," and 1943, "The Kinship System of the Contemporary United States," both in *Essays in Sociological Theory*, and 1964, *Social Structure and Personality*; Talcott Parsons and Robert F. Bales, 1955, *Family, Socialization and Interaction Process*; Eli Zaretsky, 1976, *Capitalism, the Family and Personal Life*; Peter L. Berger and Hansfried Kellner, 1974, "Marriage and the Construction of Reality," in Rose Laub Coser, ed. , *The Family: Its Structures and Functions*.

⑤ This phrase is Ruth Bloch's, 1972, "Sex and the Sexes in Eighteenth-Century Magazines. "

⑥ See Philippe Aries, 1960, *Centuries of Childhood: A Social History* of *Family Life*; William Goode, 1963, *World Revolution and Family Patterns*; Barbara Laslett, 1973, " The Family as a Public and Private Institution: An Historical Perspective," *Journal of Marriage and the Family*, 35, pp. 480-492; Peter Laslett, ed. , 1972, *Household and Family in Past Time.*

⑦ My treatment of the role-learning argument in what follows is much briefer than my treatment of the biological argument, not because it is less important but because the rest of the book provides an alternate empirical account of female development.

⑧ For good examples of the tendency to explain the reproduction and maintenance of gender-role differentiation through consciously intended socialization and training, see Lenore J. Weitzman, 1975, " Sex-Role Socialization," in Jo Freeman, ed. , *Women: A Feminist Perspective*, pp. 105-144; Jo Freeman, 1971, "The Social Construction of the Second Sex," in Michelle Garskof, ed. , *Roles Women Play*; and the Journal *Sex Roles*. For investigations of propulsion (and seduction) into motherhood by media and ideology, see Jessie Bernard, 1974, *The Future of Motherhood*; and Ellen Peck and Judith Senderowitz, eds. , 1974, *Pronatalism: The Myth of Mom and Apple Pie*. For an account of gender-role socialization as a product of a child's learning it is a girl or boy, see Lawrence Kohlberg, 1966, " A Cognitive Developmental Analysis of Sex-Role Concepts and Attitudes," in E. Maccoby, ed. , *The Development of Sex Differences*. For discussions of identification and gender-role learning, see David B. Lynn, 1959, "A Note on Sex Differences in the Development of Masculine and Feminine Identification," *Psychological Review*, 66, pp. 126-135, and 1962, " Sex Role and Parent Identification," *Child Development*, 33, pp. 555-564; Parsons and Bales, 1955, *Family*; Parsons, 1942, " Age and Sex"; Robert F. Winch, 1962, *Identification and Its Familial Determinants*; Walter Mischel, 1966, "A Social-Learning View of Sex Differences in Behavior," in Maccoby, ed. , *The Development of Sex Differences*; and Walter Mischel, 1970, "Sex Typing and Socialization," in Paul Mussen, ed. , *Carmichael's Manual of Child*

Psychology, vol. 2, 3rd ed. , pp. 3-72.

⑨ Margaret Polatnick, 1973, "Why Men Don't Rear Children: A Power Analysis," *Berkeley Journal of Sociology*, 18, p. 60.

⑩ See Parsons with Winston White, 1961, "The Link Between Character and Society," in *Social Structure and Personality*; Parsons and Bales, 1955, *Family*, *Socialization*; Frankfurt Institute, 1972, *Aspects*; Wilhelm Reich, 1966, *Sex-Pol*; Philip E. Slater, 1970, *The Pursuit of Loneliness*, and 1974, *Earthwalk*; and Warren G. Bennis and Philip Slater, 1968, *The Temporary Society*; Samuel Bowles and Herbert Gintis, 1976, *Schooling in Capitalist America*; Richard C. Edwards, 1975, "The Social Relations of Production in the Firm and Labor Market Structure," in Edwards, Michael Reich, and David M. Gordon, eds. , *Labor Market Segmentation*.

⑪ See John Bowlby, 1951, *Maternal Care and Mental Health*; Margaret S. Mahler, 1968, *On Human Symbiosis and the Vicissitudes of Individuation. Volume 1: Infantile Psychosis*; Rene Spitz, 1965, *The First Year of Life: A Psychoanalytic Study of Normal and Deviant Development of Object Relations*; Winnicott, 1965, *Maturational Processes*.

⑫ I am not talking about "maternal deprivation," as it is conventionally labeled, which implies separation from or loss of the biological or social *mother*, or that *she herself* is not providing adequate care. What is at issue is the *quality of care*, and not who provides it: "The notion that the biological mother by virtue of being the biological mother is capable of caring for her child is without foundation" (Rudolph Schaffer, 1977, *Mothering*, p. 103); "from the child's point of view, it matters little what sex mother is." (Ibid. , p. 105. For another attempt to review research which separates out the various factors involved in "maternal deprivation," see Michael Rutter, 1972, *Maternal Deprivation Reassessed*.)

⑬ My argument here is extrapolated from clinical findings on the nature of mothering. A good empirical evaluation of the argument could be drawn from investigation of black slave women's mothering of slaveowners' children or from other situations of enforced parenting by slaves, serfs, or servants. (White) folk wisdom has it that slave nurses, although in every fundamental sense coerced, were excellent mothers, whose charges remembered them fondly. Kovel speaks to some outcomes for white men of this situation, but to oedipal-sexual issues rather than to issues concerning the development of self and general relational capacities in white children of both genders (Joel Kovel, 1970, *White Racism*).

⑭ See Chapters 11 and 12 for more extended discussion.

⑮ Karl Marx, 1867, *Capital*, vol. 1, p. 577.

⑯ Claude Lévi-Strauss, 1956, "The Family," p. 269.

⑰ Ibid. , p. 277.

⑱ See, for example, Carol B. Stack, 1975, *All Our Kin*; Michael Young and Peter Willmott, 1957, *Family and Kinship in East London*.

⑲ See Lillian Breslow Rubin, 1976, *Worlds of Pain: Life in the Working-Class Family*, for discussion of women and men in the contemporary isolated working-class family.

⑳ Horkheimer, 1936, "Authority," p. 67.

㉑ Talcott Parsons, 1951, *The Social System*, p. 42.

㉒ Frankfurt Institute, 1972, *Aspects*, p. 133.

㉓ For example, David Bakan, 1966, *The Duality of Human Existence: Isolation and Communion in Western Man*; Mitscherlich, 1963, *Society Without the Father*; Slater, 1970, *Pursuit*, and 1974, *Earthwalk*.

㉔ Especially Peggy Morton, 1970, "A Woman's Work Is Never Done," *Leviathan*, 2, #1, pp. 32-37. Other Marxist feminist theorists also talk implicitly about the reproduction of male workers, but Morton is the only one to speak to the psychological dynamics I am currently discussing, rather than to physical reproduction.

㉕ Social psychological studies of the effect of "father absence" (and consequent maternal ambivalence, seductiveness, or overprotection) on development also focus almost entirely on male development. See, for example, Roger V. Burton and John W. M. Whiting, 1961, "The Absent Father and Cross-Sex Identity," *Merrill-Palmer Quarterly of Behavior and*

Development, 7, #2, pp. 85-95; John W. M. Whiting, Richard Kluckhohn, and Albert Anthony, 1958, "The Function of Male Initiation Rites at Puberty," in E. E. Maccoby, T. M. Newcomb, and E. L. Hartley, eds., *Readings in Social Psychology*; David Levy, 1943, *Maternal Overprotection*; Philip E. Slater, 1968, *The Glory of Hera: Greek Mythology and the Greek Family*, and 1970, *Pursuit*, and 1974, *Earthwalk*; William N. Stephens, 1963, *The Family in Cross-Cultural Perspective*. For exceptions, see E. M. Hetherington, 1972, "Effects of Father Absence on Personality Development in Adolescent Daughters," *Developmental Psychology*, 7, pp. 313-326, and 1973, "Girls Without Fathers," *Psychology Today*, 6, pp. 46-52; Lynn, 1959, "A Note on Sex Differences," and 1962, "Sex Role and Parent Identification"; Lynn and W. L. Sawrey, 1959, "The Effects of Father-Absence on Norwegian Boys and Girls," *Journal of Abnormal and Social Psychology*, 59, pp. 258-262; and Biller's review (1971) of the literature on "fathering and female personality development" —one short chapter of an entire book on *Father, Child and Sex Role*.

㉖ They discuss in this context the oedipus complex, the importance and effects of maternal manipulation of masculine erotism, father absence and the decline of paternal authority, masculine repression and sublimation.

5

南茜·乔德罗和苏珊·康特拉托，"对完美母亲的幻想"
Nancy Chodorow & Susan Contratto，"The Fantasy of the Perfect Mother"

《女性主义与精神分析理论》(*Feminism and Psychoanalytic Theory*)于 1989 年由耶鲁大学出版社出版。这是乔德罗继 1978 年出版《母性角色的再生：精神分析与性别的社会学》(*The Reproduction of Mothering*：*Psychoanalysis and the Sociology of Gender*)十年之后发表的又一力作。这部著作虽然没有像前一部那样引起轰动，但作者在著作中进一步发展了她在前部著作中提出的关于性别文化和心理动态学的观点，同样，她在这部书中展示了对心理学、社会学和人类学等相关学科的综合把握。

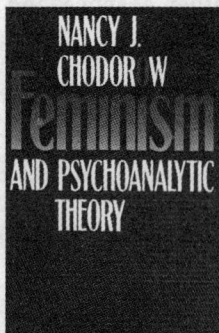

该书分三篇。第一篇，"母亲身份对性别个性和性别关系的作用"，主要讨论母亲在培养性别属性和性别身份过程中所起的重要作用，讨论不同生理性别的人如何在母亲为他们提供的角色模式下获得不同的性别身份和性别属性。第二篇，"性属、自我与社会理论"，从精神分析的角度讨论性别差异与性别关系，乔德罗再次运用了她所熟知和推荐的客体关系理论。第三篇，"精神分析、精神分析学家与女性主义"，讨论女性主义与精神分析学说的关系，提出了精神分析女性主义和女性的精神分析心理等概念。

这里选注的"对完美母亲的幻想"出自第一篇第四节，由乔德罗与苏珊·康特拉托①合著。该部分详细分析了西方思想如何把母亲形象理想化、完美化，如何使母亲沦落为受指责的对象，追溯了西方文化把母亲同死亡联系在一起的发

---

① 苏珊·康特拉托，哈佛大学教育学博士，目前在密执安大学心理学系任教。

展历程。论述中两位作者还援引了一些西方女性主义者的著述和观点。

在第一篇的开头,作者开门见山地指出,讨论男人和女人如何从僵化的性别角色中解放出来,人们必须首先弄清楚两个问题:其一,声称生理特征决定心理和个性特点从而区别男性和女性,这一观点是否真的有任何基础;其二,几乎在任何社会,女人无论是从身体、政治还是经济上都被男人驾驭,其原因究竟是什么。接着,乔德罗从文化个性的定义、不同文化中的性别差异、男性与女性行为意义的起源等方面论述说:"生理意义上的性别差别的确存在,但是,构成'女性'经验与行为或构成女性'本质'的所有特征也同样可以定义男性,只要其它种类的工作和性别角色对男性有这样的需要"①。乔德罗认为,生理意义上的性别差异往往没有人们想象的那样明显。在不同性别的人获得性别身份的过程中,"女孩成长为女人的过程相比男孩成长为男人的过程更具持续性,也更容易理解。从某种意义上说,女性身份比男性身份更容易获得"(第 32 页)。乔德罗还指出,男性对女性怀有一种恐惧,男性面对女性表现出的焦虑很像弱小的孩子面对无所不能的母亲(第 35 页)。然而,男性总是确保自己获得权力和荣耀,男性角色和男性活动相比女性角色和女性活动来讲也因此更有优势(第 37 页)。乔德罗继续她在《母性角色的再生》一书中提出的"再生"观点,认为性别角色也是循环再生的:

> 只要女性必须通过孩子谋得生活的意义,只要男性并不真正对社会化做出贡献,并不提供[下一代]容易获得的角色样板,女性持续培养出的儿子其性别身份将继续依赖于贬低女性气质,培养出的女儿不仅必须接受女性的贬值地位,而且还会继续生养更多延续这一体制并贬低女性的男性。(第 44 页)

"对完美母亲的幻想"除引言外分为 6 小节:"无所不能的母亲:指责与理想化"、"性征/性经历"、"挑衅与死亡"、"母性孤独"、"女性主义解读母性的文化与心理基础"和"女性主义与母性:超越首要过程的政治"。

---

① Nancy Chodorow, *Feminism and Psychoanalytic Theory* (New Haven: Yale University Press, 1989), p.30. 本节所引乔德罗和康特拉托观点除特别说明外均出自该书,以下只在正文标明页码,分号后第二个页码为引文在本书的页码。

作者指出,20 世纪 60、70 年代的女性主义者致力于提倡女性的生活不能被生养和抚育孩子所完全左右,到了 80 年代,更多的女性主义者关心做母亲的经历对女性产生的影响,并观察到许多女性——包括女性主义者自己——愿意生养孩子,把做母亲看做一段丰富、复杂的人生经历(第 79 页;第 91 页)。那么,母亲身份对于女性来说到底意味着什么呢? 一些女性主义者认为,由于母亲完全掌管孩子的成长经历,所以母亲是无所不能的。也正因为如此,母亲常常因孩子的状况受到责备。作者引用南茜·弗莱蒂(Nancy Friday)①在《我的母亲/我自己:女儿寻找身份的历程》(*My Mother/My Self*:*The Daughter's Search for Identity*)一书中表达的主要观点论证说:"母亲依照自己的形象培养女儿。由于母亲在成为母亲的过程中否定了自己的性征,她也因此必须阻止女儿拥有性征"(第 80 页;第 92 页)。作者继续对朱迪斯·阿卡纳(Judith Arcana)②所著《母亲的女儿》(*Our Mothers' Daughters*)和多萝西·迪纳斯坦(Dorothy Dinnerstein)③所著《美人鱼与弥诺陶洛斯怪物》(*The Mermaid and the Minotaur*)所述观点进行评论,母亲的无所不能影响了孩子的整个心理、社会和政治经历,因此母亲应该为这样一个无法控制的人类种族负责(第 82 页;第 94 页)。与妖魔化母亲的倾向相对,另一种错误观点是把母亲形象以及母亲拥有的力量过于理想化。乔德罗和康特拉托援引弗莱蒂、阿卡纳以及简·弗莱克斯(Jane Flax)④的著作,说明这些理论家都认为母亲可以变得完美,只要她们满

---

① 南茜·弗莱蒂,作家、女性主义者。代表作《我的母亲/我自己:女儿寻找身份的历程》出版于 1977 年。有关弗莱蒂的资料,访问其个人网站 http://www. nancyfriday. com。关于弗莱蒂在互联网上接受的一次访谈,参见 Alice Stamm, http://www. dearest. com/transcripts/friday720. htm, n. p. 。

② 朱迪斯·阿卡纳,诗人、教育家、女性主义者,曾在英美多所大学任教,创建位于华盛顿特区的联合学院妇女研究中心并出任第一位主任。她曾积极提倡合法堕胎,其代表著作《母亲的女儿》出版于 1979 年。关于阿卡纳的著作与思想,访问 http://www. writersontheedge. org/arcana. html, n. p. ;关于她与记者就合法堕胎问题进行的讨论,访问 http://www. uic. edu/orgs/cwluherstory/CWLUMemoir/Arcanatalk. html, n. p. 。

③ 多萝西·迪纳斯坦,美国著名女性主义理论家。代表作《美人鱼与弥诺陶洛斯怪物》出版于 1976 年。参见本书第二篇第 12 节。

④ 简·弗莱克斯,美国女性主义理论家,代表著作《思考碎片——当代西方的精神分析、女性主义和后现代主义》(*Thinking Fragments—Psychoanalysis, Feminism, and Postmodernism in the Contemporary West*)出版于 1991 年。

足孩子的各种需要(第 82 页;第 94~95 页)。作者同时也向读者展现出另一群女性主义者所持的对立观点:以亚德里安·里奇(Adrienne C. Rich)①和爱丽斯·罗茜(Alice S. Rossi)②为代表的理论家认为,母亲的完美理想只有在推翻父权制度的前提下才能充分实现,在父权体制下,母亲不是无所不能而是软弱无力的(第 83 页;第 95 页)。

乔德罗和康特拉托谈到《女性主义研究》杂志(*Feminist Studies*)③1978年第 2 期专门讨论用女性主义理论解读母亲身份,从收入这期杂志的文章可以看出,

> 表现为挑衅和愤怒的一种幻想出来的全知全能力量在母亲和孩子之间摇摆。一方面,母亲无所不能而孩子软弱无力;另一方面,孩子同无所不能的母亲产生认同,孩子的存在使母亲沦落为受害者或天使。因此……生孩子足以杀死一个女人或者迫使女人成为杀人犯。做母亲是她一生中一件生死攸关的大事,生孩子的结果要么母亲死亡要么孩子死亡。(第 86~87 页)

这样,在西方文化中,母亲总是同死亡联系在一起。

在讨论了母亲身份同性征/性经历、母亲的孤独等相关问题的关系之后,作者指出,西方文化对母性的理解具有源远流长的历史,对母亲的理想化和对母亲的责备是建构无所不能的母亲形象时不可分割的两个侧面(第 90 页;第 99 页)。对母亲的理想化来自婴孩的幻想,因为任何人都不是完美的(第 90 页;第 101 页)。至于母亲的性经历,女性主义者的观点存在分歧:罗茜和里奇认为母性同性经历可以匹配,而弗莱蒂和菲尔斯通(Shulamith Firestone)④则认为母亲应该是无性的(第 91 页;第 101 页)。乔德罗和康特拉托强调说,人们对母亲

---

① 亚德里安·里奇,美国诗人、女性主义者。详见本书第一篇第 2 节。

② 爱丽斯·罗茜,美国社会学学会第 74 任主席。主要研究领域包括性别角色、生理社会科学、家庭关系、父母与成年子女的关系问题。

③ 《女性主义研究》杂志创刊于 1972 年,首任主编是安·考德武德(Ann Calderwood)。请访问杂志网站 http://feministstudies.org。

④ 舒拉米斯·菲尔斯通,美国极端女性主义的创始人之一。其代表作《性别的辩证法:女性主义革命研究》(*The Dialect of Sex: The Case for Feminist Revolution*)出版于1970 年。

身份的理解高于生活,往往会走极端。精神分析理论和西方文化理念一直聚焦于母亲给孩子带来的伤害,一些女性主义者也延续这一理念,认为母亲应该为孩子贡献一切(第 92 页;第 101 页)。另一些女性主义者却关注母亲本人遭受的伤害,伤害先是来自于男人,后来来自于孩子。伤害导致母亲产生愤怒幻想与行为,并加剧母亲的孤独感受(第 92 页;第 101 页)。

作者总结说,女性主义在看待母亲身份和母亲经历问题上持有渐进性逻辑:

> 女性主义者要么先是与孩子认同责备母亲,要么期望母亲更加完美。文化理念和幻想也会导致从母亲的角度对母性生活持理想化倾向。……然而更多的情况是,人们往往尊崇孩子的需要和母亲的责任,同愤怒的孩子产生认同,这样的视角将导致最终同母亲认同,母亲身份因此变得充满愤怒和恐惧,父权体制彻底压迫母亲并把她们同孩子孤立起来。(第 92 页;第 102 页)

这里选注的是引言、"无所不能的母亲:指责与理想化"和"女性主义解读母性的文化与心理基础"三部分。

The Fantasy of the Perfect Mother

In the late 1960s and early 1970s, feminists raised initial questions and developed a consensus of sorts about mothering. ① We pointed to the pervasive pro-natalism of our culture; argued for safe, available abortions and birth control; criticized the health-care system; and advocated maternity and paternity benefits and leaves as well as accessible and subsidized parent- and community-controlled day-care, innovative work-time arrangements, shared parenting, and other non-traditional child-rearing and household arrangements. These consensual positions among feminists all centered on the argument that women's lives should not be totally constrained by child-care or childbearing. Women should be free to choose not to bear children; should have easy access to safe contraception and abortion; should be able to continue their other work if mothers; and should have available to them good day-care. In contrast, recent feminist writing on motherhood focuses more on the experience of mothering: if a woman wants to be a mother, what is or should be her experience? Given that parenting is necessary in any society, who should parent and how should the parenting be done? Feminist writing now recognizes that many women, including many feminists, want to have children and experience mothering as a rich and complex endeavor.

The new feminist writing has turned to mothering even while insisting on women's right to choose not to mother or to do other things in addition to mothering. Feminists often wish to speak to non-feminist or anti-feminist mothers about mothering without succumbing to heterosexism or pro-maternalism. The assumption that women have the right to mother, as well as not to mother, and the recognition that mothering, though it may be conflictual and oppressive, is also emotionally central and gratifying in some women's lives, has created a level of tension and ambivalence in recent writing that was missing in the earlier discussion.

This essay examines certain recurrent psychological themes in recent feminist writing on motherhood ②. These themes include a sense that mothers are totally responsible for the outcomes of their mothering, even if their behavior is in turn shaped by male-dominant society. Belief in the all-powerful mother spawns a recurrent tendency to blame the mother on the one hand, and a fantasy of maternal perfectibility on the other. The writings also elaborate maternal sexuality or asexuality, aggression and omnipotence in the mother-child relationship, and the isolation of the mother-child dyad. This isolation provides the supercharged environment in which aggression and, to a lesser degree, sexuality become problematic, and the context in which a fantasy of the perfect mother can also be played out.

We point to, and are concerned with, two features of these understandings of motherhood. They have an unprocessed quality; it is as if notions that the personal is political have been interpreted to mean that almost primal fantasies constitute feminist politics or theory. Further, we think there is a striking continuity between these feminist treatments of motherhood and themes found in the culture at large, even among anti-feminists. Feminists differ about the meaning of motherhood and women's mothering, but each of these themes finds its complement in non-feminist or anti-feminist writing. Both these features of the writings we discuss are problematic for feminist theory and politics.

The All-Powerful Mother: Blame and Idealization

Feminist writing on motherhood assumes an all-powerful mother who, because she is totally responsible for how her children turn out, is blamed for everything from her daughter's limitations to the crisis of human existence. Nancy Friday's *My Mother/My Self* exemplifies this genre at its most extreme. ③ The book's central argument is that mothers are noxious to daughters, and that a daughter's subsequent unhappinesses and failings stem from this initial relationship. Friday follows the daughter through the life cycle and shows at each stage how mothers forcefully, intentionally, and often viciously constrain and control daughters, keep them from individuating, and, especially, deny daughters their sexuality and keep them from men. ④ Mothers make daughters in their image. As the mother, in becoming a mother, has denied her own sexuality, so she must deny sexuality to her daughter. Friday even seems to blame mothers for the act of toilet-training their daughters. ⑤

Even when Friday points to other causes of a daughter's problems, it is still the mother's fault. Sexual information learned in school or from friends doesn't alter a mother's impact; women are ultimately responsible even for obstetrical atrocities performed by men in the interests of male power. Friday relates Seymour Fisher's finding that good female relationships with men depend on the belief that a daughter's father will not desert her, but then she asks, "But who put on the sexual brakes to begin with?" ⑥ Friday makes occasional disclaimers; for example, blaming mother is not taking responsibility for oneself. ⑦ But these disclaimers are buried in 460 pages of the opposite message. They are certainly not the message we remember from the book.

It is not clear whether Friday considers herself a feminist (though she certainly claims to be a woman's advocate and many see her as a feminist). In any event, she reflects in extreme form a widespread feminist position, one that also argues that mothers are the agents of their daughters' oppression and also pays lip-service (or more) to the fact that mothers themselves are oppressed and are therefore not responsible. Judith Arcana's *Our Mothers' Daughters*, for instance, written out of explicit feminist commitment and concern, gives us an account almost exactly like Friday's. [8] The only difference from Friday is that Arcana claims that maternal behavior is a product of mothers' entrapment within patriarchy rather than a product of their evil intentions.

While Friday and Arcana condemn mothers for what they do to their daughters, Dorothy Dinnerstein in *The Mermaid and the Minotaur* discusses the disastrous impact of maternal caretaking on sons, daughters, and society as a whole. [9] Dinnerstein claims that, as a result of "mother-dominated infancy," adult men and women are "semi-human, monstrous"—grown-up children acting out a species-suicidal pathology. [10] In Dinnerstein's account the mother is an object of children's fury and desperation, and children will put up with and create anything to escape her evil influence: "The deepest root of our acquiescence to the maiming and mutual imprisonment of men and women lies in the monolithic fact of human childhood: under the arrangements that now prevail, a woman is the parental person who is every infant's first love, first witness, and first boss, the person who presides over the infant's first encounters with the natural surroundings and who exists for the infant as the first representative of the flesh." [11]

Dinnerstein's account, like Friday's and Arcana's, confuses infantile fantasy with the actuality of maternal behavior. Thus, even as Dinnerstein describes the infantile fantasies that emerge from female-dominated child-care, she also asserts that mothers are in fact all-powerful, fearsome creatures. She emphasizes the "*absolute power*" of the "*mother's life-and-*

death control over helpless infancy: an intimately carnal control" whose *"wrath is all-potent"* and whose *"intentionality is so formidable—so terrifying and ... so alluring".* ⑫ This potency engages with the infant's totally helpless need and dependence; it humiliates, controls, and dominates as it seduces, succors, and saves. As a result, according to Dinnerstein, the mother (or whoever would care for the child) is inevitably the child's adversary.

Dinnerstein says that women's exclusive mothering affects the child's relationship to mother and father, attitudes toward the body, and adult erotic capacities. It shapes the later ambivalence toward nature and nature's resources, creates an unhealthy split between love and work, produces adults who parent differently according to sex, fosters particular kinds of destructive power and ensures patriarchal control of that power, and forms the nature of our history-making impulse. ⑬ In short, women's all-powerful mothering shapes the child's entire psychological, social, and political experience and is responsible for a species life that "is cancerous, out of control". ⑭

The other side of blaming the mother is idealization of her and her possibilities: If only the mother wouldn't do what she is doing, she would be perfect. Friday's perfect mother is self-sacrificing and giving (though ultimately in the interest of her own deferred emotional rewards): "The truly loving mother is one whose interest and happiness is in seeing her daughter as a person, not just a possession. It is a process of being so generous and loving that she will forego some of her own pleasure and security to add to her daughter's development. If she does this in a genuine way, she really does end up with that Love Insurance Policy. " "It is a noble role that mother must play here. " ⑮ Friday, the new woman's advocate, sounds like the most traditional traditionalist.

Most feminist writing does not expect mothers to change on their own. As feminists locate blame, they also focus on the conditions—those of patriarchy in which bad mothering takes place, in which mothers are victims and powerless in the perpetuation of evil. But this implies that if only we could remove these patriarchal constraints, mothering could be perfect. Arcana, in pointing to women who have broken out of the traditional mold, wants to turn these women into perfect mothers: "Such women may mother us all." [16]

These writings suggest not only that mothers can be perfect but also that the child's needs (e. g. , those of the daughters in the books by Friday and Arcana) are necessarily legitimate and must be met. Such an implication persists in the most subtle and sophisticated feminist accounts. Jane Flax, for instance, offers an analysis of the psychodynamics of the mother-daughter relationship in which she writes of the difficulties of being a mother in a male-dominant society and of the psychological conflicts that setting generates. [17] She offers perceptive insights into the contradictory needs that emerge from being mothered by a woman. But her article still implies that mothers can be perfect and that the child's felt desires are absolute needs: "As a result of all these conflicts, it is more difficult for the mother to be as emotionally available as her infant daughter needs her to be." [18] The "needs" to which she refers are those of women patients talking about their mothers, and Flax accepts their accounts. She does not suggest that a child's "needs" might be unrealistic or unreasonable.

We find the idealization of maternal possibility not only in those accounts that blame the mother but also in another strain of feminist writing on motherhood, one that begins from identification with the mother rather than with the daughter. Adrienne Rich and Alice Rossi also premise their investigations of motherhood on the assumption that a maternal ideal or perfection could emerge with the overthrow of patriarchy. [19] Both discuss mothering as it has been affected by patriarchy and describe how patriarchy has controlled—as Rich observes, even killed—mothers and children. Mothers are not powerful, but powerless under patriarchy.

Rich provides a moving account of maternal love and concern and a vision of the potential power of women's maternal bodies, which could enable women to be intellectually, spiritually, and sexually transformative, and which could forge nurturant, sexual, and spiritual linkages among women:

> The repossession by women of our bodies will bring far more essential change to human society than the seizing of the means of production by workers.... We need to imagine a world in which every woman is the presiding genius of her own body. In such a world, women will truly create new life, bringing forth not only children (if and as we choose), but the visions and the thinking necessary to sustain, console and alter human existence—a new relationship to the universe. Sexuality, politics intelligence, position, motherhood, work, community, intimacy will develop new meanings; thinking itself will be transformed. This is where we have to begin. [20]

Rossi, like Rich, turn to women's maternalism, but she focuses less on the global social and cultural implications of the freeing of motherhood from patriarchal technological constraints and more on the possibilities of the mothering experience. Rossi argues that women have a "biological edge" in parental capacities and implies that children will do best with their natural mothers if these mothers can reclaim their bodies and become in touch with their innate mothering potential, and if their experience can be removed from male-dominant social organization. Rossi stresses the natural and untutored quality of some of women's intuitive responses to infants and the potential interconnection of sexual and maternal gratification. All these qualities could be enhanced if their expression were not distorted or destroyed by doctor-centered obstetric management, by industrial threats to fetuses and pregnant women, by too-close spacing of children, by women mothering according to a male life script (i. e., self-involved instead of nurturant). The return to a more natural mothering relationship would also sustain and further connections among women, the "women's culture" that the feminist movement has emphasized. Like Rich, Rossi implies that mothering could be wonderful if women could recognize and take pleasure in their procreative and maternal capacities and if these were not taken over by institutional constraints and alienated understandings of mothering.

[……]

Cultural and Psychological Roots of Feminist Interpretations of Mothering

We have discussed four interrelated psychological themes that emerge from recent feminist work on mothering: (1) blaming and idealizing the mother, assuming that mothers are or can be all-powerful and perfect and that mothering either destroys the world or generates world perfection; (2) extreme expectations of maternal sexuality, asserting the incompatibility of motherhood and sexuality or romanticizing maternal sexuality; (3) a link between motherhood and aggression or death; and (4) an emphasis on the isolation of mother and child. All these themes share common characteristics: their continuity with dominant cultural understandings of mothering and their rootedness in unprocessed, infantile fantasies about mothers.

Our cultural understandings of mothering have a long history, but reached a peak in the nineteenth century. That century witnessed the growth of a sexual division of spheres that materially grounded mother-child isolation and bequeathed us a picture of the ideal mother who would guarantee both morally perfect children and a morally desirable world. [21] At a time when everyone's life was being affected by the frenzied growth of developing industrial capitalism, somehow mothers were seen as having total control and unlimited power in the creation of their children.

Post-Freudian psychology assumes the mother-child isolated unit that nineteenth-century industrial development produced and elaborates the notion that the early mother-infant relationship is central to later psychological development and to the psychological, emotional, and relational life of the child. As a result of this assumption, virtually all developmental research of the last thirty-five years has been directed to this early period. This has further reinforced and seemed to substantiate the popular view that the relationship of mother and infant has extraordinary significance. The assumption has also often led to a psychological determinism and reductionism that argues that what happens in the earliest mother-infant relationship determines the whole of history, society, and culture. ㉒

Both nineteenth-century cultural ideology about motherhood and post-Freudian psychological theory blame mothers for any failings in their children and idealize possible maternal perfection. Blaming the mother, a major outcome of these theories and a major theme in feminist writings, has a long social history. David Levy's *Maternal Overprotection*, the Momism of Wylie and Erikson, literature on the schizophrenogenic mother, Rheingold's analysis of maternal aggression as the primary pathogenic influence on the child, Slater's discussion of the Oedipally titillating, overwhelming mother, and Lasch's account of the mother "impos[ing] her madness on everyone else," all suggest the terrible outcome of the omnipotent mother. ㉓ With the exception of Slater, they ignore any conditions that determine or foster maternal behavior in the first place and accept a completely deterministic view of child development. ㉔

More recently, as women have entered the paid labor force and some have chosen not to become mothers, mothers have been blamed more for what is called "maternal deprivation" than for "maternal overprotection". Selma Fraiberg's *Every Child's Birthright: in defense of mothering* is a good example. ㉕ Describing herself as the child's advocate, Fraiberg has no sympathy for women who choose to work. Her message is clear: A good mother does not use regular substitute child care before the age of three.

Thus, feminists' tendency to blame the mother (the perspective of feminist-as-child) fits into cultural patterning. Feminists simply add on to this picture the notion that conditions other than the mother's incompetence or intentional malevolence create this maternal behavior. But feminists do not question the accuracy of this characterization of maternal behavior, nor its effects.

As we suggested, idealization and blaming the mother are two sides of the same belief in the all-powerful mother. In the nineteenth century, the bourgeois mother received moral training and guidance to enhance her motherly performance, guidance that, if followed, would lead children and the world to moral perfection. In contemporary child-rearing manuals, the good mother knows naturally how to mother if she will only follow her instincts,㉖ or can be perfect if she will only stay home full-time,㉗ or can provide proper stimulation and gentle teaching to her child.㉘ Feminists take issue with the notion that a mother can be perfect in the here and now, given male dominance, lack of equality in marriage, and inadequate resources and support, but the fantasy of the perfect mother remains: If current limitations on mothers were eliminated, mothers would know naturally how to be good.

Blame and idealization of mothers have become our cultural ideology. This ideology, however, gains meaning from and is partially produced by infantile fantasies that are themselves the outcome of being mothered exclusively by one woman. If mothers have exclusive responsibility for infants who are totally dependent, then to the infant they are the source of all good and evil.㉙ Times of closeness, oneness, and joy are the quintessence of perfect understanding; times of distress, frustration, discomfort, and too great separation are entirely the mother's fault. For the infant, the mother is not someone with her own life, wants, needs, history, other social relationships, work. She is known only in her capacity as mother. Growing up means learning that she, like other people in one's life, has and wants a life of her own, and that loving her means recognizing her subjectivity and appreciating her separateness. But people have trouble doing this and continue, condoned and supported by the ideology about mothers they subsequently learn, to experience mothers solely as people who did or did not live up to their child's expectations. This creates the quality of rage we find in "blame-the-mother" literature and the unrealistic expectation that perfection would result if only a mother would devote her life completely to her child and all impediments to doing so were removed. Psyche and culture merge here and reflexively create one another.

Originally, idealization of mothers is an infantile fantasy: No human being can be perfect. Thus, although the idealization of maternal life found in both Rich's and Rossi's writing is more from the perspective of mothers, their accounts are also informed by some identification with the stance of the child, who *needs* certain things in order to develop. One focus of Rossi's argument is the biological tie of infant to mother. Rich also claims that the child has powerful, strong feelings for the mother, "authentic" need—"a need vaster than any single human being could satisfy, except by loving continuously, unconditionally, from dawn to dark, and often in the middle of the night." [30] This need is evoked by the sense of uniqueness of the mother, by her singularity. This leads us to ask: What will happen to these "authentic" needs, and who will fulfill them? Does Rich think these intense feelings will disappear in a non-male-dominant world? Or are they inherent in mothering and, therefore, unavoidable? To what degree are they a product of the institution of motherhood under patriarchy and the experience of mothering it generates? And once there are "needs" and feelings like this, won't we start evaluating and idealizing mothers who do and do not meet them, and do and do not feel them? [31]

Fantasy and cultural ideology also meet in themes about maternal sexuality. An assumed incompatibility between sexuality and motherhood is largely a product of our nineteenth-century heritage, and some women psychoanalysts have helped perpetuate this cultural and psychological belief. In *The Psychology of Women*, Helene Deutsch claims clinical and literary support for the view that there is a natural and desirable psychological split between motherliness and erotic feelings. [32] Therese Benedek suggests that "mature" (i. e. , motherly) women are simply less sexual than "immature" women. [33]

Ambivalence about maternal bodies, especially around sexuality, is present in the experience of many women, both as mothers and as daughters/children or would-be mothers. The trend, ideologically and for individual women, has been to opt for asexual motherhood. Rossi and Rich argue strongly against the view that motherhood and sexuality are incompatible; other feminists, like Firestone and Friday, accept the traditional view of incompatibility yet, unlike the analysts, argue in favor of sexuality. ㉞

The understandings of motherhood we have been describing are larger than life and seen only in extremes. For Dinnerstein, women's mothering generates conditions that threaten to destroy human existence. For DuPlessis, a feminist theory of motherhood must begin with the inextricable link of motherhood and death; motherhood, she says, relates to heaven and hell, and to speech and silence; the overcoming of the institution of motherhood will be the end of dualism. For Friday, we must choose to be sexual or maternal. For Firestone, we must either accept inequality or give up our reproductive biology.

Rage is an inevitable outcome of this extremism. Psychological theory and cultural ideology have focused on the harm that mothers can do to their children, and some feminists continue to focus on this harm. We magnify the impact of one individual, the mother, and when the child in us suffers the inevitable frustrations of living, we blame our mothers. *My Mother/My Self* has been extraordinarily popular. It speaks to the daughter in all women and tells them that their problems are not political, social, personal, or, heaven forbid, caused by men; their problems are caused solely by their mothers. We are all prone to mother-hating, for we live in a society that says that mothers can and should do all for their children. Moreover, we were all mothered, and our psyches retain the imprint of these origins.

Other feminists move beyond this position. They describe aggression done to women first by men and then by children which leads to mothers' rageful fantasies and behaviors. Children's aggression in this model is expectation as much as actuality. Starting from the belief that "perfect" mothering is both centrally important and possible, if only a mother is totally devoted and attentive, as these feminists become mothers, or imagine being mothers, they fear the experience as all-consuming and come unconsciously and consciously to resent, fear, and feel devoured by their children. The outcome is the powerful aggressive feelings and behaviors and preoccupation with death we described above. The outcome also is to experience a total and overwhelming isolation of self with child.

Thus we can see a progressive logic to feminist themes about motherhood, a logic that moves woman from an identification as daughter or child to an identification as mother. Drawing from and reflecting a cultural ideology and infantile sense of infantile need and maternal responsibility for the outcomes of child rearing, feminists begin by identifying with the child and blaming the mother, or by expecting her to be more than perfect. Cultural ideology and fantasy can also lead to idealization of maternal life from the point of view of the mother, as in the writing of Rossi and Rich. More often, the belief in total infantile need and maternal responsibility, and identification with the angry child, lead to a maternal identification that is in its turn full of rage and fear, and a sense that the conditions of patriarchy totally oppress mothers and isolate them with their child.

[······]

Notes:

① We are enormously indebted to Linda Gordon, Arlie Hochschild, Sara Ruddick, Judith Stacey, Catharine Stimpson, and Barrie Thorne for their very careful reading of an earlier version of this essay. We also benefited greatly from discussions with Sherry Ortner and Norma Wikler. Although these people did not always agree with our positions, their ideas aided our ongoing explorations of the issues we examine. NIMH Training Grant MH 15 122-203 provided support for Susan Contratto during the writing of the essay.

② The authors we discuss are all white and (broadly) professional/

middle class. Thus they do not necessarily represent the whole feminist spectrum. We are focusing on certain dominant themes in several major feminist analyses of motherhood, but do not claim to discuss all aspects of these works nor all feminist writing on motherhood. Although we are often critical of the work we discuss, we have also learned from and/been moved by some of this writing.

③ Nancy Friday, *My Mother/My Self* (New York, Dell, 1977).

④ Ibid. , p. 105.

⑤ Ibid. , pp. 133, 145.

⑥ Ibid. , pp. 147, 157.

⑦ Ibid. , p. 83.

⑧ Judith Arcana, *Our Mothers' Daughter* (Berkerley, Shameless Hussy Press, 1979).

⑨ Dorothy Dinnerstein, *The Mermaid and the Minotaur* (New York, Harper & Row, 1976).

⑩ Ibid. , pp. 83, 85.

⑪ Ibid. , p. 28.

⑫ Ibid. , pp. 161, 164.

⑬ Ibid. , p. 81.

⑭ Ibid. , p. 253. Nancy Chodorow's *The Reproduction of Mothering: psychoanalysis and the sociology of gender* (Berkeley, University of California Press, 1978) has some important similarities with Dinnerstein's argument. Both books focus on the psychological meanings and consequences of women's mothering, and both argue that male and female parenting is essential for social change. Further, both take the stand that the conflicts typically found in relationships between adult men and women in our culture are grounded in the fact that both sexes are mothered by women. We are not considering Chodorow's argument here because we believe it is significantly different in ways that make it not relevant to our argument. Although Chodorow argues that women's mothering is perhaps the central feature in the reproduction of gender inequality, she also specifies the outcome of mothering in a way that leaves some autonomy to other aspects of cultural and social life. She does not take the extremist, portentous position of Dinnerstein and, in fact, has been criticized unfavorably on that score. As part of our argument holds that extremism in the analysis of mothering hurts feminist understanding and politics, we are more comfortable with this less apocalyptic approach.

⑮ Friday, *My Mother/My Self*, pp. 69, 113.

⑯ Arcana, *Our Mothers' Daughters*, p. 37.

⑰ Jane Flax, "The conflict between nurturance and autonomy in mother-daughter relationships and within feminism," *Feminist Studies*, 2 (1978),pp. 171-189.

⑱ Ibid. , p. 175.

⑲ Adrienne Rich, *Of Woman Born* (New York, W. W. Norton, 1976); Alice S. Rossi, "Maternalism, sexuality and the new feminism," in Joseph Zubin and John Money (eds.), *Contemporary Sexual Behavior* (Baltimore, John Hopkins University Press, 1973); Rossi, "A biosocial perspective on parenting," *Daedalus*, 106, no. 2 (1977), pp. 1-31; and Rossi, "Considering 'A biosocial perspective on parenting': reply by Alice Rossi," *Signs*, 4 (1979), pp. 712-717. Rich has been lauded and idealized by many feminists, whereas Rossi, also a feminist, has been criticized for making anti-feminist arguments. Rossi's work, put forth in several articles, is not nearly as theoretically complete or comprehensive as Rich's, but we cite them together because their accounts are remarkably similar in their fundamentals. Both decry the patriarchal alienation of women from their maternal bodies and mothering experiences; both link motherhood and sexuality (see below); both advocate compensatory training for men even while suggesting that women's maternal nature is in some way unique.

⑳ Rich, *Of Woman Born*, p. 292.

㉑ Ruth H. Bloch, "American feminine ideals in transition: the rise of the moral mother, 1785-1815," *Feminist Studies*, 2 (1978), pp. 100-126.

㉒ See, for instance, Dinnerstein, *The Mermaid and the Minotaur*; Norman O. Brown, *Life against Death* (New York, Vintage, 1959); and

Lloyd de Mause (ed.), *The History of Childhood* (New York, Psychohistory Press, 1974).

㉓ David Levy, *Maternal Overprotection* (New York, Columbia University Press, 1943); Philip Wylie, *Generation of Vipers* (New York, Farrar, Rinehart, 1942); Erik Erikson, *Childhood and Society* (New York, W. W. Norton, 1950); Theodore Lidz, Stephen Fleck, and Alice R. Cornelison, *Schizophrenia and the Family* (New York, International Universities Press, 1965); Joseph C. Rheingold, *The Fear of Being a Woman: a theory of maternal destructiveness* (New York, Grune & Stratton, 1964); Philip E. Slater, *The Pursuit of Loneliness* (Boston, Beacon Press, 1970); Philip E. Slater, *Earthwalk* (New York, Doubleday 1974); and Christopher Lasch, *Haven in a Heartless World: the family besieged* (New York, Basic Books, 1977), p. 153.

㉔ For a more extended discussion of the issue of maternal blame in the psychological literature, see Susan Contratto Weisskopf, "Maternal guilt and mental health professionals: a reconfirming interaction," *Michigan Occasional Papers*, no. 5 (Ann Arbor, University of Michigan Women's Studies Program, 1978).

㉕ Selma Fraiberg, *Every Child's Birthright: in defense of mothering* (New York, Basic Books, 1977).

㉖ Benjamin Spock, *The Pocket Book of Baby and Child-Care* (New York, Pocket, 1945, 1946, 1957, 1968); and D. W. Winnicott, *The Child, the Family, and the Outside World* (New York, Penguin, 1964).

㉗ Fraiberg, *Every Child's Birthright*; and T. Berry Brazelton, *Infants and Mothers: differences in development* (New York, Delacorte, 1969).

㉘ Frank Caplan, *The First Twelve Months of Life* (New York, Bantam, 1971); and Penelope Leach, *Your Baby and Child from Birth to Age Five* (New York, Knopf, 1978).

㉙ We are assuming in this argument that infants are at a stage of cognitive and ego development where they use concrete categories that are grossly affectively laden. With maturity, these categories become more elaborated, complicated, and subtle. See Jean Piaget, *The Construction of*

Reality in the Child (New York, Basic Books, 1954); Piaget, The Language and Thought of the Child (New York, Humanities, 1959); W. R. D. Fairbairn, *An Object-Relations Theory of the Personality* (New York, Basic Books, 1952); Otto Kernberg, *Borderline Conditions and Pathological Narcissism* (New York, Jason Aronson, 1975); and Kernberg, *Object-Relations Theory and Clinical Psychoanalysis* (New York, Jason Aronson, 1976).

㉚ Rich, *Of Woman Born*, p. 4.

㉛ Rich's passionate, wide-ranging work has been the inspiration for much subsequent feminist writing on motherhood (see Sara Ruddick, "Maternal thinking," in Barrie Thorne (ed.), with Marilyn Yalom, *Rethinking the Family: some feminist questions* (New York, Longman, 1981), pp. 76-94; and "Special Issue: Mothers and daughters," *Frontiers* 3 (1978)). We also see her work as a magnificent contribution. In some ways we feel that in criticizing it and expecting it to be even more perfect, we are reproducing the fantasy of the perfect mother. Nevertheless, we continue to think that it is problematic to look to the uniqueness and potential of women's maternal bodies and relationships, however broadly defined, for the perfectibility of women and society, and we are critical of theories of motherhood that begin from notions of need, as we suggest later in this essay.

㉜ Helene Deutsch, *The Psychology of Women*, vols 1 and 2 (New York: Grune & Stratton, 1944 & 1945).

㉝ Therese Benedek, untitled "Discussion of Sherfey's paper on female sexuality," *Journal of the American Psychoanalytic Association*, 3 (1968), pp. 424-448; and Benedek, "On the psychobiology of gender identity," *Annual of Psychoanalysis*, 4 (New York, International Universities Press, 1976), pp. 117-162.

㉞ See Susan (Contratto) Weisskopf, "Maternal sexuality and asexual motherhood," *Signs*, 5 (1980), pp. 766-782, for a more detailed discussion of these issues. We suspect that infantile fantasies are also part of the root of notions of asexual motherhood.

6 林恩·哈弗,"母性的过去"
Lynne Huffer, "Maternal Pasts"

林恩·哈弗(Lynne Huffer)于 1998 年由斯坦福大学出版社出版的《母性的过去,女性主义的未来:怀旧、伦理学以及差异问题》(*Maternal Pasts, Feminist Futures: Nostalgia, Ethics, and the Question of Difference*)标志着作者在性别研究领域已经具有了独到的思想和前瞻力。对法语文学的深厚功底以及直接阅读法国女性主义理论的能力使哈弗很快成为美国当代重要女性主义理论家之一。

在密执安大学获得博士学位的林恩·哈弗曾在耶鲁大学执教法语和法语文学,目前在得克萨斯州的莱斯大学(Rice University)担任女性与性别研究中心主任。她的学术专长包括女性主义理论、女性与性别研究、女同性恋研究、现代法国及法语文学、比较文学、文学批评理论以及伦理学。

哈弗的代表著作还有:

《另类克莱特①:关于性别写作的问题》(*Another Colette: The Question of Gendered Writing*),密歇根大学出版社,1992 年。

《另类面貌,另类女性:法国女性主义理论的再翻译》(*Another Look, Another Woman: Retranslations of French Feminism*),《耶鲁法国研究》(*Yale French Studies*)②1995 年第 87 期特别专刊。

---

① 克莱特(1873～1954),法国女小说家,全名 Sidonie Gabrilelle Colette。曾担任龚古尔研究院(The Goncourt Academy)院长,她是第一位担任此职务的女性。

② 关于这一期《耶鲁法国研究》的主要内容,访问 http://research. yale. edu/frenchstudies。

《母性的过去,女性主义的未来》聚焦迷失的母亲以讨论怀旧、性属以及其它基本哲学问题,作者把迷失的母亲看做性别差异的基础。"作者批评女性主义理论带有的怀旧倾向,主张思想体系的解放必须超越以母性为出发点的结构"①。该书着眼于莫里斯·布兰硕特(Maurice Blanchot)②、露丝·伊里加蕾(Luce Irigaray)③、朱丽娅·克里斯蒂娃(Julia Kristeva)④和尼科尔·布罗萨德(Nicole Brossard)⑤的著作,从文学、心理学、认识论、本体论、社会政治等多维层面阐明女性主义理论中蕴含的怀旧倾向。她同时指出,虽然约翰·朗肖·奥斯汀(John Langshaw Austin)⑥、朱迪斯·巴特勒(Judith Butler)⑦和伊里加蕾的一些思想具有反怀旧倾向,但他们却"无法为建立语言、身份和社会纽带之间的联系提供充足的模式"⑧。哈弗认为,加拿大作家尼科尔·布罗萨德的作品开创性地颠覆了传统模式并创建了新的概念,可以用来建立语言与主体性之间的关系。她呼吁女性主义著作更多地关注伦理学与文学的关系问题。

该书共分三篇。第一篇,"怀旧:迷失的母亲",评价莫里斯·布兰硕特和露丝·伊里加蕾有关母亲身份的论述;第二篇,"怀旧与伦理学:接近他者",讨论

---

① http://www.sup.org/cgi-bin/search/getmoreinfo.cgibookid = 3025 + 3026 & q = paral, n. p.

② 莫里斯·布兰硕特(1907~2003),20世纪法国著名作家、批评家、哲学家。他认为文学作品往往以许多非文学因素为特征,因此作家非常孤独。他的思想对福科(Michel Foucault)以及其他法国当代哲学家产生重要影响。关于其主要著作和观点,访问 http://www.studiocleo.com/librarie/blanchot/indexFl.htm。

③ 露丝·伊里加蕾(1932~   ),法国著名女性主义理论家、哲学家。详见本书第二篇第9节。

④ 朱丽娅·克里斯蒂娃(1941~   ),法国著名女性主义理论家、符号学家。详见本书第二篇第7节。

⑤ 尼科尔·布罗萨德(1943~   ),后现代主义和女性主义诗人、小说家、剧作家,出生在加拿大的蒙特利尔,已出版11部诗集和6部文集。关于其著作及访谈,访问 http://epc.buffalo.edu/authors/brossard。

⑥ 约翰·朗肖·奥斯汀(1911~1960),英国哲学家,曾任教于牛津大学。生前著作很少发表,身后学生结集出版《哲学文集》(*Philosophical Papers*,1961年)。

⑦ 朱迪斯·巴特勒(1956~   ),美国加州大学伯克利分校比较文学教授,著名女性主义理论家。

⑧ http://www.sup.org/cgi-bin/search/getmoreinfo.cgibookid = 3025 + 3026&q = paral, n. p.

朱丽娅·克里斯蒂娃的"穹若"(chora)理论①和伊里加蕾的行为伦理学观点;第三篇,"走向另一个模式",以尼科尔·布罗萨德的城市小说为例试图说明语言与主体性之间关系的最佳模式。该书的序言题为"母性的过去",跋题为"女性主义的未来",该著作的标题即由此而来。

序言"母性的过去"集中论述母亲如何成为西方文明的象征,母亲如何在弗洛伊德理论框架中被排斥在秩序之外,以及女性主义如何解决相互间的伦理问题。序言共分五部分:

第一部分,"起源",追溯母亲在西方文明中具有的象征意义的由来。第二部分,"行囊",论述加拿大作家尼科尔·布罗萨德如何解构西蒙·德·波伏娃②在《第二性》(*The Second Sex*)中建立的性别体系。第三部分,"追踪",表明作者所持的政治立场和研究方法。第四部分,"怀旧",评析女性主义运动和女性主义理论共同分享的怀旧倾向。第五部分,"结构",介绍该书各部分的主要内容以及各部分之间的逻辑关系。

哈弗把母亲视为"一个强有力的文化象征":"这一象征足以决定西方思想的主体结构"③。她把母亲在西方文明中的象征意义作了如下描述:

> 首先,西方传统中的母亲象征开端。母亲生育孩子,因此占据了起源的位置。引申来说,世间万物皆源于母亲。其次,由于母亲标志着起源,她也同时标志着回归。在赋予生命的同时,母亲也同时决定了最终的死亡。从象征意义上说,母性的起源其结果并非模糊不定,作为起源的母亲代表了整个生命周期,其终极目的地是死亡。(第7页;第113页)

---

① "穹若"意指"空间、处所",是具营养的母性容器,前俄狄浦斯活动的聚焦点。关于克里斯蒂娃的"穹若"理论,参见金惠敏著,《朱丽娅·克里斯蒂瓦:法国女权主义理论家》,载《中国女性主义》2004年春季卷,第135~144页。

② 关于德·波伏娃和她的《第二性》,参见本书第一篇第1节。

③ Lynne Huffer, *Maternal Pasts, Feminist Futures: Nostalgia, Ethics, and the Question of Difference* (Stanford, CA: Stanford University Press, 1998), p.7. 除特别说明,本节所引哈弗观点均出自该书,以下只在正文标明页码,分号后第二个页码为引文在本书的页码。

母亲作为起源的象征,其意义有这样两个:其一,"母亲是一个原创性符号,是意义的基础、开端的所在,一系列的相关意义可最终追溯至此"(第9页;第115页)。其二,"作为起源象征的母亲在思想和政治体系中占据的位置建构了有性别差异的意义"(第9页;第115页)。因此,母亲成为建构女性为否定因素的极端表现(第10页;第115页)。

在第二部分"行囊"中,林恩·哈弗首先简要回顾波伏娃笔下建立的"女人=母亲=子宫"这一等式的来由,说明母亲如何在西方文明中被同泥土、自然等意象联系在一起。而在加拿大作家尼科尔·布罗萨德笔下,世界首先是圆的,圆得像孕妇的肚子,一切都从这里开始:"世界是寄托在母亲体内的男性梦想"(第11页;第117页)。与此同时,恰恰是这一圆圆的形状迫使男人以扁平的状态征服圆圆的世界。因此,布罗萨德提出了世界既是圆的也是扁的这一全新理念。就好像一具行囊,既可以空空如也又可以满满如盈(第11页;第117页)。

在第三部分"追踪"中,林恩·哈弗综述自己所处时代女性主义的特点,向读者说明她力求对许多女性主义者所持的颠覆态度进行质疑,她主张重新思考父性和母性文学世系之间的对称结构(第13页)。哈弗还明确说明,虽然她的研究方法是法国式的,但其政治立场却深深植根于北美的女性主义传统(第13页)。

"怀旧"是序言中最为重要的部分。林恩·哈弗首先给"怀旧"这一概念以明确的定义和解释。她认为,怀旧具有一个基本的结构,那就是要以回归作为出发点(第14页)。父权体制确立了男性相对于女性的优势地位,因此在男性占主导地位的父权体制下,"女性已经象征性地沦落为以有生育能力的身体为表现形式的肉体的、物质的东西"(第15页)。又由于性别理念把女人简单化为母亲,那么男人追求的对象就是迷失的母亲(第15页)。哈弗引用弗洛伊德的俄狄浦斯情结理论进一步说明儿子回归母亲的怀旧欲望最终导致自我毁灭。正因为男性的怀旧探索将最终导致死亡,所以男性便成为一个不断欲望的主体(第16页)。

女性主义理论虽然各有千秋,但却拥有共同的结构,即怀旧。哈弗援引玛丽·雅各布斯(Mary Jacobus)①在其文章《弗洛伊德的记忆术:女性、屏蔽记忆

---

① 玛丽·雅各布斯,英国剑桥大学英语系教授。关于哈弗书中援引雅各布斯的文章,参见"Freud's Mnemonic: Women, Screen Memories, and Feminist Nostalgia," in Margaret A. Lourie, Domna C. Stanton, and Martha Vicinus, eds. *Women and Memory*, *Michigan Quarterly Review* 8 (1987): pp. 117-139.。

以及女性主义怀旧》("Freud's Mnemonic: Women, Screen Memories, and Feminist Nostalgia")中表达的观点,说明女性主义已经把冥王普路托强奸佩塞芬尼并迫使佩塞芬尼与母亲得墨忒耳分离的传说①当做了女性主义的起源神话。在哈弗看来,这样的怀旧模式同弗洛伊德的俄狄浦斯情结理论具有同样的缺陷,它不能指向任何有建设意义的结论。哈弗在详细讨论法国女性主义的三个代表人物——伊莲娜·西克苏(Hélène Cixous)②、朱丽娅·克里斯蒂娃和露丝·伊里加蕾——的女性主义理论以及朱迪斯·巴特勒的行为理论(Performative Theory,也译"表演理论")之后说道,行为理论虽然是反怀旧的,但同弗洛伊德理论迥异的女性主义理论仅仅反怀旧是不够的。女性主义者应该致力于建构一种女性之间的道德关系,这种关系是姐妹之间的关系,而不再是女性与母亲的关系。只有建立起一种复数的"我们"间的关系,女性主义者才有可能发展自己独立的理论体系(第28页)。

这里选注的是引言的"起源"和"行囊"两个部分。

Maternal Pasts

All this time that she remains in the story, in history, she can earn her living only by disturbing the symbolic field. Modifying the first clause, the instrument of reproduction, her only tool. The dissolution of forms, like an end of the world played out on the stage of the flat belly. Her uterus set beside her like a backpack.
— NICOLE BROSSARD, L'Amèr

I began by invoking the figure of my lesbian mother. In fact, there's a bit more to this story of women than that: I also have a sister. Alas, I must admit, the place she inhabits in the landscape I'm mapping is even less visible than that of my mother. And yet, my sister's latent presence here

---

① 传说中天神朱庇特以女儿佩塞芬尼为筹码同冥王普路托做交易以换取统治宇宙的更大权力。普路托强奸了佩塞芬尼并把她强行带入地府,从此,佩塞芬尼和母亲农业女神得墨忒耳天各一方。她们相聚时的快乐和分离时的愁苦决定了大地四季景象的更迭。

② 伊莲娜·西克苏(1937~),法国著名女性主义理论家。详见本书第二篇第8节。

promises the possibility of other maps, for reasons that I hope will become clear by the end of the book. For now, let it suffice to say that, symbolically, mother and sister stand at opposite poles of the gendered relational structures this work describes. On one end stands a conservative structure of mother-love in which nostalgia both creates and effaces the object of desire. On the other end stands a more liberatory structure of sister-love in which mutually affirming subjects of desire coexist. It is my hope that by tracing the confining boundaries of the maternal map, the book will open up future sisterly spaces for thinking about relations between women: friends, lovers, feminists in struggle.

So I began this project by asking my sister what she would want to know in reading the introduction to a book called *Maternal Pasts*, *Feminist Futures*. And she replied: "Well, to begin with, what does it have to do with anything?" One of the reasons I love her so much is that she's so direct. Unfortunately, I've had trouble responding to the skeptical curiosity embedded in her question—which I'd rather not have to answer. And yet, as usual, she's right on the mark: what *any* book has to do with anything is precisely what the introduction is supposed to spell out.

We all have mothers. Unfortunately, that will hardly suffice as an answer to my sister's question. As she or anyone else can see by simply glancing at the subtitle—"Nostalgia, Ethics, and the Question of Difference"—this is not a book about real mothers in the everyday sense of the term. Rather, to begin with, I look at the mother as a powerful cultural symbol, a symbol so powerful that it shapes the dominant structures of Western thought. When I speak of the mother as a symbol, I mean that the mother is a term—a complex cultural construct—which exists in relation to other terms. Together those terms form a nexus of semantic connections from which we make sense of the world. This book asks the question: what is the relationship between the mother and the conceptual constructs that frame our understanding of the world? How can we theorize that relationship?

Beginning

We can begin by critiquing the mother. Okay, says my sister, but just what does that mean? To talk about the mother in relation to the world is certainly impressive, but can you try to be a bit more specific? All right, I say, I'll give it a try. First of all, in the Western tradition the mother is a symbol of beginnings; as the one who gives birth, she occupies the place of the origin. Metaphorically speaking, everything begins with the mother. Second, because the mother marks the place of the origin, she also marks the place of return: in giving birth, the mother simultaneously assures the eventuality of death. Symbolically, the maternal origin does not mark a beginning whose outcome is uncertain; rather, the mother as origin represents the circle of life whose ultimate *telos* is death. As Simone de Beauvoir puts it in *The Second Sex*:

> The Woman-Mother has a face of shadows: she is the chaos whence all have come and whither all must one day return; she is Nothingness. In the Night are confused together the multiple aspects of the world which daylight reveals: night of spirit confined in the generality and opacity of matter, night of sleep and of nothingness. In the deeps of the sea it is night: woman is the Mare tene-brarum, dreaded by navigators of old; it is night in the entrails of the earth. Man is frightened of this night, the reverse of fecundity, which threatens to swallow him up. He aspires to the sky, to the light, to the sunny summits, to the pure and crystalline frigidity of the blue sky; and under his feet there is a moist, warm, and darkling gulf ready to draw him down; in many a legend do we see the hero lost forever as he falls back into the maternal shadows—cave, abyss, hell. ①

In this general sketch of the mythical meanings attached to the maternal figure, two points become clear. First, the mother is associated with an inaccessible origin; second, the structure of the maternal origin is a self-enclosed circle: its beginning is also its end. In the dominant Western

— 113 —

tradition Beauvoir describes, the mother represents the place whence we came and to which we return. Correspondingly, she also symbolizes the very foundation for everything we come to see, know, and be. She is the ground upon which the world of meaning is constructed; she is, in Beauvoir's words, the "opacity of matter" and "the entrails of the earth" upon which "the sky," "the light," and "the sunny summits" are erected. In that sense, the mother as origin is the condition of possibility of meaning itself.

At its widest level, then, this book is about the construction of systems of meaning in relation to a maternal figure. That focus may seem overly abstract to some readers; still, it is precisely by looking at those "abstract" structures of meaning that I want to elucidate the purpose of this book. To return, once again, to my sister's original question—so what does this book have to do with anything? —well, to put it simply, this work has to do with *meaning-making*: the way we make sense of the world.

I want to emphasize that the mother is not the *only* symbol of beginnings in the tradition I'm invoking here, although, as Beauvoir argues, she certainly constitutes an important, even exemplary figure of origins. Nevertheless, my argument in this book does not depend on claiming a unique or exclusive role for the mother as origin. Rather, the maternal figure functions for me as a heuristic device for uncovering and dismantling nostalgic structures of thought. Other figures may also occupy the place of the origin: a case in point is the example of Sappho in Chapter 5. And it is precisely by examining the myth of the lost mother that more general conclusions can be drawn for thinking about other originary structures of meaning.

What does it mean, then, to talk about the mother as origin? And how precisely does the maternal origin function in the making of meaning? First, it is important to remember that, within a deconstructive tradition of thought, meaning itself has no origin, no absolute ground, no place of beginning from which all other meanings stem. Ferdinand de Saussure's insight about language as a system of signs that signify *in relation* to each other is pertinent here. According to Saussure, meaning is not absolute but differential: signs acquire meaning in their difference from each other. ② And yet, in the psychoanalytically informed, deconstructive tradition of thought that has come to be known as "French theory," the term "mother" is not just one sign among many signs in an endless relay of differentially constructed meanings. Rather, as the origin, the mother becomes an originary sign, a ground of meaning, the place of beginnings to which the chain of relational meanings ultimately returns.

Second, and just as crucially, that chain of relational meanings functions within a political and ideological context. In that sense, the semiotic construction of a world of meaning around an inaccessible maternal ground has consequences that are not abstract at all, but in fact play themselves out in concrete relations of power. Specifically, the mother as origin occupies a position in the ideological and political systems through which *gendered* meanings are constructed. Not only is a world of meaning structured in relation to a maternal origin, but those meanings are given value according to the oppositional relations of gender. Further, as Beauvoir points out, across our cultural grid of gendered values, men occupy the positive and the neutral positions while women occupy the negative. ③ It follows, then, that there are connections to be made between the gendered distribution of values and the coding of the mother as the lost origin. The mother, too, occupies the negative position; she is, in fact, the most extreme expression of the construction of the feminine as negativity: absence, invisibility, meaninglessness, silence, loss. ④ In other words, as the ground of meaning, the mother can only ever be the empty foundation of meaning: she is never meaning itself, but only that which allows meaning to come to be. The political and ideological implications of such a position seem clear: she is never an agent, a subject of meaning, or a wielder of power, but rather a figure of negativity; as Beauvoir puts it, she is chaos, shadows, cave, abyss, hell. Behind the powerful men who represent that which is most valued and privileged in Western culture lies the doubled figure of both their birth and death, the source of their being as well as the specter of their negation: behind the hero lies the maternal void.

Backpacking

Given that dynamic of masculine presence and maternal absence, it is my hope that in the charting, uncharting, and recharting of this maternal map, the very logic of gender can be pushed to its breaking point. How might this happen? Let's look at this chapter's epigraph. Nicole Brossard's image of the uterus as backpack works, for me, as a figure for the disruption and transformation of the logic of gender. Indeed, writing a generation after Beauvoir and from a different place on the Francophone map—namely, Quebec—Brossard both repeats and disrupts the gendered system so forcefully articulated in *The Second Sex*. Brossard remaps what Beauvoir had already charted as one of Western culture's most powerful scripts: woman = mother = womb. "First we must ask," Beauvoir writes on the opening page of *The Second Sex*, "what is a woman? '*Tota mulier in utero*,' says one, 'woman is a womb'" (xv). The symbolic importance of the woman = mother = womb equation highlights the leap that turns the mother into the origin of all that is: from Homer's celebration of "the earth, firmly founded mother of all" to William Blake's praise of the earth as "the matron Clay" (Beauvoir, 163), the maternal womb is associated with mud, nature, the earth as source of life. In other words, the very world itself is a mother, or, as Richard Klein puts it: "the world is a dream in the body of the mother."⑤

Because their symbolic position as body, as womb, and as world relegates women to an inferior status vis-à-vis men, Brossard wants to bring about an end of that world: "like an end of the world played out on the stage of the flat belly." For Brossard, the world as woman is fecund and round, round like the belly of a pregnant mother. Everything begins in the rounded belly. Like a sentence generated from its own internal logic, the world of meaning is born out of a maternal beginning, what Brossard calls "the first clause, the instrument of reproduction". But if, symbolically, women both *generate* the world and *are* the world, the world is not something that they can possess. If woman-as-mother-as-womb is the world, that world is there for the taking. In fact, men created it so that they could take it: the world is *man's* dream in the body of the mother.

So when Brossard deflates that rounded dream, man's world becomes a stage on which other symbolic possibilities can be performed. If man's world-to-be-taken is always round like a pregnant belly, we must also be able to imagine other forms—like a flat belly, for instance—in order to play out an end of man's world. In that "dissolution of forms" Brossard modifies the masculine world perspective that creates the equation woman = mother = womb and, in so doing, challenges the very logic of gender, figured here as round versus flat. If gender gives us a world whose meaning is "round," round like the swell of a belly, it is precisely that roundness which allows men to be "flat" and to conquer our rounded world. Brossard debunks that exclusionary and essentialist meaning by making a new world that is *both* round and flat, like a backpack that can be empty or full. ("Round and flat," Jeanette Winterson writes, "only a very little has been discovered.")⑥

Let me be clear: I am not out to "destroy" the mother. Rather, my project is to trace the structures through which maternal meanings are produced and, in doing so, to unpack and challenge those meanings. In the example I'm pursuing here, one such meaning reduces woman to an organ: "*Tota mulier in utero*!" Challenging and transforming that essentializing definition of woman-as-mother-as womb can mean, as it does for Brossard, symbolically turning the womb into a backpack. In that gesture, biology becomes something that can be emptied or filled, put on or taken off at will. Further, by placing the womb beside her, Brossard's symbolic mother moves beyond a binary logic of front and back or round and flat, where to challenge gender would mean simply to reverse things. Instead, the dualistic logic of front versus back opens up toward a third, restructuring possibility: "her uterus set beside her like a backpack."

Brossard's uterus-as-backpack can thus work as a figure for the theoretical approach that frames *Maternal Pasts*, *Feminist Futures*. The uterus-as-backpack conveys, among other things, the inadequacy of mere reversal—front to back, round to flat, man to woman, father to mother— in disrupting the logic of gender. If the world is a dream in the body of the mother, I want to look at the stuff of that dream. The hero's dream might just be the mother's nightmare. And if that's the case, exposing the nightmare and shaking it up might give us a very different world.

[……]

Notes:

① Simone de Beauvoir, *The Second Sex*, trans. Howard Madison Parshley (New York: Random House, 1952), 166.

② "The linguistic entity is not accurately defined until it is *delimited*, i. e. separated from everything that surrounds it on the phonic chain. These delimited entities or units stand in opposition to each other in the mechanism of language" (103). Along the same lines, Saussure speaks of the value of the word as never "fixed": "one must also compare it [the value] with similar values, with other words that stand in opposition to it. Its content is really fixed only by the concurrence of everything that exists outside it" (115). See Ferdinard de Saussure, *Course in General Linguistics*, trans. Wade Baskin (New York: Philosophical Library, 1959).

③ "In actuality the relation of the two sexes is not quite like that of two electrical poles, for the man represents both the positive and the neutral, as is indicated by the common use of *man* to designate human beings in general; whereas woman represents only the negative, defined by limiting criteria, without reciprocity" (Beauvoir, *The Second Sex*, xviii).

④ For an influential work that attempts to recuperate the maternal sphere in order to highlight its positive cultural and political value, see Sara Ruddick's *Maternal Thinking: Toward a Politics of Peace* (Boston: Beacon Press, 1989). While I recognize the political and psychological reasons for this reversal of the dominant patriarchal script, my argument in this book points to the limitations of such an approach. For a more nuanced consideration of motherhood, see Adrienne Rich, *Of Woman Born: Motherhood as Experience and Institution* (New York: Norton, 1976).

⑤ Richard Klein, "In the Body of the Mother," *Enclitic* 7/1 (1983): p. 68.

⑥ Jeanette Winterson, *Sexing the Cherry* (New York: Random House, 1989), p. 88.

第二篇
Part 2

边缘、消音与癫狂
——女性主义框架中的母亲

Marginalization, Silencing and Madness
— Mothers in Feminist Theories

　　本篇共收入 9 部著作节选或文章,其中有 5 篇是法国女性主义理论家的代表作,4 篇出自美国女性主义理论家。这些文章从不同侧面论述母亲在西方文明的初始阶段被消音、驱逐的边缘化过程,描写母亲在男性书写中被塑造成癫狂的形象,探索女性如何通过恢复母女关系或建立姐妹情谊的途径创建独特的女性话语来表现独特的女性/母性经验。

　　法国女性主义理论家朱丽娅·克里斯蒂娃的"关于中国女性"选自其同名著作,作者追溯西方宗教的发展史论述女性如何沦落为没有话语权利的他者,母亲经验如何被视为女性身体获得愉悦的标志而被压抑,以及女性面临的认同父亲抑或母亲的两难抉择。伊莲娜·西克苏在其题为"美杜莎的浪笑"的文章中首创"女性书写"这一术语,她建议重建母女关系的纽带,指出女性的书写就是从母亲的乳汁中寻找灵感和力量的源泉。露丝·伊里加蕾似乎回应着西克苏关于创立女性话语的呼吁,她所著的"一个不会没有另一个而走动"一文探讨了女性和女性之间如何能够不受男性打扰地"讲女性话语"。伊里加蕾的另一篇文章"用身体面对母亲"通过重新阅读古希腊俄瑞斯忒亚三部曲提出了西方文明建立在杀母基础之上的惊人论断。在"被遗忘的女性祖先秘密"中,伊里加蕾再次追溯西方主要神话传说对于女性祖先的描述,重申女性祖先在创世初就已经死亡。她还因此主张,要想建立性别差异的伦理学就必须恢复女性祖先的纽带联系。

美国女性主义理论家多萝西·迪纳斯坦的"肮脏的女神"选自其著作《美人鱼与弥诺陶洛斯怪物》,她认为女性在西方文明中是肉体的替罪羊,女神的肮脏不仅由于她是人类欲望的载体和阻体,而且也因为她代表的人类从肉体得到的快感在很大程度上一直处于被压抑的状态。玛丽安·赫什的"母亲与女儿"一文聚焦母亲和女儿的关系,对多数女性主义者共同默认的女性性征和母职的认识提出质疑。她认为,女性主义的许多理论仍然被男性理论家的话语所束缚,无法描述女性存在与女性经验。苏珊·鲁宾·苏雷曼的"写作与母道"一文着眼于具有母亲身份的女性在其创作的文学作品中如何表现母性经历。安·弗古森的"母道与性"是一篇综述性文章,文章归纳了有关母道、性别与性理论中关于男性统治的作用普遍存在的几种认识,总结了女性身体对于女性主义理论家的意义以及女性具备的不同种族/民族背景和阶级与性身份的差异在建构权力关系时所起的重要作用。

7 朱丽娅·克里斯蒂娃,"关于中国女性"
Julia Kristeva,"About Chinese Women"

文学批评家、语言学家、符号学家、修辞学家、心理分析学家、作家朱丽娅·克里斯蒂娃(Julia Kristeva)①是一位当代重要的法国女性主义理论家,她把对结构语言学、符号学的研究应用于女性主义理论的建构,运用后结构主义的研究方法分析语言、社会与拥有独立心理特征和性别特征的自我的关系②,对法国女性主义的发展做出了独树一帜的贡献。

克里斯蒂娃于 1941 年出生在保加利亚的斯立文市,曾就读于索菲亚大学,1965 年移民法国,加入《原样》("Tel Quel"),随后同该组织领导人菲利普·索勒斯(Philippe Sollers)结婚。1970 年克里斯蒂娃成为该杂志编委会成员,并参加拉康心理分析培训班。她曾与罗兰·巴特(Roland Barthes)③和卢西安·戈德曼(Lucien Goldmann)④共事。1973 年克里斯蒂娃在法国高等社会科学院获得语言学博士学位,博士论文题为

---

① 照片摄影 J. Foley,取自 http://ms. cc. sunysb. edu/ ~ hvolat/kristeva/kristeva. htm。

② http://www. arlindo-correia. com/021003. html, n. p.

③ 罗兰·巴特(1915 ~ 1980),法国社会批评家、文学评论家。他最为著名的符号学理论使结构主义成为 20 世纪最为重要的思想运动之一。代表著作有《神话学》(*Mythologies*, 1957 年)、《符号学要素》(*Elements of Semiology*, 1964 年)、《符号帝国》(*The Empire of Signs*, 1970 年)和《文本的愉悦》(*The Pleasure of Texts*, 1973 年)。访问 http://www. kirjasto. sci. fi/rbarthes. htm。

④ 卢西安·戈德曼(1913 ~ 1970),生于罗马尼亚,法国哲学家、马克思主义社会学家、文学批评家、文学理论家。代表著作除对帕斯卡尔(Blaise Pascal)的《思想录》(*The Pensées*)和拉辛(Jean Racine)的悲剧进行重新解读的《隐藏的上帝》(*The Hidden God*, 1955 年)外,还有《建构小说的社会学》(*Toward the Sociology of the Novel*, 1973 年)。

《诗歌语言的革命》。1974 年起她在巴黎大学教授语言学，1979 年开始从事心理分析的实践。

克里斯蒂娃的主要著作包括：

《符号学》(*Semiotics*，1969 年)

《诗歌语言的革命》(1974 年；*Revolution in Poetic Language*，Margaret Waller 译，1984 年)

《关于中国女性》(*Des Chinoises*，1974 年；*About Chinese Women*，Anita Barrows 译，1977 年)

《语言中的欲望：文学艺术的符号学研究》(*Desire in Language：A Semiotic Approach to Literature and Art*，Leon Roudiez 编，Thomas Gora，Alice Jardine 和 Leon Roudiez 译，1980 年)

《恐怖的权力：论卑污》(*Powers of Horror：An Essay on Abjection*，Leon Roudiez 译，1982 年)

《爱在最初：心理分析与信仰》(*In the Beginning Was Love：Psychoanalysis and Faith*，Arthur Goldhammer 译，1987 年)

《黑太阳：压迫与抑郁》(1987 年；*Black Sun：Depression and Melancholia*，Leon Roudiez 译，1992 年)

《时间与意义：普鲁斯特与文学经验》(1994 年；*Time and Sense：Proust and the Experience of Literature*，1996 年)

《反抗的意义与无意义》(1996；*The Sense and Non-Sense of Revolt*，2000 年)

克里斯蒂娃创立了一门崭新的"符号分析学"(semanalysis)，即把始于索绪尔(Ferdinand de Saussure)①的符号学理论同弗洛伊德的精神分析学说结合在一起，探索语言之外的要素意义。她关注打破身份的话语，认为对身份构成挑战的三种话语模式是诗歌、母性和心理分析。诗歌指向象征过程，它的声音和韵律就是象征过程中的符号因素，象征意义就源于此。诗歌语言与日常生活中使用的语言不同，它超越逻辑法则，成为意义的生产过程。母性的身体是变化的主体性之化身，其本身蕴涵差异/相异性(alterity)。而心理分析研究主体身份的变化和差异，它细致地揭示出主体内部的符号变化/差异，展现主体内部无意识

①　费迪南·德·索绪尔(1857～1913)，瑞士语言学家，被公认为现代语言学的奠基者，他一生致力于描述语言的结构而不是追溯某一种语言的衍变历史。

作为他者的存在方式①。

纽约州立大学哲学与女性研究教授、克里斯蒂娃研究专家凯利·奥里弗（Kelly Oliver）认为，克里斯蒂娃对女性主义理论建设所做出的独特贡献主要体现在以下三个方面：

1. 她把身体重新引入人类科学的话语；

2. 她关注母性和前俄狄浦斯情结在主体建构中的作用；

3. 她提出"卑污"的概念解释压迫和歧视。②

克里斯蒂娃通过建立思想与身体、文化与自然、心理与肉身、物质与表现之间的关系主张肉体的欲望驱动力（drives）在表现中得以释放，象征的逻辑在物质意义的身体中已经运作。她强调母性在主体发展过程中所起的作用，质疑弗洛伊德和拉康对于离开母体原因的假说，认为在弗洛伊德描述的俄狄浦斯情结或拉康定义的镜像阶段之前人的主体性就已经开始建构，而西方文化中母性的作用一直被忽略，惟一的话语是宗教和科学③。克里斯蒂娃认为，身为女人和母亲的女性有情感、有欲望，因此首先是一个社会的、有话语能力的存在。在她看来，母性的作用是男、女两性都可以充当的。克里斯蒂娃反对把母性等同于自然的观点，她认为母亲首先是一个有话语能力的主体，母亲怀孕的身体恰如其分地代表了合二为一、一个包含另一个的主体关系模式。每一个个体都是这样的发展中主体（subject-in-process），从来不曾成为完全的经验主体。

《关于中国女性》的法语原文版最早于 1974 年在巴黎出版，英译版由 Anita Barrow 翻译，由纽约 Marion Boyars 出版社于 1977 年出版。该书汇集了克里斯蒂娃于 1974 年 4～5 月间在中国游历三星期的笔记和观感。该书分为两部分：第一部分较短，题为"身在此方"（"On This Side"），向读者明确讲述者以西方女性的身份观察中国的独特视角。第二部分是该书的主体，题为"中国女性"（"Women of China"），详细记录了克里斯蒂娃在中国的观感。克里

① 参见 Kelly Oliver, "Julia Kristeva", http://www. press. jhu. edu/books/hopkins_guide_to_literary_theory/julia_kristeva. html, n. p.

② Kelly Oliver, "Julia Kristeva," http://www. cddc. vt. edu/feminism/Kristeva. html, n. p.

③ Ibid. , n. p.

斯蒂娃对中国的评价带有明显的种族中心论倾向,斯匹瓦克(Gayatri Chakravorty Spivak)①也认为克里斯蒂娃对中国社会的观察有时过于傲慢②。

第一部分共分五节:"谁在讲述?"("Who Is Speaking?")、"两性战争"("The War Between the Sexes")、"话语贞节"("The Virgin of the Word")、"超越时间"("Outside Time")和"不想存在的我"("I Who Want Not to Be")。作者首先分析犹太教如何取代了先前以繁殖为目的的母性宗教。在父权的惟一神教体制下,女性沦落为没有话语权利的他者,在象征秩序中处于边缘化的地位。基督教不仅延续了犹太教的惟一神教特性,而且更强调女性贞节和女性殉难。在基督教氛围,母性或母亲经验被视为女性身体获得愉悦(*jouissance*)的明显标志,无论付出何种代价都必须压抑,生育的能力必须严格控制以屈从于父亲的名义(Father's Name)。女性因此面临两难抉择:要么认同母亲,保持被父权社会排斥的边缘地位;要么认同父亲,压抑母性欲望,试图纳入父亲代表的象征秩序。

本书选注的是第二、三两节。

第二节"两性战争"首先回顾耶和华开创天地的传说,指明在创世之初上帝就把男人和女人对立了起来③。于是,女性将充当妻子、女儿或姐妹,没有名字,"她的作用就是保证生育——为种族的繁衍生育"(第140页;第128页)。女性没有直接纽带同律法联系在一起,因为"上帝通常同男人讲话"(第140页;第128页)。女性所了解的是身体、性以及生育方面的物质条件,她的知识同肉体有关,目标是获得肉体快乐(第140页;第129页)。克里斯蒂娃紧接着追溯犹太教如何取代了以母性为中心的原始神教,得出结论说:"惟一神教压抑……女性和母亲"(第141页;第130页)。两性之间的鸿沟因此产生,这一鸿沟以男女两性同(宗教和政治)律法的不同关系而决定(第141页;第130页)。

克里斯蒂娃通过分析指出,父权体制"要求女性被排斥在惟一真实、具立法

① 斯匹瓦克(1942~),出生于印度的第三世界马克思主义、女性主义、解构主义学者,1976年翻译出版解构主义大师德里达的《论文字学》(*Of Grammatology*)一举成名。

② Gayatri Chakravorty Spivak, "French Feminism in an International Frame," *Yale French Studies* 62 (1981), pp. 154-185.

③ Julia Kristeva, "About Chinese Women," trans., Séan Hand, ed., Toril Moi, *The Kristeva Reader* (New York: Columbia University Press, 1986), pp. 139-140. 本节引自该文观点均出自此处,以下只在正文注明页码,分号后第二个页码为引文在本书的页码。

效力的原则——即话语——之外,也被排斥在赋予生育以社会价值的(父权)因素之外:总之,女性被排斥在知识与权力之外"(第143页;第132页)。她借用基督神话中上帝、亚当、夏娃和蛇的关系进一步说明女性从创世初就被剥夺了话语权利,成为相对于男性的"另类"(第143页;第132页)。父权话语得以维系是男女两性之间殊死斗争的结果,这就是惟一神教的要旨(第144页;第134页)。克里斯蒂娃提醒我们要警惕两种错误认识:一种女性主义的极端思想否认圣经中展现的两性战争;另一种虽然承认两性之间的鸿沟但却认为这一鸿沟无法逾越(第145页;第134页)。克里斯蒂娃说,要避免这两种认识,一方面应该承认性别差异,另一方面还要不停歇地继续男女两性之间的战争(第145页;第135页)。

在第三节"话语贞节"的开始克里斯蒂娃就对基督教作了如下描述:"基督教主张普救,它的确把女性同象征团体联系在一起,但前提是女性一定要保持贞节。如果女性未能做到这一点,她们也可以殉难来为肉体愉悦赎罪"(第145～146页;第135页)。在贞节和殉难这两个极端状态中间,母亲通过为孩子准备施洗参与到基督话语。在单一性别的经济秩序中,基督教对女性的期待是不言而喻的:女性应该承担话语(Word)蕴含的处女身份,只有这样她才能以与男性相同的性别来生活和思考(第147页;第137页)。

克里斯蒂娃还指出,"癫狂"("ecstatic")和"抑郁"("melancholic")是女性参与基督秩序的两种主要模式(第147页;第137页)。在"癫狂"状态中,母性特点都赋予给了父亲,女性成为缺乏性别特征的"无性人/雌雄同体"("androgynous being");而在"抑郁"状态中,女性由于拥有同男性不同的异性身体而忍受惩罚、痛苦和不幸(第147～148页;第137～138页)。克里斯蒂娃紧接着分析了女孩在这样一个惟一神教社会中经历的心理成长历程。她认为,女孩面临两种选择:要么认同母亲;要么把自己提升到父亲所代表的象征地位(第148页;第138页)。但在克里斯蒂娃看来,无论哪一种选择,女性都会丧失自我,丧失作为女性可以享受的愉悦。"做父亲的女儿? 还是做母亲的女儿?"这成为女性成长过程中面临的两难抉择(第151页;第141页)。克里斯蒂娃最后谈到被公认为"父亲女儿"的伊莱克特拉(Electra)①。她认为,伊莱克特拉杀害

---

① 古希腊剧作家埃斯库罗斯(Aeschylus)所著"俄瑞斯忒亚"三部曲之一《阿伽门农》(Agamemnon)中的人物。由于对丈夫阿伽门农把女儿依菲琴尼亚(Iphigeneia)献祭战神以换取战场上合适的风向心怀不满,克吕泰涅斯特拉(Clytemnastra)同埃癸斯托斯(Aegisthus)发生性关系作为报复,并合谋杀害了从战场归来的阿伽门农。女儿伊莱克特拉得知后,同兄弟俄瑞斯忒斯(Orestes)联手杀害了母亲。"伊莱克特拉情结"(Electra Complex)同"俄狄浦斯情结"(Oedipus Complex)相对,意指女儿爱恋父亲而仇恨母亲的复杂感情。

母亲并不是源于母亲杀害父亲从而使她无法表达对父亲的爱恋,而是因为母亲在同埃癸斯托斯的不正当关系中展现了女性身体的"愉悦"。母亲是不能享受愉悦的,父亲的女儿看到母亲在两性战争中获得了滋养而这样的较量导致父亲死亡,她无论如何也要掩盖这样的事实(第 152 页;第 142~143 页)。

About Chinese Women

[……]

2. The War Between the Sexes

Yahweh Elohim created the world and concluded alliances by *dividing* (*karath*) light from darkness, the waters of the heavens from the waters of the earth, the earth from the seas, the creatures of the water from the creatures of the air, the animals each according to their kind and man (in His own image) from himself. It's also by division that He places them opposite each other: man and woman. Not without hesitation, though, for it is said at first that "male and female created He them". But this first version is quickly corrected by the story of Adam's rib. Later, the first female creature, due to the hesitation wherein man and woman are not all that separate, makes an ephemeral appearance in the form of the diabolical Lilith, an emanation of Sodom and Gomorrah (Isaiah xxxiv, 14), who crops up in several more or less heterodox exegeses, but not in the Bible itself.

Divided from man, made of that very thing which is lacking in him, the biblical woman will be wife, daughter or sister, or all of them at once, but she will rarely have a name. Her function is to assure procreation—the propagation of the race. But she has no direct relation with the law of the community and its political and religious unity: God generally speaks only to men. Which is not to say that woman doesn't know more about Him; indeed, she is the one who knows the material conditions, as it were, of the body, sex and procreation, which permit the existence of the community, its permanence and thus man's very dialogue with his God. Besides, is the entire community not the *bride* of God? But woman's knowledge is corporal, aspiring to pleasure rather than tribal unity (the forbidden fruit seduces Eve's senses of *sight and taste*). It is an informulable knowledge, an ironic common sense (Sarah, pregnant at 90, laughs at this divine news); or else, when it serves social necessity, it's often in a roundabout way, after having violated the most ancient of taboos, that of incest (Sarah declared the sister of Abraham; Lot's daughters sleeping with their father).

Long before the establishment of the people of Israel, the Northern Semites worshipped maternal divinities. Even while such worship continued, though, these farmers and shepherds had already begun to isolate the principle of a male, paternal divinity and a pantheon in the image of the family (father-mother-son). But Judaism was founded through and beyond this tradition, when, around 2000 BC, Egyptian refugees, nomads, brigands and insurgent peasants banded together, it seems, without any coherent ethnic origin, without land or State, seeking at first merely to survive as a wandering community. Jewish monotheism is undoubtedly rooted in this will to create a community in the face of all the unfavourable concrete circumstances: an abstract, nominal, symbolic community beyond individuals and their beliefs, but beyond their political organization as well. In fact, the Kingdom of David survived only a short while after its foundation in 1000 BC, preceded by wars, and followed by discord, before becoming the vassal, and eventually the victim, of Babylonia. Devised to create a community, monotheism does not, however, accommodate itself to the political community that is the State; initially it doesn't even help it. Monotheism does survive the State, however, and determine the direction the latter will take, even much later, through Christianity up to the various forms of modern technocracies, both religious and secular. But this is not the problem that concerns us here. Let us note that by establishing itself as the principle of a symbolic, paternal community in the grip of the superego, beyond all ethnic considerations, beliefs or social loyalties, monotheism represses, along with paganism, the greater part of agrarian civilizations and their ideologies, women and mothers. The Syrian goddess who was worshipped up until the beginning of the Christian era in the Armenian city of Hieropolis-Menbidj, or the numerous sacrifices to Ishtar, survive the biblical expurgation only in the shape of Deborah, the inspired warrior who accompanied the soldiers and celebrated their deeds, or else in the mouths of prophets who deplore idolatry, such as Jeremiah, the last of the pre-exile prophets, who denounced the cult of the "Queen of the Heavens".

Consequently, no other civilization seems to have made the principle of sexual difference so crystal clear: between the two sexes a cleavage or abyss opens up. This gap is marked by their different relationship to the law (both religious and political), a difference which is in turn the very condition of their alliance. Monotheistic unity is sustained by a radical separation of the sexes: indeed, it is this very separation which is its prerequisite. For without this gap between the sexes, without this localization of the polymorphic, orgasmic body, desiring and laughing, in the *other* sex, it would have been impossible, in the *symbolic realm*, to isolate the principle of One Law—the One, Sublimating, Transcendent Guarantor of the ideal interests of the community. In the sphere *of reproductive relations*, at that time inseparably linked to relations of production, it would have been impossible to ensure the propagation of the species simply by turning it into the highest premium of pleasure.

There is one unity: an increasingly purified community discipline, that is isolated as a transcendent principle and which thereby ensures the survival of the group. This *unity* which is represented by the God of monotheism is sustained by a *desire* that pervades the community, a desire which is at once stirring and threatening. Remove this threatening desire, the dangerous support of cohesion, from man; place it beside him and create a supplement for what is lacking in this man who speaks to his God; and you have woman, who has no access to the word, but who appears as the pure desire to seize it, or as that which ensures the permanence of the divine paternal function for all humans: that is, the desire to continue the species.

This people of shepherds and nomads settled only temporarily to found their community by means of the only durable bond in the steppes and the desert: the word. The shepherd (Abel, for example) will therefore be sacrificed so that a lowly farmer can initiate the narrative of tribal wanderings. Invasions and exiles ensue: a sixth century BC of exodus, and a fifth century of temporary return to the land, with the invaders displaying a relative degree of tolerance. The word of the community will consequently oscillate between prophecy and legislation, but it will always be a word that aims to gather together this society which history is bent on dispersing. We must not employ some vulgar form of sociology in order to attribute to climatic or socio-historic conditions the privilege granted to the word and the monotheistic transcendence that represents its agency in the southern Mediterranean basin. But the discovery, by one of the peoples of this region, of the specific form of religiosity known as monotheism (which had failed in Egypt after the attempts of Amen-Hotep *IV*) on the one hand corresponds to the function of human symbolism, which is to provide an agency of communication and cohesion despite the fact that it works through interdiction and division (thing/word, body/speech, pleasure/law, incest/procreation...); while on the other hand it simultaneously represents the paternal function: patrilinear descent with transmission of the name of the father centralizes eroticism, giving it the single goal of procreation. It is thus caught in the grip of an abstract symbolic authority which refuses to recognise the growth of the child in the mother's body, something a matrilinear system of descent kept alive in the minds by leaving open certain possibilities of polymorphism, if not incest. If, with these two keys, one can consolidate a social group and make it resistant to any test of internal or external dissolution, one begins to understand that the monotheistic community acquires a vitality that allows it not only to survive geographic or historical threats, but to ensure an otherwise impossible development of productive forces by an infinite perfecting of goods and of means of production. This control ensures a productivist teleology: even if the threats of the prophets disturb this teleology and keep it from degenerating into profiteering and the enjoyment of wealth, this does not in any way preclude the advantage that the property-owning classes derive from it for the perfecting of their economic and political power.

The economy of this system requires that women be excluded from the single true and legislating principle, namely the Word, as well as from the (always paternal) element that gives procreation a social value: they are excluded from knowledge and power. The myth of the relationship between Eve and the serpent is the best summary of this exclusion. The serpent stands for the opposite of God, since he tempts Eve to transgress His prohibition. But he is also Adam's repressed desire to transgress, that which he dares not carry out, and which is his shame. The sexual symbolism helps us understand that the serpent is that which, in God or Adam, remains beyond or outside the sublimation of the Word. Eve has no relationship other than with that, and even then because she is its very opposite, the "other race".

When Yahweh says to the serpent, "I will put enmity between thee and woman, and between they seed (*zera*) and her seed (*zera*): it shall bruise thy head, and thou shall bruise (*teshufenu*) its heel (*akev*)", He established the divergence—of race or "seed"—between God and man on the one hand and woman on the other. Furthermore, in the second part of the sentence, woman disappears completely into seed: generation. But, even more essentially, Yahweh formulates the code of eroticism between the two seeds as though it were a code of war. An endless war, where *he* will lose his head (or his gland?), and *she* her trace, her limit, her succession (the threat, perhaps, to deprive her of descendants, if she takes herself to be all-powerful, and phallic?). It is a strange goal at all events, to follow on the heels of women, and one to be borne in mind when one is confronted with the bound feet of Chinese women, crushed in a way that is infinitely less decisive, but more painful and much more certain.

St Augustine returns to this function of the serpent and offers a definition when he points out that it represents the "sense of the body" but "belongs to the reason of science" and "is dependent on cognition"; and when he thinks (must we believe that this is a consequence of the double nature of the "sense of the body"?) that sexual difference, far from being a question of distinguishing between two individuals, "can be discerned in a single human being":

> *For this reason I have thought that the sense of the body should not be taken for the woman, since we see that it is common to us and beasts, and have preferred to take something which the beasts do not have, and have believed that it is more appropriate for the serpent to be understood as the sense of the body... for these are the senses of the rational nature and pertain to the intelligence, but that five-fold sense of the body by which the corporeal species and movement are perceived, not only by us but also by the beasts... Whenever that carnal or animal sense, therefore, introduces into this purpose of the mind, which uses the living force of reason in temporal and corporeal things for the purpose of carrying out its functions some inducement to enjoy itself, that is, to* enjoy itself *as a kind of* private and personal *good and not as a* public *and* common *good which is an* unchangeable good, *then the serpent, as it were, addresses the woman. But to consent to this inducement is to eat of the forbidden tree.* ①

If what woman desires is the very opposite of the sublimating Word and paternal legislation, she neither *has* nor *is* that opposite. All that remains for her is to pit herself constantly against that opposite in the very movement by which she desires it, to kill it repeatedly and then suffer endlessly: a radiant perspective on masochism, a masochism that is the price she must pay in order to be Queen. In a symbolic economy of production and reproduction centred on the paternal Word (the phallus, if you like), one can make a woman believe that she *is* (the phallus) even if she doesn't have it (the serpent, the penis): doesn't she have the child? In this way, social harmony is preserved: the structure functions, produces and reproduces. Without it, the very foundation of this society is endangered.

We must stress that this last point, for its importance is overlooked. At best one is guilty of naïvety if one considers our modern societies as simply patrilinear, or class-structured, or capitalist-monopolist, and omits the fact that they are at the same time (and never one without the other) governed by a monotheism whose essence is best expressed in the Bible: the "paternal Word" sustained by a fight to the death between the two races (men/women). In this naïvety, one forgets that whatever attacks this radical location of sexual difference, while still remaining *within the framework of our patrilinear, class-structured, capitalist societies*, is above all also attacking a fundamental discovery of Judaism that lies in the separation of the sexes and in their incompatibility: in castration, if you like—the support of monotheism and the source of its eroticism. To wish to deny this separation and yet remain within the framework of patrilinear capitalist society and its monotheistic ideology (even when disguised as humanism) necessarily plunges one back into the petty perversion of fetishism. And we know the role that the pervert, with his invincible belief in the maternal phallus and his obstinate refusal to recognize the existence of the other sex, has been able to play in anti-semitism and the totalitarian movements that embrace it. Let us recall the fascist or social-fascist homosexual community (and all homosexual communities for whom there is no "other race"), and the fact that it is inevitably flanked by a community of viragos who have forgotten the war of the sexes and identify with the paternal Word or its serpent. The feminist movements are equally capable of a similar perverse denial of biblical teaching. We must recognize this and be on our guard.

On the other hand, there are analysts who do recognize this and, faithful to Freudian pessimism, accept the abyss between the two races; yet they go on to preach the impossibility of communication between the two, the "lack of relation". Here it is no longer a question of the war between the sexes: doesn't every psychiatrist have as a companion a "dead woman", an aphasic mother, an inaudible haven of procreation, that ensures and reassures the "analytic word"?

The solution? To go on waging the war between the two races without respite, without a perverse denial of the abyss that marks sexual difference or a disillusioned mortification of the division. In the meantime, some other economy of the sexes installs itself, but not before it has transformed our entire logic of production (class) and reproduction (family). China will just be one more horizon, which we will be able to read once this transformation is complete. Before it has happened, however, that country is susceptible of functioning as just another perversion, another mortification (for example: the blindness of the left-winger who believes in Chinese chastity—the final discovery of a happiness that can be opposed to "bourgeois morality").

3. The Virgin of the Word

Universalist as it is, Christianity does associate women with the symbolic community, but only provided they keep their *virginity*. Failing that, they can atone for their carnal *jouissance* with their martyrdom. Between these two extremes, the mother participates in the community of the Christian Word not by giving birth to her children, but merely by preparing them for baptism.

St Augustine once again offers a fairly cynical explanation for the basically economic reasons for this association of women with the Christian Word, which is secured at the price of the virginity represented by Mary and imitated by the female monastic orders. Quite simply, by the time of Augustine, the survival of the European community no longer depended on the accelerated propagation of the species, but rather on the participation by all men and women in the symbolic efforts (technical as well as ideological) to perfect the means and relations of production:

> But it would be very foolish, for the sake of enjoying marriage even at the present time, when the coming of Christ is not served through carnal generation by the very begetting of children, to take upon oneself the burden of this tribulation of the

flesh which the Apostle predicts for those who marry— unless those who cannot remain continent feared that under the temptation of Satan they would fall into sins leading to damnation. ②

Between this historical constraint and the myth of the Virgin impregnated by the Word there is still a certain distance, which will be bridged by two psychoanalytical processes, one relating to the role of the mother, the other to the workings of language.

The first consists in ceasing to repress the fact that the mother is *other*, has no penis, but experiences *jouissance* and bears children. But this is acknowledged only at the pre-conscious level: just enough to imagine that she bears children, while censuring the fact that she has experienced *jouissance* in an act of coitus, that there was a "primal scene". Once more, the vagina and the *jouissance* of the mother are disregarded, and immediately replaced by that which puts the mother on the side of the socio-symbolic community: childbearing and procreation in the name of the father. This operation of false recognition—mis-recognition—of maternal *jouissance* is accomplished by a process whose origins Ernest Jones was the first to understand. Too hastily categorized simply as the biographer of Freud, Jones in fact deserves credit not only for having proposed one of the most interesting concepts of female sexuality, but for having been the first to attempt an analysis of the sexual economy of the great Christian myths. So, in the Word and Breath celebrated by many religions of which Christianity is the chief, the psychoanalyst sees an emanation not of the glottal but of the anal sphincter. This sacrilegious theory, confirmed by the fantasies of analysands, tends to prove that impregnation by the fart (hiding behind its sublimation into Word) corresponds to the fantasy of anal pregnancy, of penetration or auto-penetration by an anal penis, and, in any case, of a confusion of anus and vagina: in short, to a denial of sexual difference. Such a scenario is probably more frequent among male subjects, and represents the way in which the small boy usurps the role of the mother, by denying his difference in order to submit himself in her place and as a woman to the father. In this homosexual economy, we can see that what Christianity recognizes in a woman, what it demands of her in order to include her within its symbolic order, is that by living or thinking of herself as a virgin impregnated by the Word, she should live and think of herself as a male homosexual. If, on the other hand, this identification with the homosexual does not succeed, if a woman is not a virgin, a nun, and chaste, but has orgasms and gives birth, her only means of gaining access to the symbolic paternal order is by engaging in an endless struggle between the orgasmic maternal body and the symbolic prohibition—a struggle that will take the form of guilt and mortification, and culminate in masochistic *jouissance*. For a woman who has not easily repressed her relationship with her mother, participation in the symbolic paternal order as Christianity defines it can only be masochistic. As St Augustine again so marvellously puts it: "No-one, however, to my way of thinking, would ever prefer virginity to martyrdom" ("Holy Virginity", XLVII, 47). The *ecstatic* and the *melancholic*, two great female archetypes of Christianity, exemplify two ways in which a woman may participate in this symbolic Christian order.

In the first discourse, the maternal traits are attributed to the symbolic father, the mother is denied by this displacement of her attributes and the woman then submits herself to a sexually undifferentiated androgynous being:

But when this most wealthy Spouse desires to enrich and comfort the Bride still more, He draws her so closely to Him that she is like one who swoons from excess of pleasure and joy and seems to be suspended in those Divine arms and drawn near to that sacred side and to those Divine breasts. Sustained by that Divine milk with which her Spouse continually nourishes her and growing in grace so that she may be enabled to receive His comforts, she can do nothing but rejoice. Awakening from that sleep and heavenly inebriation, she is like one amazed and stupefied; well, I think, may her sacred folly wring these words from her: "Thy breasts are better than wine". ③

At the same time, in the second discourse, submission to the father is experienced as punishment, pain and suffering inflicted upon the heterogeneous body. Such a confrontation provokes a melancholic *jouissance* whose most emotive eulogy is perhaps to be found in Catherine of Siena's treatise on the sensuality of tears.

What is there in the psycho-sexual development of a little girl in monotheistic capitalist society that prepares her for this economy of which the *ecstatic* and the *melancholic* represent the two extremes of the attempt to gain access to the social order (to symbolism, power, knowledge)?

There is an increasing insistence on the importance of pre-Oedipal phases, oral and anal, in the subsequent development of both boy and girl. The child is bound to the mother's body without the latter being, as yet, a "separate object". Instead, the mother's body acts with the child's as a sort of socio-natural continuum. This period is dominated by the oral and anal drives of incorporation and aggressive rejection: hence the pleasure is auto-erotic as well as inseparable from the mother's body. Through language, the Oedipal phase introduces the symbolic agency, the prohibition of auto-eroticism and the recognition of the paternal function. As Jones once again points out, the boy as well as the girl must renounce his or her own pleasure in order to find an object of the opposite sex, or renounce his or her own sex in order to find a homogeneous pleasure that has no *other* as its object. But if such is the rule, it is realized differently in boys and in girls. When the boy does not identify with his mother to submit like a woman to his father, he becomes his father's rival for the mother's love, and the castration he experiences is rather a fear of "aphanisis": fear of not being able to satisfy both *her* and *himself*. The girl also finds herself faced with a choice: either she identifies with the mother, or she raises herself to the symbolic stature of the father. In the first case, the pre-Oedipal stages (oral and anal eroticism) are intensified. By giving herself a male object (a substitute for the father), she desires and appropriates him for herself through that which her mother has bequeathed her during the "female" pre-Oedipal phase—i. e. , through the oral-sadistic veil that accompanies the vaginal *jouissance* of heterosexual woman. If we perceive a sort of fundamental female "homosexuality" in this identification with the pre-Oedipal mother, we perceive at the same time that this has nothing whatever to do with male homosexuality, and is not superseded by the "female heterosexual". In the second case, identification with the father, the girl represses the oral-sadistic stage, and at the same time represses the vagina and the possibility of finding someone else as her partner. (This situation can come about, for instance, by refusing the male partner, by feminizing the male partner or by assuming either a male or a female role in a relationship with a female partner.) The sadistic component of such an economy is so violent as to obliterate the vagina. In her imagination, the girl obtains a real or imaginary penis for herself; the imaginary acquisition of the male organ seems here to be less important than the access she gains to the symbolic mastery which is necessary to censor the pre-Oedipal stage and wipe out all trace of dependence on the mother's body. Obliteration of the pre-Oedipal stage, identification with the father, and then: "I'm looking, as a man would, for a woman"; or else, "I submit myself, as if I were a man who thought he was a woman, to a woman who thinks she is a man". Such are the double or triple twists of what is commonly called female homosexuality, or lesbianism. The oral-sadistic dependence on the mother has been so strong that it now represents not simply a veil over the vagina, but a veritable blockade. Thus the lesbian never discovers the vagina, but creates from this restitution of pre-Oedipal drives (oral/anal, absorption/rejection) a powerful mechanism of symbolization. Intellectual or artist, she wages a vigilant war against her pre-Oedipal dependence on her mother, which keeps her from discovering her own body as other, different, possessing a vagina. Melancholy—fear of aphanisis—punctuated by sudden bursts of energy marks the loss of the maternal body, this immediate investment of sadism in the symbolic.

It is interesting to note that, on the level of speech, the pre-Oedipal stage corresponds to an intense echolalia, first in rhythm and then in intonation, before a phonologico-syntactic structure is imposed on the sentence. This latter is only totally achieved at the end of the Oedipal phase. It is obvious, then, that a reactivation of the pre-Oedipal phase in a man (by homosexuality or imaginary incest) creates in his pre-sentence speech an explosion of rhythm, intonation and nonsense: nonsense invades sense, and creates laughter. When he flees the symbolic paternal order (through fear of castration, Freud would say, through fear of aphanisis, Jones would say), man can laugh. But the daughter, on the other hand, is rewarded by the symbolic order when she identifies with the father: only here is she recognized not as herself but in opposition to her rival, the mother with a vagina who experiences *jouissance*. Thus, at the price of censuring herself as a woman, she will be able to triumph in her henceforth sublimated sadistic attacks on the mother whom she has repressed and with whom she will always fight, either (as a heterosexual) by identifying with her, or (as a homosexual) by pursuing her erotically. Therefore the invasion of her speech by these unphrased, nonsensical, maternal rhythms, far from soothing her, or making her laugh, destroys her symbolic armour and makes her ecstatic, nostalgic or mad. Nietzsche would not have known how to be a woman. A woman has nothing to laugh about when the symbolic order collapses. She can take pleasure in it if, by identifying with the mother, the vaginal body, she imagines she is the sublime, repressed forces which return through the fissures of the order. But she can just as easily die from this upheaval, as a victim or a militant, if she has been deprived of a successful maternal identification and has found in the symbolic paternal order her one superficial, belated and easily severed link with life.

Faithful to a certain biblical tradition, Freud saw the fear of castration as the essential moment in the formation of any psyche, male or female. Closer to Christianity, but also to the post-Romantic psychology which defines all characters according to the amorous relations, Jones proposed to find the determining element in psychic structure in aphanisis (the fear of losing the possibility of *jouissance*), rather than in castration. Perhaps it would not merely be a resurgence of Greek or logico-phenomenological thought to suggest locating this fundamental event neither in castration nor in aphanisis (both of which would be only its fantasmic derivatives), but rather in *the process of learning the symbolic function* to which the human animal is subjected from the pre-Oedipal phase onward. By symbolic function we mean a system of signs (first, rhythmic and intonational difference, then signifier/signified) which are organized into logico-syntactic structures whose aim is to accredit social communication as exchange purified of pleasure. From the beginning, then, we are dealing with a training process, an inhibition, which already begins with the first echolalias, but fully asserts itself with language-learning. If the pre-Oedipal phase of this inhibition is still full of pleasure and not yet detached from the mother/child continuum, it already entails certain prohibitions: notably the training of the glottal and anal sphincters. And it is on the foundation of these prohibitions that the superego will be built.

The symbolic order functions in our monotheistic West by means of a *system of kinship* that involves transmission of the name of the father and a rigorous prohibition of incest, and a *system of speech* that involves an increasingly logical, simple, positive and "scientific" form of communication, that is stripped of all stylistic, rhythmic and "poetic" ambiguities. Such an order brings this *inhibition constitutive of the speaking animal* to a height never before attained, one logically assumed by the role of the father. The role of the "mother" (the repressed element) includes not only the drives (of which the most basic is that of aggressive rejection) but also, through the education of the sphincters, the first training of these drives in the oral/anal phase, marked by rhythms, intonations and gestures which as yet have no significance.

Daughter of the father? Or daughter of the mother?

As the Sophoclean chorus says, "Never was a daughter more her father's daughter" than Electra. Not only does she incite vengeance; she is also the principal agent in the murder of her mother, more so than Orestes himself, for in the murder scene, is it not the voices of the daughter and the mother we hear while the son remains silent? It is a delusion to think that Orestes, an anti-Oedipus, has killed his mother to wrest himself thus from the family and move into a new community that is supra-familial and political: the *city* whose cult was already becoming an economic and political necessity in Greece. Faced with this murder, thought-out and spoken by Electra, of which Orestes is only the agent, one wonders if anti-Oedipal man is not a fiction, or, at all events, if he is not always appended to the *jouissance* of a wife-sister. There would be no unavenged dead father—no Resurrection of the Father —if that father did not have a (virgin) daughter. A daughter does not put up with the murder of a father. That the father is made a symbolic power—that is, that he is dead, and thus elevated to the rank of a Name—is what gives meaning to her life, which will henceforth be an eternal vendetta. Not that this fixation does not drive her mad: in vain Electra says that "Only a madman could forget a father killed so heartlessly"; in vain does she accuse poor Chrysothemis, "her mother's daughter", of being demented, of forgetting her father; she cannot stop herself from being driven mad by her own activity. But her own madness, contrary to Chrysothemis' passive clinging to her mother, is what the leader of the chorus will call, at the end, an "effort that crowns history", for without it, there would be no "freedom", and no "history" for the city from which, as woman, she is none the less alienated. For, in fact, this pursuit of the father's cause has a darker side to it: hatred of the mother, or, more precisely, hatred of her *jouissance*. Electra wants Clytemnestra dead, not because she is a mother who kills the father, but because she is a mistress (of Aegisthus). Let *jouissance* be forbidden to the mother: this is the demand of the father's daughter, fascinated by the mother's *jouissance*. And one can imagine how the city will depend on these fathers' daughters (given that a man can fulfil the office of daughter) in order to cover up the fact that the mother's *jouissance* is nourished by the war of the sexes in the murder of the father. The Electras—"deprived forever of their hymens"—militants in the cause of the father, frigid with exaltation—are they then dramatic figures emerging at the point where the social consensus corners any woman who wants to escape her condition: nuns, "revolutionaries", even "feminists"?

It takes a Mozart to make a comedy out of this fidelity of the daughter to the father. The dead father is retained in the guise of the Commander. Orestes is cut out and replaced with poor Ottavio. Aegisthus and Clytemnestra have no reason to exist: power and *jouissance* following one upon the other in a radiant musical infinity, will be represented by Don Giovanni. So the heroic Electra becomes the pitiful, unhappy Donna Anna: the ill-treated hysteric, passionately in love with the death of her father, commemorating his murder—but without hope of revenge—in a hallucinatory monologue of bitterness and jubilation. Since history repeats itself only as farce, Donna Anna is a comic Electra: still a slave to her father, but to a father whose political and moral law are crumbling enough, by the eighteenth century, to allow Mozart not to treat it as tragedy.

[······]

Notes:

① St Augustine, *The Trinity*, tr. S. McKenna (Washington, DC: The Catholic University of America Press, 1963), p. 362 and pp. 359-360. My emphasis.

② St Augustine, "Holy Virginity", in *Treatises on Marriage and Other Subjects*, tr. J. McQuade (New York: Fathers of the Church, 1955), p. 159.

③ St Teresa of Jesus, "Conceptions of the Love of God", in *The Complete Works*, tr. and ed. E. Allison Peers (London: Sheed & Ward, 1946), vol. 2, p. 384.

8 伊莲娜·西克苏,"美杜莎的浪笑"
Hélène Cixous, "The Laugh of the Medusa"

西克苏(Hélène Cixous)①于 1975 年发表的"美杜莎的浪笑"是 20 世纪最为重要的女性主义檄文之一,它被女性主义者广泛引用,其重要地位不容忽视。西克苏在该文中提出的"女性书写"(L'écriture féminine)概念为女性主义者摆脱男权秩序提供了一种可能的探索。西克苏一直致力于自我个性的解放,后来又关注女性的生存状况。她对生命的歌颂使她区别于许多其他知识分子的颓废②,她对性别差异、性别偏见与排斥等问题的关注促使她致力于冲破西方逻各斯中心主义(logocentrism)的局限。

西克苏于 1937 年 6 月 5 日出生在法属殖民地阿尔及利亚。父亲是法国人,有犹太血统,在西克苏幼年时辞世。西克苏的母亲来自奥地利,德语成为西克苏的第一语言。西克苏曾在法国求学,熟读各国文学作品。1959 年结婚,同年第一个孩子出世,3 年后又生了第二个孩子。与此同时她任教于波尔多大学。1965 年,离婚后的西克苏来到巴黎,先后在一些大学任教。1967 年获得博士学位,博士论文《詹姆斯·乔伊斯的流放》(The Exile of James Joyce)直至 1972 年她荣升教授才发表。1968 年学生运动后,西克苏被任命为特使到文森纳(Vincennes)组建巴黎第八大学,尝试用一种全新的理

---

① 照片来自 http://prelectur. stanford. edu/lecturers/cixous/index. html。
② http://www.egs.edu/resources/cixous. html, n. p.

念从事高等教育。热拉尔·热奈特(Gérard Genette)①、米歇尔·福柯(Michel Foucault)②、托德洛夫(Tzvetan Todorov)③、费力克斯·加塔利(Félix Guattari)④以及吉尔·德勒兹(Gilles Deleuze)⑤等人都曾先后在此任教。1969年,西克苏同托德洛夫和热奈特创办《诗论》(Poétique)杂志。1974年,西克苏创建女性研究中心(Centre d'Études Féminines)并出任主任,这是欧洲

---

① 热拉尔·热奈特(1930~   ),法国文学理论家,同结构主义运动联系密切,他把修辞学的词汇引入文学批评。代表著作有《叙事话语:论方法》(Narrative Discourse: An Essay on Method)、《虚构与行文》(Fiction and Diction)和四卷本的《隐迹稿本》(Figures)。

② 米歇尔·福柯(1926~1984),法国哲学家。他提出的理论对人们传统观念中的政治、权力、保险、福利等构成挑战,主要论著有《疯狂与文明》(Madness and Civilization,1960年)、《事物的秩序》(Order of Things, 1966年)、《纪律与惩罚》(Discipline and Punish,1975年)、《性史》(History of Sexuality, 1976年)、《愉快的作用》(The Use of Pleasure, 1984年)以及《对自我的关怀》(The Care of the Self, 1984年)。访问http://www.theory.org.uk/ctr-fouc.htm。

③ 托德洛夫(1939~   ),哲学家,出生在保加利亚,1963年后定居法国。著有近30部著作,包括《散文的诗学》(The Poetics of Prose, 1977年)、《文学观》(The Notion of Literature,1987年)等。

④ 费力克斯·加塔利(1930~1992),法国哲学家、心理分析学家,首创精神分裂分析方法。同德勒兹合作出版过《资本主义与精神分裂》(Capitalism and Schizophrenia,1969年)、《反俄狄浦斯》(Anti-Oedipus,1972年)、《一千座高原》(A Thousand Plateaus, 1980年)和《哲学是什么?》(What Is Philosophy?,1991年)。

⑤ 吉尔·德勒兹(1925~1995),法国哲学家。代表著作有《经验论与主体性》(Empiricism and Subjectivity, 1953年)、《尼采与哲学》(Nietzsche and Philosophy,1962年)、《福柯》(Foucault,1986年)、《差异与重复》(Difference and Repetition,1968年)、《哲学中的表现主义:斯宾诺莎》(Expressionism in Philosophy: Spinoza,1968年),同费力克斯·加塔利合作出版的哲学著作影响广泛。他还著有文集《批评与诊疗文集》(Essays Critical and Clinical,1993年)。访问http://www.egs.edu/resources/deleuze.html。

第一个女性研究中心,也是欧洲第一家授予女性研究领域博士学位的机构①。

由于西克苏涉猎文学、哲学、修辞与语言等多个领域,所以很难把她归入某一特定的学科。影响她思想的哲学家和文学家包括海德格尔(Martin Heidegger)②、卡夫卡(Franz Kafka)③、弗洛伊德、拉康、德里达等④。

西克苏著述众多,已出版40多部著作,发表100多篇文章。被评论家称为创作出了"几生几世的成就"⑤。其主要著作有:

《内部》(1969年;*Inside*,1986年)

《第三身体》、《开端》与《中立》三部曲(1970~1972年;*The Third Body*,*Beginnings*,*Neuter*)

《无人之名》(1974年;*Nobody's Name*)

《超越深渊的婚礼准备》(1978年;*Wedding Preparations Beyond the Abyss*)

《相伴或天真的艺术》(1981年;*With or the Art of Innocence*)

《普罗米西亚之书》(1983年;*Promethea's Book*,1990年)

《新生女性》(与Catherine Clément合著,1975年;*The Newly Born Woman*,1986年)

---

① 西克苏在接受剑桥大学三一学院教授凯瑟琳·奥格拉迪(Kathleen O'Grady)采访时说,她创建女性研究中心时有两个发现:第一,文学是局限在国家界限之内的;第二,文学正如所有的话语一样是阳性的。她身为英语教授讲授的是阳性的英语国家文学,她于是力图打破单一性别、单一语言的文学以及文学研究。她创建的女性研究中心授予的博士学位是跨学科、跨文化、跨语言的。但西克苏也承认,这一理念无论在当时还是现在都不断受到来自政府的压力和威胁。参见 Hélène Cixous, "*Guardian of Language*: An Interview with Hélène Cixous," Interviewed by Kathleen O'Grady, trans., Eric Prenowitz, http://bailiwick. lib. uiowa. edu/wstudies/cixous, n. p. 。

② 马丁·海德格尔(1889~1976),德国哲学家。代表著作是《存在与时间》(1927年)。

③ 弗兰茨·卡夫卡(1883~1924),捷克作家。代表作品有《变形记》(1915年)、《审判》(1925年)、《城堡》(1926年)等。

④ 关于西克苏如何看待影响她思想的理论家,参见 Hélène Cixous, "*Guardian of Language*: An Interview with Hélène Cixous," Interviewed by Kathleen O'Grady, trans., Eric Prenowitz, http://bailiwick. lib. uiowa. edu/wstudies/cixous, n. p. 。

⑤ Ibid., n. p.

《论写作及其它》(*Coming to Writing and Other Essays*, 1991 年)

西克苏近年来创作的戏剧作品关注殖民主义、道德腐败和社会不公正带来的现实伦理与政治问题①。

西克苏在《美杜莎的浪笑》中把拉康定义的象征秩序称为阳具中心(phallocentric)体系,因为拉康视阳具为象征中心,把女性性征排斥在象征秩序之外。女性身体——包括女性性征、女性性行为以及性快感——无法在语言体系中得以表现,无法在阳具中心的象征秩序中被书写。而在西克苏看来,由于男性书写局限在二元对立体系中,因此这一体系对于男女两性来说都是具压迫性的。西克苏认为,话语的逻辑结构保护二元对立的因素中占优势地位的一方,因为这一方可以自然地建立社会等级结构。要摆脱话语的束缚必须书写身体,因为书写身体可以打破这一线性逻辑。在西克苏看来,人类性行为和语言是紧密相连的,释放其中一个就是解放另一个。"摆脱等级纽带就可以接近西克苏称之为'愉悦'(*jouissance*)的境界,这一境界可以定义为超验地实现远远超越单纯满足的欲望"②。西克苏承认多数女性有书写的经历,但她们的书写是从男性角度出发的。如果男性用阴茎书写,女性也必须确定自己性快感的位置。她于是发明了"女性书写"的术语,并说明这一书写方式首先在诗歌中是可行的③,因为诗歌的字面意义和隐喻意义并不是一对一的关系,诗歌更接近于无意识,也因此长期以来受到压制。与男性话语体系的二元对立特征相反,女性书写处于中间的抽象地带,与处于两级的对立概念相冲突。西克苏一方面提出了这一概念,另一方面却又声明给这一概念下的任何定义都会破坏它的美感④。准确地说,西克苏并没有为她发明的"女性书写"下一个准确的定义,因为这一概念是

---

① Mary Jane Parrine, "Hélène Cixous," http://prelecture. stanford. edu/lecturers/cixous, n. p.

② Sandra M. Gilbert, "Introduction," in Hélène Cixous and Catherine Clement, *The Newly Born Woman*, trans. Betsy Wing (Minneapolis: University of Minnesota Press, 1986), p. xvii.

③ 西克苏认为她自己的理论著作也有诗歌特有的韵律和节奏,参见 Hélène Cixous, "*Guardian of Language*: An Interview with Hélène Cixous," Interviewed by Kathleen O'Grady, trans. , Eric Prenowitz, http://bailiwick. lib. uiowa. edu/wstudies/cixous, n. p.。

④ Julie Jasken, http://www. engl. niu. edu/wac/cixous_intro. html, n. p.

流动的,它超越任何定义或描述,超越现存的定义体系和知识秩序①。但这并不能说明不存在"女性书写",处于边缘地位的人(包括男性和女性)就能够排斥或拒绝阳具中心的再现体系。西克苏建议重建母女关系的纽带,女性的书写是从母亲的乳汁中寻找灵感和力量源泉。她甚至说,女性书写是用乳汁,是一首歌,有节奏和韵律的歌,同身体的节奏和运动相联系的歌。有评论家对此持有谨慎的担心,因为母性正是父权社会长期压迫女性的典型反映②。

　　西克苏正是在这时特别谈到了关于美杜莎③的神话。美杜莎是希腊神话中被称作戈尔戈(Gorgon)的三女怪之一,她名字的意思是"掌管女性智慧"④。传说中三姐妹居住在西方,是海神的后代。美杜莎曾经有着惊人的美貌,但由于她目无智慧女神雅典娜(Athena)而被后者剥夺了所有的魅力特质,变成头发如蛇、脖子长鳞、犬牙铜翅的怪模样。据说望见其面貌的人都会变成石头。她的两个姐妹斯忒诺(Stheno)和欧律阿勒(Euryale)永生不死,但美杜莎却被珀尔修斯(Perseus)杀害。后人常常把美杜莎的形象刻于盾牌或房屋的入口处以避邪⑤,雅典娜就曾把美杜莎的头固定在自己的盾牌上。人们通常认为美杜莎被砍头象征着女性智慧的最终压抑,这一男性行为"阻止她的成长,限制她的潜力、行动和文化贡献……她赋予生命、控制死亡的能力以及自然的野性被男性秩序掌握、驯服和驾驭"⑥。美杜莎在男性想象中代表恐惧,男性把女性想象成其目光会把人变成石头的美杜莎,而在西克苏看来,这表明男性对女性身体的无知。女性应该向男性展示她们的"性文本"(sexts⑦),把女性的身体、女性的性征、性经历、性快感用新的形式书写出来。

---

　　①　Mary Klages, http://www. colorado. edu/English/ENGL2012Klages/cixous. html, n. p.

　　②　Domna C. Stanton, "Difference on Trial: A Critique of the Maternal Metaphor in Cixous, Irigaray and Kristeva," in *The Poetics of Gender*, ed. N. K. Miller (New York: Columbia University Press, 1986), pp.157-182.

　　③　关于希腊神话中的美杜莎,访问 http://www. loggia. com/myth/medusa. html, n. p.。

　　④　Alicia Le Van, http://www. perseus. tufts. edu/classes/finALp. html, n. p.

　　⑤　鲁刚、郑述谱编译,《希腊罗马神话词典》,中国社会科学出版社,1984 年,第 115 页。

　　⑥　Alicia Le Van, http://www. perseus. tufts. edu/classes/finALp. html, n. p.

　　⑦　这是西克苏发明的另一个新词,是"性"(sex)和"文本"(text)两个词的结合。

西克苏称自己有两个目的:打破/摧毁并预见/建构。她要打破的是拉康描述的阳具中心的话语体系,她要建构的则是女性身体与话语之间的一种新型关系。美国科罗拉多大学教授玛丽·克雷格斯(Mary Klages)认为,西克苏理论的难度在于她同时在两个层面上论述:字面意义和隐喻意义。当西克苏主张"女性必须书写自己"、"女性必须书写女性"的时候,她一方面是说女性必须讲述她们自己的故事,另一方面作为能指符号(signifier)的"女性"必须寻找到合适的方法在象征秩序内书写自我身份/主体身份①。

《美杜莎的浪笑》,法语题目为"Le Rire de la Méduse",最先刊登在 1975 年 *L'Arc* 杂志第 39~54 页,后被《符号:文化与社会中的女性》杂志(*Signs:Journal of Women in Culture and Society*)在 1976 年夏季卷转载,英译者是基思·科恩(Keith Cohen)和保拉·科恩(Paula Cohen)。

该文分六个小部分。

第一部分,作者开篇就明确告诉读者她要谈谈女性书写:"女性必须书写她自己:她必须书写女性,必须引导女性书写,他们已经被粗暴地驱赶出了书写,就像被驱赶远离了身体一样——出于同样的原因,根据同样的律法,怀着同样的目的。女性一定要通过自己的活动把自己写进文本,写进世界与历史"②。西克苏说,她在说"女性"的时候是指"不可避免要同男性作斗争的女性",指"一个具普遍性的女性主体,她能够引导女性恢复各种感知能力并意识到她们在历史中拥有的意义"(第 875~876 页;第 152 页)。西克苏认为没有一个统一的、单一种类的女性性征(female sexuality),因为女性想象是不可穷尽的。她呼吁女性大胆地书写自己(第 877 页;第 155 页)。

---

① Mary Klages, http://www. colorado. edu/English/Engl2012klages/cixous. html, n. p.

② Hélène Cixous, "The Laugh of the Medusa," trans. Keith Cohen and Paula Cohen, *Signs:Journal of Women in Culture and Society* 1.4 (Summer 1976): p.875. 本节所引该文观点均出自此处,以下只在正文标明页码,分号后第二个页码为引文在本书的页码。

第二部分,西克苏先是指责男性犯下的最大罪孽是让女性仇恨女性,让女性不懂自恋(第 878 页;第 155 页),继而呼吁女性认识自己,把自己从旧的形象中解放出来。西克苏认为,最好的解放方式就是书写,因为"书写恰恰代表了变化的可能性",可以为女性提供一个"跳板"承载反叛的思想,预兆社会文化结构的改变(第 879 页;第 156 页)。

在第三部分的开始,西克苏首先认定"整个书写的历史同理性的历史混杂在一起"(第 879 页;第 156 页),同阳具中心传统相一致。然后西克苏明确女性书写在两个层面上具有特别的意义:第一,女性可以最后回归身体;第二,女性可以进入历史(第 880 页;第 158 页)。西克苏说,几乎每一位女性都曾经历"讲话"的痛苦:心脏怦怦乱跳,偶尔词不达意,甚至不知所措。男性总是对女性讲的话不加理会,因为他们的耳朵只能倾听男性讲的话语(第 880 ~ 881 页;第 158 页)。女性讲话时用身体,"她演讲的'逻辑'凭借身体来支撑……她用身体物化她所思,她把所思赋予身体来表达"(第 881 页;第 159 页)。从这方面讲,女性"从来就不曾远离'母亲'"(第 881 页;第 159 页),因为母亲的乳汁滋养了女性的身体。西克苏言简意赅地说:"女性用白色墨水书写"(第 881 页;第 159 页)。她主张女性同母亲的纽带赋予女性以书写的动力:

> 母亲……是隐喻。把女性自己最好的部分给予另一女性,让她能够爱自己,并怀着爱奉献"与生俱来"的身体。这不仅必要而且也足够了。……女性身体中或多或少总有母亲的影子:母亲确保一切正常,她提供营养,反对分离。……女性起源于母亲身体的所有形式和所有时期。(第 881 ~ 882 页;第 160 页)

虽然西克苏详细论述了女性书写同母亲的联系,但她却认为无法为女性书写活动下一个准确的定义:"这种不可能性还将继续,因为女性书写活动无法理论化,无法封闭,无法分类"(第 883 页;第 161 页)。但这并不意味着女性书写是不存在的。西克苏认为,女性书写终将"超越规范阳具中心体系的话语",被处于边缘地位的人所建构(第 883 页;第 161 页)。

第四部分,西克苏继续谈论女性性征——弗洛伊德理论框架中"黑暗的大陆"(Dark Continent)。她说:"黑暗的大陆既不黑暗也不是无法探索。这片大陆尚未被探索,因为我们都被迫认为它黑暗得无法探索,认为让我们感兴趣的是白色大陆,缺乏(Lack)是其纪念碑"(第884~885页)。男性认为有两种东西无法表现:死亡和女性性征,他们总是把女性性征同死亡联系在一起(第885页)。女性的书写要涵盖女性性征,书写其无限与变化的复杂性,书写女性色情意义(第885页)。

第五部分,西克苏讨论女性话语应该如何建立。她说,如果女性一直在男性话语内部运作,那么现在女性应该从这一话语中冲出来设法让这一话语为她所用(第887页)。西克苏借用法语词 voler 具有的双重含义①,提出建议说女性应该首先"偷"男性话语,然后"飞跃":"飞跃是女性的举动,在语言中飞起来,让语言飞起来"(第887页)。同男性话语相比,女性话语不是包容的,而是携带的;不是局限的,而能够开拓各种可能性(第889页)。女性力比多(libido)是具宇宙性的,正如女性无意识是全球性的。

第六部分讲述怀孕给女性生活带来的影响。西克苏说,女性体现在孩子身上的欲望并不是满足阴茎缺乏的焦渴(第890页),女性在怀孕过程中不仅其市场价值翻倍,而且其自身价值也得到加强,因为怀孕的女性同时得到了身体和性(第891页)。西克苏认为,女性缺乏的是女性与女性之间的"爱",这种爱是滋养生命的,在交换过程中可以带来相互愉悦。在这样的平等关系中,双方都将不再缺乏(第893页)。

这里选注的是该文第一、二、三部分。各部分序号为编者所加。

The Laugh of the Medusa

1

I shall speak about women's writing: about *what it will do*. Woman must write her self: must write about women and bring women to writing, from which they have been driven away as violently as from their bodies—for the same reasons, by the same law, with the same fatal goal. Woman must put herself into the text—as into the world and into history—by her own movement.

---

① 法语词 voler 有两个基本意思:"偷";"飞"。

The future must no longer be determined by the past. I do not deny that the effects of the past are still with us. But I refuse to strengthen them by repeating them, to confer upon them an irremovability the equivalent of destiny, to confuse the biological and the cultural. Anticipation is imperative.

Since these reflections are taking shape in an area just on the point of being discovered, they necessarily bear the mark of our time—a time during which the new breaks away from the old, and, more precisely, the (feminine) new from the old (*la nouvelle de l'ancien*). Thus, as there are no grounds for establishing a discourse, but rather an arid millennial ground to break, what I say has at least two sides and two aims: to break up, to destroy; and to foresee the unforeseeable, to project.

I write this as a woman, toward women. When I say "woman", I'm speaking of woman in her inevitable struggle against conventional man; and of a universal woman subject who must bring women to their senses and to their-meaning in history. But first it must be said that in spite of the enormity of the repression that has kept them in the "dark"—that dark which people have been trying to make them accept as their attribute—there is, at this time, no general woman, no one typical woman. What they have *in common* I will say. But what strikes me is the infinite richness of their individual constitutions: you can't talk about *a* female sexuality, uniform, homogeneous, classifiable into codes—any more than you can talk about one unconscious resembling another. Women's imaginary is inexhaustible, like music, painting, writing: their stream of phantasms is incredible.

I have been amazed more than once by a description a woman gave me of a world all her own which she had been secretly haunting since early childhood. A world of searching, the elaboration of a knowledge, on the basis of a systematic experimentation with the bodily functions, a passionate and precise interrogation of her erotogeneity. This practice, extraordinarily rich and inventive, in particular as concerns masturbation, is prolonged or accompanied by a production of forms, a veritable aesthetic activity, each stage of rapture inscribing a resonant vision, a composition, something beautiful. Beauty will no longer be forbidden.

I wished that that woman would write and proclaim this unique empire so that other women, other unacknowledged sovereigns, might exclaim: I, too, overflow; my desires have invented new desires, my body knows unheard-of songs. Time and again I, too, have felt so full of luminous torrents that I could burst—burst with forms much more beautiful than those which are put up in frames and sold for a stinking fortune. And I, too, said nothing, showed nothing; I didn't open my mouth, I didn't repaint my half of the world. I was ashamed. I was afraid, and I swallowed my shame and my fear. I said to myself: You are mad! What's the meaning of these waves, these floods, these outbursts? Where is the ebullient, infinite woman who, immersed as she was in her naiveté, kept in the dark about herself, led into self-disdain by the great arm of parental-conjugal phallocentrism, hasn't been ashamed of her strength? Who, surprised and horrified by the fantastic tumult of her drives (for she was made to believe that a well-adjusted normal woman has a ... divine composure), hasn't accused herself of being a monster? Who, feeling a funny desire stirring inside her (to sing, to write, to dare to speak, in short, to bring out something new), hasn't thought she was sick? Well, her shameful sickness is that she resists death, that she makes trouble.

And why don't you write? Write! Writing is for you, you are for you; your body is yours, take it. I know why you haven't written. (And why I didn't write before the age of twenty-seven.) Because writing is at once too high, too great for you, it's reserved for the great—that is, for "great men"; and it's "silly". Besides, you've written a little, but in secret. And it wasn't good, because it was in secret, and because you punished yourself for writing, because you didn't go all the way; or because you wrote, irresistibly, as when we would masturbate in secret, not to go further, but to attenuate the tension a bit, just enough to take the edge off. And then as soon as we come, we go and make ourselves feel guilty—so as to be forgiven; or to forget, to bury it until the next time.

Write, let no one hold you back, let nothing stop you: not man; not the imbecilic capitalist machinery, in which publishing houses are the crafty, obsequious relayers of imperatives handed down by an economy that works against us and off our backs; and not *yourself*. Smug-faced readers, managing editors, and big bosses don't like the true texts of women—female-sexed texts. That kind scares them.

I write woman: woman must write woman. And man, man. So only an oblique consideration will be found here of man; it's up to him to say where his masculinity and femininity are at: this will concern us once men have opened their eyes and seen themselves clearly. ①

Now women return from afar, from always: from "without," from the heath where witches are kept alive; from below, from beyond "culture"; from their childhood which men have been trying desperately to make them forget, condemning it to "eternal rest". The little girls and their "ill-mannered" bodies immured, well-preserved, intact unto themselves, in the mirror. Frigidified. But are they ever seething underneath! What an effort it takes—there's no end to it—for the sex cops to bar their threatening return. Such a display of forces on both sides that the struggle has for centuries been immobilized in the trembling equilibrium of a deadlock.

2

Here they are, returning, arriving over and again, because the unconscious is impregnable. They have wandered around in circles, confined to the narrow room in which they've been given a deadly brainwashing. You can incarcerate them, slow them down, get away with the old Apartheid routine, but for a time only. As soon as they begin to speak, at the same time as they're taught their name, they can be taught that their territory is black: because you are Africa, you are black. Your continent is dark. Dark is dangerous. You can't see anything in the dark, you're afraid. Don't move, you might fall. Most of all, don't go into the forest. And so we have internalized this horror of the dark.

Men have committed the greatest crime against women. Insidiously, violently, they have led them to hate women, to be their own enemies, to mobilize their immense strength against themselves, to be the executants of their virile needs. They have made for women an antinarcissism! A narcissism which loves itself only to be loved for what women haven't got! They have constructed the infamous logic of antilove.

We the precocious, we the repressed of culture, our lovely mouths gagged with pollen, our wind knocked out of us, we the labyrinths, the ladders, the trampled spaces, the bevies—we are black and we are beautiful.

We're stormy, and that which is ours breaks loose from us without our fearing any debilitation. Our glances, our smiles, are spent; laughs exude from all our mouths; our blood flows and we extend ourselves without ever reaching an end; we never hold back our thoughts, our signs, our writing; and we're not afraid of lacking.

What happiness for us who are omitted, brushed aside at the scene of inheritances; we inspire ourselves and we expire without running out of breath, we are everywhere!

From now on, who, if we say so, can say no to us? We've come back from always.

It is time to liberate the New Woman from the Old by coming to know her—by loving her for getting by, for getting beyond the Old without delay, by going out ahead of what the New Woman will be, as an arrow quits the bow with a movement that gathers and separates the vibrations musically, in order to be more than her self.

I say that we must, for, with a few rare exceptions, there has not yet been any writing that inscribes femininity; exceptions so rare, in fact, that, after plowing through literature across languages, cultures, and ages,[2] one can only be startled at this vain scouting mission. It is well known that the number of women writers (while having increased very slightly from the nineteenth century on) has always been ridiculously small. This is a useless and deceptive fact unless from their species of female writers we do not first deduct the immense majority whose workmanship is in no way different from male writing, and which either obscures women or reproduces the classic representations of women (as sensitive—intuitive—dreamy, etc.)③

Let me insert here a parenthetical remark. I mean it when I speak of male writing. I maintain unequivocally that there is such a thing as *marked writing*; that, until now, far more extensively and repressively than is ever suspected or admitted, writing has been run by a libidinal and cultural— hence political, typically masculine—economy; that this is a locus where the repression of women has been perpetuated, over and over, more or less consciously, and in a manner that's frightening since it's often hidden or adorned with the mystifying charms of fiction; that this locus has grossly exaggerated all the signs of sexual opposition (and not sexual difference), where woman has never *her* turn to speak—this being all the more serious and unpardonable in that writing is precisely *the very possibility of change*, the space that can serve as a springboard for subversive thought, the precursory movement of a transformation of social and cultural structures.

3

Nearly the entire history of writing is confounded with the history of reason, of which it is at once the effect, the support, and one of the privileged alibis. It has been one with the phallocentric tradition. It is indeed that same self-admiring, self-stimulating, self-congratulatory phallocentrism.

With some exceptions, for there have been failures—and if it weren't for them, I wouldn't be writing (I-woman, escapee)—in that enormous machine that has been operating and turning out its "truth" for centuries. There have been poets who would go to any lengths to slip something by at odds with tradition—men capable of loving love and hence capable of loving others and of wanting them, of imagining the woman who would hold out against oppression and constitute herself as a superb, equal, hence "impossible" subject, untenable in a real social framework. Such a woman the poet could desire only by breaking the codes that negate her. Her appearance would necessarily bring on, if not revolution—for the bastion was supposed to be immutable—at least harrowing explosions. At times it is in the fissure caused by an earthquake, through that radical mutation of things brought on by a material upheaval when every structure is for a moment thrown off balance and an ephemeral wildness sweeps order away, that the poet slips something by, for a brief span, of woman. Thus did Kleist expend himself in his yearning for the existence of sister-lovers, maternal daughters, mother-sisters, who never hung their heads in shame. Once the palace of magistrates is restored, it's time to pay: immediate bloody death to the uncontrollable elements.

But only the poets—not the novelists, allies of representationalism. Because poetry involves gaining strength through the unconscious and because the unconscious, that other limitless country, is the place where the repressed manage to survive: women, or as Hoffmann would say, fairies.

She must write her self, because this is the invention of a *new insurgent* writing which, when the moment of her liberation has come, will allow her to carry out the indispensable ruptures and transformations in her history, first at two levels that cannot be separated.

a) Individually. By writing her self, woman will return to the body which has been more than confiscated from her, which has been turned into the uncanny stranger on display—the ailing or dead figure, which so often turns out to be the nasty companion, the cause and location of inhibitions. Censor the body and you censor breath and speech at the same time.

Write your self. Your body must be heard. Only then will the immense resources of the unconscious spring forth. Our naphtha will spread, throughout the world, without dollars—black or gold—nonassessed values that will change the rules of the old game.

To write. An act which will not only "realize" the decensored relation of woman to her sexuality, to her womanly being, giving her access to her native strength; it will give her back her goods, her pleasures, her organs, her immense bodily territories which have been kept under seal; it will tear her away from the superegoized structure in which she has always occupied the place reserved for the guilty (guilty of everything, guilty at every turn: for having desires, for not having any; for being frigid, for being "too hot"; for not being both at once; for being too motherly and not enough; for having children and for not having any; for nursing and for not nursing …)—tear her away by means of this research, this job of analysis and illumination, this emancipation of the marvelous text of her self that she must urgently learn to speak. A woman without a body, dumb, blind, can't possibly be a good fighter. She is reduced to being the servant of the militant male, his shadow. We must kill the false woman who is preventing the live one from breathing. Inscribe the breath of the whole woman.

b) An act that will also be marked by woman's *seizing* the occasion to *speak*, hence her shattering entry into history, which has always been based *on her suppression*. To write and thus to forge for herself the antilogos weapon. To become *at will* the taker and initiator, for her own right, in every symbolic system, in every political process.

It is time for women to start scoring their feats in written and oral language.

Every woman has known the torment of getting up to speak. Her heart racing, at times entirely lost for words, ground and language slipping away— that's how daring a feat, how great a transgression it is for a woman to speak—even just open her mouth—in public. A double distress, for even if she transgresses, her words fall almost always upon deaf male ear, which hears in language only that which speaks in the masculine.

It is by writing, from and toward women, and by taking up the challenge of speech which has been governed by the phallus, that women will confirm women in a place other than that which is reserved in and by the symbolic, that is, in a place other than silence. Women should break out of the snare of silence. They shouldn't be conned into accepting a domain which is the margin or the harem.

Listen to a woman speak at a public gathering (if she hasn't painfully lost her wind). She doesn't "speak," she throws her trembling body forward; she lets go of herself, she flies; all of her passes into her voice, and it's with her body that she vitally supports the "logic" of her speech. Her flesh speaks true. She lays herself bare. In fact, she physically materializes what she's thinking; she signifies it with her body. In a certain way she *inscribes* what she's saying, because she doesn't deny her drives the intractable and impassioned part they have in speaking. Her speech, even when "theoretical" or political, is never simple or linear or "objectified", generalized: she draws her story into history.

There is not that scission, that division made by the common man between the logic of oral speech and the logic of the text, bound as he is by his antiquated relation—servile, calculating—to mastery. From which proceeds the niggardly lip service which engages only the tiniest part of the body, plus the mask.

In women's speech, as in their writing, that element which never stops resonating, which, once we've been permeated by it, profoundly and imperceptibly touched by it, retains the power of moving us—that element is the song: first music from the first voice of love which is alive in every woman. Why this privileged relationship with the voice? Because no woman stockpiles as many defenses for countering the drives as does a man. You don't build walls around yourself, you don't forego pleasure as "wisely" as he. Even if phallic mystification has generally contaminated good relationships, a woman is never far from "mother" (I mean outside her role functions: the "mother" as nonname and as source of goods). There is always within her at least a little of that good mother's milk. She writes in white ink.

Woman for women. —There always remains in woman that force which produces/is produced by the other—in particular, the other woman. *In* her, matrix, cradler; herself giver as her mother and child; she is her own sister-daughter. You might object, "What about she who is the hysterical offspring of a bad mother?" Everything will be changed once woman gives woman to the other woman. There is hidden and always ready in woman the source; the locus for the other. The mother, too, is a metaphor. It is necessary and sufficient that the best of herself be given to woman by another woman for her to be able to love herself and return in love the body that was "born" to her. Touch me, caress me, you the living no-name, give me my self as myself. The relation to the "mother" in terms of intense pleasure and violence, is curtailed no more than the relation to childhood (the child that she was, that she is, that she makes, remakes, undoes, there at the point where, the same, she others herself). Text: my body—shot through with streams of song; I don't mean the overbearing, clutchy "mother" but, rather, what touches you, the equivoice that affects you, fills your breast with an urge to come to language and launches your force; the rhythm that laughs you; the intimate recipient who makes all metaphors possible and desirable; body (body? bodies?), no more describable than god, the soul, or the Other; that part of you that leaves a space between yourself and urges you to inscribe in language your woman's style. In women there is always more or less of the mother who makes everything all right, who nourishes, and who stands up against separation; a force that will not be cut off but will knock the wind out of the codes. We will rethink womankind beginning with every form and every period of her body. The Americans remind us, "We are all Lesbians"; that is, don't denigrate woman, don't make of her what men have made of you.

Because the "economy" of her drives is prodigious, she cannot fail, in seizing the occasion to speak, to transform directly and indirectly *all* systems of exchange based on masculine thrift. Her libido will produce far more radical effects of political and social change than some might like to think.

Because she arrives, vibrant, over and again, we are at the beginning of a new history, or rather of a process of becoming in which several histories intersect with one another. As subject for history, woman always occurs simultaneously in several places. Woman un-thinks ④ the unifying, regulating history that homogenizes and channels forces, herding contradictions into a single battlefield. In woman, personal history blends together with the history of all women, as well as national and world history. As a militant, she is an integral part of all liberations. She must be farsighted, not limited to a blow-by-blow interaction. She foresees that her liberation will do more than modify power relations or toss the ball over to the other camp; she will bring about a mutation in human relations, in thought, in all praxis: hers is not simply a class struggle, which she carries forward into a much vaster movement. Not that in order to be a woman-in-struggle(s) you have to leave the class struggle or repudiate it; but you have to split it open, spread it out, push it forward, fill it with the fundamental struggle so as to prevent the class struggle, or any other struggle for the liberation of a class or people, from operating as a form of repression, pretext for postponing the inevitable, the staggering alteration in power relations and in the production of individualities. This alteration is already upon us—in the United States, for example, where millions of night crawlers are in the process of undermining the family and disintegrating the whole of American sociality.

The new history is coming; it's not a dream, though it does extend beyond men's imagination, and for good reason. It's going to deprive them of their conceptual orthopedics, beginning with the destruction of their enticement machine.

It is impossible to *define* a feminine practice of writing, and this is an impossibility that will remain, for this practice can never be theorized, enclosed, coded—which doesn't mean that it doesn't exist. But it will always surpass the discourse that regulates the phallocentric system; it does and will take place in areas other than those subordinated to philosophico-theoretical domination. It will be conceived of only by subjects who are breakers of automatisms, by peripheral figures that no authority can ever subjugate.

Notes:

① Men still have everything to say about their sexuality, and everything to write. For what they have said so far, for the most part, stems from the opposition activity/passivity, from the power relation between a fantasized obligatory virility meant to invade, to colonize, and the consequential phantasm of woman as a "dark continent" to penetrate and to "pacify". (We know what "pacify" means in terms of scotomizing the other and mis-recognizing the self.) Conquering her, they've made haste to depart from her borders, to get out of sight, out of body. The way man has of getting out of himself and into her whom he takes not for the other but for his own, deprives him, he knows, of his own bodily territory. One can understand how man, confusing himself with his penis and rushing in for the attack, might feel resentment and fear of being "taken" by the woman, of being lost in her, absorbed, or alone.

② I am speaking here only of the place "reserved" for women by the Western world.

③ Which works, then, might be called feminine? I'll just point out some examples: one would have to give them full readings to bring out what is pervasively feminine in their significance. Which I shall do elsewhere. In France (have you noted our infinite poverty in this field? —the Anglo-Saxon countries have shown resources of distinctly greater consequence), leafing through what's come out of the twentieth century—and it's not much—the only inscriptions of femininity that I have seen were by Colette, Marguerite Duras, ... and Jean Genêt.

④ "*Dé-pense*," a neologism formed on the verb *penser*, hence "unthinks," but also "spends" (from *dépenser*) (translator's note).

9 露丝·伊里加蕾,"一个不会没有另一个而走动"
Luce Irigaray, "And the One Doesn't Stir without the Other"

　　法国女性主义者露丝·伊里加蕾(Luce Irigaray)同伊莲娜·西克苏(Hélène Cixous)和朱丽娅·克里斯蒂娃(Julia Kristeva)一起被并列称为当代法国女性主义的三驾马车①。由于她们共同持有解构现有哲学理论体系的基本立场,也有评论家把她们称为后现代女性主义理论家。伊里加蕾的女性主义理论经过20多年的发展已逐渐形成了较为成熟、完整的理论架构,因而评论家纳奥米·斯格尔(Naomi Schor)称伊里加蕾是西蒙·德·波伏娃②的惟一继承人③。

　　伊里加蕾于20世纪30年代出生在比利时④,1955年卢旺大学(University of Louvain)硕士毕业,1956～1959年期间一直在布鲁塞尔的中学教书。伊里加蕾于60年代初期移居法国,1961年在巴黎大学获得心理学硕士学位,1962年获得心理病理学修业证书。她参加了雅克·拉康(Jacques Lacan)的心理分析研修班,成为一名心理分析学家。此后她在位于比利时布鲁塞尔的国家科学研究基金委员会工作,后到位于巴黎的法国国家科学研究中心任助理研究员。现在

---

　　① Lynne Huffer, *Maternal Pasts, Feminist Futures: Nostalgia, Ethics, and the Question of Difference* (Stanford, CA: Stanford University Press, 1998), p.21.

　　② 西蒙·德·波伏娃(1908～1986),法国重要女性主义理论家。参见第一篇第1节。

　　③ Naomi Schor, "Previous Engagements: The Receptions of Irigaray," *Engaging with Irigaray: Feminist Philosophy and Modern European Thought*, eds. Carolyn Burke, Naomi Schor and Margaret Whitford (New York: Columbia University Press, 1994), p. 4.

　　④ 一些学者称伊里加蕾出生于1932年,但似乎并未得到学术界的普遍认可。访问 Richard L. W. Clarke, "Luce Irigaray," http://humanities. uwichill. edu. bb/RLWClarke/PhilWeb/Feminist/Contemporary/Continental/(Post-) Structuralisms/Deconstruction/Irigaray/Irigaray. htm, n. p.

她是这一中心的主任。1968 年伊里加蕾荣获语言学博士学位,1970～1974 年间,她在温塞纳大学(University of Vincennes)任教,是由拉康领导的巴黎弗洛伊德学派(École Freudienne de Paris)的成员。伊里加蕾的第二篇博士论文《他者女性的反射镜》(*Speculum of the Other Woman*)重新审视"女性气质"(femininity)的概念,认为男性把女性泯灭为自己的"反射镜"①,缺乏独立主体和特质,因而主张用"女性书写"(*L'écriture feminine*)颠覆男性想象的霸权②。这部著作尚未发表就使伊里加蕾失去了在温塞纳大学的教职,这一事件不仅极具讽刺意味——她谴责阳具中心经济排斥女性,而她自己就恰恰被这一经济秩序所淘汰——而且对于她的事业来说也是毁灭性的打击——她不得不重新选择职业。伊里加蕾曾参加支持避孕、维护堕胎权利的示威,但却不愿再归属任何一个团体。20 世纪 80 年代她积极支持意大利的共产主义运动,她的学说和主张对意大利和法国的女性主义活动产生了重要影响。此后,伊里加蕾在欧洲乃至全世界演讲、著述,逐渐被世人接受为女性主义理论家、哲学家。

伊里加蕾的理论已渐成体系,她的学说发展大致经历了这样三个阶段③:

第一阶段以其著作《他者女性的反射镜》(1974 年)、《非"一"之性》(*This Sex Which Is Not One*, 1977 年,亦译作《这个不是一种的性别》)、《原始情感》(*Elemental Passions*, 1982 年)和《性别差异的道德学》(*An Ethics of Sexual Difference*, 1984 年)为主要代表。在这些著作中,伊里加蕾致力于描述男性如何建构了父权社会并用单一的男性视角诠释世界。

第二个阶段的主要代表著作包括《思考差异:为了一场和平的革命》(*Thinking the Difference*:*For a Peaceful Revolution*, 1989 年)和《我、你、我

---

① Chiara Briganti and Robert Con Davis, "Luce Irigaray", http://www.press.jhu.edu/books/hopkins_guide_to_literary_theory/luce_irigaray.html, n. p.

② John Lechte, "Luce Irigaray", http://www.envf.port.ac.uk/illustration/images/vlsh/psycholo/irigaray.htm, n. p.

③ 编者的这一划分参照了伊里加蕾于 1995 年接受美国学者采访时对自己理论发展过程的总结。参见 Luce Irigaray, "'Je—Luce Irigaray': A Meeting with Luce Irigaray," interview with Elizabeth Hirsh and Gary A. Olson, trans., Elizabeth Hirsh and Gaëton Brulotte, *Hypatia* 10.2 (Spring 1995), pp.96-97.

们:走向一种差异文化》(*I*,*You*,*We*:*Toward a Culture of Difference*,1990年)。这两部著作以及这期间伊里加蕾的演讲着重讨论女性主体存在的可能性,这一主体将有别于男性主体并独立于男性主体而存在。

第三个阶段的代表著作包括《我对你的爱》(*I Love to You*,1993年)和《二人行》(*To Be Two*,1994年)。此时伊里加蕾的目光已经转向建构尊重性别差异基础之上的主体交互性,以寻求男女之间理想的异性关系模式。

伊里加蕾最初被冠以"本质主义者"(essentialist)的标签,但随着人们对她学说的深入理解,尤其对她著作中阐释的语言学、哲学和心理学相贯通的思想精髓的了解,人们已经认识到对伊里加蕾的这一归类有欠公允①。

"一个不会没有另一个而走动"是伊里加蕾一篇非常有影响的文章,最早发表于1979年,法语原文题目为"Et l'une ne bouge pas sans l'autre",英文版发表在《符号:文化与社会中的女性》杂志(*Signs*:*Journal of Women in Culture and Society*)②1981年第1期(总第7卷),译者艾琳娜·维维安·温泽尔(Hélène Vivienne Wenzel)③。

这篇文章被认为是伊里加蕾此前发表的另一篇文章的姊妹篇④。那篇文章题为"Quand nos lèvres se parlent",是《非"一"之性》中的一节,被卡罗琳·伯克(Caroline Burke)译为"当我们的唇一起说话时"("When Our Lips Speak Together"),独立刊登在《符号:文化与社会中的女性》杂志1980年秋季卷。该文探讨女性和女性之间的关系,其途径是女性之间能够不受男性打扰地相互之间"讲女性话语"(speak female)。在"一个不会没有另一个而走动"中,伊里加蕾继续讨论女性之间的关系问题。具体说来,她以沉默的女儿的姿态设想前俄狄浦

---

① Bridget Holland,"Luce Irigaray:A Biography",http://www.cddc.vt.edu/feminism/irigaray.html,n.p.

② 《符号》杂志创刊于1975年,季刊,由哥伦比亚大学出版社出版发行。三十年的历程使这本杂志成为国际妇女研究领域最有影响的杂志之一。刊登的文章涉及性别、种族、民族、文化、阶级、国家以及性等诸多研究领域。请访问http://www.journals.uchicago.edu/signs/home.html。

③ 艾琳娜·维维安·温泽尔是耶鲁大学法语与女性研究系教授。

④ Hélène Vivienne Wenzel,"Introduction to Luce Irigaray's 'And the One Doesn't Stir without the Other'",*Signs*:*Journal of Women in Culture and Society* 7.1 (1981):pp.58-59.

斯(pre-Oedipal)阶段的母女关系①,得出结论说,女性一旦成为主体,母亲和女儿就可以成为有独立意识和独立存在的主体。

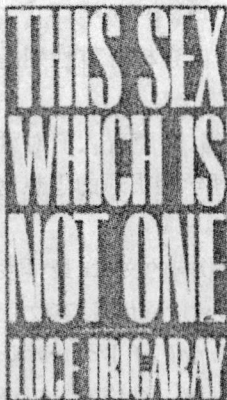

伊里加蕾用一种诗化语言、从第一人称"我"——女儿——的角度向第二人称的"你"——母亲——进行诉说。这样一个独特的角度、这样一种特殊的语言本身似乎更突显了文章的主题:母亲和女儿的关系。

文章用星号隔开三个部分。

作者首先从感觉入手,形象地描述"我"的艰难处境:"我比你走路更加艰难,也比你走动更少"②。"我"意识到没有力量奔向自己所爱,似乎被某种牢笼所束缚:"牢笼就在我自身,我成为自己的俘虏"(第60页)。紧接着,"我"感到自身内部的某种东西在慢慢苏醒,"我"看到了面前的"你":"我们之间可以分享这么多的空气、光和空间"(第61页;第169页):

> 我看上去像你,你也像我。我看着你身上的我,你看着我身上的你。你已经长得很大,我还很小。但是我是从你体内而来,现在在你眼前的,我是另一个活生生的你。(第61页;第169页)

但是,"你"的营养"我"已不再能够吸收,它令"我"窒息③。于是,"我将转向父亲,我将离开你投奔看上去比你更有活力的人。……我会用目光追寻他的身影,我会倾听他的话语,我会尝试追随他的脚步"(第62页;第170页)。伊里加蕾斩钉截铁地说:"再见了,母亲! 我永远不会成为你的同类"(第62页;第171页)。

在第二部分的开头,伊里加蕾形象地描述了身为女儿的"我"所处的三明治地位:"你看着镜子里的你,实际上你看到的也是你的母亲。不久你也会看到你的女儿,同样也是一个母亲"(第63页;第171页)。作者试图用这样形象的语

---

① Ibid. , p.56.

② Luce Irigaray, "And the One Doesn't Stir without the Other", *Signs*: *Journal of Women in Culture and Society* 7.1 (1981): p.60. 本节所引伊里加蕾该篇演讲观点均出自此处,以下只在正文标明页码,分号后第二个页码为引文在本书的页码。

③ 弗洛伊德的"缺乏"理论在这里被伊里加蕾戏虐地颠覆。

言告诉我们,无论是何种身份的女人,母亲都将是她们共同的归宿。而身为母亲的状态又是怎样的呢?

> 你走下去了,你再一次走下去,独自一人,在地下。我们好像曾经在那里一道走过。一个,还有另一个。一个或者是另一个。你放弃了自己的坚毅,放弃了自己的正直。你的脚步和你的身影在伴随孤独的决心之下变得更加坚定。你重又回到这个洞穴,入口已经无法找到。你重又回到这个地客,路径你也已分辨不清。你回到记忆深处的这个洞穴,我出生时的寂静早已被埋葬,我分离出你身体但又无法同你分离的那种寂静。回到你怀着我时的那种黑暗。(第 65 页;第 174 页)

"我"认识到,自己一旦离开,"你"就失去了生活的反射;一旦留下,又不可避免催生"你"的死亡(第 66 页;第 176 页)。"你"、"我"二人都将丧失自己的影像,我们都被母道这惟一的女性作用/价值所束缚(第 66 页;第 176 页)。

文章的第三部分最短,只有四个小段落。在这部分,伊里加蕾呼吁母女间建立真正的沟通。世世代代,女人之间不停地把自己包裹在寂静中,此时此刻是应该打破这种寂静的时候了。母女之间长期以来一直缺乏沟通:"我们从来没有互相谈话过话。如此深渊把我们分隔,我不会完完整整地离开你,因为我总是被你的子宫捆住手脚。我被裹挟在阴影中,成为我们禁锢的俘虏"(第 67 页;第 176 页)。文章的最后一段话概括了作者的思想,展现了母亲和女儿之间应该呈现的理想状态:

> 一个不会没有另一个而走动,因为我们只有在一起才能走动①。我们当中的一个来到这个世界,另一个就走入地下。当一个孕育生命的时候,另一个就会死亡。母亲,我想要的是:在给与我生命的同时,你仍然有活力。(第 67 页;第 176～177 页)

---

① 温泽尔的英语译文直译成汉语应该是:"我们不会一起走动。"但她在注释中解释说,法语原文有双重含义,另一个意思就是"我们只有在一起才能走动"。根据上下文和本篇文章的中心思想,编者认为第二个意思更符合伊里加蕾的本意。

伊里加蕾的法语在很多场合都有歧义,她仿佛刻意制造模棱两可的状态。有时我们会发现,两种意思甚或多种意思似乎都可以被接受。这是伊里加蕾试图打破父权体制惟一论断而采取的独特的话语特征,也同时体现出她采取的后现代立场。

And the One Doesn't Stir without the Other

With your milk, Mother, I swallowed ice. And here I am now, my insides frozen. And I walk with even more difficulty than you do, and I move even less. You flowed into me, and that hot liquid became poison, paralyzing me. My blood no longer circulates to my feet or my hands, or as far as my head. It is immobilized, thickened by the cold. Obstructed by icy chunks which resist its flow. My blood coagulates, remains in and near my heart.

And I can no longer race toward what I love. And the more I love, the more I become captive, held back by a weightiness that immobilizes me. And I grow angry, I struggle, I scream—I want out of this prison.

But what prison? Where am I cloistered? I see nothing confining me. The prison is within myself, and it is I who am its captive.

How to get out? And why am I thus detained?

You take care of me, you keep watch over me. You want me always in your sight in order to protect me. You fear that something will happen to me. Do you fear that something will happen? But what could happen that would be worse than the fact of my lying supine day and night? Already full-grown and still in the cradle. Still dependent upon someone who carries me, who nurses me. Who *carries* me? Who *nurses* me?

A little light enters me. Something inside me begins to stir. Barely. Something new has moved me. As though I'd taken a first step inside myself. As if a breath of air had penetrated a completely petrified being, unsticking its mass. Waking me from a long sleep. From an ancient dream. A dream which must not have been my own, but in which I was captive. Was I a participant, or was I the dream ifself—another's dream, a dream about another?

I start to breathe, or rather I start to breathe again. It's strange. I stay very still, and I feel this something moving inside me. It enters me, leaves me, comes back, leaves again. I make this movement all by myself. No one assists. I have a home inside me, another outside, and I take myself from the one to the other, from the one into the other. And I no longer need your belly, your arms, your eyes, or your words to return or to leave. I am still so close to you, and already so far away. It's morning, my first morning. Hello. You're there. I'm here. Between us so much air, light, space to share with each other. I no longer kick impatiently, for I've got time now.

The day dawns. I'm hungry. I wish I had the energy to walk. To run all by myself, near or far from you. To go toward what I love.

You've prepared something to eat. You bring it to me. You feed me/yourself. ① But you feed me/yourself too much, as if you wanted to fill me up completely with your offering. You put yourself in my mouth, and I suffocate. Put yourself less in me, and let me look at you. I'd like to see you while you nurse me; not lose my/your eyes when I open my mouth for you; have you stay near me while I drink you. I'd like you to remain outside, too. Keep yourself/me outside, too. Don't engulf yourself or me in what flows from you into me. I would like both of us to be present. So that the one doesn't disappear in the other, or the other in the one. So that we can taste each other, feel each other, listen to each other, see each other— together.

I look like you, you look like me. I look at myself in you, you look at yourself in me. You're already big, I'm still little. But I came out of you, and here, in front of your very eyes, I am another living you.

But, always distracted, you turn away. Furtively, you verify your own continued existence in the mirror, and you return to your cooking. You change yourself according to the clock. You adorn yourself depending upon the time. What time? Time for what? Time for whom? I would like you to break this watch and let me watch you. And look at me. I would like us to play together at being the same and different. You/I exchanging selves endlessly and each staying herself. Living mirrors.

We would play catch, you and I. But who would see that what bounces between us are images? That you give them to me, and I to you without end. And that we don't need an object to throw back and forth at each other for this game to take place. I throw an image of you to you, you throw it back, catch it again.

But then you seem to catch yourself, and once more you throw back to me: "Do you want some honey? It's time to eat. You must eat to become big. "

You've gone again. Once more you're assimilated into nourishment. We've again disappeared into this act of eating each other. Hardly do I glimpse you and walk toward you, when you metamorphose into a baby nurse. Again you want to fill my mouth, my belly, to make yourself into a plenitude for mouth and belly. To let nothing pass between us but blood, milk, honey, and meat (but no, no meat; I don't want you dead inside me).

Will there never be love between us other than this filling up of holes? To close up and seal off everything that could happen between us, indefinitely, is that your only desire? To reduce us to consuming and being consumed, is that your only need?

I want no more of this stuffed, sealed up, immobilized body. No, I want air. And if you lead me back again and again to this blind assimilation of you—but who are you? —if you turn your face from me, giving yourself to me only in an already inanimate form, abandoning me to competent men to undo my/your paralysis, I'll turn to my father. I'll leave you for someone who seems more alive than you. For someone who doesn't prepare anything for me to eat. For someone who leaves me empty of him, mouth gaping on his truth. I'll follow him with my eyes, I'll listen to what he says, I'll try to walk behind him.

He leaves the house, I follow in his steps. Farewell, Mother, I shall never become your likeness.

I do gymnastics. I practice the body exercises suited to my disorder. I'll become a schooled robot. I move my body, completely unmoved. I advance and move about to the rhythm prescribed for my cure. Will, not love, regulates my gestures, my leaps, my dancing about. Each hour of the day finds me applying myself: trying to obey the doctors' orders. I concur totally with their diagnosis of my condition. I give them my complete attention, all my energy. I'll be the living demonstration of the correctness of their principles. Animated, reanimated by their understanding.

See from afar how I move with measured steps, me, once frozen in anger? Aren't I good now? A nearly perfect girl? I lack only a few garments, a little jewelry, some makeup, a disguise, some ways of being or doing to appear perfect. I'm beginning to look like what's expected of me. One more effort, a little more anger against you who want me to remain little, you who want me to eat what you bring me rather than to see me dress like you, and I'll step out of the dream. Out of my disorder. Out of you in me, me in you. I'll leave us. I'll go into another home. I'll live my life, my story.

Look at how healthy I am now. I don't even have to run after a man, he comes toward me. He approaches me. I await him, immobile, rooted. He's very near. I'm paralyzed with emotion. My blood no longer circulates very well. I hardly breathe. I leave.

I can't tell you where I am going. Forget me, Mother. Forget you in me, me in you. Let's just forget us. Life continues ...

* * *

You look at yourself in the mirror. ② And already you see your own mother there. And soon your daughter, a mother. Between the two, what are you? What space is yours alone? In what frame must you contain yourself? And how to let your face show through, beyond all the masks?

It's evening. As you're alone, as you've no more image to maintain or impose, you strip off your disguises. You take off your face of a mother's daughter, of a daughter's mother. You lose your mirror reflection. You thaw. You melt. You flow out of your self.

But no one is there to gather you up, and nothing stops this overflow. Before day's end you'll no longer exist if this hemorrhaging continues. Not even a photographic remembrance as a mark of your passage between your mother and your daughter. And, maybe, nothing at all. Your function remains faceless. Nourishing takes place before there are any images. ③ There's just a pause: the time for the one to become the other. Consuming comes before any vision of her who gives herself. You've disappeared, unperceived—imperceptible if not for this flow that fills up to the edge. That enters the other in the container of her skin. That penetrates and occupies the container until it takes away all possible space from both the one and the other, removes every interval between the one and the other. Until there is only this liquid that flows from the one into the other, and that is nameless.

No one to take you into herself tonight, Mother. No one to thirst for you, to receive you into herself. No one to open her lips and to let you flow into her, thus to keep you alive. No one to mark the time of your existence, to evoke in you the rise of a passage out of yourself, to tell you: Come here, stay here. No one to tell you: Don't remain caught up between the mirror and this endless loss of yourself. A self separated from another self. A self missing some other self. Two dead selves distanced from each other, with no ties binding them. The self that you see in the mirror severed from the self that nurtures. And, as I've gone, you've lost the place where proof of your subsistence once appeared to you.

Or so you thought. But by pouring your ice into me, didn't you quench my thirst with your paralysis? And never having known your own face, didn't you nourish me with lifelessness? In your blood, in your milk there flowed sandy mirages. Mixed in with these was the still-liquid substance which would soon freeze in all our exchanges, creating the impossible between us. Of necessity I became the uninhabitable region of your reflections. You wanted me to grow up, to walk, to run in order to vanquish your own infirmity.

So that your body would move to the rhythm of your desire to see yourself alive, you imprisoned me in your blindness to yourself. In the absence of love that provoked or accompanied the mobility of your features, your gestures. You desired me, such is this love of yours. ④ Imprisoned by your desire for a reflection, I became a statue, an image of your mobility. ⑤

In the place where you wanted yourself seen you received only transparency or inertness. An atmosphere indefinitely void of any reflection of you, a body uninhabited by self-knowledge. You could traverse every landscape or horizon, over and over again, without ever encountering yourself. Or bump up against this thing that you are, and that you have made me, hindering your/my progress. Opacity eclipsing any movement toward the light.

Who are you? Who am I? Who answers for our presence in this translucency, before this blind obstacle?

And if I leave, you no longer find yourself. Was I not the bail to keep you from disappearing? The stand-in for your absence? The guardian of your nonexistence? She who reassured you that you could always find yourself again, hold yourself, at any hour, in your arms? Keep yourself alive? Nurture yourself indefinitely in your attempt to subsist? Feed yourself blood and milk and honey over and over again (I never wanted your meat), to try to restore yourself to the world? ⑥

But so it is when one waits; ⑦ this evening no one comes. You move toward a future that is lacking. There is no one in whom to remember the dream of yourself. The house, the garden, everywhere is empty of you. You search for yourself everywhere in vain. Nothing before your eyes, in your hands, against your skin to remind you of yourself. To allow you to see yourself in another self. And this makes you empty yourself even more into my body—to maintain the memory of yourself, to nourish the appearance of yourself. No, Mother, I've gone away.

But have I ever known you otherwise than gone? And the home of your disappearance was not in me. When you poured yourself into me, you'd already left. Already become captive elsewhere. Already entered into someone else's gaze. You were already moving into a world to which I had no access. I received from you only your obliviousness of self, while my presence allowed you to forget this oblivion. So that with my tangible appearance I redoubled the lack of your presence.

But forgetfulness remembers itself when its memorial disappears. And here you are, this very evening, facing a mourning with no remembrance. Invested with an emptiness that evokes no memories. That screams at its own rebounding echo. A materiality occupying a void that escapes its grasp. A block sealing the wall of your prison. A buttress to a possible future, which, taken away, lets everything crumble indefinitely.

Where are you? Where am I? Where to find the traces of our passage? From the one to the other? From the one into the other?

You go down, you go down again, alone, under the ground. Under the ground where we seemed to be walking. The one, the other. The one or the other. You abandon your firmness, your uprightness. Your steps, your features hardened by the determination that accompanies solitude. You return to this cave whose entrance you couldn't find. To this cellar whose doorway you've forgotten. To this hole in your memory where the silence of my birth from you was buried—the silence of my separation, inseparable from you. To the obscurity of your conception of me.

What happened in the nighttime of your belly to make you no longer know I existed? Of the two of us, who was the one, who the other? What shadow or what light grew inside you while you carried me? And did yon not grow radiant with light while I lived, a thing held in the horizon of your body? And did you not grow dim when I took root in your soil? A flower left to its own growth. To contemplate itself without necessarily seeking to see itself. A blossoming not subject to any mold. An efflorescence obeying no already known contours. A design that changed itself endlessly according to the hour of the day. Open to the flux of its own becoming. Turning, turning away, turning around as it was drawn or pushed toward the burst of growth, or held back near the hiding place of its first watering; unfolding in an atmosphere as yet free of images. Becoming ecstatic with its own rhythm and measure, not yet under the constraint of eyes in quest of its mystery. Full-blossomed, bound by the ring of a lost vision. Encircled in the blind periphery of a question without answer.

Was I not your predestined guarantor? The profile of yourself that another would have stolen from you? The skin that another would have taken away? Wandering without identity, discharging upon me this endless, and at each step excruciating, wandering of yours. In me, shaping your destiny of an unknown. The yet-undeveloped negative images of your coming to yourself/me.

Here is she who I shall be, or was, or would like to be—was that not your response to my birth? What place remained for me into which to be born? Where to start my birth outside of you? For even when I was yet inside you, you kept me outside yourself.

With your milk, Mother, you fed me ice. And if I leave, you lose the reflection of life, of your life. And if I remain, am I not the guarantor of your death? Each of us lacks her own image; her own face, the animation of her own body is missing. And the one mourns the other. My paralysis signifying your abduction in the mirror.

And when I leave, is it not the perpetuation of your exile? And when it's my turn, of my own disappearance? I, too, a captive when a man holds me in his gaze; I, too, am abducted from myself. Immobilized in the reflection he expects of me. Reduced to the face he fashions for me in which to look at himself. Traveling at the whim of his dreams and mirages. Trapped in a single function—mothering.

* * *

Haven't you let yourself be touched by me? Haven't I held your face between my hands? Haven't I learned your body? Living its fullness. Feeling the place of its passage—and of the passage between you and me. Making from your gaze an airy substance to inhabit me and shelter me from our resemblance. From your/my mouth, an unending horizon. In you/me and out of you/me, clothed or not, because of our sex. In proportion to our skin. Neither too large nor too small. Neither wide open nor sutured. Not rent, but slightly parted.

And why would any other hurt be inflicted upon me? Didn't I already have my/your lips? And this body open on what we would never have stopped giving each other, saying to each other? This breach of silence where we constantly reenvelope ourselves in order to be reborn. Where we come to relearn ourselves and each other, in order to become women, and mothers, again and again.

But we have never, never spoken to each other. And such an abyss now separates us that I never leave you whole, for I am always held back in your womb. Shrouded in shadow. Captives of our confinement.

And the one doesn't stir without the other. But we do not move together. ⑧ When the one of us comes into the world, the other goes underground. When the one carries life, the other dies. And what I wanted from you, Mother, was this: that in giving me life, you still remain alive.

Notes:

(All notes are translator's comments.)

① The French here—*Tu melte donnes à manger*—carries several nuanced meanings: "You give me [something] to eat"; "You give yourself [something] to eat"; and "You give me yourself to eat".

② The word in French, *la glace*, has the second meaning of "ice" that carries more strongly than the English "mirror" a sense of movement frozen and rigidified.

③ The French is more elegant than the English can be: *Nourir a lieu avant toute figure*. Implied also in the word *figure* is the concept of "face" and of "identity."

④ The phrase *tel cet amour de toi* carries the meaning "such is this love of yours," but also suggested is "such is this love *of yourself*," underlining the confusion/fusion of identities between mother and daughter.

⑤ Irigaray's own words—*j'étais pétrifiée dans la représentation de ta mouvance*—brings together ideas of fear and immobility as the English cannot. In these passages Irigaray creates a locus of coexisting opposites that contrast actual paralysis and potential movement: *paralysie*, *inanimée*, *gel*, *infirmité* , *enfermée*, *figée*, *petrifiée*; and *coulait*, *fluide*, *marche*, *coure*, *meuve*, *mobilité*, *mouvance*.

⑥ The phrase used by Irigaray—*se remettre au monde*—carries the implication of physical birth (*mettre an monde*) as well as of giving birth to the self or of self-restoration.

⑦ The phrase *telle l'attente de toi* carries the meaning "such is your wait," but also suggested is "so it is when one waits *for you*," in recognition of the daughter's waiting for the mother.

⑧ The sentence in French—*Mais ce n'est ensemble que nous nous mouvons*—creates a sense of ambiguity since it suggests as well that "it is only together that we (can) move".

10 露丝·伊里加蕾,"用身体面对母亲"
Luce Irigaray,"The Bodily Encounter with the Mother"

"用身体面对母亲"是伊里加蕾最有影响的文章之一,已经被视为女性主义的经典之作。这是伊里加蕾于 1981 年 5 月参加在加拿大蒙特利尔召开的以"女性与疯狂"("Women and Madness")为主题的国际学术研讨会上所作的发言。法语原文,"Le corps-à-corps avec la mère",最早收入文集《性别与世系》(*Sexes et Parentés*),由法国 Les Éditions de Minuit 出版社于 1987 年出版。《性别与世系》收入的文章是伊里加蕾在加拿大和欧洲巡回讲学期间所作的演讲。作者把性别差异看做社会性别和意识形态双重作用的结果,这一相互作用不可避免地涉及了宗教、法律、心理学、社会学、人类学等相关领域。该书英文版 *Sexes and Genealogies* 由季兰·吉尔(Gillian C. Gill)翻译,由哥伦比亚大学出版社于 1993 年出版。在这个版本中,这篇文章的题目被英译成"Body Against Body: In Relation to the Mother"。

本书选取的英译文由大卫·梅西(David Macey)翻译,选自惠特福德(Margaret Whitford)编辑的《伊里加蕾读本》(*The Irigaray Reader*),由布莱克威尔出版社(Blackwell Publishers)于 1991 年出版。该文通过重新阅读古希腊

SEXES AND
GENEALOGIES

LUCE IRIGARAY
TRANSLATED BY GILLIAN C. GILL

俄瑞斯忒亚三部曲（Oresteia trilogy）①而对传统的父权体制提出了挑战。

该文可以分为四个部分。这一划分为编者所作。

伊里加蕾在第一部分首先指出，在关于女性的学术研讨会上，通常男性是缺席的。而这种缺席恰恰解释了女性的疯狂，因为"无人倾听她们的话语"②。事实上，男女两性以各自不同的方式同疯狂相联系，所有的欲望都同疯狂联系在一起（第 35 页；第 183 页）。伊里加蕾接着把目光聚焦在母亲的欲望和疯狂的关系上。她说，"同母亲的关系是一种疯狂的欲望，因为这一关系是最经典的'黑暗的大陆'"（第 35 页；第 183 页），不被父权文化所展示。

母性的作用支撑着社会秩序和欲望秩序，但这一作用总是被控制在需要的层面。就欲望而言，尤其是宗教意义上的欲望，女性——母性力量的作用常常在满足个人和集体需要的过程中被消灭了。

对母亲的欲望以及母亲的欲望，这是父亲律法所禁止的，是所有父亲律法所禁止的：家庭的父亲、国家的父亲、宗教意义上的父亲、做教授的父亲、做医生的父亲、做情人的父亲，不一而足。不管符合道德与否，父亲总是会

---

① 俄瑞斯忒亚三部曲为古希腊著名悲剧作家埃斯库罗斯（c. 525 B.C. ~456 B.C.）所作，由《阿伽门农》（*Agamemnon*）、《奠酒人》（*Choëphoroe*，亦译"Libation-Bearers"）和《善好者》（*Eumenides*，亦译"The Furies"，也译《复仇女神》）三部情节连续的剧作组成，其中最为著名的是第一部《阿伽门农》。《阿伽门农》主人公阿伽门农的妻子克吕泰涅斯特拉（Clytemnastra）对丈夫把女儿依菲琴尼亚（Iphegeneia）献祭战神的举动不满，联合阿伽门农家族的世仇埃癸斯托斯（Aegisthus）杀死了刚从特洛伊战场得胜归来的阿伽门农以及他带回的情妇卡桑德拉（Cassandra）。在《奠酒人》中，阿伽门农的儿子俄瑞斯忒斯（Orestes）在姐妹伊莱克特拉（Electra）的怂恿和支持下，杀死埃癸斯托斯和母亲为父报仇。由于此举引起复仇女神的愤怒，他们一起到阿波罗神庙请众神裁决。《善好者》讲述在阿波罗神庙中雅典娜如何面对复仇女神的起诉裁决俄瑞斯忒斯无罪，并承诺复仇女神可以永久居住雅典城。

② Luce Irigaray, "The Bodily Encounter with the Mother," trans. David Macey, in *Margaret Whitford, ed., The Irigaray Reader* (Cambridge, Mass.: Blackwell Publishers, 1991), p.35. 本节所引伊里加蕾该篇演讲观点均出自此处，以下只在正文标明页码，分号后第二个页码为引文本书的页码。

干涉进来监控并压制母亲的欲望和对母亲的欲望。（第 35 ~ 36 页；第 183
~ 184 页）

伊里加蕾做出惊人论断说：弗洛伊德在《图腾与禁忌》（*Totem and Taboo*）
中把杀父视作文化起源的时候，他忘却了一个更为古老的谋杀，即杀母
（matricide），这才是建构城邦秩序的基础（第 36 页；第 184 页）。

伊里加蕾在第二部分通过重新解读俄瑞
斯忒亚悲剧中母亲克吕泰涅斯特拉被谋杀的
情节论证自己关于西方文化基于杀母的观点。
她解释说，人们早已忘记克吕泰涅斯特拉杀害
阿伽门农的初衷——丈夫把女儿作为牺牲以
赢得战场的胜利，而一味把克吕泰涅斯特拉塑
造成了一个有外遇的不忠诚女人，因此，俄瑞
斯忒斯的杀母报仇被视为一种正义行为。所
以，虽然在此事件之后，俄瑞斯忒斯和伊莱克
特拉兄妹都疯了，但俄瑞斯忒斯却在阿波罗和雅典娜的帮助下恢复了神志，这也
是维持父权秩序所必需（第 37 页；第 185 页）。同样，在雅典娜——根据伊里加
蕾的解释，雅典娜是"女性气质最完美的模式"，"迷人"但不"诱人"——的帮助
下，儿子杀母的行为并没有受到惩罚（第 37 页；第 186 页）。可以得出结论说：
"父亲阻止用身体面对母亲"（第 39 页；第 188 页）。

在文章第三部分，伊里加蕾进一步指出，西方文化不仅禁止用身体接触母
亲，而且母亲往往成为"一个有吞噬能力的怪物"（第 40 页；第 189 页）。父亲拒
绝母亲具有的生殖能力，他要做惟一的造物主，于是就把一整套语言和象征系统
强加在女性身上（第 41 页；第 189 ~ 190 页）。

> 子宫……被许多男人幻想成一张有吞噬能力的嘴巴、一个排泄孔或肛门及
> 尿道的外脱、一个阳物威胁，最多不过是有生育能力的。在没有对女性性征
> 进行坚实再现的情况下，子宫便淹没在女性的整体性别概念之中了。（第
> 41 页；第 191 页）

伊里加蕾认为，弗洛伊德所说的杀父恰恰是为了让男性有机会继续保持对

世界、尤其是对女性的控制权力(第 42 页;第 191 页)。明确的性别身份没有建立起来,这时的男人"把他的阴茎转变为统治母性力量的工具"(第 42 页;第 191页)。

在文章第四部分,伊里加蕾试图提出改变现状的一些办法。她说,女性应该认识到,她们的价值不仅是生育孩子,她们还给世界带来爱情、欲望、语言、艺术以及有关社会、政治、宗教等领域的许多东西:"女性在这些领域的创造力在许多世纪一直被禁止发挥"(第 43 页;第 192 页)。伊里加蕾提醒我们:

> 我们必须小心对待另一件事:我们一定不能再次谋杀母亲了,她已经为我们文化的起源牺牲过一次了。我们必须赋予她新的生命,赋予母亲以新生命,赋予我们内心的母亲和我们之间的母亲以新生命。我们必须拒绝让她的欲望被父亲律法所消灭。我们必须给她追求快乐的权利,享受愉悦(*jouissance*)的权利,拥有激情的权利,我们必须恢复她讲话的权利,甚至间或哭泣和愤怒的权利。(第 43 页;第 192～193 页)

除此之外,女性还必须发现一种属于女性自己的语言(langage),这一语言"不取代身体面对",而且还能够表达肉体需要(第 43 页;第 192～193 页)。对于女性来说,至少有两种模式的愉悦:"一种设计在符合某一阳具秩序的男性力比多经济程序内;另一种则与女性的真实面目更相和谐,与女性的性别身份相和谐"(第 45 页;第 194 页)。在演讲的最后,伊里加蕾呼吁说:"人类也许应该开始清洗自己的罪恶了"(第 46 页;第 195 页)。只有女性分享劳动果实,摈弃仇恨和忘恩负义,她们之间才能建立起一个"女性世系"(female genealogy)(第46 页;第 195 页)。

The Bodily Encounter with the Mother

1

I would like to begin by thanking the organizing committee of the colloquium on mental health for having chosen as the theme for this meeting "Women and Madness", that is to say for having helped to bring out of the silence large-scale suffering on the part of women that is all too often kept hidden.

I am astonished—and, unfortunately!, not astonished, but I like to go on being astonished— that so few men-practitioners are here to listen to what women have to say about their madness. Given that the vast majority are the doctors of these women patients, their absence is a sign of their practice, especially their psychiatric practice. What women say appears to be of little importance to them. When it comes to knowing how things stand with women and what treatment should be prescribed them, they are self-sufficient. No need to listen to women. That no doubt explains their therapeutic choices.

But I have so often heard men getting angry about women—only meetings, wanting to penetrate them at all cost, that I find their absence today all the more significant. They have not been excluded from this colloquium, where most of the speakers will be women. How is it that their curiosity has not brought them here to listen? It is up to those men who are here to understand why and in what sense they are the exception!

Could it be something to do with the register of power that has kept away the others, the majority of practitioners? They do not dominate this colloquium. Or is it a matter of shame, given the statistics presented this morning, revealing the impressive number of women interned in psychiatric hospitals (most of them non-voluntary patients committed by families: hospitals function as a place of incarceration for women), and the fact that they are treated by chemotherapy and not psychotherapy? Unless it is a question of scorn because the colloquium is organized by and for women? Or of sexual indifference? I leave the interpretation open.

In any case, this absence is in itself an explanation for the madness of women: their words [*leur parole*] are not heard. What they say is illegitimate in terms of the elaboration of diagnoses, of therapeutic decisions that affect them. Scientific discourses and serious scientific practices are still the privilege of men, as is the management of the political in general and of the most private aspects of our lives as women. Their discourses, their values, their dreams and their desires have the force of law, everywhere and in all things. Everywhere and in all things, they define women's function and social role, and the sexual identity they are, or are not, to have. They know, they have access to the truth; we do not. Often, we scarcely have access to fiction.

As a particularly "honest" man friend told me not so long ago, not without some astonishment at his discovery, "It's true, I have always thought that all women were mad." And he added, "No doubt I wanted to avoid the question of my own madness."

That is indeed how the question is posed. Each sex relates to madness in its own way. All desire is connected to madness. But apparently one desire has chosen to see itself as wisdom, moderation, truth, and has left the other to bear the burden of the madness it did not want to attribute to itself, recognize in itself.

This relationship between desire and madness comes into its own, for both man and woman, in the relationship with the mother. But all too often, man washes his hands of it and leaves it to woman—women.

The relationship with the mother is a mad desire, because it is the "dark continent" *par excellence*. It remains in the shadows of our culture; it is its night and its hell. But men can no more, or rather no less, do without it than can women. And if there is now such a polarization over the questions of abortion and contraception, isn't that one more way of avoiding the question: what of the imaginary and symbolic relationship with the mother, with the woman-mother? What of that woman outside her social and material role as reproducer of children, as nurse, as reproducer of labour power?

The maternal function underpins the social order and the order of desire, but it is always kept in a dimension of need. Where desire is concerned, especially in its religious dimension, the role of maternal-feminine power is often nullified in the satisfying of individual and collective needs.

Desire for her, her desire, that is what is forbidden by the law of the father, of all fathers: fathers of families, fathers of nations, religious fathers, professor-fathers doctor-fathers, lover-fathers, etc. Moral or immoral, they always intervene to censor, to repress, the desire of/for the mother. For them, that corresponds to good sense and good health, when it's not virtue and sainthood!

Perhaps we have reached a period in history when this question of domination by fathers can no longer be avoided. This question is determined, or furthered, by several causes. Contraception and abortion raise the question of the meaning of motherhood, and women (notably because of their entry into and their encounters within the circuits of production) are looking for their sexual identity and are beginning to emerge from silence and anonymity.

And what is now becoming apparent in the most everyday things and in the whole of our society and our culture is that, at a primal level, they function on the basis of a matricide.

When Freud describes and theorizes, notably in *Totem and Taboo*, the murder of the father as founding the primal horde, he forgets a more archaic murder, that of the mother, necessitated by the establishment of a certain order in the polis.

2

Give or take a few additions and retractions, our imaginary still functions in accordance with the schema established through Greek mythologies and tragedies. I will therefore take the example of the murder of Clytemnestra in the *Oresteia*.

Clytemnestra certainly does not obey the image of the virgin-mother that has been held up to us for centuries. She is still a passionate lover. Moreover, she will go as far as a *crime passionnel*: she will kill her husband. Why?

He had been abroad for years and years, having gone off with other men to win back the beautiful Helen. This may be the forgotten prototype for war between men. In order to bring his military and amorous expedition to a successful conclusion, he ordered the sacrifice of Iphigenia, the adolescent daughter he had by Clytemnestra. When he comes back, it is with another woman, his slave, and no doubt his mistress.

Clytemnestra, for her part, has taken a lover. But she had heard nothing from her husband for so long that she thought he was dead. So she kills Agamemnon when he returns in glory with his mistress. She kills him out of jealousy, out of fear perhaps, and because she has been unsatisfied and frustrated for so long. She also kills him because he sacrificed their daughter to conflicts between men, a motive which is often forgotten by the tragedians.

But the new order demands that she in her turn must be killed by her son, inspired by the oracle of Apollo, the beloved son of Zeus: God the father. Orestes kills his mother because the rule of the God-Father and his appropriation of the archaic powers of mother-earth require it. He kills his mother and goes mad as a result, as does his sister Electra.

Electra, the daughter, will remain mad. The matricidal son must be saved from madness to establish the patriarchal order. It is the handsome Apollo, a lover of men rather than women, the narcissistic lover of their bodies and their words, a lover who does not make love much more than Athena, his sister in Zeus, who helps him to recover from his madness.

This madness is, moreover, represented in the form of a troop of enraged women who pursue him, haunt him wherever he goes, like the ghosts of his mother: the Furies. These women cry vengeance. They are women in revolt, rising up like revolutionary hysterics against the patriarchal power in the process of being established.

As you might have gathered, all this is still extremely contemporary. The mythology underlying patriarchy has not changed. What the *Oresteia* describes for us still takes place. Here and there, regulation Athenas whose one begetter is the head of the Father-King still burst forth. Completely in his pay, in the pay of the men in power, they bury beneath their sanctuary women in struggle so that they will no longer disturb the new order of the home, the order of the polis, now the only order. You can recognize these regulation Athenas, perfect models of femininity, always veiled and dressed from head to toe, all very respectable, by this token: they are extraordinarily seductive [*séductrices*], which does not necessarily mean enticing [*séduisantes*], but aren't in fact interested in making love.

The murder of the mother results, then, in the non-punishment of the son, the burial of the madness of women—and the burial of women in madness—and the advent of the image of the virgin goddess, born of the father and obedient to his law in forsaking the mother.

When Oedipus makes love with his mother, it will in fact do him no harm to start with, if I can put it that way. On the other hand, he will go blind or become mad when he learns she was his mother: she whom he has already killed in accordance with his mythology, in obedience to the verdict of the Father of the gods.

This interpretation is possible, but never happens. The event is always related to borrowing the place of the father, to the symbolic murder of the father. Now, Oedipus is no doubt re-enacting the madness of Orestes. He is afraid of his mother when she reveals herself to him for what she is. His primal crime comes back to him like an echo, he fears and detests his act, and the woman who was its object. Secondarily, he has infringed the law of the father.

Isn't all analytically inspired theory and practice based upon Oedipus's ambivalence towards his father? An ambivalence focused on the father, but which is retroactively projected on to the archaic relationship with the body of the mother. When it concerns itself with the life of the drives, psychoanalysis certainly talks to us of the mother's breast, of the milk she gives us to drink, of the faeces she accepts (a "gift" in which she may or may not be interested), and even of her gaze and her voice. It takes too little interest in them. What is more, isn't this bodily encounter [*corps-à-corps*] with the mother—and it is probably not without its difficulties—fantasized post-Oedipally, reprojected after the Oedipus? Hasn't the mother already been torn to pieces by Oedipus's hatred by the time she is cut up into stages, with each part of her body having to be cathected and then decathected as he grows up? And when Freud speaks of the father being torn to pieces by the sons of the primal horde, doesn't he forget, in a complete misrecognition and disavowal, the woman who was torn apart between son and father, between sons?

Partial drives appear to be concerned mainly with the body which brought us *whole* into the world. The genital drive is said to be the drive thanks to which the phallic penis takes back from the mother the power to give birth, to nourish, to dwell, to centre. The phallus erected where once there was the umbilical cord? It becomes the organizer of the world of and through the man-father, in the place where the umbilical cord, the first bond with the mother, gave birth to the body of both man and woman. That took place in a primal womb, our first nourishing earth, first waters, first envelopes, where the child was *whole*, the mother *whole* through the mediation of her blood. They were bound together, albeit in an asymmetrical relationship, before any cutting, any cutting up of their bodies into fragments.

Psychoanalysts take a dim view of this first moment—and, besides, it is invisible. A foetal situation or foetal regression, they say, and there is not a lot to be said about that. A taboo is in the air. If the father did not sever this over-intimate bond with the primal womb, there might be the danger of fusion, of death, of the sleep of death. Putting the matrix of his language [*langue*] in its place? But the exclusivity of his law forecloses this first body, this first home, this first love. It sacrifices them so as make them material for the rule of a language [*langue*] which privileges the masculine genre [*le genre masculin*] to such an extent as to confuse it with the human race [*le genre humain*].

According to this order, when a child is given a proper name, it already replaces the most irreducible mark of birth: the *navel*. A proper name, even a forename, is always late in terms of this most irreducible trace of identity: the scar left when the cord was cut. A proper name, even a forename, is slipped on to the body like a coating—an extra-corporeal identity card.

Yet, no matter what use he makes of the law, the symbolic, language [*langue*] or proper names (the name of the father), in practice the psychoanalyst usually sits behind the analysand, like the mother he should not look back at. He should make progress, advance, go outside and forget her. And if the patient did look back, perhaps she would have disappeared? Could he have annihilated her?

The social order, our culture, psychoanalysis itself, want it this way: the mother must remain forbidden, excluded. The father forbids the bodily encounter with the mother.

3

I feel like adding: if only it were true! We would be much more at peace with our bodies, which men need so badly to feed their libido and, first and foremost, their life and their culture. For the prohibition does not preclude a certain number of exemptions, a certain blindness.

The imaginary and the symbolic of intra-uterine life and of the first bodily encounter with the mother... where are we to find them? In what darkness, what madness, have they been abandoned?

And the relationship with the placenta, the first house to surround us, whose halo we carry with us everywhere, like some child's security blanket, how is that represented in our culture?

In the absence of any representation of it, there is always the danger of going back to the primal womb, seeking refuge in any open body, constantly living and nesting in the bodies of other women.

And so, the openness of the mother [*ouverture de la mère*], the opening on to the mother [*ouverture à la mère*], appear to be threats of contagion, contamination, engulfment in illness, madness and death. Obviously, there is nothing there that permits a gradual advance, one step at a time. No Jacob's ladder for a return to the mother. Jacob's ladder always climbs up to heaven, to the Father and his kingdom.

And besides, who could believe in the innocence of this bond with the mother when anyone who tries to establish a new bond with her is responsible for the crime that has been committed and perpetuated against her?

The mother has become a devouring monster as an inverted effect of the blind consumption of the mother. Her belly, sometimes her breasts, are agape with the gestation, the birth and the life that were given there without any reciprocity. Except for a murder, real and cultural, to annul that debt? To forget dependency? To destroy power?

The unchanging character of what is known in analytic therapies as orality, infinite thirst, the desire to be gratified by her that we hear so much about and which, it is said, makes some analyses impossible... the bottomless nature of an infant's mouth—or of a woman's genitals [*sexe*]—... hasn't that been thought or fantasized on the basis of Oedipus's hatred? There is no reason why either the hunger of a child or the sexual appetite of a woman should be insatiable. Everything proves the contrary. But this buccal opening of the child and all desire become an abyss if the sojourn *in utero* is censored and if our separations from that first home and the first nurse remain uninterpreted, unthought in their losses and scars. So when the child makes demands of the breast, isn't it demanding to receive all? The all that it received in its mother's belly: life, the home in which it lived, the home of its body, food, air, warmth, movement etc. For want of being situated in its time, its space and their exile, that all is displaced on to oral avidity.

The unavoidable and irreparable wound is the cutting of the umbilical cord. When his father or his mother threatens Oedipus with a knife or with scissors, he or she forgets that the cord has already been cut, and that it is enough to take note of that fact.

The problem is that, by denying the mother her generative power and by wanting to be the sole creator, the Father, according to our culture, superimposes upon the archaic world of the flesh a universe of language [*langue*] and symbols which cannot take root in it except as in the form of that which makes a hole in the bellies of women and in the site of their identity. In many patriarchal traditions, a stake is therefore driven into the earth to delineate the sacred space. It defines a place for male gatherings founded upon a sacrifice. Women may be tolerated within it as non-active bystanders.

The fertility of the earth is sacrificed to delineate the cultural horizon of the father tongue [*langue*] (wrongly termed the mother tongue). But that is never talked about. A hole in the texture of language corresponds to the forgetting of the scar of the navel.

Certain men and women would like to attribute this capture-net to maternal power, to the phallic mother. But when it is attributed to her, it is like a defensive network projected by the man-father or his sons on to the abyss of a silent and threatening belly. Threatening because silent?

The womb, unthought in its place of the first sojourn in which we become bodies, is fantasized by many men to be a devouring mouth, a cloaca or anal and urethral outfall, a phallic threat, at best reproductive. And in the absence of valid representations of female sexuality, this womb merges with woman's sex [*sexe*] as a whole.

There are no words to talk about it, except filthy, mutilating words. The corresponding affects will therefore be anxiety, phobia, disgust, a haunting fear of castration.

How can one not also feel them on returning to what has always been denied, disavowed, sacrificed to build an exclusively masculine symbolic world?

Might not castration anxiety be an unconscious memory of the sacrifice which sanctifies phallic erection as the only sexual value? But neither the postulate nor the name of the Father are enough to guarantee that the penis [*sexe*] of the son will remain erect. And it is not the murder of the father that supports and threatens the phallic erection, as psychoanalysis asserts to us in a sort of act of faith in the patriarchal tradition.

Unless—and this remains unthought—this murder of the father signifies a desire to take his place, a rival and competitive desire, but a desire to do away with the one who artificially cut the link with the mother in order to take over the creative power of all worlds, especially the female world.

No longer omnipotent, the phallic erection could, then, be a masculine version of the umbilical bond. It would, if it respected the life of the mother—of the mother in all women, of the woman in all mothers— reproduce the living bond with her. Where once was the cord, then the breast, there shall come in its time, for man, the penis which binds, gives life to, nourishes and recentres bodies, recalling in penetration, in touching beyond the skin and the will, in the outpouring, something of intra-uterine life, with detumescence evoking the end, mourning, the ever-open wound. This would be a preliminary gesture of repetition on man's part, a rebirth allowing him to become a sexuate adult capable of erotism and reciprocity in the flesh.

This rebirth in necessary for women too. It cannot take place unless it is freed from man's archaic projection on to her and unless an autonomous and positive representation of her sexuality exists in culture.

Woman has no reason to envy either the penis or the phallus. But the non-establishment of the sexual identity of both sexes [*sexes*] results in the fact that man, the people of men, has transformed his penis [*sexe*] into an instrument of power so as to dominate maternal power.

4

What use can all these descriptions be to us, as women? For us, understanding and describing all that is a way of escaping a world of madness which is not ours, a fear of the dark, of the non-identifiable, a fear of a primal murder which is culturally not ours. I think that it is very important to realize this because, again and again, we are placed in the sites of those projections. Again and again, we become the captives of these fantasies, this ambivalence, this madness which is not ours. We would do better to take back our own madness and return men theirs!

As for us, it is a matter of urgency not to submit to a desubjectivized social role, that of the mother, governed by an order subordinated to a division of labour—man produces/woman reproduces—which confines us to a mere function. Have fathers ever been asked to renounce being men? Citizens? We do not have to renounce being women in order to be mothers.

One other point. I am going to make a certain number in order to open up or institute exchange between us. It is also necessary for us to discover and assert that we are always mothers once we are women. We bring something other than children into the world, we engender something other than children: love, desire, language, art, the social, the political, the religious, for example. But this creation has been forbidden us for centuries, and we must reappropriate this maternal dimension that belongs to us as women.

If it is not to become traumatizing or pathological, the question of whether or not to have children must be asked against the background of an other generating, of a creation of images and symbols. Women and their children would be infinitely better off as a result.

We have to be careful about one other thing: we must not once more kill the mother who was sacrificed to the origins of our culture. We must give her new life, new life to that mother, to our mother within us and between us. We must refuse to let her desire be annihilated by the law of the father. We must give her the right to pleasure, to *jouissance*, to passion, restore her right to speech, and sometimes to cries and anger.

We must also find, find anew, invent the words, the sentences that speak the most archaic and most contemporary relationship with the body of the mother, with our bodies, the sentences that translate the bond between her body, ours, and that of our daughters. We have to discover a language [*langage*] which does not replace the bodily encounter, as paternal language [*langue*] attempts to do, but which can go along with it, words which do not bar the corporeal, but which speak corporeal.

It is important for us to guard and keep our bodies and at the same time make them emerge from silence and subjugation. Historically, we are the guardians of the flesh; we do not have to abandon that guardianship, but to identify it as ours by inviting men not to make us "their bodies", guarantors of their bodies. Their libido often needs some wife-mother to look after their bodies. It is in that sense that they need a woman-wife [*femme*] at home, even if they do have mistresses elsewhere. This question is very important, even if it seems minor.

It is therefore desirable, for us, to speak within the amorous exchange. It is also good to speak while feeding a child, so that it does not experience feeding as violent force-feeding, as rape. It is also important to speak while caressing another body. Silence is all the more alive in that speech exists. Let us not be the guardians of silence, of a deadly silence.

It is also necessary, if we are not to be accomplices in the murder of the mother, for us to assert that there is a genealogy of women. There is a genealogy of women within our family: on our mothers' side we have mothers, grandmothers and great-grandmothers, and daughters. Given our exile in the family of the father-husband, we tend to forget this genealogy of women, and we are often persuaded to deny it. Let us try to situate ourselves within this female genealogy so as to conquer and keep our identity. Nor let us forget that we already have a history, that certain women have, even if it was culturally difficult, left their mark on history and that all too often we do not know them.

Throughout all this, what we have to do (not that we necessarily have to do one thing before the other) is discover our sexual identity, the singularity of our desires, of our auto-erotism, of our narcissism, of our heterosexuality and of our homosexuality. In that connection, given that the first body they have any dealings with is a woman's body, that the first love they share is mother love, it is important to remember that women always stand in an archaic and primal relationship with what is known as homosexuality. For their part, men always stand in an archaic relationship with heterosexuality, since the first object of their love and desire is a woman.

When analytic theory says that the little girl must give up her love of and for her mother, her desire of and for her mother so as to enter into the desire of/for the father, it subordinates woman to a normative hetero-sexuality, normal in our societies, but completely pathogenic and pathological. Neither little girl nor woman must give up love for their mother. Doing so uproots them from their identity, their subjectivity.

Let us also try to discover the singularity of our love for other women. What might be called (though I do not like these label-words) " ' secondary homo-sexuality ' ", with lots of inverted commas. I am trying here to outline a difference between archaic love of the mother and love for women-sisters. This love is necessary if we are not to remain the servants of the phallic cult, objects to be used by and exchanged between men, rival objects on the market, the situation in which we have always been placed.

It is important that we discover the singularity of our *jouissance*. Of course, it is possible for a woman to come [*jouir*] in accordance with the phallic model, and there will never be any shortage of men and pornographers to get women to say that they have amazing orgasms [*jouissent extraordinairement*] within such an economy. The question remains: aren't they being drawn out of themselves, left without any energy, perceptions, affects, gestures or images to relate them to their identity? For women, there are at least two modes of *jouissance*. One is programmed in a male libidinal economy in accordance with a certain phallic order. Another is much more in harmony with what they are, with their sexual identity. Many women are guilty, unhappy, paralysed, say they are frigid, because, within the norms of a phallocratic economy, they do not succeed in living their affects, their sexuality, whereas they could do so if they tried to go back to a *jouissance* more in keeping with their bodies and their sex. This does not mean that they must renounce the other for ever, or immediately. I have no wish to make anyone choose between these alternatives, which could be repressive. But if we are to discover our female identity, I do think it important to know that, for us, there is a relationship with *jouissance* other than that which functions in accordance with the phallic model.

We have a lot of things to do. But it is better to have the future before us than behind us. Let us not wait for the Phallus god to grant us his grace. Yes, the Phallus god, because whilst many repeat that "God is dead", they rarely question the fact that the Phallus is alive and well. And do not many bearers of the said phallus now increasingly take themselves for gods in the full sense? Everywhere, and also, even—I will end with this question—in the holy Catholic Church, whose sovereign pontiff now thinks fit, once more, to forbid us contraception, abortion, extramarital relations, homosexuality, etc. So when this minister of the so-called one God, of the Father-God, pronounces the words of the eucharist: "This is my body, this is my blood" in accordance with the rite of celebrating the sharing of food, which is our age-old rite, perhaps we might remind him that he would not be there if our body and our blood had not given him life, love and spirit. And that it is us, women mothers, that he is giving to be eaten too. But no one must know that. That is why women cannot celebrate the eucharist... Something of the truth which is hidden therein might be brutally unmasked.

Humanity might begin to wash itself clean of a sin. A woman celebrating the eucharist with her mother, sharing with her the fruits of the earth she/ they have blessed, could be delivered of all hatred or ingratitude towards her maternal genealogy, could be consecrated in her identity and her female genealogy.

11 露丝·伊里加蕾,"被遗忘的女性祖先秘密"
Luce Irigaray, "The Forgotten Mystery of Female Ancestry"

　　"被遗忘的女性祖先秘密"是伊里加蕾的一篇演讲,首次发表在 1989 年 3 月 31 日美国的锡拉丘兹(Syracuse),后来又于同年 4 月和 6 月在意大利的巴勒莫(Palermo)和特尔尼(Terni)演讲。在本篇演讲中,伊里加蕾追溯了西方主要神话传说对于女性祖先的描述,得出结论认为,女性祖先在创世初就已经死亡。她还因此主张,要想建立性别差异的伦理学就必须恢复女性祖先的纽带联系①。

　　本书选段出自伊里加蕾的文集《思考差异:为了一场和平的革命》。这部著作的法文原版 Le Temps De La Différence: Pour une révolution pacifique 由巴黎法国大图书馆于 1989 年出版,由卡琳·蒙田(Karin Montin)翻译成英文,英译本于 1994 年由英国阿狮龙(The Athlone Press)出版社出版。该书收集了伊里加蕾于 1986～1989 年所作的四篇演讲,这些演讲讨论语言、宗教、法律、艺术和科学技术如何未能充分认识和表现女性以及女性利益,这对人类的生存和发展至关重要。针对这些误区伊里加蕾还提出了一些具体建议,希望真正的性别差异伦理学能够在此基础上建立起来。

　　"被遗忘的女性祖先秘密"可以分为四个部分,这一划分为编者所作。

---

　　① Luce Irigaray, Thinking the Difference: Toward a Peaceful Revolution, trans. Karin Montin (London: The Athlone Press, 1994), p. 109. 本节所引伊里加蕾该篇演讲观点均出自此处,以下只在正文标明页码,分号后第二个页码为引文在本书的页码。

伊里加蕾在第一部分首先指出,在某些古老然而却很发达的传统中,女性首先引导男性进入爱情(第 91 页),但这样的行为在现代社会却被认为是淫秽的举动而为人所不齿。弗洛伊德把男性主动的爱情模式理论化为惟一可能的两性关系,爱情于是成为混沌、黑暗、兽性、罪恶和虚无的代名词(第 91 页)。既然女性在爱情中的角色不被认同,那么女性就被混同于男性,至少在性冲动上男女两性没有分别,他们是"统一性的"(unisex)。

在第二部分,伊里加蕾追溯创世纪初男女两性如何在生育子女的过程中产生了性别的区分(第 92 ~ 93 页)。她以希腊神话中爱与美的女神阿芙罗狄蒂

(Aphrodite)①为例说明她如何像鱼一样无需交配、在母亲子宫外的大海中孕育并出生(第 93 页),也因此象征爱情可以转变为人类的自由和欲望(第 95 页)。爱情于是成为一种罪恶,因为它能毁灭人类的身份,它能消灭肉体与精神(第 96 页)。在这样的情况下,生育就被转化为一种宗教的或平民的义务(第 96 页)。伊里加蕾说,混沌状态是生命驱动力,是男性回归母亲子宫并从此享受子宫绝对

---

① Sandro Botticelli, "The Birth of Venus", c. 1485-1486, http://www.webtheo.com.

肥沃营养以维持自身活力的欲望(第 96 页)。在两性关系中男人应该占据主动,这是人们普遍接受的事实和规范,两个个体间的相互爱恋是不存在的(第 98~99 页)。女人做母亲,这是"女性惟一有价值的命运","通常意味着通过为自己的丈夫、为国家、为男性文化权力生育孩子的方式延续父权世系"(第 99 页)。对于女性来说,做母亲的经历代表着恢复同自己母亲以及其他女性的纽带(第 99 页)。

在第三部分,伊里加蕾回顾了古希腊神话中女性祖先的纽带如何被摧毁的诸多实例,其中最为重要的是关于主管丰饶的女神得墨忒耳(Demeter)和女儿珀尔塞福涅(Persephone)如何被宙斯(Zeus)强行分离的故事①。宙斯为获得统治宇宙的更大权力单方面同冥王哈德斯(Hades)达成协议,把自己的女儿珀尔塞福涅卖给哈德斯为妻。身为母亲的得墨忒耳对此毫不知情。珀尔塞福涅被强行掠到地府时发出的惊天动地的哭声却无法让宙斯和得墨忒耳听到。在得墨忒耳的强烈要求下,宙斯和哈德斯才同意让这对可怜的母女在一年当中见一次面。于是,母女分离的季节,得墨忒耳的悲痛使得土地荒芜,寸草不生;而在母女相聚的秋季,大地才呈现出丰饶的景象。"女性的世系就这样被中断"(第 106 页;第 204 页)。

在演讲的第四部分,伊里加蕾总结说,"身为处女的女孩要想成为女人就必须屈服于一种文化,尤其是一种爱的文化。对于她来说,这种文化就是哈德斯"(第 110 页;第 207 页)。她认为,女儿对母亲说的话是最具伦理模式的一种语言,因为这些话语尊重女性之间的主体关系(第 111 页;第 208 页)。伊里加蕾话语犀利地指出,

> 父权制建立在对女儿处女身份的偷窃和侵害之上,建立在使用女性贞节完成男人之间的商品交易,包括宗教交易。……父权体制就是在这样一个原罪的基础之上建构了自己的一片天地。(第 111~112 页;第 208~209 页)

---

① Frederic Leighton, "The Return of Persephone", c. 1890-1891, http://www.loggia.com/art/19th/leighton16.html.

在伊里加蕾看来，正是通过这样的途径，父权制摧毁了最为宝贵的母女关系，而这却是爱情和丰饶之所在(第112页；第209页)。在演讲的最后，伊里加蕾说道：

> 要重新建立基本的社会公正，要拯救地球使之不完全屈服于男性价值观念……我们必须恢复文化中这一缺失的支柱：即母女关系以及对女性话语和女性贞节的尊重。这需要改变象征代码，尤其是语言、法律和宗教。(第112页；第209页)

本书选注的是该演讲的第三、四两个部分。

The Forgotten Mystery of Female Ancestry

[……]

How have we come to this—all of us, and especially we women? One of the lost crossroads of our becoming women lies in the blurring and erasure of our relationships to our mothers and in our obligation to submit to the laws of the world of men-amongst-themselves.

The destruction of female ancestry, especially its divine aspect, is recounted in a variety of ways in the Greek myths and tragedies. Aphrodite's mother is no longer mentioned; she is supplanted by Hera, and Zeus remains the God who has many lovers, but no female equivalent. The goddess Aphrodite can thus be said to have lost her mother. Iphigeneia is separated from her mother to be offered as a sacrifice in the Trojan War. And though oracular speech was originally passed on from mother to daughter, beginning with Apollo it is often assimilated to the oracle at Delphi, which still has a place for Pythia, but not for mother-daughter relationships. Antigone's uncle, the tyrant Creon, punishes by death her faith, her loyalty to her maternal ancestry and its laws, in order to safeguard his power in the polis. The Old Testament does not tell us of a single happy mother-daughter couple, and Eve comes into the world motherless. Although Mary's mother, Anne, is known, the New Testament never mentions them together, not even at the moment of the conception of Jesus. Mary goes to greet Elizabeth, not Anne, unless Elizabeth is Anne, as in Leonardo da Vinci's interpretation. Mary's leaving her mother for a marriage with the Lord is more in keeping with the tradition that was already several centuries old.

Perhaps the best illustration of the fate of the mother-daughter relationship is to be found in the myths and rites surrounding Demeter and Kōrē. You are probably fairly familiar with these myths. You live in a place that still bears traces of them, memories of them. As is almost always the case, there are several versions of the myths. This means that they appeared at different times and in different places.

Most ancient Greek myths are of Asian or unknown origin. This is true of those concerning Aphrodite, Demeter and Kōrē/Persephone. Their evolution should be understood as the result of migrations to different places where they were adapted to varying degrees, and the effect of historical developments. For myth is not a story independent of History, but rather expresses History in colourful accounts that illustrate the major trends of an era. The temporality of History is expressed in this form because in those days, speech and art were not separate. As a result, they retained a special relationship to space, time and the manifestation of the forms of incarnation. History as expressed in myth is more closely related to female, matrilineal traditions.

In myths concerning mother-daughter relationships and myths about the goddess/lover and god couples, the story, setting and interpretation were masked, disguised to varying degrees by the patriarchal culture that was growing up. This culture erased—perhaps out of ignorance, perhaps unwittingly—the traces of an earlier or contemporaneous culture. Thus many sculptures were destroyed or buried in the ground, rites were eliminated from traditions or transformed into patriarchal rituals, myths and mysteries were interpreted from the patriarchal perspective, or simply as representing the

Prehistory of the patriarchal era.

The same applies to the myths of Demeter Kōrē/Persephone. It seems to me that there are at least two different versions. In one, Demeter's daughter is abducted by the god of shadows, fog and the Underworld, and then seduced by him despite herself, so that she cannot return to her mother for good. When she is first carried off by Hades—also called Erebus or Aidoneus by Homer—she is looking at spring flowers with other maidens, and just as she is about to pick a narcissus, the earth opens up, and the prince of the Underworld takes her away with him. He has not yet made her his wife when Hermes, Zeus' messenger, comes to fetch her at the request of Demeter, her mother, who in her grief has made the earth barren. The god of the Underworld has no choice but to obey, but he gives Persephone a poisoned gift behind Hermes' back: he gives her pomegranate seeds to eat, and anyone who accepts a gift from Hades becomes his captive.

This is the version of the Homeric hymn. In later versions or interpretations, Kōrē/Persephone has become more or less responsible for her own fate, and is thus more like Eve the seductress, who leads man to his fall. It was nothing like that in the initial versions. But the story of Demeter and Kōrē/Persephone is so terrible and so exemplary that it is understandable that the patriarchal era wished to make the seductive woman bear the responsibility for its crimes.

It seems that Kōrē/Persephone's only sin was to reach out to pluck a narcissus. Of course it is preferable to leave flowers rooted in the earth rather than pick them, especially in spring, but should the girl be punished for picking a flower, even a marvellous narcissus, by being carried off to the Underworld?

Whatever the reasons cited for blaming Kōrē/Persephone, it is clear that her fate is decided by men-gods. Jupiter [Zeus], Poseidon and Hades' must divide up the heavens, the sea and the Underworld. The episode of Kōrē/Persephone's abduction involves a power struggle between Zeus and Hades, two brothers of different parentage who can neither meet nor see each other because of their ancestral ties. Zeus is a descendant of Gaia, and Hades is a descendant of Chaos. Zeus is a child of the female pole, conceived with one of her first sons; Hades, or Erebus, is the offspring of the initial Chaos, or the male pole of the origin of the world. Zeus wishes to become God of gods despite the infernal male powers that wanted to annihilate him as an individual more differentiated than Chaos. He wants to overturn the divine male omnipotence of the initial Chaos.

To do this, Jupiter, Kōrē/Persephone's father, gives his daughter in marriage to Hades, who none the less steals and rapes her. This episode, like many others, takes place at the time of the shift from matrilineality to patrilineality. Jupiter trades his daughter's virginity for affirmation of his male omnipotence. His father did not want him to be born as a human manifestation having a sex; he agrees to yield his daughter's virginity, her female identity, as the price of his recognition as God of the Olympian gods. To exist as God in the eyes of all, he agrees to give his daughter in marriage to the god of the Underworld. This transaction takes place without the consent of either his laughter or her mother. Two things are thus sacrificed to establish Zeus' power: Kōrē/Persephone's virginity and the love between Demeter and her daughter. Jupiter has no right to use his daughter and her mother this way. Demeter tries to tell him so, but Kōrē/Persephone no longer dares, except by crying for help. Jupiter breaks off the exchange of words between his daughter and himself at the same time as he deprives her of her virginity, a good bartered with Hades.

This sacrifice of Kōrē/Persephone's virginity and language, including that used in her relationship with her mother, seems to show that Jupiter does not yet have access to either fulfilled humanity or the divinity of his male identity. Yet not only does he make Hades bear this imperfection, but he continues to commit incest and to have many lovers, which indicates that he is not fully embodied.

By affirming himself as sovereign of the world above, he creates or maintains the existence of a sovereign of the world below. If he reduplicates heaven, Jupiter must also reduplicate the earth. According to the patriarchal hierarchy, both human and divine, Jupiter is above Uranus in access to the celestial, but this above implies a below. The infernal Hades corresponds to the sovereign Zeus. The two of them can neither see nor meet each other. The God of the world above is the resplendent, dazzling, yet thundering God of lightning, of the violent relationship between heaven and earth. The god of the world below is the god of indifferentiation transformed into the Underworld, fog, abyss. This infernal power of the realm of the male gods, this god of the invisible, is a thief, a rapist, the black man all little girls fear. Is he not Jupiter's dark double? Is he not the shadow of sovereignty? Is he not the inverse [envers] or inferno [enfer] of his absolute power without tender sharing with the other sex? Does this Hades not correspond to the dark underside, or, in current parlance, the disordered unconscious of his brilliance?

So the black man takes her, little girl or adolescent. He cloaks her in shadow. He carries her off to his underground domain. She refuses to give herself to her lover.

She cries out when he drags her down to the Underworld, but neither her mother nor her father, Zeus, hears her. It is said that the sun hears her, and perhaps Hecate does, unless it is the sun that tells Hecate of Kōrē/Persephone's abduction.

It is Hecate who, ten days later, tells Demeter where her daughter is. She also tells her that the abduction took place with the connivance of Zeus, husband of the one and father of the other. Demeter then becomes angry with the gods. She leaves Olympus and goes among the mortals. Grief-stricken, she tries to console herself by becoming the wet-nurse to another child. Without revealing her identity, she offers her services at a house where a woman has just given birth to an unhoped—for younger son, a late son, perhaps a son of a god, of Zeus. Her offer is accepted.

She is given a little boy to care for in place of her daughter, and for a while she is content. But she has plans for this child. She wants to make him immortal. She therefore brings him up in a strange manner: she does not feed him, but rubs him with ambrosia, blows on him while clasping him to her heart, and at night holds him in the fire. That is how someone is made immortal. Indeed, the child grows up like a god. But his mother watches Demeter tending her son. She becomes frightened and cries out, giving away her presence. Demeter, vexed at the mortal woman's lack of confidence in her, drops the infant, leaves him on the ground, and decides to stop working for the household. She then reveals who she is and demands that the husband make amends for the offence.

The essence of her demand is that a sanctuary to her should be erected at Eleusis, and this is done. Demeter retires there and thinks of nothing but her daughter. Her grief causes the earth to become barren, which means no more food for the mortals, and therefore no mortals to honour the gods.

After a year of famine, Zeus becomes worried. He tries to persuade Demeter to change her mind. First he sends Iris, then all the gods in existence, as messengers of peace, bearing magnificent gifts and all the privileges she could want. But Demeter accepts nothing. She wants to see her daughter's face again. In this regard, it should be noted that she never turns to her mother in her grief. Like Kōrē/Persephone, like Iphigeneia, like Antigone, like Mary and like Eve; none of these women has a mother in whom to confide. The female line of descent is already interrupted.

The story of Kōrē/Persephone shows that the daughter is not responsible. The mother is a little more responsible, for she begins to console herself for the disappearance of her daughter by nursing a boy-child. But her acceptance of this substitute is also a form of revenge. A god has stolen her daughter, so she renounces life among the immortals and tries to force a mortal upon them as a god. When this solution fails, she refuses any proposition from the God of gods, unless he gives her back her daughter. Zeus understands that there is no other way to save the mortals and the immortals. He sends Hermes to Erebus [Hades] to fetch Persephone. Hades must obey, but he is still plotting to keep his mastery: he induces

Persephone to eat a pomegranate seed, which, unknown to her, makes her a hostage of the Underworld.

Mother and daughter are happily reunited. Demeter asks Persephone to tell her everything that has happened to her. She does so, beginning at the end. In a way, she goes back in time, as must any woman today who is trying to find the traces of her estrangement from her mother. That is what the psychoanalytical process should do: find the thread of her entry into the Underworld, and, if possible, of her way out.

But let us return to the reunion of Demeter and Persephone. They spend all day pouring their hearts out to each other, comforting each other, expressing their joy to each other. Hecate joins them and, ever since, she has held an important place in the mysteries surrounding Kōrē/Persephone. In particular, she follows her when she descends to the Underworld and precedes her on her return to earth.

Indeed, the poisoned gift that Persephone accepted from Hades is apparently enough to make her his captive at least a third of the year, the cold season. Similarly, yet differently, eating an apple is all it later took to be excluded from earthly paradise. Then, it is true, the prohibition was clearly stated before the sin was committed, which was not the case for Kōrē/Persephone. But both are stories of fairly similar traps or taboos involving flowers or fruits; in one, the prince of darkness is clearly responsible, and in the other, a woman is blamed. It is true that Eve is no longer a woman, since she is made from Adam's rib. Eve is only part of Adam, created without a mother; this is not the case of Kōrē/Persephone, who is a goddess, a daughter of a goddess, of a god couple. The bond between humanity and divinity is thus unbroken. Sometimes it is woven in one direction, sometimes in the other, with curious tests or tricks, strange prohibitions imposed upon women to establish a patriarchally transmitted ancestry and theology.

All these codes are beyond the little girl. She may make a mistake, but she does not decide to do so. She is caught up in the dealings, contractual or otherwise, between men, between men and male gods. According to their agreements, she should refuse everything from men and gods so that she will not be seduced through a mistake on her part. She should keep well away from mankind, men's contracts, men's relationships, until her virginity is no longer a subject of negotiations between men. She should remember that virginity signifies her relationship to her physical and moral integrity, and not the price of a deal between men. She should learn to keep herself for herself, for her gods and her love, for the love of which she is capable if she is not taken outside herself, abducted, raped and deprived of freedom of action, speech, thought. Obviously this freedom must be real and not controlled; the freedom to seduce in accordance with male instincts or to gain equality of rights within a unisex male order is only a superficial freedom that has already exiled woman from herself, already deprived her of any specific identity. She thus becomes a sort of puppet, or movable object, reduced to being subjected to basic drives with passive goals. She thinks she needs to be "screwed" by a man, she suffers from a basic oral need (partially an inverted projection stemming from male desire), Freud writes learnedly, without considering that this need might be symptomatic of woman's submission to male instincts. According to Freud, this need is a sort of relic of the initial chaos that male desire opened up in the earth's womb.

Indeed, this chaos still exists. It is manifested in the libido's economy of drives without genitality, the economy in which woman is imprisoned. One of the two—he—is stuck in incestuous regression and anal possession, while the other—she—is reduced to oral mendicancy. Woman supposedly always hungers for him without any return to herself. She thus eventually becomes hungry from the abyss that he has opened up in her; she becomes ill with a bottomless hunger, because it is not her hunger, but the abyss inside her of the natural and cultural hunger of the other.

None of this could happen if she had not been separated from her mother, from the earth, from her gods and her order. This is the original sin that makes woman a seductress against a backdrop of nothingness. But why abduct her from her mother? Why destroy female ancestries? To establish an order man needed, but which is not yet an order of respect for and fertility of sexual difference.

To make an ethics of sexual difference possible once again, the bond of female ancestries must be renewed. Many people think or believe that we know nothing about mother-daughter relationships. That is Freud's position. He asserts that on this point, we must look beyond Greek civilization to examine another erased civilization. Historically, this is true, but this truth does not prevent Freud from theorizing on and imposing, in psychoanalytical practice, the need for the daughter to turn away from the mother, the need for hatred between them, without sublimation of female identity being an issue, so that the daughter can enter into the realm of desire and law of the father. This is unacceptable. Here Freud is acting like a prince of darkness with respect to all women, leading them into the shadows and separating them from their mothers and from themselves in order to found a culture of men-amongst-themselves: law, religion, language, truth and wisdom. In order to become a woman, the virgin girl must submit to a culture, particularly a culture of love, that to her represents Hades. She must forget her childhood, her mother; she must forget herself as she was in her relationship to Aphrodite's *philotes*.

If the rationale of History is ultimately to remind us of everything that has happened and to take it into account, we must make the interpretation of the forgetting of female ancestries part of History and reestablish its economy.

The justifications given for breaking up mother-daughter love are that this relationship is too conducive to fusion. Psychoanalysis teaches us that it is essential to substitute the father for the mother to allow a distance to grow between daughter and mother. Nothing could be further from the truth. The mother-son relationship is what causes fusion, for the son does not know how to situate himself in regard to the person who bore him with no possible reciprocity. He cannot conceive within himself. He can only artificially identify with the person who conceived him. To separate himself from his mother, man must therefore invent all sorts of objects for himself, even transcendental ones—gods, truth—in order to resolve this insoluble relationship between the person who carried him inside her and himself.

The situation is different for the daughter, who is potentially a mother and can live with her mother without destroying either one of them even prior to the mediation of specific objects. To them, nature is a preferred environment; the ever-fertile earth is their place, and mother and daughter coexist happily there. They, like nature, are fertile and nurturing, but this does not prevent them from having a human relationship between them. This relationship depends upon the establishment of female lines of descent, but not solely. Therefore the daughter's words to the mother may represent the most highly evolved and most ethical models of language, in the sense that they respect the intersubjective relationship between the two women, express reality, make correct use of linguistic codes and are qualitatively rich. For little girls, education, the social world of men-amongst-themselves and the patriarchal culture function as Hades did for Kōrē/Persephone. The justifications offered to explain this state of affairs are inaccurate. The traces of the story of the relationship between Demeter and Kōrē/Persephone tell us more. The little girl is taken away from her mother as part of a contract between men-gods. The abduction of the daughter of the great Goddess serves to establish the power of male gods and the structure of patriarchal society. But this abduction is a rape, a marriage with the consent of neither the daughter nor the mother, an appropriation of the daughter's virginity by the god of the Underworld, a ban on speech imposed on the girl/daughter and the woman/wife, a descent for her (them) into the invisible, oblivion, loss of identity and spiritual barrenness.

Patriarchy is founded upon the theft and violation of the daughter's virginity and the use of her virginity for commerce between men, including religious commerce. Carrying on this commerce involves money changing hands, but also exchanging real property; at stake are either symbolic or narcissistic powers. Patriarchy has constructed its heaven and hell upon this original sin. It has imposed silence upon the daughter. It has dissociated her body from her speech, and her pleasure from her language. It has dragged her down into the world of male drives, a world where she has become invisible and blind to herself, her mother, other women and even men, who perhaps want her that way. Patriarchy has thus destroyed the most precious site of love and its fertility: the relationship between mother and daughter, the mystery of which is guarded by the virgin daughter. This relationship does not separate love from desire, or heaven from earth, and it knows nothing of hell. Hell appears to be a result of a culture that has annihilated happiness on earth by sending love, including divine love, into a time and place beyond our relationships here and now.

To re-establish elementary social justice, to save the earth from total subjugation to male values (which often give priority to violence, power, money), we must restore this missing pillar of our culture: the mother-daughter relationship and respect for female speech and virginity. This will require changes to symbolic codes, especially language, law and religion.

12　多萝西·迪纳斯坦,"肮脏的女神"
Dorothy Dinnerstein, "The Dirty Goddess"

　　使迪纳斯坦(Dorothy Dinnerstein)①一夜成名并在历史上占据不可替代地位的是她于 1976 年出版的《美人鱼与弥诺陶洛斯怪物:性别分工与人类痼疾》(*The Mermaid and the Minotaur: Sexual Arrangements and Human Malaise*)。这部书被誉为"最为重要的女性主义著作之一",同时也是常常被忽视和低估的著作之一②。著作中提倡的让男性分担养育孩子责任的平等抚养精神让许多男性视为对父权体制的根本挑战。也正是这样的一个主张让奥立瑞(Stephen O'Leary)认为这将是改变我们生活的一本书③。

　　迪纳斯坦在位于纽瓦克的鲁特格斯大学(Rutgers University)工作了近 20 年。她的一生在默默无闻中度过,20 世纪 90 年代初期在一场车祸中不幸丧生。她利用实验室考察人的认知过程,同时用心理分析方法对人类生活进行社会与哲学的分析。

　　《美人鱼与弥诺陶洛斯怪物》把核心家庭视为父权的、充满性别的歧视。迪纳斯坦解释说,女人是男人第一个爱恋的对象、第一个见证人、第一个老板,这使

---

　　①　照片摄影 Freda Leinwand, 取自 http://www.usc.edu/isd/archives/womens_salons/photos/dinnerstein.html。

　　②　Christopher Schmitz, http://www.amazon.com/gp/cdp/member-reviews/A3CM1CDUSWYDIO/104-9915692-6092755?%5Fencoding = UTF8&display = public&page = 4, n. p.

　　③　Stephen O'Leary, http://www.amazon.com/gp/cdp/member-reviews/A2LM0I6AJ00Y25/ref = cm_cr_auth/104-9915692-6092755, n. p.

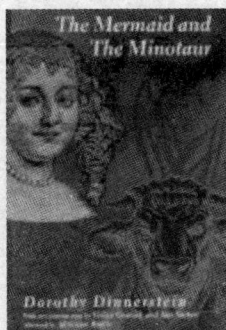

得男人反过来寻找机会让女人感到低人一等。这是造成核心家庭中女性处于低下地位的根本原因。又由于母亲或其他女性主要承担了抚养孩子的任务，这使得孩子在成年以后对女性产生了普遍的厌恶和仇恨。迪纳斯坦因此提倡男人和女人分担养育孩子的责任。毫无疑问，男人和女人在孩子成长过程中发挥着同样重要的作用，但这并不意味着他们应该承担同样的义务和工作。迪纳斯坦在书中还探讨了性在人类性格形成过程中所起的重要作用，让人们重新思考男人和女人、父母和孩子之间的关系。

迪纳斯坦认为男人和女人在养育孩子过程中可以承担相同的角色，施密兹（Christopher Schmitz）认为这个想法纯属纸上谈兵，在实际生活中却不可行①。实际上，男人和女人在家庭中的角色应该是互补的。

该书分为三个部分：

第一部分："美人鱼与弥诺陶洛斯怪物"。在这一部分，迪纳斯坦主要解释了她在书中将频繁使用的一些术语的含义，算作全书的引言。在谈到书的题目中包含的两个形象时，迪纳斯坦解释说：

美人鱼②与弥诺陶洛斯怪物③两个意象关系到一般意义上的人类痼疾

---

① Christopher Schmitz, http://www. amazon. com/gp/cdp/member-reviews/ A3CM1CDUSWYDIO/104-9915692-6092755?%5Fencoding = UTF8&display = public&page = 4, n. p.

② 美人鱼是一种传说中的海洋生物，长有女人的头部和上身，却生有一条鱼尾巴。丹麦作家安徒生的童话故事《海的女儿》（"The Little Mermaid"，1836 年）给这一故事赋予了美丽的想象。迪纳斯坦这里的用意显然与安徒生的故事无关。插图来自 http://www. mermaid. net。

③ 弥诺陶洛斯是半人半牛的怪物。传说弥诺斯（Minos）国王向海神波塞冬求救以拥有不寻常的力量同兄弟抗衡。波塞冬赠给他一头雪白的公牛，弥诺斯食言，没有用这头牛作牺牲。波塞冬知道后非常生气，他设计让弥诺斯的妻子帕西法厄（Pasipha）爱上了这头公牛。帕西法厄让建筑师代达罗斯（Daedalus）造了一个逼真的木制母牛以吸引公牛，他们欢爱的结果便是半人半牛的弥诺陶洛斯。弥诺斯下令在克里特岛造了一座迷宫，使弥诺陶洛斯无法逃脱。此后 9 年，弥诺陶洛斯每年吃掉雅典进贡的童男童女各 7 人，直至被忒修斯（Theseus）杀死。访问 Micha F. Lindemans, http://www. pantheon. org/articles/m/ minotaur. html, n. p. 插图来自 http://homepage. mac. com/cparada/GML/Minotaur. html。

[……]也关系到具体的性别分工。背信弃义的美人鱼充满女性诱惑，不可渗透，引诱航行者走向毁灭，它女性般地象征黑暗而魔幻的水下世界，我们的生命源于此，但又无法生活其中。令人恐惧的弥诺陶洛斯怪物身材庞大，是母亲非凡肉欲所生的永恒婴儿，男性般地象征着愚笨无知又欲壑难填的权力，贪婪地吞噬鲜活的人类生命。

本书的题目总体来说有两个含义：其一，它代表人们长期以来对自己在动物王国中所处的动摇不定、模糊不清的地位的认识；其二，如果人们不彻底改变两性之间有害的合作关系，男人和女人将永远半人半兽，怪异恐怖。①

第二部分："推动摇篮与统治世界"。迪纳斯坦着重讨论女性在孩子成长过程中承担的重要而惟一的作用。

第三部分："性别分工与人类痼疾"。迪纳斯坦分析男人不参与抚养孩子将直接造成目前畸形的性别分工以及性别歧视，从而提倡男人和女人分担养育责任。

"肮脏的女神"是该书第二部分的第7节。

这一节包括引言和6个部分。

作者在引言中首先承认女性是肉体替罪羊，这一点普遍存在于西方文化中。作者详细引述德·波伏娃②的观点，认为男性对所有神秘的、强有力的事物怀有一种敬畏和恐惧，女性可繁殖的身体是这样一种事物最基本的象征（第125页）。

第一部分，"母性、死亡、肉欲与事业"（"Maternity, Mortality, Carnality, and Enterprise"）。由于母亲在赋予生命的同时也决定了走向死亡的道路，男性对女性因而怀有一种恐惧的心理。母性同死亡相联系，同肉欲相联系，并在孩

---

① Dorothy Dinnerstein, *The Mermaid and the Minotaur: Sexual Arrangements and Human Malaise* (New York: Harper & Row, Publishers, 1976), p. 5. 本节所引迪纳斯坦观点除特别说明外均出自此书，以下只在正文标明页码，分号后第二个页码为引文在本书的页码。

② 德·波伏娃，法国女性主义理论家。参见本书第一篇第1节。

子成长过程中独占了抚养的工作(第 130 页)。这反过来又导致人们对身体的看法充满矛盾。

第二部分，"肉体：人类愿望的载体和阻体"("The Flesh as Vehicle-Saboteur of Human Wishes")。性别分工与无法排解的肉体矛盾来自孩子发现肉欲既具有神秘的快感又具有窘迫的局限，这一发现是孩子同女人接触时产生的。这一早期发现同后来习得的知识融合为一体(第 130 页)。

第三部分，"肉体：压抑的回归"("The Flesh as 'Return of the Repressed'")。作者详细引述诺曼·奥立佛·布朗(Norman Oliver Brown)①的观点论证对于身体的复杂感情使女性埋葬并否定对于身体的爱，以一种病态的、令人汗颜的情感取而代之，这使本来简简单单的愤怒变得复杂化了(第 134～135 页)。

第四部分，"性别分工与肉体的复杂性"("Gender Arrangements and Ambivalence to the Flesh")。女神是肮脏的，不仅仅由于她是人类欲望的载体和阻体，而且也因为她代表积极的一面——人类从肉体得到的快感——在很大程度上一直处于被压抑的状态(第 147 页；第 214 页)。

第五部分，"母道与父道"("Motherhood and Fatherhood")。同母亲相比，父亲在孩子幼小时所起的作用要小得多。如果父亲能像母亲一样参与孩子的幼年生活，他那男性的身体构成的现实对于成长中的孩子来说会更为坚实(第 150 页；第 216 页)。

第六部分，"可能性"("Possibilities")。如果打破女性对抚养孩子的垄断，女性将不再被视为肮脏的女神、替罪羊或是半人半兽的怪物(第 155 页；第 222 页)，女性也将不再同死亡联系在一起(第 156 页；第 223 页)，人类在性别关系上的痼疾也才有可能消除(第 156 页；第 223 页)。

本书选注的是该节的第四、五、六部分。

---

① 诺曼·奥立佛·布朗(1913～   )，美国社会理论家，曾在多所大学教授古典文学。使他闻名遐迩的两部代表作是《面对死亡的生活：历史的心理分析意义》(*Life Against Death*：*The Psychoanalytical Meaning of History*，1959 年)和《爱的身体》(*Love's Body*，1966 年)。访问 Ellen Myers，"Forerunner of New Age Madness：A Critique of Norman O. Brown"，http://www.creationism.org/csshs/v13n1p07.htm，n. p.。

The Dirty Goddess

[······]

Gender Arrangements and Ambivalence to the Flesh

To recapitulate: The dirty goddess is dirty not simply because the flesh that she represents is the vehicle-saboteur of our wishes, and because its meaning as hateful saboteur—split of from and thus unmodified by its meaning as lovely vehicle—makes our tie to it feel degrading. She is dirty also, more deeply dirty, for another reason: the positive side of what she embodies—our old joy in the flesh and the capacity we still have to feel the kind of contact with life that the flesh originally carried—has been largely suppressed. The side of what she embodies which, when it emerges, gives her real, radiant goddess status—the mystic carnal truth that underlies the biblical use of the verb "to know" and makes the nude body in art the most telling visual symbol of full human majesty—is not only dissociated, compartmentalized; it is also in large degree denied and discounted.

Our stubborn interest in this discounted carnal truth forces it back into consciousness, but in debased form. The love of the flesh that woman stands for thus includes (in varying degrees, of course, depending on personal and cultural differences) an ashamed love for something actively loathsome. The flesh carries this loathsomeness not because it humbles us with its hungers, reminds us of our tie to the earth, makes us fall asleep when we want to go on playing: these distresses are inherent in the flesh's beauty as a miraculous temporary organization of inorganic matter; our failure to integrate them with our sense of the flesh's beauty keeps our feeling for life shallow, but it is not what makes the flesh loathsome. What debases the flesh is our repression of our sense of the flesh's beauty so as to avoid the pain that this sense carries, and the return of the repressed in a form that includes our reproach to ourselves for failing to bury it altogether.

We are able to go on debasing the flesh in this way, and to live on without rebelling constructively against what we are doing to ourselves, only because woman is available for the dirty-goddess role, and man can thus be relatively exempt (an exemption that comforts her as well as him) from the baseness that she carries.

In sum, human ambivalence toward the body of woman arises from, and at the same time helps perpetuate, incompetence to reconcile our inevitable mix of feelings for the flesh itself. The unreconciled mix is projected onto the first parent. Worse still, much of the positive side of this ambivalence is suppressed and what has been suppressed is converted into an obscene preoccupation; this means that even the love that is part of the prevailing attitude toward woman's body is to some degree a dirty love. The shame that for many people tinges carnal attraction is made possible by, and at the same time deepens, woman's general human degradation.

Both this failure to integrate our feelings toward the flesh and this debasement of what is positive in these feelings express our helplessness to cope with carnality, a helplessness that has so far permeated the death-denying, and therefore death-dominated, life of our enterprising species. Woman's status as scapegoat-idol is maintained by, and at the same time works to maintain, this helplessness. And what keeps her available for this status is her child *rearing*, not her child *bearing*, contribution.

When the child, once born, is as much the responsibility of man as of woman, the early vicissitudes of the flesh—our handling of which lays the basis for our later handling of mortality—will bear no special relation to gender. Both sides of the double fact that we are born mortal and born of woman will then change their meaning.

That we are born mortal now gets its meaning from other grievances against the body, which develop before we discover that it was born and will therefore die, and which later melt together with this discovery into one global rage. For this rage woman, who both bore and raised the body, is at present the natural target. When these early grievances develop as much under male as under female auspices, when they can no longer be foisted off on the female and must be integrated instead, their character, and therefore the character with which they later endow the fact of mortality, will be cleaner, less necrophilic. When our love for the mortal flesh has learned to incorporate our hate for it, we will have learned to live without marching to meet death halfway.

That we are born of woman now gets its meaning from other features of our early relation with her, which take shape before we absorb the strange news that we came out of her belly. Woman's prenatal and postnatal parental contributions are at present so deeply fused together in our thinking that a grievance which in fact stems from the latter can seem connected to the former. When the early experience that later gives mortality its meaning has been discovered not solely in contact with the sex that turns out, amazingly, to have borne the child, but also in equally intimate contact with the sex that turns out to have played an equally amazing part in its conception, the special link between woman and death will dissolve. This link has depended on our child-care arrangements, not on the sheer abstract fact that those who are born die.

Motherhood and Fatherhood

Because pre- and postnatal mothering are now fused in our thinking, the former now has an exaggerated emotional weight for us, as compared with prenatal fathering (which normally includes not only the initial planting of seed but a long period of protective, expectant, imaginative waiting afterward). It is true that man's procreative role is less visible and tangible, and in a physical sense immeasurably less strenuous, than woman's. But it has for that very reason its own specific poignance. When males are as directly involved as females in the intensely carnal lives of infants and small children, the reality of the male body as a source of new creatures is bound to become substantial for us at an earlier age than it does now, and to remain emotionally more salient forever after.

I see no reason to doubt that woman's body, even after it is freed of its special tie to the conscious self-discovery of the mortal flesh, will still have a special post-hoc significance for us as the original nurturer of that flesh, as the heart that sent blood through it before it saw light. But this significance will be changed once the body, and therefore birth itself, no longer seems obscene. The change will not make woman's procreativity less miraculous than it is now, only less horrifying to the spirit that wants to assert its bright distinctness, its non-identity with mucus and blood; the spirit that at present still resonates to the image of Athena springing (fully formed and presumably dry) from the forehead of Zeus. And there will be another change as well: once fatherhood, like motherhood, means early physical intimacy, man's procreativity will seem in its own way as concretely miraculous, as fraught with everyday magic, as woman's. For man's body will carry for us as intense an emotional charge, a charge as pervaded with primitive pre-verbal feeling, as woman's.

We know very well already what this charge will be. We already recognize, though so far in principle only, the symmetry between man's peculiar procreative magic and woman's. Her breast, her hidden womb and the dark grotto that leads to it, are dramatic, in a sense sacred: powerful, yet vulnerable, violable. Her superfluous clitoris, vividly alive on its own, is uncannily moving. But so are his superfluous nipples strangely moving. His proud, vulnerable, untamable external genital is no more and no less dramatic than the belly it fertilizes and the breasts that need it to make them flow. And it is no more or less a sacred carnal truth, for his burst of fertile fluid is as powerful, and at the same time as vulnerable and violable, as the part of her that it bursts into: The fragility of his tie to the seed that he buries for so many months in the dark center of another, independent, body balances the fragility of her claim on him to help take responsibility for the child she carries. His life-extending biological link with the past and future rests with her. If he cares about this link, he can be betrayed, just as she can be betrayed if she relies on him to act as a parent to the child. But see Box I.

Box I

It is true that woman can betray man by carrying away in her body—or denying that it is his, or not knowing whose it is—the seed that he has to trust her to carry, and that if the bodily link with the dead and the still unborn which this seed represents is important to him, this betrayal can be as hurtful to him as his refusal to act as father to the child can be to her. But these two possibilities cannot really be regarded as evenly balanced unless additional, more subtle matters are taken into consideration as part of the balance.

The imbalance in an immediate sense is that, though both are vulnerable, his situation is by and large much easier to slip out of, psychologically, than hers is. The difference, of course, is that if lie betrays her it is because he is choosing not to be emotionally a parent on that particular occasion, while this is a choice that she, regardless of who does or does not betray whom, is less free to make. It is easier, in other words, for him to impregnate her and then dodge the emotional significance of fatherhood than it is for her to get pregnant and then dodge the emotional significance of motherhood. Even in cases (and these are still rare) in which she avails herself of freely accessible abortion and feels no conscious heaviness of heart, what she is refusing to let herself feel solemn about is a process that is going on in her own body, not in someone else's. And needless to say if she bears the child she can neither abandon it nor keep it without heavy, lasting personal consequences.

This is part of what underlies the problem that Margaret Mead considers in her wonderfully lucid essay Fatherhood Is a Social Invention," in *Male and Female*. That essay is oriented mainly to those social conditions (virtually universal in our species' past, and still in force for most humans now) in which the only reliable alternative to uncontrolled fertility is abstinence from copulation. But even under our own conditions, where parenthood is (relatively) optional, its emotional meaning remains in some irreducible way harder for woman to side-step than for man. Even if she is celibate, or homosexual, she is the one who bleeds every month, and this bleeding (with the uterine contractions and the swelling and tenderness of breasts that often go with it) is more directly tied to gestation and gestation only than any purely bodily experience of his can be. And if they do copulate it is of course she who—if precautions fail, or are not taken—can find herself pregnant. What this means is that so long as we continue to be live-bearing mammals, she has to be more callous than he does to escape experiencing the impact of parenthood. And experiencing this impact (whether we choose or refuse to be parents) means feeling through in a peculiarly primitive and intimate way what it is to be human: to be knowingly part, that is, of a process that started before we were born and continues after we die. Humanness itself, then, is in this particular sense more firmly forced on woman than on man.

But there is another sense (and here it is she, not he, whose link with the past and future is in greater danger of being stunted or mutilated) in which humanness is more firmly forced on him than on her: If he *does* allow himself to feel the impact of parenthood, he (since he does so under less direct, bodily, duress) is more surely bound than she is to recognize that he has done so voluntarily.

An anthropologist once told me about a talk with a Puerto Rican cane cutter whose young manhood was being poured into grueling labor to keep his family alive. He thought, this trapped father said, about just taking off; but he did not do it: "I'd miss the kids" was his rueful explanation. He and the anthropologist then shared a sentimental moment of feeling what it is like to be male and human. The kids' mother, I assume (it is implied in the way he explained himself: not that they would die but that he would miss them), never dreamed of taking off. Women sometimes do, but not often: as *they* are apt, ruefully, to remind each other, when a creature has spent nine months inside your body, it is possible, but more difficult, to consider leaving it to starve. Life, then, neither left her so free as her man was to toy with inhumanity nor pushed her so hard into clear awareness that on balance she chose—preferred—to be human. Again, a symmetry of differentness.

But it should be added that the difference between these two parents was enhanced by the fact that she had not only borne, but also spent more time afterward in intimate contact with, the children. The more contact the father has, and the more helpless his attachment to them becomes, the smaller this difference becomes. It is not, then, only the attractiveness of the young (which male baboons, for instance, also seem strongly to feel) that makes men want more contact with babies. It is also their need to share the opportunity this contact offers for consolidating one's *involuntary*, un-thought-out, humanness.

Conversely, women also wish, from their direction, to reduce this difference. They need to share the opportunity for developing the *voluntary*, conscious side of the humanness that parenthood carries: this (together with the more often expressed feeling that control over one's body, to the full extent that existing technology makes such control possible, is a basic human right) is what makes women want safer, less troublesome birth control, and free—that is, unquestioned, dignified, respected, as well as economically non-punitive—access to abortion. It is also what makes them want child-care arrangements that let the time they spend with their children feel as optional to them as it does to men.

Such changes would surely not erase all difference between male and female parenthood. But there is no reason to want such erasure: the bodily contrasts between the sexes, and many of the ramifications of these contrasts, are a source of joy that we do not need to give up to achieve what is essential in the project of sexual liberty. All we need to make sure of—and this is a matter of social inventiveness, not of renouncing cherished features of our physique—is that what is the *same* in men and women can be freely and fully lived out by both. What they share is a capacity for the kind of intelligence, imagination, and will that draws on many layers of sentience at once; the capacity to be abstractly reasonable and at the same time intuitively empathic; the capacity, in other words, to contribute to the self-maintenance and self-creation of human life in two ways that interpenetrate only as they can be contained within a single personality: on the one hand planfully, deliberately, and on the other hand involuntarily, inarticulately.

We are aware of this potential emotional balance, but we do not live by it. If we did, woman would seem no dirtier and no more sacred than man, man no more a human authority than woman. The sexes would be drawn to

each other's bodies, and respect each other's personalities, symmetrically. ①
Women would be overtly, not secretly and half-contemptuously, protective
of what is vulnerable in men. And men would protect what is vulnerable in
women in a spirit of mutuality, not of condescension, since they would be
conscious of, and unashamed of, needing the protection they were getting
from women.

Possibilities

It is true, then, that we are born mortal and born of woman. But it is
also true that we are born ignorant of both these facts. What we make of
each of them, and of the connection between them, depends on what
happens before we discover them. Woman is now the focus for our
ambivalence to the flesh not because she gives birth to it but because she is
in charge of it after it is born. This mutable fact is by far the more important
one, for it impinges upon our awareness at an earlier, less rational, more
impressionable stage of development, and we are coping with it long before
we can learn, or even wonder, where babies come from.

When woman's lone dominion over the early flesh is abolished, she will
no longer be peculiarly available as a dirty goddess, a scapegoat-idol, a
quasi-human being toward whom we have no obligation to make the painful
effort to see her steadily and see her whole. Once we give up this easy way
out, we will have to try to reconcile, and live out more directly, the mixed
feelings about carnality which we now handle in a split-off, life-denying way.
This in turn will help force us to come to more conscious terms with death.
Not only the meaning of death, but death's relation to birth, and the
meaning of birth itself, will change. Because of our increased early contact
with him, man's procreative role will become real for us sooner, and
therefore more deeply, than it does now. That rounded complementarity of
the male and the female in the production of children toward which we have
all along been groping—a complementarity resting on mutual awareness of
feeling that only an imaginative, reflective, purposefully pro-creative species

could want to achieve—will start coming into stable focus for us. Woman and man will start at last stably to share the credit, and stably to share the blame, for spawning mortal flesh. ②

For our sexual arrangements, the main point here is that we become aware both of mortality and of birth against a prior emotional background whose nature bears crucially upon their impact; and that woman's role in this background, and therefore the meaning-link between mortality and the maternal flesh, is now open to radical change.

For human malaise, the main point is that when this change has been achieved, we may find ourselves able to free the potentially pure human joy in exercising competence, exerting will power, making things happen, from the joyless, corrupting burden of carnal denial that it now carries. We may find out how to handle the memory of the first separation without rejecting the opportunities for direct, effortless erotic flow between the self and the environment that life continues, episodically, to offer; and how to handle the prospect of the final separation without despising the body's simple wishes, without robbing the body of the poignant, cherished status that rightly belongs to loved and perishable things. We cannot be sure that we will be able to do this. But we can be sure that we will remain *unable* to do it until children's first efforts to cope with the irreducible isolation of individual existence, their first steps toward independent enterprise, their first discovery of the mixed blessings of carnality, are felt through as intimately in relations with male as with female adults. At that point, we will have a chance.

Notes:

① De Beauvoir is eloquent about the special magic of female flesh, and as she describes it this magic seems an inevitable aspect of our situation as self-aware mammals. But in fact it is inevitable only to the extent that our greater early intimacy with woman makes her body more significant to us than man's is. And it is from this fact that our more intense and ambivalent awe of her procreativity follows. We put more energy, under present conditions, into imagining just what it takes less energy to imagine. Our genesis in her loins preoccupies us more passionately than our genesis in his because her body has mattered to us more than his since long before the question of genesis could occur to us. And so the more strenuous leap of imagination that is needed to take emotional hold of our bodily link with him is just the leap for which early childhood has prepared us less well.

Yet this is a leap that we badly want to make: Since we, unlike other creatures, are able to know intellectually that the procreative link between fathers and children exists, the felt abstractness of the link is painful to us: Its emotional inaccessibility makes us suffer. Its unsubstantiality drives men to unsatisfying and therefore escalating compensatory measures, and makes them seem, to each other and to women, in a certain animal sense nearly reachable yet always out of reach.

This is a dilemma that exists only because we are intellectually complex enough to experience it; and we arrived at this complexity, as a species, as an adaptation to an environment that our own inventiveness was cumulatively creating. So it is a dilemma that our own inventiveness is called upon to solve.

② This changed meaning of femaleness and maleness will of course extend then, as the meaning of gender extends now, to people who do not in fact spawn flesh. People's bodies have procreatively tinged significance for us mainly because we all *had* parents, not because we all *are* parents.

13 玛丽安·赫什,"母亲与女儿" Marianne Hirsch, "Mothers and Daughters"

1989 年出版的《母亲/女儿合谋》使玛丽安·赫什(Marianne Hirsch)①声名鹊起,引起批评界的注意,她后来撰写的女性主义著作,尤其是对于母亲和女儿关系的研究,已经扎实地奠定了她在女性主义研究领域的地位。

赫什于 1975 年在布朗大学荣获比较文学博士学位。现任达特默思学院(Dartmouth College)法语和意大利语教授,比较文学系系主任。她的主要女性主义著作有:

《母亲/女儿合谋:叙事、心理分析与女性主义》(*The Mother/Daughter Plot*: *Narrative*, *Psychoanalysis*, *Feminism*, 1989 年)

《女性主义的冲突》(*Conflicts in Feminism*, 1990 年,与伊芙琳·福克斯·凯勒②合著)。该书针对女性主义的冲突提出了一些崭新的策略,试图协调女性主义理论的千差万别,追溯差异的根源,并倡导建立有建设性意义的差异话语模式。

《家庭框架:摄影、叙事与后记忆》(*Family Frames*: *Photography*, *Narrative and Postmemory*, 1997 年)

《家庭注视》(*The Familial Gaze*, 1998 年)

---

① 照片取自 http://www.dartmouth.edu/~jewish/faculty/hirsch.html。

② 伊芙琳·福克斯·凯勒(Evelyn Fox Keller)在加利福尼亚大学伯克利分校的修辞与女性研究系任教。她还著有《关于性别和科学的思考》(*Reflections on Gender and Science*)以及诺贝尔奖获得者麦克林托克(B. McLintock)的传记《感受机体》(*A Feeling for the Organism*,又译《情有独钟》)。

本书选注的"母亲与女儿"一文刊载于《符号：文化与社会中的女性》（*Signs：Journal of Women in Culture and Society*）杂志 1981 年第 1 期（总第 7 卷）。文章对多数女性主义者共同默认的女性性征和母职的认识提出质疑。作者认为，女性主义的许多理论仍然被男性理论家的话语所束缚，用这样的话语描述出的女性存在与女性经验从本质上说仍然是男性理论的反映，也因此很难逃脱男性的视角。

该文除引言外分五个部分。

在引言中，赫什指出是里奇①首先于 1976 年明确指出母女关系是沉默的。此后的几年间有许多文章问世，讨论母亲与女儿的关系。赫什告诉我们，她的这篇文章目的在于揭示评论界为什么会突然关注母女关系，并描述人们关注焦点的走向。

在文章第一部分，赫什首先指出，里奇在《生于女性》一书中表述的观点——母职是父权体制下的一个体制，女性经验被男性期待所塑造，而没有被女性自己所记录——毫无疑问是具革命性的②。赫什继而把注意力集中在里奇著作中题为母亲身份和女儿身份的章节，援引里奇著作最为核心的思想："母亲失去女儿，女儿失去母亲，这是女性最为根本的悲剧"（第 202 页；第 231 页）。里奇还曾指出，每一位女性都将参与母职的经验和体制，她迟早都会身兼母亲和女儿两种身份（第 202 页；第 231 页）。通过分析赫什发现，对于母亲与女儿关系的研究一定是跨学科的，它不仅仅是女性研究的课题，而且还需要社会学、人类学、宗教学、历史、哲学、心理学和文学批评等学科的相关知识（第 202 ~ 203 页；第 232 ~ 233 页）。其中，女性主义精神分析学说对诠释母女关系做出了特别的贡献。

在文章第二部分，赫什描述了女性主义精神分析学说在诠释母女关系上呈现的三个趋势。第一个趋势以多萝西·迪纳斯坦③所著《美人鱼与弥诺陶洛斯怪物：性别分工与人类痼疾》、南希·乔德罗所著《母性角色的再生：精神分析与

---

① 亚德里安·里奇，美国女性主义理论家，诗人。参见本书第一篇第 2 节。

② Marianne Hirsch，"Mothers and Daughters"，*Signs：Journal of Women in Culture and Society* 7.1（1981）：p. 201. 本节所引该文观点均出于此处，以下只在正文标明页码，分号后第二个页码为引文在本书的页码。

③ 多萝西·迪纳斯坦，美国著名女性主义理论家。代表作《美人鱼与弥诺陶洛斯怪物》出版于 1976 年。参见本书第二篇第 12 节。

性别的社会学》(*The Reproduction of Mothering*：*Psychoanalysis and the Sociology of Gender*)、简·弗莱克斯(Jane Flax)①所著《母女关系和女性主义内部的抚育与自立之争》("The Conflict between Nurturance and Autonomy in Mother/Daughter Relationships and within Feminism")和让·贝克·米勒(Jean Baker Miller)②所著《走向女性的新心理》(*Toward a New Psychology of Women*)为代表,这些著作和学说直接引用弗洛伊德的俄狄浦斯关系模式来诠释母女关系(第204页;第234页)。作者一致认为,母亲较与女儿产生认同,把女儿看做自己生命的延续,而鼓励儿子成为独立的存在。她们把父母共同分担养育孩子的责任看做对父权律法的挑战,母性角色给女性的身份制造了混乱(第208页;第237页)。

第二个趋势的代表是诺·霍尔(Nor Hall)③所著《月亮与处女:对原型女性的思考》(*The Moon and the Virgin*：*Reflections on the Archetypal Feminine*)和其他一些以荣格的精神分析和原型理论以及埃里克·纽曼(Erich Neumann)④和卡尔·柯林伊(Carl Kerényi)⑤的原型理论为理论依据的文章与著作。由于这一趋势的理论基础较为个性化和个人化,尤其是在分析原型形象的时候,因此这一理论在做文学批评时更为有效(第209页;第239页)。

---

① 简·弗莱克斯,美国女性主义者,代表作《思考碎片——当代西方的心理分析、女性主义和后现代主义》(*Thinking Fragments—Psychoanalysis, Feminism, and Postmodernism in the Contemporary West*)出版于1991年。

② 让·贝克·米勒,美国女性主义者,代表作《走向女性的新心理》出版于1976年。她还创办了米勒培训学院(Jean Baker Miller Training Institute),致力于心理诊疗。

③ 诺·霍尔,美国心理诊疗师,诗人。代表作《月亮与处女:对原型女性的思考》出版于1981年。

④ 埃里克·纽曼,心理分析医生,荣格(C. G. Jung)的学生。代表作有《起源与意识的历史》(*The Origins and History of Consciousness*, 1954年)、《爱神与普绪克:女性的心理发展历程》(*Amor and Psyche*：*The Psychic Development of the Feminine*, 1971年)、《伟大的母亲:原型分析》(*The Great Mother*：*An Analysis of the Archetype*, 1972年)和《对女性的恐惧及其他女性心理札记》(*The Fear of the Feminine*：*And Other Essays on Feminine Psychology*, 1994年)。

⑤ 卡尔·柯林伊(1897~1973),是对希腊神话进行现代研究的先驱者之一,出生在匈牙利,后入籍瑞士。他是荣格的朋友和长期合作者。代表作《依洛西斯:母亲与女儿的原型形象》(*Eleusis*：*Archetypal Image of Mother and Daughter*)首先以德语出版于1960年。依洛西斯是古希腊的一座城市名。古希腊每年在这座城市举行秘密的宗教仪式,祭祀谷物和繁殖女神得墨忒耳(Demeter)和女儿珀尔塞福涅(Persephone)。

第三个趋势主要体现在一些法国女性主义理论家的著述中,尤其是伊里加蕾①、西克苏②和克里斯蒂娃③的著作,她们的理论都以雅克·拉康(Jacques Lacan)的思想为基础。伊里加蕾认为,女性间的关系既不是相同性的关系,也不是差异性的关系,而是相互漠视/差异间(in-difference)的关系(第 209~210 页;第 239 页)。她认同女性身份的相互渗透。克里斯蒂娃认为,女儿对母亲的仇恨奠定了父权政治秩序的基础(第 211 页;第 240 页)。西克苏则主张用母亲的乳汁书写才能表达女性的特殊经验(第 211 页;第 240~241 页)。

赫什在分析了三个趋势各自不同的主张所基于的理论基础之后说,虽然这些趋势的方法和话语截然不同,但在分析女性身份的问题上,她们却有着惊人的认同:前俄狄浦斯阶段母亲和女儿之间的关系决定了女性的存在具有延续、复数、变化的特征(第 211 页;第 241 页)。

在文章第三部分,赫什以南茜·弗莱蒂(Nancy Friday)④的《我的母亲/我自己:女儿寻找身份的历程》、希纳·哈默(Signe Hammer)⑤的《女儿与母亲:母亲与女儿》以及朱迪斯·阿卡纳(Judith Arcana)⑥的《母亲的女儿》为例探讨理论如何应用于女性的个人经验。

赫什在文章的第四部分讨论女性主义理论与个人经验的冲突在文学作品中如何得以表现。她以许多文学作品为例追溯了母亲与女儿的关系在文学作品中的描写是如何发展变化的。在 19 世纪的许多作品中,母亲是缺席的(第 215~216 页)。到了 20 世纪初,虽然有一些作品塑造了强势的母亲形象,但却并没有削弱女儿的形象(第 216 页)。而到了 20 世纪中叶,母女关系的描写趋向多元

---

① 露丝·伊里加蕾,法国女性主义理论家。参见本书第二篇第 9 节。
② 伊莲娜·西克苏,法国女性主义理论家。参见本书第二篇第 8 节。
③ 朱丽娅·克里斯蒂娃,法国女性主义理论家。参见本书第二篇第 7 节。
④ 南茜·弗莱蒂,作家、女性主义者。代表作《我的母亲/我自己:女儿寻找身份的历程》出版于 1977 年。有关弗莱蒂资料,访问其个人网站 http://www. nancyfriday.com。
⑤ 希纳·哈默,作家、编辑、社会活动家、女性主义理论家。代表作《女儿与母亲:母亲与女儿》出版于 1975 年。有关哈默资料,访问其个人网站 http://signehammer.com。
⑥ 朱迪斯·阿卡纳,诗人、教育家、女性主义理论家,曾在英美多所大学任教,创建位于华盛顿特区的联合学院妇女研究中心并出任第一位主任。她曾积极提倡合法堕胎,代表著作《母亲的女儿》出版于 1979 年。关于阿卡纳的著作与思想,访问 http://www. writersontheedge. org/arcana. html, n. p. 。

化,作家探讨不同的女性心理范式,女性之间的关系也成为许多作品主要情节背后的潜情节线索(第218页)。赫什总结说:"母女关系渐渐融合到更为广泛的对女性发展与经验所作的文学研究领域……我们已经充分认识到母女关系对女性文学至关重要"(第219页)。

在文章的第五部分,赫什通过详细分析萨拉·鲁迪克(Sara Ruddick)①的《母性的思考》和里奇的《强制异性恋与同性关系存在》两篇文章试图为我们预见母女关系的未来发展趋向。在赫什看来,鲁迪克的贡献是把母性视为一个社会概念,她设想的母亲角色将来由男性和女性共同承担,他们生活在同一个社区,具有母亲的思想,共同养育下一代(第220页;第242页)。里奇的文章提出了一个惊人的主张,作者认为女性之间的同性关系是女性力量与知识的来源,这是彻底颠覆父权体制的途径(第220页;第242页)。

赫什总结说,许多女性主义理论对表现女性经验具有重要意义,但同时也具有局限性。应该彻底打破思维模式,即超越父权神话和男性观察,发明全新的理论框架来表现男女关系和女性之间的关系(第221页;第244页)。在这方面,里奇提倡的建立女性之间同性关系的观点的确为在父权观念之外研究女性之间的关系提供了一种可能(第222页;第244页)。

本书选注的是该文的引言和第一、二、五部分。

Mothers and Daughters

In 1976 Adrienne Rich alerted us to the silence that has surrounded the most formative relationship in the life of every woman, the relationship between daughter and mother: "The cathexis between mother and daughter—essential, distorted, misused—is the great unwritten story. Probably there is nothing in human nature more resonant with charges than the flow of energy between two biologically alike bodies, one of which has lain in amniotic bliss

---

① 萨拉·鲁迪克,美国哲学家。代表作《母性的思考:走向和平的政治》(*Maternal Thinking: Towards a Politics of Peace*)出版于1989年,她还曾与哈尼伯格(E. Hanigsberg)和考德威尔(Amy Caldwell)合编《母亲的麻烦:对当代母亲困境的再思考》(*Mother Troubles: Rethinking the Contemporary Maternal Dilemmas*, 1999年)。

inside the other, one of which has labored to give birth to the other." ①
Since Rich demonstrated the absence of the mother-daughter relationship
from theology, art, sociology, and psychoanalysis, and its centrality in
women's lives, many voices have come to fill this gap, to create speech and
meaning where there has been silence and absence. In fact, the five years
since the publication of Rich's book have seen a proliferation of writings that
have both documented the relationship from its most personal resonances to
its most abstract implications and uncovered a variety of precedents for their
inquiry. Books, articles in scholarly journals, essays in popular magazines,
novels, poems and plays, films and television scenarios, discussion groups at
national and international conferences, and courses in universities, junior
colleges, and high schools throughout the country all attest to the dramatic
reversal of the silence Rich deplores. It is the purpose of this essay first to
account for this reversal and the subsequent centrality of the mother-daughter
relationship at this particular point in feminist scholarship and then to
delineate the range and direction of the work done in this area. Although I
shall concentrate primarily on major psychoanalytic and literary studies that
have appeared since Rich, I shall by necessity go back to some of their
conceptual and theoretical sources. ②

I

It seems appropriate to begin with Rich's extraordinary and
controversial book itself, *Of Woman Born: Motherhood as Experience and
Institution*, the first systematic study of the fact that "all human life on the
planet is born of woman. The one unifying, incontrovertible experience
shared by all women and men is that months-long period we spent unfolding
inside a woman's body... . Most of us first knew love and disappointment,
power and tenderness, in the person of a woman" (p. 11). Rich's analysis
of motherhood as an institution in patriarchy—a female experience that is
shaped by male expectations and structures, and virtually unrecorded by
women themselves to date—is revolutionary not only in its content but also in

its methodology: "It seemed to me impossible from the first to write a book of this kind without being often autobiographical, without often saying 'I'" (p. 15). Rich's voice, both personal and scholarly, resting on research in various academic fields, as well as on her own experience as a mother and a daughter, has helped create a novel form of feminist discourse which, I would like to argue, has freed scholars to consider extremely personal experiences as valid objects of scholarly inquiry.

Rich's chapter on "Motherhood and Daughterhood" is, as she says, "the core of my book" (p. 218). It contains, in fact, the germs of many of the other studies I shall mention in this essay. It is both an evocation of the desire that connects mother and daughter, of the knowledge they share, "a knowledge that is subliminal, subversive, pre-verbal: the knowledge flowing between two alike bodies, one of which has spent nine months inside the other" (p. 220), and an account of what Lynn Sukenick has called "matrophobia," the "desire to become purged once and for all of our mother's bondage, to become individuated and free" (p. 236). It traces a relationship "minimized and trivialized in the annals of patriarchy" (p. 236), as well as the close female bonds that seem nevertheless to have persisted. It deplores the silences surrounding this relationship: "The loss of the daughter to the mother, the mother to the daughter, is the essential female tragedy. We acknowledge Lear (father-daughter split), Hamlet (son and mother), and Oedipus (son and mother) as great embodiments of the human tragedy; but there is no, presently enduring recognition of mother-daughter passion and rapture" (p. 237). And it reminds us of the Eleusinian mysteries that celebrated the reunion of mother and daughter, the assertion of a maternal power that could "undo rape and bring her [daughter] back from the dead" (p. 240). Most important, Rich reminds us forcefully and persuasively of every woman's participation in the experience and institution of motherhood: "The 'childless woman' and the 'mother' are a false polarity, which has served the institutions both of motherhood and heterosexuality.... We are, none of us, 'either' mothers or daughters; to our amazement, confusion, and greater complexity, we are both" (pp. 250, 253).

In drawing on literature, theology, psychology, anthropology, myth, and history, Rich's book announces in both content and form the work that has followed on mother-daughter relationships. Its emergence at this particular moment can be explained by a glance at prevalent trends in feminist scholarship. There can be no systematic and theoretical study of women in patriarchal culture, there can be no theory of women's oppression, that does not take into account woman's role as a mother of daughters and as a daughter of mothers, that does not study female identity in relation to previous and subsequent generations of women, and that does not study that relationship in the wider context in which it takes place: the emotional, political, economic, and symbolic structures of family and society. Any full study of mother-daughter relationships, in whatever field, is by definition both feminist and interdisciplinary.

The study of mother-daughter relationships situates itself at the point where various disciplines become feminist studies, as well as at the point where the feminist areas of a number of disciplines intersect: sociology, where it concentrates on sex-role differentiation, where it attempts to distinguish between the individual and the roles she has to assume, and where those roles are studied in relation to their social determinants; anthropology, where it examines theories of matriarchy and their validity, matrilineal social organizations, matrilocal residence, and the effects of these different kinship structures on gender configurations and power distributions; religious studies, where it seeks evidence for a mother-goddess and attempts to develop a female-centered spirituality; history, where it examines the private stories of women's lives in journals, letters, and autobiographies that document family relationships; philosophy, where it challenges the dominant Western dualistic thought that banishes woman into the position of nature to man's culture, matter to man's spirit, emotion to man's reason, object to man's subject; [3] and psychology and literary criticism, where the focus is so specific and where the points of intersection are so numerous that they demand detailed analysis.

The most complete and complex work on mother-daughter relationships to date has been undertaken in the area of feminist psychoanalysis. As Juliet Mitchell has demonstrated, psychoanalysis is particularly useful to feminist scholarship in that it shows us "how we acquire our heritage of the ideas and laws of human society within the unconscious mind". ④ In spite of certain limitations to which I shall return, it helps us to understand how the laws underlying and underwriting patriarchy function within each of us, whether male or female, and how they affect our most intimate relationships. Moreover, feminist revisions of psychoanalytic texts allow us to appreciate the specificity of female, as distinguished from male, development and the effect of those differences on relationships among women.

Female writers' accounts of the mother-daughter bond are the most articulate and detailed expressions of its intimacy and distance, passion and violence, that we can find; they are the most personal and at the same time the most universal. Recent critical studies of works written by women have answered Rich's charge: the story of mother and daughter has indeed been written, although it is not often found on the surface but in the submerged depths of literary texts. The question now becomes the analysis of its intricacies and complexities, and especially of its influence on literary forms and structures. For as Mary Carruthers wrote in "Imagining Women: Notes toward a Feminist Poetic," "Language is the medium in which we carry our past, determine our present, and condition our future." ⑤

II

Three trends have emerged in recent feminist psychoanalytic works about mothers and daughters. Dorothy Dinnerstein's *The Mermaid and the Minotaur: Sexual Arrangements and the Human Malaise*, Nancy Chodorow's *The Reproduction of Mothering: Psychoanalysis and the Sociology of Gender*, Jane Flax's "The Conflict between Nurturance and Autonomy in Mother/Daughter Relationships and within Feminism," and

Jean Baker Miller's *Toward a New Psychology of Women* all draw, more or less directly, on the Freudian oedipal paradigm and on neo-Freudian theory, especially object-relations psychology. ⑥ A second trend is represented by Jungian studies; Nor Hall's *The Moon and the Virgin: Reflections on the Archetypal Feminine*—as well as a number of literary studies—draw on Jung, on Erich Neumann's *The Great Mother: An Analysis of the Archetype*, and on Carl Kerényi's *Eleusis: Archetypal Image of Mother and Daughter.* ⑦ A third trend emerges in the work of French feminist theory, in particular Luce Irigaray's *Et l'une ne bouge pas sans l'autre*, but also at crucial points in the writings of Julia Kristeva and Héléne Cixous; all are based in Jacques Lacan. ⑧

This brief and sketchy introduction already reveals the problem I perceive to be inherent in these analyses: at the source of each of these important and useful feminist theoretical studies we find not only a male theorist but a developed androcentric system, which, even if deconstructed and redefined, still remains a determining and limiting point of departure. I shall return to this criticism; first, however, it is useful to summarize these three trends and their points of intersection.

In his three late essays on female sexuality, Freud revises his equilateral theory of early individual development, and he stresses, for both boys and girls, the importance of the pre-oedipal attachment to the mother. ⑨ The significance for women of this pre-oedipal phase and of the resultant bond to the mother had for Freud the surprise that archaeologists experienced when they discovered the Minoan-Mycenaean civilizations behind the Greek. All three of his essays revolve around the central mystery of female development—the source of a girl's transfer of attachment to her father. Freud himself admits that his numerous theoretical explanations (mostly based in the girl's supposed hostility for having been deprived of a penis) are not ultimately satisfying. His admission clearly disproves the perceived notion that Freud outlines the Electra complex; in fact, he rejects the term, even while insisting, as best he can, on the idea of natural heterosexuality. Boys experience only rivalry with the same-sex parent; threatened with castration, they resolve the oedipal conflict very rapidly. Girls, in contrast, feel ambivalent toward the mother who is both rival and object of desire. In fact, Freud emphasizes that the pre-oedipal attachment to the mother is never totally superseded by the desire for the father; neither is the oedipal rejection of the mother ever overcome. This ambivalent relationship dominates a woman's entire life, especially her relationship with her husband or lover.

Dinnerstein, Chodorow, and Flax take as their starting points the formative importance of the pre-oedipal period and the female parent's domination of that period for both sons and daughters. In studying the consequences of exclusive parenting by women for adult personality and for the gender configurations of our culture generally, Chodorow and Flax rely not so much directly on Freud but on the work of object-relations psychologists, in whose theory the pre-oedipal period is seen not as a stage through which infants progress instinctually (drive or *Trieb* theory), but as an interpersonal field of relationships internalized by the infant and therefore configurative in the adult personality. ⑩ The mother thus remains an important inner object throughout adult life. Chodorow and Flax find that this interpersonal field functions differently for male and female infants: mothers identify more strongly with female infants seeing them more as extensions of themselves, whereas they encourage boys to become separate and autonomous. Ego boundaries between mothers and daughters are more fluid, more undefined. The girl is less encouraged to be autonomous, but she is also less nurtured, since the mother projects upon her daughter her own ambivalence about being female in patriarchal culture. Chodorow finds in these dissatisfactions the source of the "reproduction of mothering"—a woman becomes a mother in order to regain a sense of being mothered and in order to compensate for a heterosexual relationship with a man who values separation while she values connection and continuity. In her relationship with her daughter, a mother works out her unresolved relationship to her own mother. Differences in adult male and female personality are based, according to Chodorow, Flax, and Dinnerstein, on the different interpersonal configuration that occurs in the pre-oedipal phase:

> *Feminine personality comes to be based less on repression of inner objects, and fixed and firm splits in the ego, and more on retention and continuity of external relationships. From the retention of pre-Oedipal attachments to their mother, growing girls come to define themselves as continuous with others; their experience of self contains more flexible and permeable ego boundaries. Boys come to define themselves as more separate and distinct, with a greater sense of rigid ego boundaries and differentiations. The basic feminine sense of self is connected to the world, the basic masculine sense of self is separate.* [11]

Chodorow's and Flax's conclusions about the continuity and the lack of separation or differentiation between mother and daughter has tremendous implications for anyone studying female identity. In *Toward a New Psychology of Women*, Jean Baker Miller concurs: "Women's sense of self becomes very much organized around being able to make and then to maintain affiliations and relationships"; her term "affiliation," of course, points to the connections between the relation to mother and all subsequent interpersonal relationships in a woman's life. [12] Dinnerstein's view of these pre-oedipal differences and of exclusive female parenting provides us with the most far-reaching analysis to date of the sources of woman's exclusion from history, of her own collusion in the perpetuation of patriarchy. She convincingly argues that woman is the "other" only because she is the "mother," that patriarchy itself is a reaction against female dominion in infancy. Maternal omnipotence is so great a threat that we are willing to acquiesce to male rule in adulthood; even to women, paternal authority looks like a reasonable refuge.

In a recent article, "The Bonds of Love: Rational Violence and Erotic Domination," Jessica Benjamin interprets the same fundamental asymmetry we all experience in early infancy differently; yet her conclusions are, in fact, quite similar to Dinnerstein's. [13] According to Benjamin, "Selfhood is defined negatively as separateness from others" (p. 148). Because of the ways boys and girls relate to and differentiate from their mothers, they grow up to play different roles in the relationships of submission and domination, object and subject. We all seem to need these oppositions in order to perpetuate a "false" sense of differentiation. As a result of the "false" differentiation we all choose instead of equality, "a whole, in tension between negation and recognition, affirming singularity and connectedness, continuity and discontinuity at once" (p. 161), our culture is dominated by a form of rational violence that is the basis of sadomasochism. "The male posture ... prepares for the role of master.... The female posture disposes the woman to accept objectification and control .... He asserts individual selfhood, while she relinquishes it" (p. 167). Benjamin and Dinnerstein both demonstrate the disastrous, the lethal effects of the asymmetry of the pre-oedipal period.

Chodorow and Dinnerstein perceive shared parenting in early infancy as the most important challenge to patriarchal rule, as the only way to balance the severely skewed "sexual arrangements" in which we live now, the only way to make us "fully human" (Dinnerstein's term). Shared child rearing, in Dinnerstein's rather global vision, will lead us to conquer the ambivalence we now feel toward carnal mortality, toward self-creation and autonomy, toward treating others as sentient beings, toward growing up and becoming adults. As all these writers point out so convincingly, women, like men, need the nurturance that will allow them to become creative, productive adults, and as long as mothers carry the burden of child rearing alone, they will not be able to nurture and support their daughters in their struggle for self-realization: the maternal role creates too much ambivalence about their own and their daughters' female identity. Although these writers disagree about the details of the interaction between mother and child (where Dinnerstein talks of the mother's power, for example, Benjamin perceives her weakness and frailty), the bases of their arguments as well as their conclusions are quite similar.

Since the publication of their books, Chodorow and Dinnerstein have received criticism from many sides, much of it in the pages of this journal, most of it centering on the limitations of the psychoanalytic paradigm on which their theory rests. ⑭ Yet it is important to perceive the far-reaching implications of their work, as well as that of Flax and Benjamin; it is important to recognize the significance of a theory that links the most private family structures to social, economic, and political structures, a theory that treats women's mothering as a "social structure which affects all other structures." ⑮ Because of its wide scope, this psychoanalytic work is as pertinent to scholars in the humanities as to social scientists; it is interdisciplinary in the fullest sense. Even though I have reservations about aspects of this work, my training as a literary critic makes me particularly sensitive to a usefulness in it that I shall shortly demonstrate.

The points of intersection between the Chodorow-Flax-Dinnerstein model of mother-daughter relationships and the model created by Jung-Kerényi-Neumann in their studies of the archetype of the Great Mother, Eleusinian archaeological evidence, and other maternal or female symbolism are most illuminating. All stress the continuity between mother and daughter. Demeter and Kore are merely two sides of woman, the mother and the maiden. As Jung says, "Every mother contains her daughter within herself, and every daughter her mother.... Every woman extends backwards into her mother and forwards into her daughter. This participation and intermingling gives rise to that peculiar uncertainty as regards *time*: a woman lives earlier as a mother, later as a daughter. The conscious experience of these ties produces the feeling that her life is spread out over generations." ⑯ Nor Hall's recent book *The Moon and the Virgin*, a "quest for origins" that begins with the Mother, with the preconscious matriarchal phase in order to "remember ... the mother-daughter body," proposes thereby to "cure the void felt these days by women—and men—who feel that their feminine nature, like Persephone, has gone to hell." ⑰ Again it is a question of reaching a balance or of correcting an asymmetry. However, because the Jungian approach to mother-daughter relationships is highly individualistic, particularly in its analysis of symbols and archetypes, it seems at this point to have more resonance in literary analysis than in critiques of social structures.

Even more illuminating are new points of intersection between French and American psychoanalysis, two traditions that have come more and more to be seen as divergent. In Luce Irigaray's "And the One Doesn't Stir without the Other" (*Et l'une ne bouge pas sans l'autre*), we find a similar insistence on the ultimate lack of separation between daughter and mother and an emphasis on multiplicity, plurality, and continuity of being. It is important to situate this short, lyrical address in the context of Irigaray's work, until recently a dense, heavily abstract deconstruction of Western philosophy from Plato to Freud and Lacan. As Carolyn Burke shows, it is only in the last section of *This Sex Which Is Not One*, entitled "When Our Lips Speak Together," that Irigaray begins to explore a different discourse, a "parler-femme," a "female-centered signification" that could express women's speech to each other. [18] Relationships between women are neither relationships of sameness nor of difference, but of in-difference. [19] This new language and syntax must reflect the mutuality and interdependence of female being(s): therefore Irigaray insists on using the double pronoun "You/I" ("toi/moi"). "And the One Doesn't Stir without the Other" is Irigaray's first full work in this new, exploratory, and experimental mode. Desperately trying to untangle herself from within her mother and her mother from within herself, Irigaray comes to acknowledge and to accept the interpenetration that characterizes female identity.

Although this short text is the only French theoretical work directly concerned with the mother-daughter relationship, this relationship surfaces at crucial points in much current French feminist writing. Irigaray's project, based in part on Lacan and Jacques Derrida, is an attack on phallogocentrism and aims, like the work of Julia Kristeva and Hélène Cixous, to deconstruct what she so aptly calls "that sameness in which for centuries we have been the other", and to define the specificity of the female experience, which is to be found in the silences and absences, in all that our culture has repressed and suppressed. ⑳ The mother-daughter relationship is crucial in this process of exploration and definition. For Julia Kristeva, the repressed space—not exclusively female, but also to be found in the breaks that occur in avant-garde writing—is called "the semiotic" (*le sémiotique*) and is opposed to the symbolic-logic, logos, Name-of-the-Father. The semiotic is pre-oedipal, chronologically anterior to syntax, a cry, the gesture of a child. In adult discourse it is rhythm, prosody, pun, non-sense, laugh. ㉑ It is a break in the paternal order and woman, in large part because of her pre-oedipal relationship with her mother, has special access to it, at once privileged and dangerous. According to Kristeva, woman's access to the symbolic paternal order depends on her repression of her connection to her mother, her censoring of the woman within herself, her denial especially of maternal sexuality, or, as she calls it, maternal "jouissance". Woman in the symbolic order is the Virgin, impregnated by the Word. Woman has access to the semiotic through the functions of her body, pregnancy and childbirth. ㉒ Yet that access is dangerous, and Kristeva recalls the suicide of so many female writers: "For a woman, the call of the mother is not only a call beyond time, beyond the socio-political battle…. This call troubles the Word. It generates voices, madness, hallucinations. After the superego, the ego, that fragile envelope, founders and sinks. It is helpless to stave off the eruption of this conflict, this love which has bound the little girl to her mother and then lain in wait for her—black lava—all along the path of her desperate attempt to identify with the symbolic paternal order. " ㉓ Kristeva reminds us of Electra, her "father's daughter" whose hatred of her mother, and especially of her mother's "jouissance," is the basis of a larger order of the city and politics. The deconstruction of that larger symbolic order depends on the reunification of mother and daughter.

Cixous's excursus in "feminine" writing also emphasizes the mother-daughter bond. Her medium is white ink, or mother's milk, and in every woman, Cixous insists, "there is always more or less of 'the mother' who repairs and sustains and resists separation, a force that won't be severed. "㉔

The project in which all three of these writers are engaged, that of dismantling the sameness and unity of the symbolic order that has excluded woman, of creating a discourse of plurality, depends on a redefinition of the individual subject: it must be seen not as unified, integrated, whole, and autonomous, but as multiple, continuous, fluid, or, as Kristeva calls it, "in-process. " It is interesting that although American psychoanalysis is essentially based on ego psychology and French psychoanalysis insists on the explosion of the unified ego, they intersect where female identity is concerned; for woman the delimited, the autonomous, separated, individuated self does not exist (although much of our discourse still functions as if it did). In their analysis of female identity, Chodorow, Flax, Dinnerstein, and Miller, in spite of their radically different methodology and discourse, find themselves in surprising agreement with Irigaray, Kristeva, and Cixous. Woman's being, because of the quality of the pre-oedipal mother-daughter relationship, is, according to both traditions, continuous, plural, in-process: "And what I love in you, in myself, no longer takes place for us: the birth that is never completed, the body never created once for all time, the face and form never definitely finished, always still to be molded. The lips never open or closed upon one single truth. "㉕

[......]

V

It is not only in literary criticism that the study of mother-daughter relationships is being integrated into broader perspectives on female experience. Two recent essays will permit me to conclude with a comment on some new methodological directions and on some of the methodological and ideological divisions that surround all of this scholarship about mothers and daughters. Sara Ruddick's "Maternal Thinking" is an attempt to identify a "coherent and benign account of maternal power and influence." ㉖ "Maternal," for Ruddick, is a social and not a biological category: she concentrates on what mothers do rather than on what they are; thereby her essay enables us more fully than any other study to break out of biological necessities. Ruddick insists on a privileged identification between maternal and female; thus, even those of us who are not mothers think "maternally" because we are daughters. The aim of Ruddick's essay, based in the terminology of Habermas and other philosophical relativists, is to identify how mothers think and to bring that form of thought (thought which responds to the demands of preservation, growth, and acceptability) into the public eye and the public world. To do so is to insist that the characteristically "womanly" be valued, thus freeing women from the "ideology of womanhood [which] has been invented by men". ㉗ Ruddick's clear and straightforward exposition of the conceptual and emotional ways in which mothers approach their work frees motherhood and consequently mother-child relationships from mythic and psychoanalytic visions of maternal power and powerlessness that tend to obscure the more practical realities of the work involved in mothering. Ruddick looks forward to a world where children will be raised not by "parents" but by "mothers of both sexes who live out a transformed maternal thought in communities that share parental care". ㉘ Ruddick's extension of the term "mother" is a valuable breakthrough.

The second essay I want to mention here, Adrienne Rich's "Compulsory Heterosexuality and Lesbian Existence" is more explicit in criticizing recent feminist scholarship, which, she says, confirms and participates in the mystification it aims at attacking. Feminist psychoanalysis in particular, Rich maintains, fails to deal with lesbian existence as a reality and as a source of power and knowledge available to women. According to Rich, Miller writes "a new psychology of women" as if lesbians did not exist, and Dinnerstein emphasizes so strongly women's collusion in their own oppression that she is led to ignore all those women who have resisted and refused to internalize the "values of the colonizer". Rich's critique of Chodorow is more qualified because, she says, Chodorow "does come close to the edge of an acknowledgement of lesbian existence" by implying that women find heterosexual relationships "impoverishing and painful". Yet Rich insists that "mothering-by-women is [not] a sufficient cause of lesbian existence". [29]

Rich's own vision of compulsory heterosexuality as an institution enforced by physical violence and false consciousness calls many of our assumptions into question; she demonstrates rather convincingly that much of feminist scholarship is a part of that institution. Her accusation points out dissatisfactions and limitations fundamental to the research on mother-daughter relationships. Rooted so strongly in Freudian psychoanalysis, Chodorow's and Dinnerstein's theoretical framework makes it difficult for us to envision relationships between women outside of the context of patriarchal oppression, of competition between women for men, of male identification. Firmly based in the nuclear family, their framework makes it difficult for us to see and analyze the varieties of "families" in which children are raised today: adoptive families, single-parent families, lesbian and communal households, or multiple families in the case of shared custody. Despite their far-reaching and incisive analysis, despite their usefulness for literary critics, these works suffer from these limitations.

This debate within the feminist scholarly community is a serious one. It is important for us to be able to see and recognize ourselves and each other without the blinders imposed by the traditional paternal order. At the same time, it is important to foster whole and healthy relationships between women, between women and men, between men. As Nancy Chodorow says, "I think that children who live exclusively with women or men, gay or straight, need to be given every opportunity for developing ongoing close relationships with people of the opposite gender from that of their primary caretakers."[30] Although none of us can predict what a generation raised by "mothers of both sexes" will be like, Chodorow's and Dinnerstein's confidence that they will be "whole human beings," that changes in family structure will produce fundamental social changes, is our only hope.

I have found the work of Chodorow and Dinnerstein, Flax, Benjamin, and Ruddick, Irigaray and Kristeva useful in the most generous sense; I hope to have shown that I have also found it frustrating. The last five years have revolutionized our thinking but have also convinced me of the need to transform more radically the paradigms within which we think, to invent new theoretical frameworks that allow us, in our study of relationships between women, truly to go beyond patriarchal myths and perceptions. Rich suggests one such direction when she outlines the notion of a "lesbian continuum": "If we consider the possibility that all women—from the infant suckling her mother's breast, to the grown woman experiencing orgasmic sensations while suckling her own child, perhaps recalling her mother's milk-smell in her own; to two women like Virginia Woolf's Chloe and Olivia, who share a laboratory; to the woman dying at ninety touched and handled by women— exist on a lesbian continuum, we can see ourselves as moving in and out of this continuum, whether we identify ourselves as lesbian or not."③ This is one way to envision and to study the relationships between women outside of patriarchal conceptions, to approach perhaps the power and value they hold in themselves. There are other ways. Again Adrienne Rich has cut out our work for us.

Notes:

① Adrienne Rich, *Of Woman Born: Motherhood as Experience and Institution* (New York: W. W. Norton & Co. , 1976), p. 225.

② For an earlier review of some of this literature, see Judith Kegan Gardiner, "The New Motherhood," *North American Review* 263, no. 2 (Fall 1978): 72-76.

③ Jessie Bernard's important book *The Future of Motherhood* (New York: Dial Press, 1974) studies motherhood as a social institution, not as a fact of nature. It is a role that women learn, a role subject to certain cultural imperatives, and, at this point, a role that is being changed profoundly by factors such as women's increased participation in the labor force, an ever-decreasing birthrate, and the isolation of the nuclear family. Bernard studies, as well, the effects of all-female mothering on our society where it fosters a polarization of nurturance and power. On matriarchy, see J. J. Bachofen, *Myth, Religion and Mother-Right: Selected Writings*, trans. Ralph Manheim (Princeton, N. J.: Princeton University Press, 1967); and Robert Briffault, *The Mothers* (New York: Johnson Reprint Corp., 1969). See also Joan Bamberger, "The Myth of Matriarchy: Why Men Rule in Primitive Society," in *Woman, Culture, and Society*, ed. Michelle Zimbalist Rosaldo and Louise Lamphere (Stanford, Calif.: Stanford University Press, 1974), pp. 263-280; and Gayle Rubin, "The Traffic in Women: Notes on the Political Economy of Sex," in *Toward an Anthropology of Women*, ed. Rayna Rapp Reiter (New York: Monthly Review Press, 1975). In religious studies, see, e. g., Carol Christ and Judith Plaskow, eds., *Womanspirit Rising: A Feminist Reader in Religion* (New York: Harper & Row, 1979); Carol Christ. *Diving Deep and Surfacing: Women Writers on Spiritual Quest* (Boston: Beacon Press, 1980); and the critique by Rosemary Ruether, "A Religion for Women: Sources and Strategies," *Christianity and Crisis* 39, no. 19 (1979): 307-311. In history, see. e. g., Carroll Smith-Rosenberg, "The Female World of Love and Ritual: Relations between Women in Nineteenth-Century America," *Signs: Journal of Women in Culture and Society* 1, no. 1 (Autumn 1975): 1-29; Gerda Lerner, ed., *The Female Experience: An American Documentary* (Indianapolis: Bobbs-Merrill Co., 1977); and Mary Kelley, "Peculiar Circumstances: Literary Domesticity in Nineteenth-Century America" (Hanover, N. H.: Department of History, Dartmouth College). On woman as the "other," see Dorothy Dinnerstein, *The Mermaid and the Minotaur: Sexual Arrangements and the Human Malaise* (New York: Harper & Row, 1976); and Simone de Beauvoir, *The Second Sex*, trans. and ed. H. M. Parshley (New York: Alfred Knopf & Sons, 1953).

④ Juliet Mitchell, *Psychoanalysis and Feminism* (New York: Random

House, 1975), p. xiv.

⑤ Mary Carruthers, "Imagining Women: Notes toward a Feminist Poetic," *Massachusetts Review* 20 (1979): 281-307. Carruthers analyzes three main themes in women's poetry in the 1960s and 1970s: the mother-daughter relationship, the tradition of romantic love, and the nature of the powerful woman.

⑥ Nancy Chodorow, *The Reproduction of Mothering: Psychoanalysis and the Sociology of Gender* (Berkeley and Los Angeles: University of California Press, 1978). See also Chodorow's earlier essay, "Family Structure and Feminine Personality," in Rosaldo and Lamphere, eds., pp. 43-66, which includes a cross-cultural comparison of mother-daughter relationships that she unfortunately does not pursue in her book. Other essays by Chodorow include "Mothering, Object-Relations and the Female Oedipal Configuration," *Feminist Studies* 4, no. 1 (February 1978): 137-158, and "Feminism and Difference: Gender, Relation and Difference in Psychoanalytic Perspective," *Socialist Review* 46 (July-August 1979): 51-69, also reprinted in Hester Eisenstein and Alice Jardine, eds., *The Future of Difference* (Boston: G. K. Hall, 1980). See too Jane Flax, "The Conflict between Nurturance and Autonomy in Mother/Daughter Relationships and within Feminism," *Feminist Studies* 4, no. 1 (February 1978): 171-189. (This special issue of *Feminist Studies* is devoted to delineating "a feminist theory of motherhood". I shall mention some of the essays included in it.) See also Jane Flax, "Mother-Daughter Relationships: Psychodynamics, Politics and Philosophy," in Eisenstein and Jardine, eds.; Jean Baker Miller, *Toward a New Psychology of Women* (Boston: Beacon Press, 1976).

⑦ Nor Hall, *The Moon and the Virgin: Reflections on the Archetypal Feminine* (New York: Harper & Row, 1980); Erich Neumann, *The Great Mother: An Analysis of the Archetype*, trans. Ralph Manheim (Princeton, N. J.: Princeton University Press, 1955); and Carl Kerényi, *Eleusis: Archetypal Image of Mother and Daughter*, trans. Ralph Manheim (New York: Schocken Books, 1976).

⑧ Luce Irigaray's work, translated by Hélène Vivienne Wenzel and entitled "And the One Doesn't Stir without the Other," appears in *Signs*: *Journal of Women in Culture and Society* 7, no. 1 (Autumn 1981): 60-67. The original French version, *Et l'une ne bouge pas sans l'autre*, was published in Paris by Editions de Minuit in 1979.

⑨ These three essays—"Some Psychical Consequences of the Anatomical Distinction between the Sexes" (1924), "Female Sexuality" (1931), and "Femininity" (1931)—are conveniently reprinted in Jean Strouse, ed., *Women and Analysis* (New York: Dell Publishing Co., 1974).

⑩ See esp. D. W. Winnicott, "Mirror-Role of Mother and Family in Child Development," in *Playing and Reality* (New York: Basic Books, 1971); Margaret Mahler, Fred Pine, and Anni Bergman. *The Psychological Birth of the Human Infant* (New York: Basic Books, 1975); and W. R. D. Fairbairn, *An Object-Relations Theory of Personality* (New York: Basic Books, 1952).

⑪ Chodorow, *Reproduction of Mothering*, p. 169.

⑫ Miller, p. 83.

⑬ Jessica Benjamin, "The Bonds of Love: Rational Violence and Erotic Domination," *Feminist Studies* 6, no. 1 (Spring 1980): 144-174, also reprinted in Eisenstein and Jardine, eds. See also Benjamin, "The Oedipal Riddle: Authority, Autonomy, and the New Narcissism," in Kahn and Diggins, eds., *Authority in America: The Crisis of Legitimacy* (Philadelphia: Temple University Press, in press).

⑭ In an early essay, "Mothers and Daughters in the World of the Father," *Frontiers* 3, no. 2 (1978): 16-21, Marcia Westkott criticizes the "fatalism that informs the psychoanalytic mode Chodorow uses in her essays." This special issue of *Frontiers* is devoted to *Mothers and Daughters* and contains a number of informative essays, as well as poems, stories, and a play. See also Judith Lorber et al., "On *The Reproduction of Mothering*: A Methodological Debate," *Signs*: *Journal of Women in Culture and Society*

6, no. 3 (Spring 1981): 482-514; and Adrienne Rich, " Compulsory Heterosexuality and Lesbian Existence," *Signs: Journal of Women in Culture and Society* 5, no. 4 (Summer 1980): 631-660.

⑮ Chodorow, "On *The Reproduction of Mothering*," p. 501.

⑯ "The Psychological Aspects of the Kore," in Carl G. Jung and Carl Kerényi, *Essays on a Science of Mythology: The Myths of the Divine Child and the Mysteries of Eleusis* (Princeton, N. J.: Princeton University Press, 1969), p. 162.

⑰ Hall, pp. xvi, 68.

⑱ Luce Irigaray, "When Our Lips Speak Together," trans. Carolyn Burke, *Signs: Journal of Women in Culture and Society* 6, no. 1 (Autumn 1980): 69-79. This essay, "Quand nos lèvres se parlent," first appeared in *Ce sexe qui n'en est pas un* (Paris: Editions de Minuit, 1977).

⑲ Irigaray's use of *indifférence* and *indifférente* is a good example of her word play, as she shifts its meaning from "detached" to "nondifferent" or "undifferentiated"; see "When Our Lips Speak Together," p. 71n.

⑳ Ibid., p. 71. For an overview of this work, see Elaine Marks, "Women and Literature in France," *Signs: Journal of Women in Culture and Society* 3, no. 4 (Summer 1978) 832-842; Carolyn Burke, "Report from Paris: Women's Writing and the Women's Movement," *Signs: Journal of Women in Culture and Society* 3, no. 4 (Summer 1978): 843-855; Elaine Marks and Isabelle de Courtivron, eds., *New French Feminisms: An Anthology* (Amherst: University of Massachusetts Press, 1980), an anthology of these and other French theorist and writers; and Julia Kristeva, *Desire in Language: A Semiotic Approach to Literature and Art*, ed. Léon Roudiez (New York: Columbia University Press, 1981). See also Domna Stanton "Language and Revolution: The Franco-American Disconnection," and Jane Gallop and Carolyn Burke, "Psychoanalysis and Feminism in France," both in Eisenstein and Jardine, eds. My own sketchy summary cannot do justice to these extremely complex concepts.

㉑ Julia Kristeva, *Polylogue* (Paris: Seuil, 1977), p. 14. See also

"L'Herétique de L'amour," *Tel Quel* 74 (Winter 1977): 30-49.

㉒ Kristeva, *Polylogue*, p. 412.

㉓ Julia Kristeva, *About Chinese Women*, trans. Anita Barrows (New York: Urizen Books, 1977), p. 39.

㉔ Hélène Cixous, "Sorties," in *La Jeune Née*, by Catherine Clément and Hélène Cixous (Paris: Union Générale d'Editions, 1975), p. 172.

㉕ Irigaray, "When Our Lips Speak Together," p. 78.

㉖ Sara Ruddick, "Maternal Thinking," *Feminist Studies* 6, no. 2 (Summer 1980): 342-367.

㉗ Ibid., p. 345.

㉘ Ibid., p. 362.

㉙ Rich, "Compulsory Heterosexuality," pp. 634, 635, 636, 638.

㉚ Chodorow, "On *The Reproduction of Mothering*," p. 512.

㉛ Rich, "Compulsory Heterosexuality," p. 651.

14 苏珊·鲁宾·苏雷曼,"写作与母道"
Susan Rubin Suleiman, "Writing and Motherhood"

苏雷曼(Susan Rubin Suleiman)①是美国哈佛大学教授,教法国文明和比较文学。她兴趣广泛,研究的领域主要有文学、自传和电影。近年来她主要致力于关于记忆与犹太文化的研究。

她的主要著作包括:

《颠覆的意图:性别、政治与先锋派》(*Subversive Intent: Gender, Politics and the Avant-Garde*,哈佛大学出版社,1990年),该书探讨男性先锋派艺术家作品中的性关系和政治关系,被《纽约时报书评》称为"全面综合运用不同的女性主义理论解读广泛的文本,是这一方法令人震惊的一个范例"②。

《冒险:与当代艺术和文学面对面》(*Risking Who One Is: Encounters with Contemporary Art and Literature*,哈佛大学出版社,1994年)

《布达佩斯日记:寻找母亲之书》(*Budapest Diary: In Search of the Motherbook*,内布拉斯加大学出版社,1996年)

她还编著有:

《文本中的读者:论受众与解读》(*The Reader in the Text: Essays on*

---

① 关于作者简介,访问 http://www. fas. harvard. edu/ ~ rll/people/faculty/suleiman. html。作者照片来自 http://shc. stanford. edu/shc/1996-1997/96-97events/suleiman. html。

② 访问 http://www. hup. harvard. edu/reviews/SULSUB_R. html。

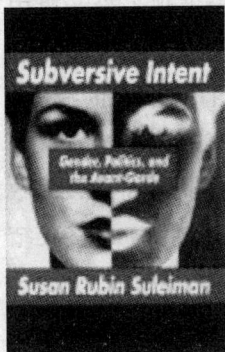

Audience and Interpretation，普林斯顿大学出版社，1980年）

《西方文化中的女性身体》(*The Female Body in Western Culture*，哈佛大学出版社，1986年）

《书写的生活：萨特、波伏娃与传记/自传》(*Writing Lives: Sartre, Beauvoir and (Auto) Biography*)

《流放与创造性：路标、游客、外来者与回顾的目光》(*Exile and Creativity: Signposts, Travelers, Outsiders, Backward Glances*，杜克大学出版社，1998年）

本书选编的"写作与母道"（"Writing and Motherhood"）选自由贾纳（Shirley Nelson Garner）、卡黑恩（Claire Kahane）和斯普林内德（Madelon Sprengnether）编辑的《他者/母亲的话语：女性精神分析解读文集》(*The (M) other Tongue: Essays in Feminist Psychoanalytic Interpretation*)，康乃尔大学出版社1985年出版。

该文除引言外被作者分为三个部分。

在引言中，苏雷曼告诉读者她将在本文中用自己的方式讲述写作与母道的关系。

第一部分，"母亲/写作：精神分析的解释"。苏雷曼从弗洛伊德的精神分析入手，详细阐述精神分析如何消音了母亲的话语。在弗洛伊德看来，女性成长的过程是由身体、生理决定了的，因而也是必然的①。母亲的形象与作用完完全全被她与孩子的关系联系起来（第355页）。苏雷曼在分析后断然得出结论说："母亲不书写，她们被书写"（第356页）。在剖析精神分析缘何不能允许母亲书写、也看不到母亲在试图书写的原因后，作者指责精神分析为母亲的沉默找到了冠冕堂皇的借口（第359页）。她说，精神分析已经凭借科学的优势建立了一个广泛的文化偏见，不断加强并使之最终成为一个"自然"的律法（第360页）。在这部分的最后，苏雷曼呼吁说，"该到了让母亲说说话的时候了"（第359页）。

---

① Susan Rubin Suleiman, "Writing and Motherhood," in Shirley Garner, Claire Kahane, and Madelon Sprengnether eds., *The (M) other Tongue: Essays in Feminist Psychoanalytic Interpretation* (Ithaca, NY: Cornell University Press, 1985), p.354. 本文所引该文观点均出自此书，以下只在正文标明页码，分号后第二个页码为引文在本书的页码。

第二部分,"写作与母道:母亲的视角"。苏雷曼在这部分展现了母亲眼中的书写是怎样的。她详细引用并分析了一些母亲作家的观点,进而观察说:"负罪感、绝望、自我分裂、疏离的角色扮演……成就甚微以及对自我书写的放弃"(第 361~362 页;第 254 页),这些构成了母亲作家生活的现实。就母亲作家的作品所表现的主题来讲,主要有两类:对立,即母道成为障碍和冲突的源泉;融和,即母道成为连接母亲与外面世界的纽带(第 362 页;第 255 页)。苏雷曼结合几位女性作家——菲里丝·契斯勒(Phyllis Chesler)①、亚德里安·里奇(Adrienne Rich)②和朱丽娅·克里斯蒂娃(Julia Kristeva)③——的观点对这两个倾向作了详细阐述。她最后指出,男性书写把女性书写置于边缘化的地位,使之成为权力关系中位于中心外(ex-centric)的现象(第 371 页;第 264 页)。她表示忧虑说:法国女性主义理论家试图规范女性书写,把女性书写定义为惟一的一种模式——以展现女性身体为中心,表现女性同自然的亲近,流动的书写特征,自然的基本韵律等等,这显然是错误的(第 371 页;第 265 页)。

第三部分,"写作与母道:母亲的小说"。苏雷曼在这部分探讨的是身为母亲的作家在作品中如何表现母道。她以美国诗人、小说家罗萨琳·布朗(Rosellen Brown)④的短篇小说《好管家》("Good Housekeeping")和长篇小说《我母亲的自传》(*The Autobiography of My Mother*)为例,展现了身为母亲的女作家布朗如何在作品中表现了母亲身份。相比之下,被誉为"母性小说家"

---

① 菲里丝·契斯勒,美国女性主义心理学家,主要论著有《女性与疯狂》(*Women and Madness*, 1972 年)、《与孩子相伴》(*With Child*, 1979 年)和《女性主义的死亡》(*The Death of Feminism*, 2005 年)。

② 亚德里安·里奇,美国女性主义理论家、诗人。参见本书第一篇第 2 节。

③ 朱丽娅·克里斯蒂娃,法国女性主义理论家。参见本书第二篇第 7 节。

④ 罗萨琳·布朗,美国当代诗人、小说家,在芝加哥艺术学院教书。主要作品有《我母亲的自传》(*The Autobiography of My Mother*)、《温柔的怜悯》(*Tender Mercies*)、《内战》(*Civil Wars*)、《从前与今后》(*Before and After*)、《半颗心》(*Half a Heart*)。她曾荣获欧·亨利短篇小说奖。

("the novelist of maternity") 的英国作家玛格丽特·德拉布尔 (Margaret Drabble) ① 作品中的母亲身份却总是同男人或孩子联系在一起 (第 377 页)。如果说布朗揭示了母道那梦魇般的现实,德拉布尔则展示了它理想的侧面 (第 377 页)。

本书选注的是该文的第二部分。

Writing and Motherhood

[⋯⋯]

Writing and Motherhood：As Mothers See It

The picture is not all rosy.

> *Try telling a child that Mamma is working, when the child can see with its own eyes that she is just sitting there writing.... I dare not have music on when I am in the basement, writing, lest upstairs they think I am just sitting here loafing. I feel that to be respected I must produce pancakes and homebaked bread and have neat, tidy rooms.* [*Liv Ullman*] ①

> *Since I had begun writing, I had sought time alone. That very self I had once sought to flee, ... that dangerous, frightening self was precisely what I had learned to treasure, what I had begun to understand.*
>
> *In order to tame [the dangerous self], I had to write, regularly and consistently, and in order to write I had to be alone.*
>
> *Now suddenly I was always with Benjamin.* [*Jane Lazarre*] ②

---

① 玛格丽特·德拉布尔 (1939 ~　　　),英国当代小说家。主要作品有《夏日鸟笼》(*A Summer Bird Cage*, 1964 年)、《磨盘》(*The Millstone*, 1966 年)、《金色的耶路撒冷》(*Jerusalem the Golden*, 1967 年)、《瀑布》(*The Waterfall*, 1969 年)、《针眼》(*The Needle's Eye*, 1972 年)、《黄金领地》(*The Realms of Gold*, 1975 年)、《冰河时代》(*The Ice Age*, 1977 年)、《天生的好奇心》(*A Natural Curiosity*, 1989 年)、《象牙门》(*The Gates of Ivory*, 1992 年)、《七姐妹》(*The Seven Sisters*, 2002 年)、《红皇后》(*The Red Queen*, 2004 年)。

For me, *poetry was where I lived as no-one's mother*, *where I existed as myself*. [*Adrienne Rich*] ③

I just started pecking away at this story set during the American Revolution. It wasn't anything I could get completely absorbed in. I had three boys at home, and there were always dishes to put in the dishwasher. [*Kathleen Woodiwiss*] ④

Children need one now. *The very fact that these are real needs, that one feels them as one's own (love, not duty); that there is no one else responsible for these needs, gives them primacy.... Work interrupted, deferred, relinquished, makes blockage—at best, lesser accomplishment*. [*Tillie Olsen*] ⑤

Every time I thought something would do, in the old days I'd race to the writing pad... and really be excited. Now I kept thinking: "*Oh no, I don't think that's very good.*" *Then one morning I woke up and I thought*: "*It's gone ... and I don't want it to come back.*" [*Susan Hill*] ⑥

Guilt, desperation, splitting of the self, alienated role playing ("My writing is not serious, don't be offended by it, just look at my three children"), resignation to lesser accomplishment, renunciation of the writing self—these are some of the realities, some of the possible choices that writing mothers live with.

Kathleen Woodiwiss is a rich woman, the author of historical romances for the "housewife market." Her last book has sold more than two million copies. She calls herself "an ordinary housewife": "I enjoy cooking and cleaning, my family and home. Right now my husband is remodeling one of the bathrooms." ⑦ She represents what some would call the perfect accommodation between writing and mother-wifehood. Perhaps she has no serious talent or ambition; perhaps she has never allowed herself to ask whether she does.

Susan Hill was a highly respected "younger" British novelist—for the cultivated reader, not the best-seller type. In her late thirties she married, and she became pregnant soon after. She was working on a novel at the time, but never finished it. She no longer writes fiction.

Between these two extremes, each of which is in its own way a renunciation of the writing self, are manifold ways of coping—some we know about because they have been written, others we can only guess at. We need to have more information—more interviews, more diaries, more memoirs, essays, reminiscences by writing mothers. I am sure I have missed many as it is, but exhaustiveness is not what I am aiming for. I wish merely to glimpse the possibilities, the principal recurrent themes in what some contemporary writing mothers have said discursively (poetry and fiction are a later question) about, or out of, their own experience of the relationship between writing and motherhood.

What are the major themes? I see them clustered into two large groups: opposition and integration, motherhood as obstacle or source of conflict and motherhood as link, as source of connection to work and world. The oppositional themes—guilt vs. love, mother's creative self vs. child's needs, isolation vs. commitment—are the ones I emphasized in the above quotations. The daily conflict and self-doubt, the waste of creative energies these oppositions engender cannot be overestimated. What is involved here, furthermore, is not simply an institutional or social problem; alternate nurturers will not necessarily relieve it (although they may eventually help) because the conflicts are *inside* the mother, they are part of her most fundamental experience. One can always argue, as Rich and others have done, that the internal conflicts are the result of institutional forces, the result of women's isolation, women's victimization by the motherhood myth in patriarchal society. But while this argument can help us understand *why* the conflicts are internal, it does not eliminate them. *At the present time*, any mother of young children (and I don't mean only infants, but children of school age and beyond) who wants to do serious creative work—with all that such work implies of the will to self-assertion, self-absorption, solitary grappling—must be prepared for the worst kind of struggle, which is the struggle against herself. Here I am reminded of Karen Horney's description of a certain type of neurotic disturbance in work—the disturbance she sees as typical of the "self-effacing type":

Without being aware of it, he is up against two kinds of chronic handicaps: his self-minimizing and his inefficiency in tackling the subject matter. His self-minimizing largely results... from his need to keep himself down in order not to trespass against the taboo on anything "presumptuous". It is a subtle undermining, berating, doubting, which saps the energies without his being aware of what he is doing to himself.... As a result he works with the oppressive feeling of impotence and insignificance.... His inefficiency in tackling the subject matter is caused mainly by taboos on all that implies assertion, aggression, mastery.... His difficulty is not in being unproductive. Good original ideas may emerge, but he is inhibited in taking hold of them, tackling them, grappling with them, wrestling with them, checking them, shaping them, organizing them. We are not usually aware of these mental operations as being assertive, aggressive moves, although the language indicates it; and we may realize this fact only when they are inhibited by a pervasive check on aggression. [8]

Mothers, or women, are of course not the only ones to whom Horney's description applies. [9] She herself obviously had both men and women in mind. But I would suggest that in the case of the writing mother, the subtle undermining, the oppressive feeling of impotence and insignificance, the pervasive check on aggression that Horney talks about are intimately linked to a sense of guilt about her child. Jean-Paul Sartre once said in an interview, when asked about the value of literature and of his own novels in particular: "En face d'un enfant qui meurt. *La Nausée* ne fait pas le poids" (freely translated: "When weighed against a dying child, *La Nausée* doesn't count"). [10] If this statement reflects the well-known guilt of the bourgeois writer with left-wing sympathies (Sartre being a specialist on *that* question),

— 256 —

what are we to say about the guilt of a mother who might weigh her books not against a stranger's dying child but merely against her own child who is crying?

One way to appease the crying child (and my contention is that whether or not the child actually cries while the mother writes, s/he always cries in the mother's nightmares) is to tender her/him the book as a propitiatory offering. Phyllis Chesler's *With Child*, a diary of her first pregnancy and childbirth at the age of 37, is dedicated to her son: "To my son Ariel, this handmade gift to welcome you." (I am a good mother, I make my own presents.) Liv Ullman's autobiography, from which I quoted above, is dedicated to her daughter, Linn, with a frontispiece photograph of mother and child forehead to forehead. The back cover is a close-up photo of Liv, somber, alone. The last pages are a letter to Linn—a series of self-reproaches by the mother, culminating in the astonishing question: "Do you understand that I really have no valid reason not to run out to you and live your life?" This from one of the most serious actresses of our time, who is also a genuine writer.

Another way to propitiate the crying child is not to write the book, or to write it less well than one could. "Almost no mothers—as almost no part-time, part-self persons—have created enduring literature … so far." That was Tillie Olsen writing, in 1972. ⑪

So much for the dark side. There is also a lighter one.

> *Through you, Ariel, I'm enlarged, connected to something larger than myself. Like falling in love, like ideological conversion, the connection makes me feel my existence.* [*Phyllis Chesler*] ⑫

> *And yet, somehow, something, call it Nature or that affirming fatalism of the human creature, makes me aware of the inevitable as already part of me, not to be contended against so much as brought to hear as an additional weapon*

against drift, stagnation and spiritual death. [*Adrienne Rich*] ⑬

A mother can be any sort of person, great or ordinary, given to moderation or intensity, inclined toward amazonian aggression or receptivity. But whatever type you are, being a mother forces you to accept your limitations. And when you accept your limitations as a mother, you begin to accept your limitations in other areas of life as well. The daily grinding friction of motherhood will give you the chance, at least, of relinquishing some of your egotism. You will finally cease to be a child. [*Jane Lazarre*] ⑭

... through the coming of the child and the beginning of a love, perhaps the only genuine feminine love for another ... one has the chance to accede to that relationship so difficult for a woman, the relationship to the Other: to the symbolic and the ethical. If pregnancy is a threshold between nature and culture, motherhood is a bridge between the singular and the ethical. . . . [*Julia Kristeva*] ⑮

What does it mean to love, for a woman? The same thing as to write. . . . WORD/FLESH. From one to the other, eternally, fragmented visions, metaphors of the invisible. [*Julia Kristeva*] ⑯

Integration, connection, reaching out; a defense against drift and spiritual death, a way of outgrowing the solipsism of childhood, a way to relate, a way to write—this too is motherhood as seen by mothers, often by the very same mothers who at other times feel torn apart by the conflicting pulls of work and child. Jane Lazarre, at the end of *The Mother Knot*, invents a debate between "the mother" and "the dark lady," the one urging Jane to have a second child, the other arguing against it. The dark lady says: "I am not speaking about mere details and practical responsibilities. It is the effect of those continuous demands on the spirit to which I commend your attention." The mother counters: "Don't you want the feeling of a baby moving inside you again?" But it turns out that the dark lady is the mother in disguise, the mother the dark lady. And Jane is both of them, they are inside her head.

Have we simply arrived here at the point where Adrienne Rich began? "My children cause me the most exquisite suffering of which I have any experience. It is the suffering of ambivalence: the murderous alternation between bitter resentment and raw-edged nerves, and blissful gratification and tenderness."[17] Yes and no. For Rich, as she expresses it in this diary entry, ambivalence is an *alternation* between resentment and tenderness, negation of the child and reaching out for the child—as if these two impulses were unconnected to each other, locked in an insurmountable opposition, corresponding perhaps to the opposition between the mother's need to affirm her self as writer and the child's need (or her belief in the child's need) for her selflessness. There is something of this struggle in Lazarre's parable, but the parable also suggests a possibility of reconciliation rather than conflict between the warring elements. If the mother is the dark lady and the dark lady the mother, then the energies and aspirations of the one are also those of the other. The mother's tenderness and the dark lady's urge for self-expression may support, not hinder, each other.

This is precisely what is implied by Chesler, by Rich in another diary entry (the one I quoted above), and especially by Kristeva, who goes beyond implication to explicit statement: "Far from being in contradiction with creativity (as the existentialist myth still tries to make us believe), motherhood can—in itself and if the economic constraints are not too burdensome—favor a certain feminine creation. To the extent that it lifts the fixations, makes passion circulate between life and death, self and other, culture and nature ..."[18] Kristeva is prudent, she makes no absolute claims (motherhood *can* favor creation, it doesn't necessarily do so); she is aware of the material obstacles (how will mother write if there is no one else to care for baby, or if she must work at other jobs to support baby? —Tillie Olsen's questions). Yet, in an important turn of French feminist theory, which we also see appearing in a less abstract version in current American feminist thinking, Kristeva rejects the either/or dilemma and suggests that motherhood and feminine creation go hand in hand.

Kristeva's argument, as stated in two essays in the Winter 1977 issue of *Tel Quel*, is a very complex one and would deserve a long analysis unto itself. This is not the appropriate place for that, but I wish to pause at least briefly in order to take a closer look.

Kristeva's argument can be summed up approximately as follows: the order of the symbolic, which is the order of language, of culture, of the law, of the Name-of-the-Father (to use Lacan's terminology), is especially difficult for women to accede to, whether for historical or other reasons. Motherhood, which establishes a *natural* link (the child) between woman and the social world, provides a privileged means of entry into the order of culture and of language. This privilege belongs to the mother (if I read Kristeva correctly here) not only in contrast to women who are not mothers but also in contrast to men, whose relationship to the symbolic order is itself problematical, characterized by discontinuity, separation, absence. The symbolic, whether for men or for women, functions as the realm of the (unattainable) Other, the realm of arbitrary signs rather than of things; it is by definition the realm of frustrated relations, of impossible loves. The love of God, that ultimate sign of the Other, is of the order of the impossible. But for the mother, according to Kristeva, the Other is not (only) an arbitrary sign, a necessary absence: it is the child, whose presence and whose bodily link to her are inescapable givens, material facts. If to love (her child) is, for a woman, the same thing as to write, we have in that conjunction a modern, secular equivalent of the word made flesh.

This straightforward summary is in a sense a betrayal, however, for the most interesting thing about Kristeva's argument is its quasi-byzantine indirection. The first of the two essays, placed as an introduction to the special issue of the journal devoted to "*recherches féminines*," is not ostensibly about motherhood at all, or even about women, but about the possibilities of intellectuals and of intellectual dissidence in Western culture.

The remarks about motherhood and its relation to feminine creation form part of a section on the possibly dissident role of women in relation to patriarchal law. Since the more elemental law of the reproduction of the species is essentially in women's hands, Kristeva wonders whether mothers are not, in fact, at the very opposite pole of dissidence—whether by maintaining the species they do not also maintain and guarantee the existing social order. She does not answer this question directly, but my sense is that, if pressed, her answer would be: "Yes and no." The mother's body, being a place of fragmentation, cleavage, elemental pulsations that exist *before* language and meaning, is necessarily a place of exile, a place of dis-order and extreme singularity in relation to the collective order of culture. At the same time, the mother's body is the link between nature and culture, and as such must play a conserving role.

What interests me, however, is another question that Kristeva poses: "After the Virgin [Mary], what do we know about the inner discourse of a mother?" The question is both provocative and bizarre, its bizarreness residing in the opening words. Do we know more about the Virgin's inner discourse than about any other mother's? At best we know the discourse that has been attributed to her, that has in fact *created* her—it is the discourse of Christianity, of the *Fathers* of the Church.

Kristeva is aware of this. Her second and much longer essay ("Hérétique de l'amour") is devoted precisely to the question of how the myth of the Virgin Mother was gradually elaborated by Christian discourse, and how it has functioned in the imagination of the West. Above all, she seeks to answer this question: What is it about the Christian representation of ideal motherhood, as embodied in the Virgin, that was satisfactory to women for hundreds of years, and why is that representation no longer satisfactory today? Her tentative conclusion is that in the image of the Virgin Mother, Christianity provided what for a long time was a satisfactory compromise solution to female paranoia: a denial of the male's role in procreation (virgin birth), a fulfillment of the female desire for power (Mary as Queen of

Heaven), a sublimation of the woman's murderous or devouring desires through the valorization of her breast (the infant Jesus suckling) and of her own pain (the *Mater dolorosa*), a fulfilling of the fantasy of deathlessness or eternal life (the Assumption), and above all a denial of other women, including the woman's own mother (Mary was "alone of all her sex")—all of this being granted upon one condition: that the ultimate supremacy and divinity of the male be maintained in the person of the Son, before whom the Mother kneels and to whom she is subservient.

According to Kristeva, the compromise solution represented by the Virgin Mother provided a model that women could, however indirectly, identify with, and at the same time allowed those in charge of the social and symbolic order to maintain their control. (It may be worth noting that the Christian representation of the Virgin Mother has some affinities with, but is much more powerful than, the representation of ideal motherhood in psychoanalytic discourse: in both cases the mother is elevated precisely to the extent that she prostrates herself before her son; for Freud, the mother's greatest satisfaction is to see her favorite son attain glory, which then reflects back on her.) For today's women, however, Kristeva argues, the myth of Mary has lost its positive powers: it leaves too many things unsaid, censors too many aspects of female experience, chief among them the experience of childbirth and of the mother's body in general, the relationship of women to their mothers (and to their daughters), and the relationship of women to men (not to male children, but to adult men). As far as all of these relationships are concerned, motherhood provides a central point from which to ask the questions and to make a first step toward answering them.

As if to demonstrate this very thing, Kristeva intersperses her analytical, discursive text with lyrical, discontinuous fragments of an "other" text—this "other" text being the inner discourse of a mother, Kristeva herself. Since the lyrical fragments are surrounded, enveloped by the discursive text, it is tempting to see the two as "mother" and "child," with the lyrical fragments representing the child. (This idea was suggested to me by Carolyn Burke).

But paradoxically, in the "child-text" it is a *mother* who writes other experiences: childbirth, playing with her infant, watching over the child sick for the first time, feeling separated from and at the same time united with the child, memories of her own mother (the "other woman"), her relationship to language, to the Law. The lyrical fragments are thus in counterpoint, both stylistically and on the level of content, to the discursive text, as the mother's *inner* discourse is in counterpoint to the discourse given to her, constructed about her, by Christianity, the dominant order of Western culture.

These essays by Kristeva seem to me to be especially important for three reasons: she seeks to analyze and show the limitations of Western culture's traditional discourse about motherhood; she offers a theory, however incomplete and tentative, about the relation between motherhood and feminine creation; finally, she *writes* her own maternal text as an example of what such creation might be. This ambitious undertaking is part of the much broader context of contemporary French feminist theory, which over the past several years has been trying both to elaborate a theory of and to exemplify the specificity of *l'écriture féminine*. Luce Irigaray and Hélène Cixous (who is a mother) have insisted on the essentially subversive, dis-orderly nature of women's writing in patriarchal culture, without attempting to differentiate between the feminine and the maternal. This may be because—at least for Cixous—the very fact of being a woman means that one is "never far from the 'mother,'" that is, from a force of reparation and nourishment that is fundamentally "other" in relation to the desiccated rationalism of male discourse. [19]

Chantal Chawaf, on the other hand, much more radically than Kristeva, has tied the practice of feminine writing to the biological fact of motherhood. Chawaf is the mother of two children and the author of several books written in a lyrical autobiographical mode. The central experience around which all her writing turns is the physical and emotional experience of motherhood and of maternal love, which she endows with quasi-cosmic significance. One other recent books, *Maternité*, is a series of sensuous prose poems celebrating the love between a mother who is on the verge of emotional breakdown and her two children, whom she perceives as her only link to communication and light, in opposition to solitude and eternal darkness. Chawaf has stated in interviews and in commentaries on her work that for her motherhood is the only access to literary creation. In *Maternité* she speaks of a "new syntax with fatty nouns, infinitive thighs," a language so physical that it would be a nourishment and "would make every sentence the close relative of the skin and of the mucous membranes...."[20]

The work of the French radical feminists represents without a doubt the most ambitious attempt so far to theorize the relationship between writing and femininity, and more or less directly between writing and motherhood. Personally, my one reservation about their work—which is clearly a work in progress, and therefore too early to make definitive pronouncements about—concerns its exclusionary aspects. To recognize that women, mothers, have been excluded from the order of patriarchal discourse, and to insist on the positive difference of maternal and feminine writing in relation to male writing, can only be beneficial at this time. But it would be a pity if the male gesture of exclusion and repression of the female "other" were to be matched by a similar gesture in reverse. I do not mean by that only the obvious exclusion of men, for some French feminists (Héléne Cixous among them) are willing to admit that certain male poets have attained a "feminine" status in their writing. Rather, I mean the exclusion of a certain *kind* of writing and discourse arbitrarily defined as "male," repressive, logical, the discourse of power, or what have you. Such a gesture necessarily places "feminine" writing in a minority position, willfully ex-centric in relation to power. I am not wholly convinced that that is the best position for women to be in.

I also have reservations about what might be called that fetishization of the female body in relation to writing. It may be true that femininity and its quintessential embodiment, motherhood, can provide a privileged mode of access to language and the mother tongue. What would worry me would be the codification, on the basis of this insight, of women's writing and writing style. In recent French feminist theory and practice, one sees tendencies toward just such codification, both on the level of themes and on the level of style: the centrality of the woman's body and blood, her closeness to Nature, her attunement to the quality of *voice* rather than to "dry" meaning; elemental rhythms, writing as flow (of menstrual blood, of mother's milk, of uterine fluid), "liquid" syntax, lyricism at all costs, receptivity, union, nonaggression.... We are reaching the point where a new genre is being created, and that may be all to the good. But to see in this genre the one and only genuine mode of feminine writing would, I think, be a mistake. ㉑

[……]

Notes：

① Liv Ullman, *Changing* (New York: Bantam, 1978), pp. 36, 37.

② Jane Lazarre, *The Mother Knot* (New York: Dell, 1977), pp. 55-56.

③ Adrienne Rich, *Of Woman Born: Motherhood as Experience and Institution* (New York: Bantam, 1977), p. 12.

④ Kathleen E. Woodiwiss, Interviewed by Judy Klemensrud, *New York Times Book Review*, November 4, 1979, p. 52.

⑤ Tillie Olsen, *Silences* (New York: Doubleday, 1979), p. 19.

⑥ Susan Hill, "On Ceasing to Be a Novelist" (interview with Robert Robinson), *The Listener*, February 2, 1978, p. 154.

⑦ Woodiwiss, interviewed by Klemesrud.

⑧ Karen *Horney*, "Neurotic Disturbances in Work," in *Neurosis and Human Growth: The Struggle toward Self-Realization* (New York: Norton, 1970), pp. 319-320 (my emphasis).

⑨ I am struck, however, by how closely Horney's description corresponds to Simone de Beauvoir's explanation for the lack of audaciousness in women writers：

— 265 —

To please is her first care; and often she fears she will be displeasing as a woman from the mere fact that she writes .... The writer of originality, unless dead, is always shocking, scandalous; novelty disturbs and repels. Woman is still astonished and flattered at being admitted to the world of thought, of art—a masculine world. She is on her best behavior; she is afraid to disarrange, to investigate, to explode; *she feels she should seek pardon for literary pretensions through her modesty and good taste. She stakes on the reliable values of conformity....* [The Second Sex, *trans. and ed.* H. M. Parshley (New York: Bantam, 1961), *p.* 666; *my emphasis*]

⑩ Quoted by Jean Ricardou in Simone de Beauvoir et al. , *Que peut la littérature?* (Paris: Union Générale, 1965), p. 59.

⑪ Olsen, *Silences*, p. 19.

⑫ Phyllis Chesler, *With Child: A Diary of Motherhood* (New York: Crowell, 1979), p. 246.

⑬ Rich, *Of Woman Born*, p. 9.

⑭ Lazarre, *Mother Knot*, p. 216.

⑮ Julia Kristeva, "Nouveau Type d'intellectuel: Le dissident," *Tel Qual*, no. 74 (Winter, 1997), p. 6.

⑯ Julia Kristeva, "Héréthique de l'amour," *Tel Quel*, no. 74 (Winter 1977). p. 31. Reprinted as "Stabat Mater" in Kristeva, *Histoires d'amour* (Paris: Denoël, 1983). English translation to appear in special issue of *Poetics Today* titled *The Female Body in Western Culture: Semiotic Perspectives*, ed. Susan Rubin Suleiman, forthcoming.

⑰ Rich, *Of Woman Born*, p. 1.

⑱ Kristeva, "Nouveau Type d'intellectuel," p. 6.

⑲ See Cixous's essay "Sorties," in Catherine Clément and Hélène Cixous, *La Jeune Née* (Paris: Union Générale, 1975), esp. pp. 169-180.

⑳ Chantal Chawaf, *Maternité* (Paris, 1979), p. 20.

㉑ The debate over *l'écriture féminine*, whose implications have properly been seen as political rather than merely stylistic, has been long and sometimes acrimonious among French feminists. The issues are clearly defined in the dialogue that concludes Cixous's and Clément's *Jeune Née*, as well as in Clément's essay "Enslaved Enclave" and Cixous's "Laugh of the Medusa," in *New French Feminisms*, ed. Elaine Marks and Isabelle de Courtivron (New York: Schocken, 1981). Like Clément, but from a different perspective, Kristeva has criticized the concept of *l'écriture féminine*; see in particular "A partir de *Polylogue*," *Revue des sciences humaines*, no. 168 (December 1977), pp. 495-501.

15 安·弗古森,"母道与性"
Ann Ferguson, "Motherhood and Sexuality"

安·弗古森(Ann Ferguson)①是位于阿莫斯特(Amherst)的马萨诸塞大学哲学系教授。她于 1959 年毕业于斯瓦斯莫尔学院(Swarthmore College),主修哲学,辅修政治学和心理学。她于 1961 年在布朗大学(Brown University)获得哲学硕士学位,1965 年在同一所大学获哲学博士学位。

她的研究领域主要包括女性主义理论、伦理学、性的哲学、社会哲学和政治哲学,尤其对福柯(Michel Foucault)②的理论感兴趣。她教授的课程包括女性主义理论、女性哲学、女性研究导论、性别哲学等。

她的代表著作有:

"根本的血腥:母道、性与男性统治"(Blood at the Root: Motherhood, Sexuality and Male Dominance, 1989 年)

《性的民主:女性、压迫与革命》(Sexual Democracy: Women, Oppression and Revolution, 1991 年)

---

① 访问 http://www.umass.edu/philosophy/faculty/ferguson.htm。

② 福柯(1926~1984),法国哲学家。他提出的理论对人们传统观念中的政治、权力、保险、福利等构成挑战,主要论著有《疯狂与文明》(Madness and Civilization, 1960 年)、《事物的秩序》(Order of Things, 1966 年)、《纪律与惩罚》(Discipline and Punish, 1975 年)、《性史》(History of Sexuality, 1976 年)、《愉快的作用》(The Use of Pleasure, 1984 年)以及《对自我的关怀》(The Care of the Self, 1984 年)。访问 http://www.theory.org.uk/ctr-fouc.htm。

编著有文集《敢于为善:女性主义伦理政治研究》(*Daring to Be Good：Essays in Feminist Ethico-Politics*,1998 年)

《母道与性:一些女性主义问题》(*Motherhood and Sexuality：Some Feminist Questions*)发表于《希帕蒂亚:女性主义哲学》杂志(*Hypatia：A Journal of Feminist Philosophy*)①1986 年秋季卷。该文讨论了女性主义理论同弗洛伊德精神分析理论的关系,涉及母道和性的女性主义伦理问题,探讨社会建构的性欲如何同男性统治相联系以及身体在女性主义理论中发挥的作用。

文章分为六个部分:

第一部分,"引言"(Introduction)。弗古森首先归纳在有关母道、性别与性理论中关于男性统治的作用大致有四种认识:第一种认识主要是那些接受福柯后结构主义思想的理论家,她们认为弗洛伊德的理论太过一般化和西方化了②。第二种认识以乔德罗③和迪纳斯坦④为代表,她们认同男性统治在社会建构性别和性的过程中所起的作用,这使得父母承担的养育责任不平衡(第 4 页;第272 页)。第三种认识为以里奇⑤为代表的激进女性主义者所持有,她们认同父权制的跨文化基础,但却坚持异性恋关系是男性统治的必备机理。第四种观点结合了弗洛伊德的跨文化视角和当今有关男性统治和女性抵抗的概念。弗古森

---

① 该杂志由印第安纳大学出版社出版,季刊,致力于讨论女性研究和哲学研究的交叉问题。杂志以亚历山大城著名女数学家、天文学家和哲学家希帕蒂亚(Hypatia, 370 ~ 415)的名字命名,据说这位才女以学问和美貌著称。访问 http://muse.jhu.edu/journals/hyp。

② Ann Ferguson, "Motherhood and Sexuality：Some Feminist Questions," *Hypatia：A Journal of Feminist Philosophy* 1.2 (Fall 1986)：p.4. 本文所引该文观点均出自此处,以下只在正文标明页码,分号后第二个页码为引文在本书的页码。

③ 南茜·乔德罗,美国心理学家和女性主义理论家。见本书第一篇第 4 节。

④ 多萝西·迪纳斯坦,美国女性主义理论家。见本书第二篇第 12 节。

⑤ 亚德里安·里奇,美国诗人、女性主义理论家。见本书第一篇第 2 节。

把这种观点又细分为拉康学派(以米歇尔①和盖洛普②为代表)、法国女性主义学派(以克里斯蒂娃③、伊里加蕾④和西克苏⑤为代表)以及鲁宾⑥关于性别/性属体系的理论三种类型(第 4～5 页;第 272～273 页)。弗古森在梳理这些理论的基础上提出自己的"性/情感生产体系"("sex/affective production systems"),即关于父母责任、性与养育的历史体系的理论(第 7 页;第 276 页)。她坚持认为,今日美国社会运作的机制是三重的:阶级、种族/民族和性别,每一重机制都是半自主的,都有不同的运作机理(第 7 页;第 276 页)。

第二部分,"母道与性的女性主义伦理学"(Feminist Ethics of Motherhood and Sexuality)。关于女性主义的性伦理理论主要呈现两种趋势:一种为激进女性主义者所持有,她们过分强调父权体制如何建构虐待狂男人和受虐狂女人;另一种可以称作自由意志女性主义者(libertarian feminists),她们过分强调自由行为,否定统一的性关系实践(第 8 页;第 278 页)。

第三部分,"性与欲望"(Sexuality and Desire)。弗古森认为人类性爱倾向中具有一种与生俱来的对于同他人的社会关系的偏好(第 10 页;第 281 页)。她说,人类的性能量既是情绪的也是情感的,弗古森把它称之为"性/情感能量"("sex/affective energy")。这一能量有双重目的:一方面具有同其他社会主体

---

① 朱丽叶·米歇尔,心理分析学家、女性主义理论家,剑桥耶稣学院社会与政治学教授。代表著作有《女性的庄园》(*Women's Estate*, 1972 年)、《心理分析与女性主义》(*Psychoanalysis and Feminism*, 1975 年)和《疯狂的男人与美杜莎》(*Mad Men and Medusas*, 2000 年)。访问 http://www.sps.cam.ac.uk/stafflist/jmitchell.html 和 http://www.sps.cam.ac.uk/stafflist/jmitchell_profile.html.

② 简·盖洛普,美国心理分析学家、女性主义理论家。代表著作有《交叉路口》(*Intersections*, 1981 年)、《女儿的诱惑:女性主义与心理分析》(*The Daughter's Seduction: Feminism and Psychoanalysis*, 1982 年)、《阅读拉康》(*Reading Lacan*, 1985 年)、《通过身体思考》(*Thinking Through the Body*, 1988 年)、《1981 年前后》(*Around 1981*, 1991 年)和《散佚理论》(*Anecdotal Theory*, 2002 年)。访问 http://www.uwm.edu/~jg.

③ 朱丽娅·克里斯蒂娃,法国女性主义理论家、符号学家。见本书第二篇第 7 节。

④ 露丝·伊里加蕾,法国女性主义理论家。见本书第二篇第 9 节。

⑤ 伊莲娜·西克苏,法国女性主义理论家。见本书第二篇第 8 节。

⑥ 盖尔·鲁宾,美国人类学家、女性主义理论家。以《女性交易:关于性的"政治经济学"笔记》("The Traffic in Women: Notes on the 'Political Economy' of Sex", 1975 年)一文著称于世。

结合的欲望,另一方面通过结合实现身体上的愉悦(第 11 页;第 282 页)。在弗古森看来,历史上呈现出不同的家庭形式和社会实践,这源于不同的性/情感生产过程,又与不同的生产经济模式结合在一起(第 11~12 页;第 282 页)。

第四部分,"概念化母道与性理论中的身体"(Conceptualizing the Body in Motherhood and Sexuality)。在这部分里,弗古森综述了一些女性主义理论家对于女性身体意义的不同理解,指出女性主义理论家致力于概念化女性身体,其目的旨在建立一种女性独有的社会生理学(第 13 页)。既然多数女性还是会选择做生理意义上的母亲,那么,女性主义理论家一定要寻找实用的方法影响当前的生育技术发明,并设法挑战男性对生育技术的控制(第 16 页)。

第五部分,"自我、性别和机制"(Self, Gender and Agency)。弗古森认为,自我包括两个侧面:一个侧面是可结合的侧面,容许同他人认同和结合;另一个侧面是以自我利益为中心的、对立的侧面,把自己的利益同他人的相分离(第 18 页)。这决定了人们在性别、种族和阶级上的差异,决定了由自我的不同侧面参与的社会实践有所不同(第 18~19 页)。

第六部分,"权力"(Power)。弗古森首先追溯马克思和福柯关于权力的论述,分析他们的偏颇,然后指出,激进女性主义和社会主义女性主义理论在建构权力理论时应该注意到女性不同的种族/民族背景和阶级与性身份的差异(第 21 页)。并建议说,只有在把女性同其他女性的友谊关系作为女性主义差异理论关键的时候,女性主义理论和女性主义政治才能得到真正的发展。只有通过这样的途径,才能建立起一个持久的女性主义联合关系,从而形成一种能够消除差异的共同性(第 22 页)。

这里选注的是该文的第一、二、三部分。

Motherhood and Sexuality:
Some Feminist Questions

I. Introduction

There is a sense in which my mother will always be a central part of me. After all, in my young days when I developed as a self, she was my all. Good and bad were defined by her. So, at one level, even when I disagree with her, she is my touchstone of value. In the same way my daughter will always be a part of that part of me that is defined through motherhood-and-childhood. In spite of my ambivalence about mothering and being mothered, childraising and being childraised has been an intrinsic value. Having a child (and stepchildren too) has given me an emotional security that no relations with lovers (male or female) or husbands have done. After all, motherhood is forever if one wants it to be: no other commitment in our society can provide such assurance! No marxist or liberal economic theory that tries to grasp the relation between my children and I or my mother (or grandmother) as simply a relationship of exchange (and thus of dominance or oppression) will have got it all (From my diary, 11/26/85).

Reading this entry today, I hear my contrary voice disagreeing. After all, there is another way to see my self, or should I say another aspect of my self? This alter aspect is not defined in terms of either my mother or my children. Neither the same or in opposition is this aspect, just different as a leftist, a lesbian, a feminist and an academic, I am unlike both my mother and my daughter. How then can I understand how such a divided self gains or loses power? This is the way that my own personal quest for mental health connects to one of the important questions for feminist theory, i. e. the role of male dominance in relation to motherhood, gender and sexuality.

One important direction to look for the answer is toward an appropriation of some aspects of Freudian theory. There seem to be four popular positions here. Feminists by and large agree that Freud's ideas cannot be saved as is, for they incorporate a biologistic and patriarchal theory of "penis envy" to explain gender identity. Those who are very concerned to emphasize cultural, racial and class differences in the social construction of parenting, gender and sexuality reject Freud outright as too Western-oriented and too universalistic in his theories. Feminists who are influenced by the work of post-structuralists such as Foucault are in this camp and Jana Sawicki's paper in this issue reflects this tendency.

The second tendency is represented by Nancy Chodorow (1978) and Dorothy Dinnerstein (1976). These theorists accept the idea that there is a universal cross-cultural base for male dominance rooted in the social construction of gender and sexuality in asymmetrical parenting arrangements. Patriarchy thus has an unconscious psychological basis independent of economic, political and social structures which can only be eliminated by a radical reorganization of the sexual division of labor in the family and kin networks.

The third tendency, radical feminism, accepts the idea of a universal cross-cultural base for patriarchy and also certain aspects of Freud's thought (Firestone 1971). However, since most radical feminists are also lesbian-feminists, they are much more sharply critical of Chodorow and Dinnerstein's stress on co-parenting as the solution to male dominance. Instead, they take compulsory heterosexuality to be the key mechanism of male dominance, by which means the original woman-identified erotic tie between mother and infant daughter is broken and patriarchy is installed. Adrienne Rich (Rich 1976, 1980) was the groundbreaking radical feminist thinker on the connection between motherhood and compulsory heterosexuality. Jan Raymond (1979) emphasizes in her new book, *A Passion for Friends: A Philosophy of Female Affection* (1986) and in her article here, "Female Friendship Contra Chodorow and Dinnerstein," that Chodorow's emphasis on women's mothering and sexual relations with men ignores the more important base of patriarchy, which is the coercive nature of *hetero-relations*, whether of kinship, sexuality or friendship. Since *male bonding* is the key mechanism for reproducing male dominance, Raymond argues that women's friendships are the key to female resistance to patriarchy.

The fourth contemporary feminist use of Freudian though is a revision which combines some of his cross-cultural insights with concepts which allow us to historicize different types of male dominance and female resistance. We can divide these theorists further into three groups: Lacanians (Juliet Mitchell 1974, Gallop 1982), French feminists Kristeva (1979, 1980),

Irigaray (1974, 1977, 1979), and Cixous (1976), and Gayle Rubin's sex/gender systems theory (Rubin 1975).

Mitchell and Lacan (in Mitchell and Rose 1982) give a quasi-historical rendition of Freud by combining his theory with that of Levi-Strauss on the cross-cultural male exchange of women in marriage which defines kinship ties. According to these thinkers, women then become defined as *objects* rather than *subjects* of language. Children, when developing gender identity and forming their sexual desire come to define the masculine position as the object of the mothers desire, hence desirable and powerful, and the feminine position as a lack of power, hence undesirable. Though the exchange of women in kin ties is no longer the central organizing principle of society, patriarchy continues to be reproduced by the unconscious structure of masculine and feminine Desire.

Lacan's interpretation of Freud has been appropriated by some French feminists to suggest a way of challenging patriarchy. Lacan suggests that the woman who passively allows herself to be loved, to be the object rather than the subject of Desire, may attain a type of jouissance, mystical sexual pleasure, not available to women or men who seek actively to satisfy sexual Desire. The truly feminine woman, being *outside* the assumptions of patriarchal language, has another way of being, enjoying and knowing not bound by these limitations. Kristeva, Irigaray and Cixous, while challenging many of Lacan's assumptions, all accept the idea that woman's unique relation to our bodies as subjects outside the assumptions of phallic language, our unique relation to our mothers and our sexuality, created the possibility for a radically new feminine writing and sensibility outside the patriarchy.

Cynthia Freeland challenges this view in her article in this issue, "Woman Revealed or Reveiled?" She takes on the obscure Lacanian theories of Desire, Self and Gender by using them to interpret the feminine roles juxtaposed in Nathanial Hawthorne's *The Blithedale Romance*. Lacan's views both romanticize and devalue women, she argues, since he presents women as universal victims of patriarchy who unconsciously always desire their own oppression. The only way out of the circle of phallic desire, he suggests, is for women to eschew active sexuality (always phallic) and to revel passively in their bodily Otherness to men, for in not actively seeking sexual pleasure it may happen to them unexpectedly! Freeland points out how this indirect approach to feminine liberation mars the strategies of Lacan's erstwhile follower, Luce Irigaray, who seems to suggest that women should not seek to describe, generalize or articulate their desire for fear of falling into phallocentric logic.

While I accept Freeland's criticisms of Lacan and of one "natural" reading of Irigaray's work, I think there is another way of reading Irigaray which saves her enterprise from fatalist conclusions Freeland sees in it. I read Irigaray as seeking to revalorize women's bodies by reconstructing their meaning, while acknowledging the hold that phallic signifiers have had in coding the Unconscious.

Irigaray wants to open a descriptive space for women which is ironic, that is, a discourse which seems to provide a universal description of the multiple and diffuse nature of women's bodily sexuality as opposed to men's, but in actuality invites women to consult our own individual, diverse and multiple bodily experiences in order to reconceptualize the individual "body and its pleasures" (as Foucault might say). Thus there is a nonessentialist reading of Irigaray in which her work, unlike Lacan's, points us in the important direction of reconceptualizing the role of our bodies in gender and sexuality in individual and relative terms. Irigaray's work is important as a part of a more general feminist project of re-assessing the role that bodily differences between men and women play in reproducing patriarchy and also, potentially, in undermining it.

While Mitchell and the French Feminists try to reconstruct Freud in a way that can allow us to take historical differences and changes into account, ultimately it seems to me that they fail in this task. Gayle Rubin's appropriation of Lacan is more promising as an overall theoretical paradigm than either Mitchell or Irigaray because of her innovative concept of "sex/ gender systems". Rubin defines a "sex/gender system" in a manner analogous to a "mode of production," that is as a historically based set of categories of kinship, gender and sexuality whereby a socially produced sexuality and gender is created out of biological sexuality. However, her own work does not apply her concept of sex/gender systems to allow us to understand and periodize historical types of male dominances. Isaac Balbus (1982) comes closer to a historical application but his paradigm is too neo-Hegelian, in my opinion, in his concentration of the dialectic between autonomy and merging that different types of parenting practices create.

In my own work I try to carry Rubin's analytical insights further (Ferguson 1981a, 1981b, 1984a, 1984b, 1985, 1986 forthcoming). I coin the idea of "sex/affective production systems," i. e. historical systems of parenting, sexuality and nurturance (friendships, kin relations, work bonding). I agree with Folbre (1983, 1984) that the question of biological reproduction (fertility rates) is a key factor of economic production that mainstream and Marxist economists have ignored. The historically variable need for children's labor, and the work necessary for childrearing, are part of the material base for socially constructed patriarchal modes of sex/ affective production. These systems organize the social practices of marriage, prostitution, kin networks and stigmatization of homosexual practices that allow men's control of women's bodies. In the process men dominate women's sexuality, nurturance, an unequal exchange of gender labor and control of the key product, children.

I argue that there are tri-systems of social domination (class, race/ ethnic and gender) operating in American society today, each of which is semi-autonomous and which have separate dynamics. Although I have criticized Chodorow in the past, as of this moment I think it may be possible to historicize some of both Chodorow and Mitchell's reconstruction of the Freudian theory of gender development so as to understand the cross-cultural base for male dominance along her lines while at the same time not erasing important differences in how race, ethnic, class and sexual identity position may differently construct gender dynamics (Ferguson 1985, mss.).

II. Feminist Ethics of Motherhood and Sexuality

Should there be a feminist ethics of sexuality and motherhood? This question is more central than it might otherwise seem to the American women's movement today. It is to be expected that a social movement demanding liberation of women from patriarchal values would be called upon to develop its own values, not only to confront conservatives with a coherent vision of an alternative set of ethical standards for personal life, but to provide guidelines for a feminist oppositional culture to show forth its values by attempting to exemplify them.

Problems have immediately arisen, however, with the demand for a set of feminist alternative values and the insistence that the personal is the political. It is much easier to reject male breadwinner-female housewife marriage as the ideal way to organize parenting and sexuality than it is to decide which alternative life styles are feminist! Should we be monogamous or non-monogamous? Live alone, in couples or in communal households? Be lesbian or straight? And whatever happened to bisexuality in the shuffle to claim a vanguard feminist sexual identity? Or celibacy? Or prioritizing friendships over one's love life? Is prostitution a life-style that any self-respecting feminist should reject? Since motherhood as an institution has been so infused with male dominance, should feminists reject motherhood altogether? Or at least avoid committing themselves to bringing up boys? (After all, motherhood involves self-sacrifice enough, and if, as some radical feminists suggest, men are incorrigible, why should one sacrifice time to bring up boys which might better be spent helping women (including oneself)?

The decision to mother unavoidably requires one to define a feminist ethic by which to guide one's parenting choices. For example, should being a mother be a commitment that one makes independently of a commitment to a lover or mate? How should children best be brought up to have feminist values? Should we commit ourselves to co-parenting with a father (when he is available) on the grounds that this is most desirable for the children even when it may limit our own options, as when the mother has a new lover-mate-partner but has previously engaged in co-parenting with the father? (This is often particularly difficult when the new lover is a woman.) What about the situation of the child who has a number of co-parents, each subsequent lovers of (one of her) mothers? (My former "house" daughter has one biological mother, one biological father and three subsequent co-parenting mothers!) What do we teach them (and think ourselves) about the issues of sex education, incest, adult/child sexuality, child/child sexuality, erotica, pornography, fantasies of rape, S/M sex? Can one be feminist and engage in and/or recommend such practices to others?

With respect to a feminist sexual morality, the recent debate has been dominated by radical feminists on one pole and those I call "libertarian" feminists on the other (Ferguson 1984b). While the former can be criticized for overemphasizing the power of patriarchy to construct men with sadistic and women with masochistic desires (cf. Dworkin 1974, 1982, MacKinnon 1979, 1982, 1983), the latter end up validating any consensual practice at all, thus sliding into a "do your own thing" mentality (Califia 1981, Rubin 1982, 1984, Rubin, English and Hollibaugh 1981). While this stance has a certain plausibility for consenting adults, it is unworkable as a guide for dealing with children about sex. Part of the commitment of motherhood after all is to form one's children's values in a way one considers healthy until the point where they are considered mature enough to make their own choices. While the vagueness of what counts as achieving this "maturity" creates the possibility of much misuse of parental power, the dilemma is a real one which is not dissolved by those who argue that mutual consent, not age, is the sole criterion on which sexual practices should be approved. For the question simply pops up again in trying to establish under what conditions it is plausible to assume consent is really present.

Cheryl Cohen, in "The Feminist Sexuality Debate Ethics and Politics," challenges the libertarian position, arguing that feminists cannot eschew the political task of attempting to construct a feminist sexual morality. She argues that the current sex debate in the Women's Movement needs to take account of Gilligan's distinction between a masculine "rights" ethic and a feminine "responsibilities" morality. Using the latter approach we must insist on reconstructing the distinction between public and private that early feminist theory broke down with its insistence that the personal is the political. While feminists should support public policy which guarantees individuals the right to many forms of sexual expression in their private life it does not necessarily follow that what is *privately* morally acceptable (that is, should be protected from being restricted by state policy) is *politically* liberatory from a feminist ethical point of view.

While I agree with Cohen that we must reject the relativist "do your own thing" implications of the libertarian sexual liberation strategy, she herself seems to underemphasize this strategy's historical importance to counteract a certain smug puritanism of radical lesbian-feminist thought. Even if we agree to make the distinction she urges between feminist *state* policy on sexuality and our prescriptions for an oppositional liberatory feminist sexual ethics, we must find a way to permit people to challenge status quo norms in their personal sexual interactions. Libertarians are on the right track when they insist on the value of sexual pleasure for its own sake. But this does not imply that there are not other values (emotional intimacy, autonomy, equality, self-respect, etc.), which are also ends in themselves. We must examine sexual practices contextually and not abstractly to seek which of them can better achieve not *merely* pleasure but these other ends as well. The search for a feminist sexual liberatory ethics must find a middle ground between a "nothing goes but lesbian vanilla sex" moralism and an "everything goes" sexual experimentalism. We seek not merely a *transitional* sexual morality, one which allows us autonomy from the sexual repression characteristic of 20th century capitalist patriarchy, but also a theory of self-development, tactics and strategy to change ourselves and a vision of where we are going.

Other papers in this issue attempt to develop theories of autonomy, reproduction and self-development to provide the groundwork for an ethics of motherhood and sexuality. Marjorie Weinzweig develops a Heideggerian notion of "autonomous-being-with-others" as the ideal mode of combining the feminist values of equality, freedom and self-development. She combines this with a three stage theory of development which then yields answers to when and how to engage in marriage, couple relationships and parenthood. Anne Donchin in "The Future of Mothering Reproductive Technology and Feminist Theory" defends what she calls a "moderate interventionist" position on the question of what feminists' stance should be on the development of reproductive technology. In "Possessive Power" Janet Farrell-Smith argues that feminists should demand rights against the state which allow for parenthood under conditions of autonomy. And Jan Raymond argues, at least by implication, that heterosexual co-parenting should never take precedence over women's friendships, and thus that the ethical injunction to co-parent, regularly drawn from Chodorow and Dinnerstein's work, should be rejected. For further discussion of these claims I refer the reader to sections below.

III. Sexuality and Desire

Ironically, American radical feminist theories of motherhood and eroticism of Rich (1976, 1980) and Daly (1978, 1984) manifest some of the same over-simplifications of the relation as does Freud's work. Eroticism in mothering is assumed to be a natural given, an otherwise unproblematic joyous connection between mothers and children which patriarchy and compulsory heterosexuality represses. Like Irigaray and Flax my alternative reading of sexuality assumes that there is a problematic inherent to mother/child erotic relations which has little to do with the power of the father or adult lover (male or female) or the mother. This is that the inevitable power differential between mother and child creates an autonomy/eroticism conflict for children of both sexes which will tend to lead them to attempt to find other erotic objects in order to establish a sense of independence from the mother.

My view of sexuality differs from Freud in that I theorize an inherent predilection for social relations with others built into human eroticism. I agree with the emphasis of Objects Relations theory that human understandings of self are construction from relations with others. But unlike the Chodorowian version, I would hold that masculine and feminine gender personalities have no cross-cultural, cross-class and cross-racial *content*. Rather, they depend importantly on the nature of the family structure (extended, nuclear, male or female headed, etc.) in which children are raised. In nuclear families where the opposition between an erotic relation to the mother and a distanced relation to the father is present, children of either sex who identify with the father may assume such identification carries the consequence that no erotic relation is possible with a person of the male sex. In nuclear families where the mother herself has a suppressed or ambivalent eroticism toward the children and the father a more erotic one, the consequences may be the converse. Extended families where there is more than one significant female kin doing mothering may provide children with a choice of erotic objects and self-identifications.

Another way that Freud's theory of gender and sexual identity development is mistaken is the deterministic emphasis it puts on family relations and childhood development as opposed to childhood, adolescent and adult peer and community interactions. Like the symbolic interactionists (Simon and Gagnon 1973, Plummer 1975) I hold that gender and sexual identity is a process subject to constant change by one's relations with one's peer reference groups as one's early family experiences. Freud's emphasis on the latter ignores the key importance of whether one is defined as "normal" or "deviant" by one's peers.

In my view, what follows from the emphasis on gender and sexual identity as an ongoing process is that oppositional cultural networks for heterosexual and lesbian-feminists which redefine the meaning and value of "femininity," feminine sexual pleasure, and lesbian identity thus become extremely important modes of resistance to dominant identifications which tie women to patriarchal and heterosexist values.

What explains the apparent universality of male dominance and compulsory heterosexuality cross-culturally? Rather than locating the persistence of these features in a repressed or tabooed mother/child sexuality, my reading of sexuality rejects the idea of a sexual drive whose major aim is bodily satisfaction, and a secondary, or sublimated, interest in emotional or affectionate relations with others. Rather, human sexual energy is always both emotional and affectionate energy, what I would call "sex/affective energy". Sex/affective energy has a double-sided aim: the desire to be incorporated/united with other social subjects and in doing so to achieve bodily pleasure (e.g. not merely orgasm: simple touching, as in hugging, satisfies this desire). Although tension reduction is achieved when orgasm is achieved, tension reduction per se is not, as Freud thought, the ultimate *aim* of human sexuality but a healthy side effect. Although emotional incorporation with others is a key aim of sex/affective energy, partial satisfaction of this desire can be attained by sexual practices that substitute an imaginary relation with others or with oneself, e.g. as in masturbation.

It is my view that historically different forms of the family, embedded in different modes of sex/affective production, mesh together with different economic modes of production to yield different social practices with respect to motherhood, friendship and sexuality. These in turn have different general implications for the strength of patriarchy in that period, as well as for opportunities for oppositional practices of feminist resistance (Ferguson 1984a). For example, in New England colonial families motherhood and sexuality were assumed to go together by Calvinist ideology. Since this was evil, fathers were expected to intervene in the mother/child relationship in order to break the will of the child, since it was assumed that the mother by herself would encourage the child to be lustful. Female resistance in this period no doubt consisted in persisting in eroticism with young children in spite of paternal interdictions and, more generally, by prioritizing the needs of the body (through "witchcraft," taught by elders to youngsters) over the presumed needs of the soul.

Other examples of a changed ideological relation between motherhood, friendship and sexuality, and hence different forms of feminist resistance, can be drawn from what I term 19th century "husband patriarchy" and 20th century "public patriarchy" (Ferguson 1984a). In the 19th century bourgeois family, "true" women in natural motherhood were presumed to be asexual. Women's sole goal in life was to the high vocations of wife and motherhood. Feminine resistance in this period included sexual abstinence which led to a reduction in fertility rates for women (called by some "domestic feminism," (cf. Scott-Smith 1974), prostitution (for working class women) and female spiritual and presumably asexual friendships that allowed for women's peer bonding outside of patriarchally controlled families (Faderman 1981, Smith-Rosenberg 1975).

Conditions for public patriarchy in the 20th century have included the expansion of wage labor to include fulltime work for married women, public welfare provisions for poor single mothers and the expansion of state control of childhood socialization by public schooling and social service agencies. Psychoanalysis created the category of a homosexual identity as well as the new ideal of the heterosexual sexually passionate companionate marriage (Jackson 1983). These changes have weakened the patriarchal control of individual men over women and children in families while strengthening the power of men to control women and children through wage labor, the state and sexual liaisons. One result has been the expansion of the feminization of poverty through the increase of single mother-headed families. Women have escaped oppressive marriages only to fall into increased exploitation as the sole parent assuming both domestic and breadwinner responsibility for childrearing.

There are many forms of feminist resistance to this contemporary form of patriarchy. Many women have delayed or bypassed motherhood as a primary life goal. In the sexual sphere some have consciously expressed feminist resistance by choosing a lesbian identity and lifestyle. For others feminist independence has involved separating heterosexual sexuality and motherhood by contraceptive use. The permanent monogamous family has been challenged by increasing divorces, extramarital sex, single motherhood and singles lifestyles in general.

The point of these historical examples is to suggest that since compulsory heterosexuality and sexual repression take different forms in different modes of sex/affective production, we must develop a new paradigm of sexuality and sexual liberation that itself is more social than the Libido that Freud assumes. Sexual Desire is determined by specific, not general conditions of patriarchy, that is, by specific forms of the family, schooling, and the sexual division of wage labor. The Unconscious is continually being created and modified, not only in childhood but by the implicit "sex/affective" assumptions of our ongoing friendship, romantic and sexual relations with each other.

Such a paradigm of Sexuality will allow us to highlight the current importance of a lesbian-feminist identity as a type of feminist sexual liberation without supposing that this is the universal vanguard resistance to patriarchy as Rich (1980) seems to suggest. It will also allow us to focus on the specific historical drawbacks and opportunities that single motherhood in the 20th century raises both with advanced reproductive technologies (cf. the Donchin article in this issue) and the changed nature of male exploitation of women in the asymmetrical relations of parenting and childcare (Brown 1981, Ferguson 1984a).

[……]

第三篇
Part 3

科技、解构与后现代
——后现代语境下的母亲身份

Technology, Deconstruction and Postmodernity
— *Motherhood in Postmodern Context*

    本篇收入的 5 篇文章从不同角度探讨了后现代语境下母亲身份的改变,尤其是生育技术的开发和临床使用给传统母亲身份、对传统家庭观念带来的冲击与挑战。这 5 篇文章的作者来自不同的国家,拥有迥异的文化背景和学术、职业经历,她们的观点代表了后现代社会呈现的多元视角。

    戴安·埃伦萨福特的"当男人和女人共同做母亲的时候"一文从心理学和社会学的角度研究男人和女人共同分担做母亲的职责给男女双方、给孩子带来的影响,指出分担养育是一项有意义的政治变革,将会改变原有性别差异导致的性别体制的循环再生。安·丹琴所著"母性的未来:生育技术与女性主义理论"从生育技术在美国的开发和使用这样的大背景入手,分析了人们对待生育技术所持的不干涉主义、适度干涉主义和激进干涉主义等几种不同态度,她还分析了女性主义对待生育技术的反响。在此基础上,作者提出应在充分对话的基础上合理引导生育技术的使用。米歇尔·斯坦沃思的"生育技术与母亲身份的解构"探讨了生育技术的使用如何解构了传统的母亲身份，如何改变了自然的生育过程，如何打破了家庭、父母、性行为等传统观念。正因为生育技术在很大程度上影响女性的生活，所以作者主张女性应该积极参与对生育技术的评价过程。伊莲娜·瑞萍也承认生育技术改变了许多传统的观念，她指出，女性主义者对生育技术的使用大多持悲观的否定态度，但她认为，应该看到生育技术的使用目前还没有做到完全平等，而且也不能对生育技术持简单的批评态度，因为技术对人类社会仍然具有潜在的促进和改善作用（"母道的未来：一些不切实际的幻想"）。罗斯·布雷多蒂在"母亲、魔鬼与机器"一文中寻找到母亲、魔鬼和机器之间的四个连接点，讨论母亲如何同魔鬼这样既令人恐怖又令人艳羡的东西在文化上具有联系，男人对生育过程的控制如何从古代炼金术士的实验室转移到了现代化的医院，魔鬼这样的畸形人形象又如何在当代流行文化中衍变为机器人、半机械人和仿生人。作者提出应该建立一种游牧式的女性主义风格允许女性多元化地重新思考她们在后现代社会的地位。

16

戴安·埃伦萨福特,"当男人和女人共同做母亲的时候"
Diane Ehrensaft, "When Women and Men Mother"

戴安·埃伦萨福特(Diane Ehrensaft)是一位临床心理学家,加利福尼亚大学伯克利分校心理学系和行为与健康科学学系教授。她在 20 世纪 80 年代积极倡导男人应更多参与养育孩子的新理念,并用亲身经历讲述和评价父母在孩子成长过程中所起的作用。埃伦萨福特目前在奥克兰市(Oakland)任儿童心理专家,主要对父母离婚后的孩子提供诊疗、咨询、监护评估、协调等工作①。

埃伦萨福特的代表著作有三部:

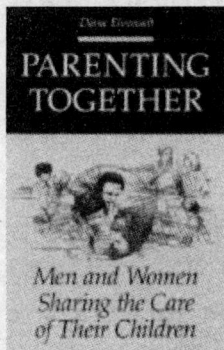

《共同养育:男人和女人分担养育孩子的责任》(*Parenting Together*: *Men and Women Sharing the Care of Their Children*,1987 年)。这部书记录了作者自己和她的患者在家庭中尝试男女共同抚养孩子的经历,探索这样的经历对孩子性属形成具有的意义,以及这样的家庭模式对父母个人生活和双方关系产生的影响②。

《娇惯的童年:父母给予孩子太多——本意善良但却非孩子所需》(*Spoiling Childhood*: *How Well-Meaning Parents Are Giving Children Too Much—But Not What They Need*,1997 年)。作者旨在给父母以及幼儿教育专家就孩子成长过程中父母发挥的作用提出建议,她提出了"成年婴儿"("kinderdult")的概念,试图表明

---

① 访问 http://www.unex.berkeley.edu/dept/bhs/instructors.html。

② 访问 http://www.amazon.de/exec/obidos/ASIN/0029094402/ref%3Dnosim/asearch/028-6862001-3070907。

孩子成长过程中被给予了太多关爱和太多权利。这种过分以孩子为中心的现象既困惑了父母又迷惑了孩子,她呼吁父母不要过多陷入关注孩子的境地①。

《妈妈、爸爸、捐赠者、代理人:解答疑难问题,建设稳固家庭》(*Mommies*, *Daddies*, *Donors*, *Surrogates*:*Answering Tough Questions and Building Strong Families*,2005 年)。作者在书中解答了人工辅助生育技术(assisted reproductive technology)给家庭带来的新问题,以便帮助代理父母处理好同捐赠者的关系、同养子的关系以及其他家庭成员的关系。

本书选注的《当男人和女人共同做母亲的时候》最早发表于《社会主义评论》(*Socialist Review*)杂志 1980 年 1、2 月合刊,后被选入由汉森(Karen V. Hansen)和菲利浦森(Ilene J. Philipson)编选的《女人、阶级和女性主义想象:社会主义-女性主义读本》(*Women*,*Class*,*and the Feminist Imagination*:*A Socialist-Feminist Reader*)一书,该书由坦普尔大学出版社于 1990 年出版。

文章分为五个部分:

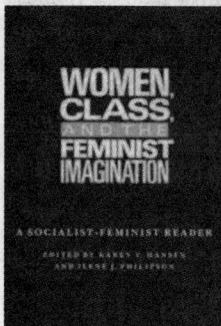

引言。作者首先谈到 20 世纪六七十年代间妇女解放运动给女性家庭生活带来的影响,一些女性倡议建立一种新型的模式——男女双方共同承担养育孩子的责任,即"分担养育"(shared parenting)②,这样可以避免随着越来越多的女性外出工作而使得她们实际上在做两份全职工作的现象。作者认为,男女共同承担养育孩子的责任,其政治意义在于:第一,如果母职是女性受压迫的主要来源,那么,男女共同承担母亲的职责将会对这一情况构成挑战;第二,由于生产和生育紧密相关、互相影响,因此,在美国资本主义体制下,男女分担养育责任的过程中完全的平等是无法实现的(第 401 页)。

第一部分,"资本主义背景下的分担养育"("Shared Parenting in a

---

① 访问 http://www.amazon.com/gp/product/1572304502/104-6855247-8176717?v=glance&n=283155&tagActionCode=infoline-20。

② Diane Ehrensaft, "When Women and Men Mother," in Karen V. Hansen and Ilene J. Philipson, eds. *Women*, *Class*, *and the Feminist Imagination*:*A Socialist-Feminist Reader* (Philadelphia:Temple University Press, 1990), p.399. 本节所引该文观点均出自此处,以下只在正文标明页码,分号后第二个页码为引文在本书的页码。

Capitalist Context"）。埃伦萨福特首先引用霍莉（Nancy Press Hawley）①的语言对分担养育作了准确定义（第 401 页），然后指出，在实际生活中分担养育的情况并不多见，反而越来越多的家庭成为双职工家庭（two-working-parent families）（第 402 页）。与此同时，来自社会要求女性继续承担母亲职责的压力也越来越大，激进的社会主义女性主义者和自由意志女性主义者之间产生了很大分歧（第 403～404 页）。但作者认为，分担养育对母道的神秘性和传统的性别分工提出了挑战，具有几个层面的政治、社会意义（第 405 页）。

第二部分，"尿布与工资的辩证关系：分担养育中的性别分工"（"The Dialects of Pampers and Paychecks：The Sexual Division of Labor in Shared Parenting"）。这一部分分为以下小节：1. 男人能当妈吗？2. 权力与养育；3. 养育中身体和心理的劳动分工。作者首先定义母亲责任的含义（第 405～406 页；第 290～291 页），然后指出，女性的生理、生殖结构并不能证明她们比男人更适合做母亲（第 406 页；第 290～291 页）。虽然作者承认分担养育说起来容易做起来难（第 407 页；第 292 页），但对于女性来说这至少意味着：其一，从 24 小时的全职母亲身份中解放出来；其二，使女性有机会同男人一样进入公众领域（第 408 页；第 293 页）。与此同时，男性分担家庭责任也有两个方面的收获：其一，他能有机会多和孩子在一起；其二，他能体会养育孩子的愉快（第 408 页；第 293 页）。埃伦萨福特认为，分担养育给男性和女性心理上造成了不同的影响（第 412～414 页；第 298～301 页），这种不同的心理状态又反过来影响了男女双方在养育孩子过程中的行为（第 415 页；第 301～302 页）。

第三部分，"孩子会怎么样？"（"What Happens to the Children?"）。埃伦萨福特指出，由于父母双方在孩子的成长过程中共同分担责任，过去由母亲一人养育带来的孩子心理和个性差异的问题有望消除（第 418 页），而当分担养育下成长起来的男孩子长大后，可能比父辈更愿意分担母亲的责任（第 421 页）。不仅如此，分担养育下长大的孩子在社会责任感、同情心和爱心以及政治、社会意识等方面也会更具强势（第 421～424 页）。

结论。作者再次重申分担养育是一项具有政治意义的变革，它挑战传统核

---

① 埃伦萨福特所引观点出自霍莉著，《分担养育责任》（"Shared Parenthood"），收入波士顿女性健康丛书（Boston Women's Health Book Collective）《我们以及我们的孩子》（*Ourselves and Our Children*，1978 年）。

心家庭的压迫特征,把女性从母亲身份的普遍性中解放出来,并有可能因此改变原有男女性别差异导致的性别体制的循环再生(第 427 页)。

这里选注的是该文的第二部分,"尿布与工资的辩证关系:分担养育中的性别分工"。

When Men and Women Mother

[……]

The Dialectics of Pampers and Paychecks:

The Sexual Division of Labor in Shared Parenting.

Can Men Mother?

In this argument, the word "mothering" is used specifically to mean the day-to-day *primary* care of a child; it involves the consciousness of being *directly* in charge of the child's upbringing. It is to be differentiated from the once-a-week baseball games or twenty-five minutes of play a day that characterize the direct parenting in which men have typically been involved. One mother put it aptly: "To a child Mommy is the person who takes care of me, who tends my daily needs, who nurtures me in an unconditional and present way. Manda has two mothers; one is a male, Mommy David, and the other a female, Mommy Alice. "[1]

According to recent psychological studies, anyone can "mother" an infant who can provide frequent and sustained physical contact, soothe the child when distressed, be sensitive to the baby's signals, and respond to a baby's crying promptly. Beyond these immediate behavioral indices, psychoanalysts argue that anyone who has personally experienced a positive parent-child relationship that allowed the development of both trust and individuation in his or her own childhood has the emotional capabilities to parent. However much as sociobiologists would take issue there is no conclusive animal or human research indicating that female genitals, breasts, or hormonal structure provide women with any better equipment than men for parenting. ② Yet years in female-dominated parenting situations and in gender-differentiated cultural institutions can and do differentially prepare boys and girls for the task of "mothering". ③ And in adulthood social forces in the labor market, schools, media, and so on, buttress these differential abilities. To understand what happens when two such differentially prepared individuals come together to parent, two issues have to be addressed: parenting and power, and the psychic division of labor in parenting.

Power and Parenting

I recently read four articles in the popular press acclaiming a shifting in family structure. Women, they said, have become more and more interested in and committed to extrafamilial lives, while men have fled from the heartless world to the haven of the family. Knowing that theirs is not the only paycheck coming in, more men walk off the job, come late to work, rebel against the work ethic. The articles speak optimistically of a new generation of "family men" and "career women" and a greater sharing among men and women in both family and work life. ④

But we who know the behind-the-scenes story take a moment of pause. We women who have shared parenting with men know the tremendous support and comfort (and luxury) of not being the only one there for our children. We see opportunities to develop the many facets of ourselves not easily afforded to our mothers or to other women who carried the primary load of parenting. We watch our children benefit from the full access to two rather than one primary nurturing figure, affording them intimacy with both women and men, a richer and more complex emotional milieu, role models that challenge gender stereotypes. We see men able to develop more fully the nurturant parts of themselves as fathers, an opportunity often historically denied them. And we develop close, open, and more equal relationships between men and women as we grapple with the daily ups and downs of parenting together. The quality of our lives no doubt has been improved immensely by the equalization of parenting responsibilities between men and women.

Yet we also know that shared parenting is easier said than done. Because it has remained so unspoken, it is this latter reality I speak to here, while urging the reader to keep in mind the larger context of the successes, the improvements in daily life, and the political import that accompany the shared parenting project.

Men and women are brought up for a different position in the labor force: the man for the world of work, the woman for the family. This difference in the sexual division of labour in society means that the relationship of men as a group to production is different from that of women. For a man the social relations and values of commodity production predominate and home is a retreat into intimacy. For the woman the public world of work belongs to and is owned by men. ⑤

While men hold fast to the domination of the "public sphere," it has been the world of home and family that is woman's domain. Particularly in the rearing of children, it is often her primary (or only) sphere of power. For all the oppressive and debilitating effects of the institution of motherhood, a woman *does* get social credit for being a "good" mother. She also accrues for herself some sense of control and authority in the growth and development of her children. As a mother she is afforded the opportunity for genuine human interaction, in contrast to the alienation and depersonalization of the workplace:

A woman's desire to experience power and control is mixed with the desire to obtain joy in childrearing and cannot be separated from it. It is the position of women in society as a whole, their dependent position in the family, the cultural expectation that the maternal role should be the most important role for all women, that make the exaggerated wish to possess one's child an entirely reasonable reaction. Deprived and oppressed, women see in motherhood their only source of pleasure, reward, and fulfillment. ⑥

It is this power and control that she must partially give up in sharing parenting equally with a father.

What she gains in exchange is twofold: a freedom from the confines of twenty-four-hour-a-day motherhood and the same opportunity as her male partner to enter the public world of work and politics, with the additional power in the family that her paycheck brings with it. But that public world, as Rowbotham points out, is still controlled and dominated by men and does not easily make a place for women within it. The alteration in gender relations within the "shared parent" family is not met by a simultaneous gender reorganization outside the home. A certain loosening, of societal gender hierarchies, the opening of new job opportunities for women, no doubt has prefigured and created the structural conditions that have allowed a small number of men and women to share parenting at this historical moment. But those structural changes are minor in contrast to the drastic alteration of gender relations and power necessary for shared parenting to succeed. So the world the sharing mother enters as she walks out her door will be far less "fifty-fifty" than the newly created world within those doors.

For men taking on parenting responsibilities, the gain is also twofold: he gains access to his children and is able to experience the pleasures and joys of child rearing. His life is not totally dominated by the alienated relations of commodity production. He is able to nurture, discover the child in himself. But he too loses something in the process. First, in a culture that dictates that a man "make something of himself," he will be hard pressed to compete in terms of time and energy with his male counterparts who have only minimal or no parenting responsibility. In short, parenting will cut into his opportunities for "transcendence". Second, the sharing father is now burdened with the daily headaches and hassles of child care which can (and do) drive many a woman to distraction: the indelible scribble on the walls, the search for a nonexistent good child-care center, the two-hour tantrums, and so on. He has now committed himself to a sphere of work that brings little social recognition—I'm *just* a housewife and a mother.

In *shared* parenting the gains and losses are not equal for men and women. Mom gives up some of her power only to find societally induced guilt feelings for not being a "real" mother and maybe even for being a "bad" mother. (Remember: she may have grown up believing that she should and would be a full-time mommy when she was big.) The myth of motherhood remains ideologically entrenched far beyond the point when its structural underpinnings have begun to crumble. She is giving up power in the domestic sphere, historically her domain, with little compensation from increased power in the public sphere. Discrimination against women in the labor force is still rampant. She will likely have less earning power, less job opportunity, less creative work, and less social recognition than her male partner. When push comes to shove, she is only a "*working mother*" There is as yet no parallel term "working father".

The power dynamic for Dad is quite different and more complicated. On one level he gains considerable authority in the daily domestic sphere of child rearing, a heretofore female domain. But by dirtying his hands with diapers he also removes himself from his patriarchal pedestal as the breadwinning but distant father, a position crucial to men's power in the traditional family. He now does the same "debasing" work as the mother, and she now has at least some control of the purse strings. Nonetheless, as the second "mother," the father has encroached on an arena of power that traditionally belongs to women, yet he most likely retains more economic and social power vis-à-vis Mom in the public world of work and politics.

The societal reaction is also double-edged for the sharing father. Given the subculture that most current sharing parents come from, in his immediate circles Dad often receives praise for being the "exceptional" father so devoted to his children or so committed to denying his male privileges. In challenging a myth so deeply embedded as motherhood, the man who marches with baby bottle and infant in arm can become quite an antisexist hero. But in the larger culture reactions are often adverse. A man who stays home to care for children is assumed by many to be either disabled, deranged, or demasculinized. One father, pushing his child in a stroller past a school on a weekday afternoon, was bemused by a preadolescent leaning out the school window yelling, "Faggot, Faggot". Some time ago my grandmother, in response to my mother's praise of my husband's involvement with our children, snapped, "Well, of course, he doesn't work." But as pressures of shifting family structures increase, popular response is rapidly swinging in the sharing father's favor, at least among the middle classes; and the response to his fathering from his most immediate and intimate circles is most likely a positive or even laudatory one.

When the results are tabulated, the gains and losses for men and women are not comparable: women come out behind. Where does this newly experienced power imbalance leave mothers and fathers vis-à-vis their commitment to shared parenting? Women can feel deprived of status both at home and at work. The experienced sexual inequalities in the world outside the family can create a tension in the "sharing" mother to reclaim dominance as primary parent in order to establish control and autonomy *somewhere*:

I was angry and I was jealous. I was jealous because he not only had the rewards of parenthood, he was into work he could relate to. I think one reason I nursed as long as I did was to keep myself as Amanda's most special person. It was also difficult to share one area of competence I felt I had…. After all, if she prefers David, what else do I have. I am woman therefore mother. I held on to my ambivalent identity as student in order to have something of my own. ⑦

Structural forces dictate that she'll be much more successful in claiming control in the family sphere than in the public sphere. For some women, particularly those who start as primary parents and then move to shared parenting, it is not a question of reclaiming but of giving up control of parenting in the first place. As expressed by one woman:

Neither of us could find a satisfactory way to increase his involvement. The children would have nothing to do with him. This situation probably came about because he was home less often and also because for many years the children were my own arena and thus my main base of power. At some level I probably did not want Ernie to be equally important in the lives of the children. ⑧

The reclaiming of or unwillingness to give up a more primary role in parenting is not easy. It often culminates in frustration or anger (self- or other-directed) when a woman sees herself as doing more or too much parenting in comparison with her male partner.

The man, on his part, can feel a number of things when his female partner claims more parenting responsibility for herself: resistant to being shut out, inadequate in his own seeming lack of parenting skills, relieved to relinquish 50 percent of control in a sphere that he was never meant or prepared to participate in anyway. This is not to say that father merely reacts to mother's power tactics. As I discuss more fully in the next section, he is often quite active in " granting" women increased power in the sphere of parenting to give him the time he wants, needs, or has been conditioned to devote to extrafamilial activities.

The underlying point is this: powerful tensions arise when the sexual divisions of labor and power in the family are altered without simultaneous sweeping restructuring of gender-related power relations outside the family. Women under advanced capitalism spend too much time feeling powerless to relish a situation where, under the auspices of liberation, they find themselves with less power. I have watched many a sharing mother—undervalued, sexually harassed, or discriminated against in the workplace—waffle on her outside work identity and refocus on the pleasure, reward, and fulfillment to be found in identity as a mother. This is not to say that she relinquishes her paid work but that indeed she becomes a *working mother*. Fathers, for their part, are not often prepared for the arduous, but undervalued task they take on in becoming the other mommy:

I get an empty feeling when people ask me what I'm doing. Most of my energy in the last six months has focused on Dylan, on taking care of him and getting used to his being here. But I still have enough man-work expectations in me that I feel uncomfortable just saying that. ⑨

Even if he, too, balks at the alienation of the workplace, the flight into parenthood is not a likely one.

The tension between men and women over this issue was illustrated by the marked female-male differences in response to the first draft of this article. Women, whether mothers or non-mothers, urged me to emphasize how *rare* it is for men to involve themselves in parenting or for shared parenting actually to work. Men, on the other hand, wanted me to put more emphasis on the growing involvement of men in family life and the actual fathering that men have done historically *and continue to do*. Both are true, and both reflect the unresolved dialectic between women and men regarding parenting responsibility.

Physical vs. Psychic Division of Labor in Parenting

The tensions in shared parenting cannot, however, be reduced to power politics in personal relationships. External expectations, attitudes, and ideology collide with deeply internalized self-concepts, skills, and personality structures to make the breakdown of the sexual division of labor in parenting an exciting but difficult project. Often the sharing *of physical* tasks is easily implemented: you feed the baby in the morning, I'll do it in the afternoon; you give the kids a bath on Mondays, I'll do it on Thursdays. What is left at least partially intact is the sexual division of the *psychological* labor in parenting. There is the question "Who carries around in their heads knowledge of diapers needing to be laundered, fingernails needing to be cut, new clothes needing to be bought?" Answer: mothers, because of years of socialization to do so. Vis-à-vis fathers, sharing mothers often find themselves in the position of cataloguer and taskmaster—We really should change the kids' sheets today; I think it's time for the kids' teeth to be checked. It is probable that men carry less of the mental load of parenting, regardless of mutual agreements to share the responsibility; this leaves the women more caught up in the psychic aspects of parenting.

The more significant division of psychological labor, however, is the different intrapsychic conflict that men and women experience in integrating their parent and nonparent identities. We have already looked at the power imbalance that pulls mothers back into the home and fathers away from it. A tremendous ambivalence or guilt in relinquishing full-time mothering responsibilities is common among women who depart from full-time mothering, either by working outside the home or sharing parenting responsibility with other(s):

> The myth of motherhood takes its toll. Employed mothers often feel guilty. They feel inadequate, and they worry about whether they are doing the best for their children. They have internalized the myth that there is something their children need that only they can give them.
>
> To have children but turn over their rearing to someone else—even their father—brings social disapproval: a mother who does this must be " hard," "unloving," and of course, "unfeminine."⑩

Numerous studies negating any ill effects to children who are not totally mother-raised pale in the public light in contrast to sensationalist reports of the delinquency, psychopathology, and emotional deficiencies that befall children who are not provided with the proper "mother-love". And this love is "naturally" woman's duty and domain. Raised in this culture, even the most committed feminist "sharing" mother will experience doubt. Doubts and fears are profound because the stakes are so high. By sharing parenting, we are experimenting with the growth and development of our children, adopting new child-rearing structures in the face of reports from psychologists, pediatricians, and politicians that we will only bring ruin to our young.

These fears are fueled by pressures from individuals in the sharing mother's immediate life. *Her* mother is often appalled or threatened by her daughter's deviation from her own parenting model. Relatives are often resistant to the notion that a man should hang around the house taking care of a kid. People will inadvertently (or deliberately) turn to mother rather than father in asking information about the children. Letters from school come addressed to "Dear Mother." From the point of view of the outside world, even though men are being given more and more attention for their participation in family life, the father remains an invisible or minimal figure in the daily rearing of children. A feeling so deeply internalized as "mother guilt," constantly rekindled by these external pressures and messages, creates in the sharing mother a strong ambivalence. Our intellectual selves lash out at the Alice Rossis telling us that we as women are the best-made parents, but our emotional selves struggle hard to calm the fear that our feminist views on motherhood may be ill founded.

As if mother guilt were not enough, women confront two additional conflicts. First, the traditional structures of child rearing have produced in a woman a psychological capacity to mother. With personal observations and experience to back her up, she may have a hard time believing that a father, with no parallel long-term preparation, is really capable of fulfilling "mothering" responsibilities. As she watches her male partner stick the baby with a diaper pin (even though she as a new parent may have done the same thing the day before) or try unsuccessfully to calm a screaming child, her suspicions are confirmed. Thus, internal forces pressure the mother to reclaim control over parenting in order to be assured that her children will survive intact. Men are often accomplices in this process: "Some men act out unconscious resistance to shared parenting by accentuating their ignorance, asking a lot of questions they could figure out themselves." ⑪ Sometimes women are not willing to be teachers. In the short run, they find it easier to do it themselves.

The second conflict arises from a woman's establishment of an "extra-mother" identity. We've already mentioned that women do not accrue much social recognition at the workplace, that they are seen as mothers first and workers second, and that when they attempt shared parenting they sometimes retreat from the world of paid work back into the female sphere of family life. Within her own psyche the sharing mother has a hard time integrating a work identity with being a mother: "When you go out to work, the job is something you *do*. But the work of a housewife and mother is not just something you do, it's something you *are*."[12]

For men, however, the experience is quite different. Historically, since the advent of industrialization, fathers' daily involvement with the kids in the nuclear family has been peripheral—usually concentrated on evening, weekend, and holiday play or instructional activities. There is no doubt that fathers have always been important figures in their children's lives and socialization experiences, even if as a result of their absence. The traditional father is very actively involved in his child's life as breadwinner as role model, as disciplinarian, but not in the day-to-day nurturant fashion that shared parenting dictates. The challenge for the man in shared parenting is to move from being a "father" to a "mother".

The growing participation of men in the birth experience of their children still often stops at the delivery room doors. Contrasted to mothers, the sharing father more likely enters the parenting experience with a nation that parenting is something you *do* rather than someone you are. In early preparation for this consciousness, preschool boys in a recent study not once reported "Daddy" as something they would be when they grew up, while a majority of girls named "Mommy" as a projected adult identity.[13] In popular writing today, involved fathering is often presented as a *choice*: "only if the man wants to."

Only this consciousness could yield an article in the *San Francisco Chronicle* about a football coach who "tossed in the towel" after a sixty-eight-day attempt at mothering: "Peters said yesterday he's convinced 'motherhood' is an impossible *task* [my emphasis] for a normal human being. "⑭ If parenting is something you *do*, then it is something you can stop doing. But it is much harder to stop being someone you are ⑮.

The guilt that the sharing father experiences is markedly different from the mother guilt reported above. Often he feels caught up in his own inadequacies, his own lack of socially molded "intuition" in handling the everyday intrapsychic and interpersonal aspects of parent-child relationships. It was mentioned earlier that men often resist shared parenting by accentuating their ignorance. But often they feel genuinely ignorant, lacking the psychological skills to meet their children's emotional needs. Learning practical skills like changing diapers or administering nose drops is one thing. Developing the traits of "empathy," "nurturance," "taking the role of the other" necessary to good "mothering" is a far more challenging task. These are the very traits that often remain underdeveloped or atrophy in the man's life history and are not easily reinstated at a later developmental period. The shared father's male guilt parallels the guilt felt more generally by men who feel accountable for the oppression of women (or a woman) and for the perpetuation of sexism. But within a relational context it can become magnified in shared parenting because the object of the father's guilt is not just the women he lives with but also the children he loves and feels responsible for. This is not to say that father guilt is limited only to the *sharing* father. Given that all fathers are involved in some parenting functions, any man who feels he is shirking his responsibilities (not spending enough time with the kids, not providing enough of an income) can experience guilt.

But the guilt is felt in relationship to something he does, in contrast to a more central and deep-seated guilt in mothers for something she is. Because of this the "sharing" man is less likely to be consumed by father guilt than the woman by mother guilt. Instead, he feels caught between parenting responsibilities and extrafamilial identity. When people ask him what his paid work is, nobody asks him, as they do his female partner, who takes care of the kids while he works. No one is awestruck by his dual responsibilities as worker and father; on the contrary, people and institutions will pin pressure on him to perform as if he had no child-care responsibilities. And as a child who grew up believing he should make something of himself that aspiration can gnaw at him. In Beauvoir's sense of "transcendence," being a successful parent does not qualify. Being successful or fulfilled in one's paid work or in public life does. Even when a man repudiates the work of public success ethic, as some men in our generation have done, he seldom turns to parenting as the locus of fulfillment and positive identity. This is well illustrated in the *San Francisco Chronicle* account of a financial wizard on Wall Street, a father of three, who took a year off to find himself. He spent his time lying on the couch, talking on the phone, collecting tropical fish, setting himself a "schedule bristling with physical, intellectual, and cultural self-improvement projects," and "marveling" at his wife's frantic schedule as homemaker and mother. His only parenting activity during this year was watching his son from behind a tree when his class had sports in the park. [16] Does this represent, at least in part, the actual content of "men's growing involvement in the family," which is making such a media splash? Coming home to a haven where one's own psychological needs can be nurtured is a far cry from taking on new responsibilities for the nurturance of others.

Gender-differentiated intrapsychic conflicts of sharing parents do not necessarily remain quietly within the mother's and father's heads. They appear in subtle male-female differences in actual parenting. The obvious difference often cited is that because of years of dolls and playing house, women will continue in our generation to make better parents than men because of their preparation and social induction into parenting. The woman, grappling with the repudiation of socially induced guilt that to mother less than full time is to abandon one's intimate relationship with the child, often vacillates among three stances: (1) overinvolvement with her child, often to prove to the world, her child, and herself that she is "supermom"; [17] (2) respectful human interaction with her children based on her ability to explore both her parent and nonparent self and not carry the whole weight of parenting on her shoulders; (3) tension, frustration, or underlying resentment directed at the child (or other parent), reflecting her own struggle, in the face of institutional and ideological obstacles, to integrate her identity as both a mother and a nonparenting adult.

The sharing father is less likely to experience such a tension-ridden relationship or overinvolvement with the children. He is not consumed by guilt for not parenting enough; more likely, he is being raised to the level of sainthood in certain of his immediate circles for parenting at all. He can maintain effective boundaries between himself and his child and provide unconflicted warmth and narturance. But with doing rather than being as the basis of day-to-day fathering, and with pressures to do something loftier than change diapers all day, the pull on the man may manifest itself instead in a psychic (or physical) disappearing act vis-à-vis the children, a phenomenon reminiscent of men's general coping style in other emotional relations. Instead of an overtly conflict-ridden relationship, the father's relationship with the children may be somewhat diluted in contrast to the mother's, or it may periodically dissipate. A father may feel the same frustration as a mother in trying to integrate parenting with other parts of his life, but he has a safety valve not as easily accessible to women. With more power in the outside world than women have and less indoctrination in the inevitability of parenthood as his primary adult role, he is freer to pull back from his parenting and direct more energy elsewhere. One mother reports that she had to leave town to accomplish the same redirection of energy away from parenting. The gender-related differences in handling this conflict are further exemplified in the following account. A mother was responsible for arranging child care for her child one year; the father was responsible the next year. Because she didn't have a paid job and felt it would allow her time with her child, the mother had consciously limited the number of days her child would attend child care during her year. In handling child-care arrangements for the following year, with the option of three or five days of child care per week, the father responded, "Five days of child-care, of course. It's my freedom we're talking about."

The foregoing mother-father differences are most representative of sharing couples who try to balance parenting and outside work. It is somewhat different for the "one year on, one year off" parenting pair. Here, when Dad is "on," he is more firmly planted in his parenting seat; Mom is out working and just isn't there to take over. And Mom, by periodically finding herself structurally in the traditional fathering role, can theoretically make a cleaner break from being a hovering mother in her "working" year. ⑱ But the advantages of this model must be weighed against its problems: (1) It is becoming increasingly difficult as more people discover that one parent's income is financially insufficient. (2) Often the mother's "year on" is during the child's infancy, when mother is recovering from pregnancy and breastfeeding. It is also when strong infant-parent bonding is developing, bonding that carries into later years and makes Mom more central than Dad in the child's psyche. (3) Even with the "on again, off again" parenting model, both parents are integrally involved in the child's life, and for all the reasons cited above Mom is still often more involved in her children during her "off" years than Dad in his "off" times.

In sum, both women and men in shared parenting relationships find themselves in a dialectical tension between breaking away from and retreating back into gender-differentiated parenting. The challenge and success in breaking away from traditional fathering and mothering is one of the most exciting social projects for our generation. The parents of those of us who come from second-generation left families look at our own shared parenting relationships with admiration and some sense of loss and frustration that their historical moment did not open up the same consciousness and opportunities for them. At the same time, the difficulties we encounter in actually implementing shared parenting bring home to us the long-term nature of our project and the necessity of working on all three fronts at once—production, social reproduction, and ideology—in the reorganization of personal life.

In this project we remind ourselves that shared parenting is necessary not just for the development of healthier relationships between mothers and fathers but also for the elimination of destructive engenderment and the provision of healthier socialization experiences along socialist-feminist principles for our children. What reflections can be made about the possible outcomes for the children of sharing parents?

[……]

Notes:

① Abarbenal, "Redefining Motherhood," p. 366.

② Cf. Ann Oakley, *Women's Work* (New York: Vintage Books, 1974), Chapter 8, "Myths of Woman's Place, 2: Motherhood"; Wini Breines, Margaret Cerullo, and Judith Stacey, "Social Biology, Family Studies, and Antifeminist Backlash," *Feminist Studies*, February 1978, pp. 43-68.

③ Nancy Chodorow, *The Reproduction of Mothering: Psychoanalysis and the Sociology of Gender* (Berkeley: University of California Press, 1978).

④ See, e. g. , Betty Friedan, "Feminism Takes a New Turn," *New York Times Magazine*, 16 November 1979; Caroline Bird, *The Two-Paycheck Marriage* (New York:Rawson-Wade,1979);Jane Geniesse, "On Wall Street: The Man Who Gave Up Working," *San Francisco Chronicle*, 13 November 1979;Lindsy Van Gelder, "An Unmarried Man," *Ms.* , November 1979.

⑤ Sheila Rowbotham, *Woman's Consciousness*, *Man's World* (Baltimore, Md. : Penguin, 1973), p. 61.

⑥ Oakley, *Woman's Work*, p. 220.

⑦ Abarbenal, "Redefining Motherhood," p. 360. This reaction is paralleled in the public sphere of work by the resistance of female child-care workers to allowing men in their field, as it is one area of paid work where women do have control (and can get jobs).

⑧ Quoted interview in Hawley, "Shared Parenthood," p. 134. This desire to maintain parenting within woman's sphere as a source of power may have had some influence, conscious or unconscious, on the feminist movement's tendency to avoid demands for fathers' involvement in parenting.

⑨ David Steinberg, "Redefining Fatherhood: Notes after Six Months," in Louise Kappe Howe, ed. , *The Future of the Family* (New York: Simon and Schuster, 1972), p. 370.

⑩ Oakley, *Woman's Work*, pp. 211, 189.

⑪ Hawley, "Shared Parenthood," p. 139.

⑫ Rowbotham, *Woman's Consciousness*, p. 76.

⑬ Barbara Chasen, "Sex Role Stereotyping and Pre-Kindergarten Teachers," *Elementary School Journal*, 1974, pp. 74, 225-235.

⑭ "A Father Who Failed as a Mother," *San Francisco Chronicle*, 6 September 1978.

⑮ In the general population, the large number of desertions or failures to pay alimony or child payments by fathers testifies to the male-female difference in "parenting permanence"; the number of women who similarly desert their parenting role is infinitesimal in comparison.

⑯ Jane Geniesse, "On Wall Street: The Man Who Gave Up Working," *San Francisco Chronicle*, 13 November 1979. *Ms*. magazine has reported similar situations.

⑰ This is parallel to the phenomenon that many lesbian mothers feel even more strongly. To answer society's accusations that they are unfit mothers, they are constantly under pressure to be even better than the best moms.

⑱ The importance of this structural position, often outweighing the saliency of gender, is highlighted in the account of a lesbian parent who holds a paid job while her partner, the actual biological mother of the child, stays home to care for the baby. She reports feeling just like a father when she arrives home, wanting to be cared for and attended to by her partner after a long day at work.

安·丹琴,"母性的未来:生育技术与女性主义理论"
17
Anne Donchin,"The Future of Mothering:Reproductive Technology and Feminist Theory"

安·丹琴(Anne Donchin)①是美国印第安纳大学—印第安纳波里斯普渡大学(Indiana University-Purdue University Indianapolis)哲学系名誉教授,女性研究和博爱研究系兼职教授。她主要研究生物医学伦理、女性主义理论以及其它相关的跨学科理论。

丹琴于1953年在芝加哥大学获哲学学士学位,1954年在威斯康星大学获文学学士学位,1965年获莱斯大学文学硕士学位,1970年获得克萨斯大学哲学博士学位。1981～1982年荣获国家人文基金(National Endowment for the Humanities),1989～1990年获黎黎基金(Lilly Endowment)②。她于1992年创办女性主义生物伦理学国际网站,并一直担任协调员至1998年。

丹琴的代表著作是与劳拉·珀蒂(Laura M. Purdy)③合编的《再现生物伦

---

① 访问 http://w3. liberalarts. iupui. edu/faculty/fgMain. asp? action = view&FacultyNumber =60。

② 黎黎基金是一项私人慈善基金,由黎黎家族的三个成员于1937年创立,资金来源于艾里·黎黎公司(Eli Lilly and Company)的医药股票盈利,旨在资助印第安纳州的宗教、教育、社区发展等活动。访问 http://www. lillyendowment. org。

③ 劳拉·珀蒂是威尔斯学院(Wells College)哲学系教授,她于1974年获哈佛大学哲学博士学位。主要研究领域有伦理学、应用伦理学、生物伦理学、女性主义理论、家庭及教育问题等。访问 http://aurora. wells. edu/ ~ lpurdy。

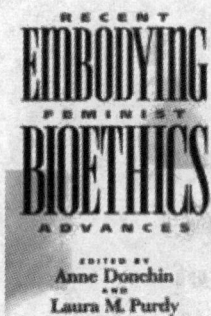

理：女性主义的新进展》(*Embodying Bioethics：Recent Feminist Advances*,1999 年)。该书汇集了 14 篇杰出女性主义理论家对生物伦理学的重要问题展开的讨论,文章均发表在 1996 年在旧金山召开的女性主义生物伦理学国际研讨会。

丹琴发表的文章中比较重要的是在《生物伦理学》(*Bioethics*)杂志 2000 年第 3 期(总第 14 卷)上发表的《独立自主、相互依赖与借力自杀：尊重界限与跨越分歧》("Autonomy, Interdependence, and Assisted Suicide：Respecting Boundaries/Crossing Lines")。文章通过讨论借助于医生自杀的行为考察自主性的界限。

本书选注丹琴所著"母性的未来：生育技术与女性主义理论"一文首先发表于《希帕蒂亚：女性主义哲学》杂志(*Hypatia：A Journal of Feminist Philosophy*)1986 年秋季卷。

文章分为六个部分：

引言。丹琴从玛吉·皮厄茜(Marge Piercy)所著《时间边缘的女人》(*Woman on the Edge of Time*, 1976 年)①和赫胥黎(Aldous Huxley)所著《美丽新世界》((*Brave New World*, 1932 年)②中从未来世界的乌托邦和反乌托邦

---

① 玛吉·皮厄茜,美国诗人、小说家、理论家。已出版诗集 17 部、小说 17 部以及数部散文集、回忆录。代表小说有《生活的昂贵代价》(*The High Cost of Living*, 1978 年)、《走向士兵》(*Gone to Soldiers*, 1987 年)、《他、她和它》(*He, She and It*, 1991 年)和《女人的憧憬》(*The Longings of Women*, 1994 年)。重要杂文集有《与猫同眠》(*Sleeping with Cats*, 2002 年)和《两性战争》(*Sex Wars*, 2005 年)。《时间边缘的女人》发表于 1976 年,是皮厄茜创作的一部科幻小说。小说描写一位被送入精神病院的母亲在精神被控制下几次访问未来世界,这是一个用非中心化的无政府主义思想组织的社会,人们对科技怀有积极的、环保主义的态度。孩子在人造子宫中孕育,每个孩子都有三个父母。小说中描写的理想社会折射出现实社会的弊端。访问 http://www.margepiercy.com。

② 阿道斯·赫胥黎(1894～1963)出生在知识分子世家,是倡导进化论的托马斯·赫胥黎的孙子。他在 1931 年用 4 个月时间写成《美丽新世界》,这部书成为他的代表作。这是一部反乌托邦作品,故事发生在 600 年后的未来,此时的社会由实用主义思想治理以保证最大的稳定和幸福。生育由技术控制,被人为地根据需要设定,这样,人的命运在出生前就已经被决定了。访问 http://somaweb.org。

的描写出发,说明他们作品中描述的生育技术已经逐渐在生活中越来越广泛地应用:人工授精、体外受精、卵子移植以及正在进行的模拟胎盘功能的试验、子宫外受孕等技术的发明和试验成功,说明谁控制这些技术谁就将有权力控制未来的世界①。丹琴告诉读者她将在文中梳理女性主义中间面对生育技术的出现产生的几种主要思想立场,分析其利弊,并尝试找到解决这些理论分歧的中间道路(第 123 ~ 124 页;第 314 ~ 315 页)。

第一部分,"当今的社会背景"("The Present Social Context")。丹琴指出,同英国和澳大利亚不同,美国对于生育技术的使用和研发没有立法限制,也因此对由此产生的道德和伦理问题缺乏规范(第 124 页;第 315 页)。到目前为止,生育技术的使用基本依赖于使用者的经济能力和医务工作者自身的道德准则(第 124 页;第 315 页)。对于创新的生育技术,社会反响差距很大,这将在以下的部分详细解释。

第二部分,"不干涉主义"("The Noninterventionists")。持不干涉主义论调的代表人物是新教神学家保罗·兰姆兹(Paul Ramsey)②,他反对除用医学或外科手段治疗不孕不育以外的所有形式的生育技术(第 125 ~ 126 页;第 317 ~ 318 页)。他关注对自然的权力和对人类的权力之间的关系,这一点引起许多女性主义理论家的共鸣(第 127 页;第 319 页)。另一位代表人物是雷昂·卡斯(Leon Kass)③,他认为,生育技术将使人类生活处于危险状态,因此,他倡议建立相关立法来规范体外受精和胚胎移植(第 127 页;第 319 页)。

第三部分,"适度干涉主义"("Moderate Interventionists")。生育权力深

---

① Anne Donchin, "The Future of Mothering: Reproductive Technology and Feminist Theory", *Hypatia* 1.2 (Fall 1986): pp. 122-123. 本节所引该文观点均出自此处,以下只在正文标明页码,分号后第二个页码为引文在本书的页码。

② 保罗·兰姆兹被认为是 20 世纪最为重要的伦理学家,他的《基督教基本伦理》(*Basic Christian Ethics*, 1950 年)决定性地影响了 20 世纪后半叶西方政治、宗教、医学、道德和伦理的走向。

③ 雷昂·卡斯(1939~),哈佛大学生物化学博士,芝加哥大学教授,曾任外科医生并在国家科学院任医学伦理学研究员。代表著作有《走向更加自然的科学:生物学与人类事务》(*Toward a More Natural Science: Biology and Human Affairs*, 1988 年)和《饥饿的灵魂:吞噬和完善我们的自然》(*The Hungry Soul: Eating and the Perfecting of Our Nature*, 1994 年)。2001 年 8 月,卡斯被美国总统布什任命为生物伦理学委员会主任。访问 http://olincenter. uchicago. edu/kass_cv. html 和 http://www. alteich. com/links/kass. htm。

深植根于西方传统(第 128 页;第 320 页),如果利用生育技术使想要生一个"自己的孩子"的愿望延伸至家庭以外,就会产生严重的问题(第 129 页;第 321 页)。乔治·阿纳斯(George Annas)①在 1985 年曾指出,如果不对生育技术的使用进行合理的立法,将会危及家庭的稳固和孩子的利益(第 129 页;第 322 页)。他建议在孩子出生时刻对父亲和母亲身份进行定义,并提出保护人类胚胎不用作商业用途(第 129 页;第 322 页)。

第四部分,"激进干涉主义"("Radical Interventionists")。正如皮厄茜小说中描写的那样,过度地干涉人类自然的生育过程将颠覆对母亲身份的传统定义。激进干涉主义的代表是舒拉米斯·费厄斯通(Shulamith Firestone)②,她在《性别的辩证法》(*The Dialectic of Sex*)一书中提倡用生育技术消除两性间的生理差异,从而消除所有的文化分类(第 130 页;第 323 页)。她把人类的生理状况视为必须克服的局限,把科学技术看做征服自然的有力武器(第 130 页;第 323~324 页)。但丹琴认为,如果没有文化角色作媒介,我们将很难确定自己经验的价值到底在哪里(第 130 页;第 323 页)。

第五部分,"女性主义的反响"("Feminist Reaction")。丹琴指出,费厄斯通的理论在女性主义理论家中间引起了争论,一些人认为费厄斯通的理论对后来的女性主义理论影响重大,另一些人则不以为然,因为她们看到技术也经常被用来加强男性的统治(第 131 页;第 324 页)。阿尔-希布利(Azizah Y. al-Hibri)③主张,男性控制技术,从而也将继续对女性实施控制,这一点重新定义了压迫和权力关系,这一观点得到乔德罗④和迪纳斯坦⑤的认同(第 132 页;第

---

① 乔治·阿纳斯是波士顿大学公共卫生学院教授,波士顿大学法学院法律与健康科学中心主任,是一位知名的医学与法律专家和公众人物。代表著作有《患者的权利》(*The Rights of Patients*, 1989 年)和《选择:法律、医学与市场》(*Some Choice: Law, Medicine and the Market*, 1998 年)。访问 http://www. meta-library. net/bio/annas-body. html。

② 舒拉米斯·费厄斯通(1945~   ),著名女性主义理论家,芝加哥女性解放联合会的创建者。代表著作是《性别的辩证法》(*The Dialectic of Sex*, 1970 年)。

③ 阿尔-希布利是里奇蒙大学法律学教授,宾夕法尼亚大学哲学博士,曾创办《希帕蒂亚:女性主义哲学》杂志(*Hypatia: A Journal of Feminist Philosophy*)。访问 http://religion. ciweb. org/biobox_hibri. html。

④ 南茜·乔德罗,美国心理学家、女性主义理论家。参见本书第一篇第 4 节。

⑤ 多萝西·迪纳斯坦,美国女性主义理论家。参见本书第二篇第 12 节。

326 页）。一些学者对费厄斯通建议的针对技术的补救措施提出质疑（第 132 ~ 133 页；第 326 页），卡罗尔·麦克米兰（Carol McMillan）①就是这样的一位代表。里奇②似乎也把母亲身份截然地分割成理论意义上的和实践意义上的，把母亲经历从社会环境中孤立开来。这在丹琴看来有待仔细研究（第 135 页；第 330 页）。简奈特·塞厄斯（Janet Sayers）③就对里奇提出了批评。她认为，把女性之间的关系等同于婴儿与母亲间的关系，这纯属幻想，实际上，女性之间的关系是以冲突为特征的（第 136 页；第 330 页）。

丹琴认为，目前没有任何女性主义理论可以引导生育技术的发展，她因此提出这样几条道路供选择：其一，支持里奇的观点，反对所有生育技术的使用；其二，支持费厄斯通的观点，不计后果地使用生育技术；其三，综合女性主义各方观点以形成中间立场，加强对话，并试图影响目前生育技术的走向（第 136 ~ 137 页；第 331 ~ 332 页）。显然，这第三条道路是丹琴力主的。

The Future of Mothering:
Reproductive Technology and Feminist Theory

An exploration of (i) alternative perspectives toward recent innovations in reproductive technology support for new techniques for the sake of the kind of feminist future they facilitate, unqualified opposition despite therapeutic benefit to individual women, or qualified opposition depending upon specific threats to women's interests and (ii) relationships between these positions and values bound

---

① 卡罗尔·麦克米兰，美国女性主义理论家。代表著作是《女性、理性与自然：关于女性主义的一些哲学问题》（*Women, Reason and Nature: Some Philosophical Problems with Feminism*, 1982 年）。

② 亚德里安·里奇，美国诗人、女性主义理论家。参见本书第一篇第 2 节。

③ 简奈特·塞厄斯，英国肯特大学社会政策、社会学和社会研究学院心理分析学和心理学教授。代表著作有《生理政治：女性主义与反女性主义视角》（*Biological Politics: Feminist and Anti-Feminist Perspectives*, 1982 年）、《性别冲突：心理学、心理分析与女性主义》（*Sexual Contradictions: Psychology, Psychoanalysis, and Feminism*, 1986 年）和《心理分析的母亲》（*Mothers of Psychoanalysis*, 1991 年）。访问 http://www. kent. ac. uk/sspssr/staff/sayers. htm。

up with mothering practices.

The nurse said I would have to show you, but you reached right for my breast. You suckled right away I remember how you grabbed with your small pursed mouth at my breast and started drawing milk from me, how sweet it felt. How could anyone know what being a mother means, who has never earned a child nine months heavy under her heart, who has never borne a baby in blood and pain, who has never suckled a child. What do they know of motherhood?

Connie Ramos, a mother of our time

It was part of women's long revolution. When we were breaking all the old hierarchies. Finally there was that one thing we had to give up too, the only power we ever had, in return for no more power for anyone. The original production the power to give birth 'Cause as long as we were never biologically enchained, we'd never be equal. And males never would be humanized to be loving and tender. So we all become mothers. Every child has three. To break the nuclear bonding.

Luciente, a "mother" from a possible future

Connie's dialogue with Luciente takes place within the imaginative territory explored by Marge Piercy in *Woman on the Edge of Time* (1976, 105-106). Hers is a culturally androgynous society based on feminist values and organized about a commitment to the extinction of all systematic sex-role distinctions and the elimination of biological reproduction by females. Instead genetic material taken from human males and females is stored in "brooders" where it is fertilized and the embryos are grown until ready for birth. The bond between genes and culture is deliberately broken. Knowledge of genetic origin is obliterated. Still the citizens of Luciente's world remain divided over the desirability of genetic intervention. They watch for birth defects, for genes linked with disease susceptibility, but they do not yet breed for selected traits. The "shapers" among them push for selective breeding, the "mixers" "don't think people can know objectively how people should become." They see the "shapers" proposal as a "power surge" (Piercy

1976, 226).

The breeding practices adopted in Piercy's utopian society bear a remarkable resemblance to the reproductive arrangements instituted in Aldous Huxley's dystopian *Brave New World* (1932), though in this imaginative future, not only eugenics, but dysgenics, as well, is practiced systematically. In their laboratories they gestate both biologically "superior" embryos and, in far larger numbers, biologically "inferior" embryos which are subjected to the Bokanosky Process (ninety-six identical twins from a single ovum) and treated prenatally with toxins. When decanted they are barely recognizably human, but are useful in performing unskilled work and, with appropriate conditioning, can be relied upon to docilely follow the commands of superiors. Reproduction has been brought wholly within control of the state.

Since Huxley's dystopian fantasy appeared, the feasibility of such a world has drawn increasingly nearer to us. Researchers have made substantial strides in both genetic research and reproductive technologies. Artificial insemination has become a commonplace occurrence. *In vitro* fertilization and ovum transfer, though only marginally successful, are widely practiced. Economically disadvantaged women are readily available to serve as surrogate mothers for a modest fee. When mastery of the processes of extra-uterine gestation is achieved, they will be dispensible too. Already extra-corporeal membrane oxygenation (an adaptation of the heart-lung machine) is being applied successfully to infants weighing even less than one kilogram (Bartlett 1984). Once the functions of the placenta have been successfully mimicked, perpetuation *in vitro* to viability (ectogenesis) will render the biological process of pregnancy technically obsolete. Though the mere fact of technological feasibility might suggest possible development within either a Piercean or a Huxleyan social framework, subsequent achievement of effective political control over larger, more diffuse populations than even Huxley envisaged only sharpens the vision of the more portentous future. And were extra-uterine gestation to become available, the potential for such a concentration of political power would be immeasurably enhanced. Those who control the instrumentalities of power would command the means to bring either future into being.

If women's long-term interests are to be represented in determining the future direction of reproductive technology, women will need to participate collectively in shaping public policy. Unfortunately, there has been too little discussion among women about either the fundamental values at stake or the social goals that would best promote women's well-being. Though many feminist writers have expressed concern *retrospectively* about the increased dominance of medically controlled childbirth technologies and some have pointed to the direction in which prevailing interests are pushing reproductive technology, this discussion has taken place in virtual isolation from both the general context of feminist theorizing and the background of social theory with which feminist theory is intertwined ①. There is need now to integrate grass-root feminist concerns about medically controlled reproduction with feminist theorists' attempts to reconstruct the social framework of women's collective past and draw out connections to possible feminist futures. We need to think collectively about the sort of social policy that would best serve women's most fundamental interests whether the capacity to give birth is of such paramount value that no social aim achievable in any technological future could supplant it, whether *all* technological innovations in reproductive practices should be opposed despite their therapeutic benefit to some women individually, or if specific technological advances might be supported step by step until their deleterious social effects become clearly manifest.

In the following pages I should like to sketch out a framework within which such a feminist dialogue might proceed. First, I shall briefly discuss the utilization of reproductive technologies within the present social context, then describe the principal ethical and social positions regarding emerging reproductive technologies, considering the social values and policy alternatives implicit in each position, attempting to ferret out the implications of these developments for the interests of women. Next I will raise some conceptual and theoretical questions about the very idea of a utopian feminist future, considering first, the arguments of feminist theorists who have taken exception to the sort of utopian analysis Shulamith Firestone offers and then those feminist commentators who share Huxley's dystopian prognosis of a future where the bond between pregnancy and procreation has been severed. Finally, I will contrast their positions with the utopian feminists in order to better understand the basis of present feminist reaction to reproductive innovation, whether it stems principally from reservation about the nature of technological intervention itself or from fears about the more probable consequences of such a technological future I will end with some observations about the presuppositions underlying theoretical differences among feminists and suggest an interim course of action to meet the present situation.

The Present Social Context

Although Great Britain and Australia have established national commissions to investigate the ethical and social implications of the new reproductive technologies and recommend appropriate social policy, in the United States the development and utilization of reproductive innovations is left to the discretion of individuals and physicians. Though there has been some consideration at the federal level of ethical issues involving *in vitro* fertilization and embryo transfer, the Ethics Advisory Board which undertook this work was disbanded after submitting its initial report in 1979. Though federally supported research into these processes cannot proceed without the approval of the disbanded committee, both private research efforts and commercial marketing of new reproductive techniques continue to go forward with virtually no ethical constraints other than those researchers themselves choose to impose. ② Individuals seeking to benefit from the fruits of reproductive research are left free to negotiate with individual physicians subject only to the constraints of private conscience and economic resources.

In instances of artificial insemination, a low-tech "cottage" industry, medical and economic constraint virtually fall out and individual choice becomes the exclusive determinant. Recipient choice is limited, however, by available information which lies principally within the control of "donors" (more accurately "sperm vendors," since in most instances they are paid for their product). Because of possible legal liability their anonymity is usually protected. Though most recipients would prefer to receive sperm from genetically screened donors, access to such information is frequently denied them. Where women attempt to procure sperm through non-medical channels from *known* donors, they risk the possibility that the donor may later claim paternity.

Hence some controls are desirable both from the perspective of those seeking to suppress the dissemination of reproductive technologies altogether and in the interests of unmarried and infertile women who hope to benefit from reproductive innovations. The principal issues, then, center around the nature of these controls and the goals toward which they are to be directed. Would women's interests be better served by continuing along the present freewheeling course that maximizes "reproductive freedom," limited only by the capacity to find a cooperative physician and by the patient's ability to bear the cost of the service? Or should the available options be limited by circumscribing choices, either at the level of service delivery or in the process of further research development.

Both of these positions are defended by their supporters as options which maintain continuities with social and political traditions. One emphasizes individual freedom, the other gives centrality to traditional patterns of reproduction and parenting. However, emphasis upon individualistic values tends to push in the direction of technological innovation. Attention to the focal role of the biological family in social organization, in effect, subordinates individual interests and would suppress unfettered technological development.

Social reactions to innovative reproductive practices divide roughly into three camps: the noninterventionists, who question the advisability of any practice which tampers with either nature's way of doing things or traditional social institutions; the moderate interventionists, who give primacy to reproductive freedom while acknowledging that some weight should be attached to other values as well; and the radical interventionists who divide into two distinctive factions: those who support advances in knowledge of reproductive processes for their own sake without regard to possible technological applications and those who favor reproductive research for the sake of the technological future such research will facilitate. Advocates of the first version of the radical position are to be found principally among researchers and some philosophers who argue that we should push the frontiers of knowledge forward now and concern ourselves about undesirable applications only as the need becomes manifest. ③ Most conspicuous among supporters of the second version are Marge Piercy and her model, Shulamith Firestone whose 1970 work *The Dialectic of Sex: The Case for Feminist Revolution*, first focused feminist attention on the political significance of reproductive biology. Ursula LeGuin's fantasy *The Left Hand of Darkness* (1976) and Joanna Russ' *The Female Male* (1975) also borrow their central themes from Firestone's proposal. All look with favor upon reproductive innovations which free women from their traditional biological role.

The Noninterventionists

Among the most eloquent and articulate of the noninterventionists is Protestant theologian Paul Ramsey, who participated in the deliberations of the now defunct Ethics Advisory Board. He objects to all forms of reproductive innovation other than medical or surgical treatment of infertility (Ramsey 1972). In support of his position he offers three arguments: (1) It is a violation of the received canons of medical ethics to expose a possible human being to any unnecessary risk. Since a merely possible human cannot grant consent, there is no ground upon which it is morally permissible to jeopardize its future well being. (2) The proper role of medicine is the correction of "medical conditions," such as infertility. However, if there are no remedies for the physical condition itself, then it is not appropriate to intervene further. (3) Procreation and parenthood are "courses of action" appropriate to humans as natural objects toward whom an attitude of "natural piety" is appropriate. They cannot without violation be disassembled and put together again. Instead we should work according to the functions operating in the whole of the natural order of which we are a part Increasing mastery over nature brings increased power over humans and even greater risk of abuse.

Each of Ramsey's arguments incorporates controversial presuppositions: (1) that the canons of medical ethics are extendable to merely *possible* humans, and (2) that medicine's proper function is the reversal of a physical condition. Many physical deficits cannot be reversed, but where the function is highly valued, ways are found to circumvent the incapacity, e. g. prosthetic limbs, or eyeglasses, etc.

Many women experience sterility as such an incapacity. Having learned from infancy to associate femininity with fertility they look upon their barrenness as a mutilation. The apparent eagerness of many women to endure considerable pain and suffering at the hands of technological experts in an often futile attempt to bring about a pregnancy cannot be understood apart from this larger social context. Others fully intend to bear children but are victims of "family planning" technologies or environmental pollutants injurious to their reproductive capacities. The social obligation to such women cannot be dismissed merely on the ground that patient *desire* is not the proper object of medical intervention. That argument fails to speak to the morally relevant features of the situation. ④

Ramsey's final argument is complex, incorporating presumptions about both the place of humans in nature and the tendencies of human nature. There are serious ambiguities here which merit careful examination. It is not clear why the bare fact that something is natural should give it any moral weight. Why moral force should be attributed selectively to normal procreation while human intervention, say, in the use of respirators for premature infants is unquestioningly supported calls for further explanation. For such an appeal to nature to stand it would have to rest on some other ground, possibly the fear that human power over reproduction, in particular, would invite serious abuse. ⑤

Despite the fragmentary character of Ramsey's arguments they do point to several widely shared concerns about the direction in which reproductive innovation is leading technologically advanced societies. His allusion to a relationship between power over nature and power over humans, in particular, captures a concern widely shared by feminist critics of technological innovation, a theme which I shall return to later and examine in detail within the context of feminist criticism.

Leon Kass, a physician and influential writer on medical ethical issues, also frames his principal objection to reproductive innovations on traditionalist grounds, but unlike Ramsey who sees the principal threat in the violation of "nature," Kass emphasizes values attached to human respect. However, his notion of "respect" bears the mark of an origin closely linked to Ramsey's conception of "nature". Though he claims that what is at stake is the idea of the humanness of human life and the meaning of human embodiment, these conceptions appear to borrow their meaning from their affinity with social practices assumed to be naturally given rather than socially derived.

On the basis of these assumptions Kass favors legislative intervention to regulate the dangers of *in vitro* fertilization and embryo transfer which, he argues, "erode fundamental beliefs, values, institutions and practices" (Kass 1979). He proposes that the use of embryo transfer be restricted to the married couple from whom the embryo derives in order to sustain traditional bonds among sexuality, love and procreation.

Like Ramsey, Kass proposes that further research be restricted to the treatment of infertility or other measures that support the desire to have a child of "one's own" (by implication presupposing a distinction between legitimate and inappropriate desires). He opposes use of embryos in investigative research, donation to other couples or commercial transactions (such as surrogate mothering arrangements), claiming that such practices violate the traditional human sense of our sexual nature and the experience of relatedness to our ancestors and descendants. He, too, fears the concentration of power such technological developments would place within the control of researchers and special interests, but his fear, unlike Ramsey's, is couched within an appeal to cultural practices rather than to nature. However, since his cultural arrangements seemingly owe their authority to what is "natural" the differences between them are not so great as would first appear. Though Kass is undoubtedly correct in observing that certain innovative practices, were they to become widespread, would threaten present conceptions of historical connectedness, it is not self-evident either that such innovations would be widely adopted or that prevailing norms are more desirable than any that might supplant them. Moreover, there are other well established traditions which tend to give primacy to individual autonomous decision-making over collective social interests, traditions frequently appealed to by advocates of innovative reproductive practices.

Moderate Interventionists

The right to procreate is firmly imbedded in the Western liberal tradition. However, the *desire* to have a child of "one's own" is not harbored exclusively by couples as pairs, as Kass' view suggests, but may extend to individuals one by one Noel Keane (1981), ⑥ an attorney involved in facilitating surrogate mothering arrangements, relates the story of a 59 year old lawyer who came to his office. He and his 61 year old wife had no children. She had been infertile throughout their marriage. He had planned to leave his estate to his nieces and nephews but then became intrigued by the renewed possibility that he might still be able to will his property to a child of his own. He asked Keane to find a couple willing to assist him. The wife would be artificially inseminated with his semen and bear his child. He would guarantee financial arrangements for the child and provide for its education. Keane pursued his request and made suitable arrangements. He has also established a surrogate mothering agency and is lobbying for legislative reform that would facilitate legal enforcement of surrogate contracts ⑦. Decisions either to support such individualistic practices within the law or discourage options of this kind will have an important bearing on future social policy determinations, marking the boundary between the permissible exercise of personal desire and the sphere of collective social interests. Though the desire to pass on one's genetic endowment seems a predominantly male preoccupation, women's interests in bearing and rearing children outside the institution of marriage might also be served by a social policy that allows individuals free space to construct alternative childrearing arrangements. However, the legal advantages presently available to married couples, such as Keane represents, are not so readily extended to the unmarried who seek to fulfill comparable desires.

Recent judicial decisions have repeatedly affirmed the "right" of individuals, at least within marriage, to control their own reproductive activity. This freedom is taken to be derived from the right to privacy, to a domain within which individuals may pursue their own life plans with a minimum of societal interference. Supporters of innovative reproductive technologies are by implication advocating application of these individualistic norms to an increasingly broader range of circumstances. Extension of the scope of reproductive freedom to gratification of a desire to parent (either biologically or socially) by technological intervention is highly problematic. Legal rulings supporting reproductive freedom have leaned principally on rights of *noninterference*, on the liberty *not* to procreate. However, at issue here, is legal support for service demanded from *other* parties. In such instances, the use of innovative technologies is likely to impinge on other persons' rights of noninterference and on other social values, some that are preconditions for the very exercise of personal autonomy and others that would command comparable weight in any just social ordering.

George Annas, in testimony to the U. S. House of Representatives Committee on Science and Technology (U. S. 1985), recently pointed out that if children resulting from such techniques as surrogate embryo transfer (to a woman other than the egg donor) and the use of frozen embryos are to be adequately protected, government will have to intervene into the arena of human reproduction. Failure to regulate private contractual agreements, he argues, jeopardizes the integrity of the family and threatens the interests of children. The claims of some infertile couples, he contends, are outweighed by the interest of the potential child. For the sake of protecting these interests he advocates legal action (1) defining maternity and paternity at the moment of birth, preserving the current legal presumption that the gestation mother is the legal mother so that it will be conclusive and cannot be overridden by private contractual arrangements, and (2) protecting the human embryo from commercial exploitation by restricting the freedom to use frozen embryos to the purpose specified by the donors (Annas 1984). The Warnock Commission Report incorporates comparable recommendations.

However, some object to the modesty of such regulatory recommendations, particularly those noninterventionists who accept Ramsey's and Kass ' arguments in defense of early embryos and traditional conceptions of the family Some feminists reach the same conclusions, too, though for other reasons. They fear further erosion of women's decisionmaking powers if reproductive technologies are allowed to proliferate so freely.

Radical Interventionists

Incorporation of Marge Piercy's thought-experiment into consideration of policy options for the more immediate future should promote us to consider more carefully the grounds for hesitancy to support reproductive innovations, where what is principally at issue is the nature of the activity itself or fears about the likely consequences to follow Luciente, Piercy's protagonist from Mattapoisett, her utopian feminist world, readily acknowledges that the institution of their new reproductive arrangements required women to relinquish the power to give birth. However, they judge the benefit well worth the sacrifice since all power relations have been abolished as well. Within such a social context the choice seems obviously sensible.

There is reason to wonder, though, whether such a social framework is plausible, or even intelligible? Apart from the obvious difficulty in understanding a set of social circumstances under which the socially and politically advantaged would agree to relinquish power, it is far from clear that we can even comprehend the meanings of the radically new roles envisaged for such a society. The astonishment of Marge Piercy's character, Connie Ramos, is shared by all her readers who wonder what the word "mother" could mean divorced from both the facts of biological mothering and the set of social expectations imbedded in traditional mothering practices. Within a social tradition that ungrudgingly grants women little status and few gratifications apart from the mothering role, there is no solid ground upon which so radically novel a conception can get a foothold. Presented with such a set of facts about alternative social structures Connie is at a loss to understand what value to place upon them. Her plight dramatizes the reaction of many feminists to Shulamith Firestone's case for feminist revolution *The Dialectic of Sex*. Firestone's proposals for the "abolition of all cultural categories" (1970, 182) and the transformation of procreation so that "genital distinctions between the sexes would no longer matter culturally" (1970, 11) boggle the imagination, for without the mediation of a set of cultural roles and expectations we cannot know what value to place upon our experiences.

Though Firestone's advocacy of technological reproduction aims to serve feminists interests, it rests on conceptual foundations that have much in common with the presuppositions of researchers and policymakers who would pursue goals antagonistic to her own, who would support technological intervention for the sake of the monopoly of power it would make possible. Both sorts of interests view technology as "a victory over nature". They favor not only *reproductive* technology but the technological transformation of production and the elimination of labor as well. Both see human biology as a limitation to be overcome—for Firestone, because she takes the relations of procreation to be the base of society and the source of women's oppression, for those who would support "a brave new world," because the diffusion of power among women and families threatens their own power hegemony.

Feminist Reaction

In this section I will try to isolate the issues of deepest concern to feminist thinkers who see advances in reproductive technology as further encroachments on the social status of women. Some of these concerns relate to the theoretical underpinnings of Firestone's theory and, by implication, to similar analyses of the causes of and correctives for women's cultural subordination. Others focus instead on the more probable consequences of technological transformations within a social context still dominated by male power structures. In most feminist commentaries both kinds of concerns are intertwined. However, here I will attempt to disentangle them so that detachable claims can then be examined one by one on their own merits. I will focus first on one issue that enters importantly into the expression of these concerns the presumptive neutrality of technology to gender specific social practices. Then I will briefly allude to a second significant issue the possibility of making meaningful distinctions between the biologically given and the culturally acquired. Finally I will offer a tentative interpretation of the importance of the mothering debate for feminist theory, ending with some remarks about conditions for the participation of feminist theorists in shaping reproductive policy.

Firestone's influence on subsequent feminists is a matter of some controversy, particularly with regard to her principal claims that mothering is more a barrier to women's self-fulfillment than a vehicle for it and that biological motherhood lies at the heart of women's oppression. Hester

Eisenstein, in her most recent work, *Contemporary Feminist Thought* (1983), credits Firestone with considerable influence over subsequent feminist theorists, particularly in the early 1970's when feminism and motherhood were widely held to be in diametrical opposition. She attributes opposition to Alice Rossi's (1977) advocacy of women's nurturing role (the position that the capacity to nurture is shaped by *biological* as well as social factors) to sympathy for Firestone's position. However, Alison Jaggar in her *Feminist Politics and Human Nature* (1983) points to a lack of enthusiasm for Firestone among grass-roots feminists, probably springing, she speculates, from a widespread suspicion of advanced technology, from the observation that technology has so often been used to reinforce male dominance. Hence these feminists do not see how women could take control of technology and use it for their own ends. This latter position is given further support by Azizah al-Hibri, who argues that

> *Technological reproductive does not equalize the natural reproductive power structure—it* inverts it. *It appropriates the reproductive power from women and places it in the hands of men who now control both the sperm and the reproductive technology that could make it indispensable it " liberates" them from their humiliating dependency" on women in order to propagate.* (1984, 266)

Further, she argues, were cloning techniques to be perfected as well, men would finally be freed from their need to share their genes with women.

Her argument challenges both the claim that it is women's biological function that lies at the root of their oppression and the derivative implication that technological reform can eliminate oppressive social practices. It rests on a very different analysis of the basis of male domination, the presumption that *envy* of women's reproductive capacities and fear of their powers create a male need to control women, limiting the free exercise of those powers. Several features of the present situation support such an alternative analysis. If the root of women's oppression were their biological role, then enormous male resistance to the technologization of procreation might be expected, for each step toward its perfection would further threaten male power. However, the contrary is the case male dominated social institutions provide the principal basis of support for technological transformation of reproductive practices. Moreover, al-Hibri's analysis is compatible with conclusions reached by numerous other feminist theorists Though some, like Mary O'Brien (1981), share a similar starting point, others such as Nancy Chodorow (1978) and Dorothy Dinnerstein (1976), reach the same conclusion by very different routes, deriving support from disciplines as disparate as psychoanalysis and anthropology.

Recent criticism of Firestone's position has not focused solely on her analysis of the *sources* of women's social subordination but extends to her remedy as well. Of course, exposure of weaknesses in the argument for the biological basis of social stratification would, itself, undermine support for Firestone's solution. But the remedy is also suspect on independent grounds Carol McMillan (1982), for instance, has noted that Firestone's theory of social institutions presupposes that relations between individuals and society are exclusively *functional*. Firestone sees all barriers to the achievement of desired goals as *technical* problems, presuming that the ends sought can be fully known in advance and we need only figure out the most technically efficient way to get there. This presupposition stems, McMillan thinks, from the presumption that reproduction is analogous to the production and manufacture of goods, where the means to bring about a desired end have no significance of themselves apart from their instrumental value (McMillan 1982, 77). Once the expertise to accomplish the aim more efficiently is at hand, earlier more 'primitive' methods can be abandoned with no loss of value.

Close reading of Firestone supports this interpretation. She compares development of artificial reproduction to the future of cybernetics and speculates that the same reticence underlying reservations about the benefits of artificial reproduction pervades our thinking about a work world where machine thinking and problem solving have displaced human efforts. She attributes this reticence to the presently prevailing distribution of power, to envisage either possibility "in the hands of present powers is to envisage a nightmare" (Firestone 1970, 90). But within "post-revolutionary" systems both reproductive technology and cybernetics would be left free to play a wholly different role in social life. Hence, within Firestone's conceptual framework technology plays an instrumental role twice over, first by transforming the means to achieve socially desired goals without itself affecting the character of the goal, and second, by neutrally serving the interests of whichever party happens to control the means of production or reproduction.

McMillan shares company with the vast predominance of both feminist and nonfeminist women who presently hold a markedly different assessment of values bound up with childbearing and rearing practices as human activities. Unlike Firestone and the utopian feminists who presume that the values attached to mothering can be detached, lifted off and reapplied to a radically different set of social practices, they see the values identified with mothering as *integral* to procreation and nurturing. Robyn Rowland, for instance, has remarked that

> *a groundswell of women within the movement has begun to reasses the value of biological maternity. Reacting against the feeling that the women's movement coerced them to give up having children, many feminists are striving to create the experience of maternity and family in a non-exploitive way.* (Rowland 1984, 358)

She points to Adrienne Rich's contention that the problem is not motherhood itself but the patriarchal *institutionalization* of motherhood (Rich 1976, 369) and argues that the sources of women's oppression lie in the nature of the social structures within which motherhood is experienced rather than in motherhood itself—which embodies within it a network of affirmative values which women ought not to abandon. She and the many women writers she cites all see technological control of these practices as usurpation of a body of values central to the fundamental interests of women She appropriates Leon Kass' (1979) arguments to her own cause, citing his admonition that "some men may be destined to play God, to recreate other men in their own image," in support of her own fear that the new reproductive technologies will ultimately be used for the benefit of men and to the detriment of women (Rowland 1984, 356).

Writing in the same volume Janice Raymond (1984) not only decries the technological *future* that new modes of reproduction will impose on women, but the present social context "in which women supposedly 'choose' such debilitating procedures" as *in vitro* fertilization and embryo transfer. Such technologies, she believes, only give scientific and therapeutic support to female adaptation to the patriarchal ideology that reproduction is women's prime commodity, thereby reinforcing women's oppression. She, too, echoes the fears first voiced by noninterventionists, such as Paul Ramsey and Leon Kass, that submission even to presently established modes of technological intervention dehumanizes women, imposing upon them "choices" not of their own making and forcing them to submit to a technology whose developers seek ultimately to render their mothering role obsolete. The arguments of Rowland and Raymond draw together both issues that women's historical and social capabilities incorporated within childbearing and childrearing practices possess independent value wholly apart from their patriarchal context and that technological intervention into reproduction would only remove from women occasion to develop these capabilities under the guise of serving their interests. Recognizing this, women need to voice their *own* interests in accord with the moral and social values that support their sense of the good life. Unlike noninterventionists from Ramsey's background or critics of feminism such as Carol McMillan, their "conservatism" attempts to avoid appeal to women's natural function. Their objections to alternative forms of reproduction are not couched in allusions to their supposed "unnaturalness" but focus on a profound sense of disease, stemming from the threat of further consolidation of power structures which purport to speak *for* women while simultaneously undermining women's control of their own reproductive activities. Nonetheless, despite their deliberate effort to base their case on a direct appeal to women's own expression of their interests, their arguments appear to rely on a theoretical distinction very like Adrienne Rich employs in her analysis of motherhood. She wrote,

> *I try to distinguish between two meanings of motherhood, one superimposed on the other the potential relationship of any woman to her powers of reproduction and to children, and the institution which aims at ensuring that that potential—and all women—shall remain under male control.* (*Rich* 1976, 13)

If the *institution of* motherhood—the "symbolic architecture" that derives from male control—could be lifted off, the *experience* of motherhood would be revealed in its true nature, grounded, Rich believes, in women's *biology.*

> *In arguing that we have by no means yet explored or understood our biological grounding, the miracle and paradox of the female body and its spiritual and political meanings, I am really asking whether women cannot begin, at last, to think through their body, to connect what has been so cruelly disorganized—our great mental capacities, hardly used, our highly developed tactile sense, our genius for close observation, our complicated, pain-enduring multi-pleasured physicality.* (*Rich* 1976, 24)

Rich's argument, like Firestone's, presupposes that we can think intelligibly about mothering experiences detached from their social context and that they can be lifted off and opened to view apart from *any* institutional structures. She assumes, too, that we can imagine them transposed into a radically different context, within which the affirmative values imbedded in mothering would be freed from the negative associations bound up with present mothering arrangements.

The foundation for these presumptions needs closer scrutiny. Despite her penetrating criticism of "male created dualisms" her own work appears to reintroduce analogous dualisms, relying, as it does, on the distinguishability of the sources of women's experiences, on the assumption that we can trace the derivation of certain experiences to women's biology and that others owe their origin to patriarchal institutions. Though such scrutiny of the logic of her work might seem to overlook its most obvious intent to prepare a space within which to celebrate motherhood as a source of women's most cherished experiences, I wonder whether this aim can be given secure support on such a foundation. I would like to suggest now that a common thread links Rowland, Raymond and Rich's positions together and, whether or not that thread connects them all to a nature/culture dualism, they do share certain common *psychological* assumptions that hold all of them together and apart from Firestone and her company.

Like many other contemporary feminists they see the relation between the infant and mother as essentially a positive one and look to this relationship for images of what relations between woman and woman might be once women have been freed to give expression to their own values and shape social institutions that foster their unfettered expression. Their vision stands in marked contrast to the perceptions of Firestone and her generation of feminists who looked to sources outside of the mother-child relationship for models on which to build sense of the unity and solidarity of women.

In a recent paper critical of Rich's position, Janet Sayers (1984) has argued that any attempt to ground relationships between women in images of the infant-mother bond rests upon a fantasy, that in reality this relationship is marked by *contradiction*, by both positive and negative elements. She writes:

The merits of Melanie Klein's work as far as feminism is concerned is that it draws attention to the way we often deny contradictions in personal relationships through the defensive mechanism of splitting, and draws attention to the hatred as well as love that inheres in the early infant-mother relationship—an ambivalence that is not only overlooked in feminist writing that celebrates this relation as the basis of women's solidarity as a sex, but that is also overlooked in that writing which by contrast sees in this relation the very source of women's oppression and alienation. (*Sayers* 1984, 240)

By way of example she cites Luce Irigaray as illustrative of the latter view, though she could as easily have cited many other feminists, including Firestone. Though her reliance on the Kleinian perspective might be called into question, her cautionary warning ought not to go unheeded. Both attitudes toward the mother-infant relation are amply represented within feminist writing. Neither can be claimed to capture the *true* expression of feminism. Her appeal to Klein is an attempt to draw together both positions within a more inclusive framework. The development of such a framework leaves much theoretical work to be done but the need for feminist action cannot be delayed until we have worked out an adequate theory of intergenerational relationships.

For the present, lacking any feminist theory capable of providing unambiguous direction in guiding the development of reproductive technology, these options lay before us (1) we might commit ourselves unequivocally to a Richian position, accept Rowland and Raymond's analysis of the consequences of reproductive innovation and oppose all use of reproductive technology despite its short-term benefits to some women individually, [8] (2) we could join forces with the heirs of Shulamith Firestone, though it is by no means clear what implications this might have for *present* social policy considering the extent to which powerful institutional and commercial interests currently control these technologies, or (3) we could work to integrate the plurality of feminist positions into an *interim* policy, commit ourselves to intensified dialogue and attempt to influence the present direction of reproductive innovation in much the same pragmatic ways feminists are now participating in framing economic policies. Though pursuit of the third option is likely to put the cohesiveness of the feminist community to its most severe test, adoption of either of the remaining options would already presuppose a cleavage far more irreconcilable. Over this issue either the current "wave" of the feminist movement will lose its momentum and disintegrate or feminism will emerge a far stronger, more unitary force for social transformation than ever in its prior history.

Notes:

① A notable exception is a recent collection edited by Joan Rothchild (1983).

② In the summer of 1984 the U. S. House of Representatives Subcommittee on Investigations and Oversights heard testimony on the new reproductive technologies with the intent of eventually introducing appropriate regulative legislation (U. S. 1985).

③ See, for instance, two recent philosophical works *Glover* (1984) and *Singer and Wells* (1984).

④ Comments of Simone Novaes have been most helpful to me in efforts to understand the complex motivations of women seeking these technologies. I am grateful, too, for the valued insights of two unnamed reviewers.

⑤ This argument was first suggested to me in a discussion of Ramsey's position by Samuel Gorovitz (1982).

⑥ I do not discuss other individual "moderate interventionists" at length here only because their arguments are not directly pertinent to the issues I emphasize. However, the regulatory bodies that I do refer to—the British Warnock Committee and the Australian and Canadian commissions—all adopt versions of a moderate interventionist position. Also, most legal commentators and scientific researchers fall into this category. Some have no principled objections to the new technologies at all, others support innovations only selectively. All of them seek regulation principally to maintain continuity with prevailing liberal values.

⑦ Several states have already considered legislation that would bind both parties to surrogate contracts. Both Kentucky and Michigan have ruled against it.

⑧ Gena Corea (1985) offers much empirical evidence in support of this position.

18 米歇尔·斯坦沃思,"生育技术与母亲身份的解构"
Michelle Stanworth, "Reproductive Technologies and the Deconstruction of Motherhood"

米歇尔·斯坦沃思(Michelle Stanworth)①是一位著名的女性主义理论家,她从女性主义的视角研究社会学问题,提出了许多崭新的见解。斯坦沃思曾在剑桥郡艺术与技术学院(Cambridgeshire College of Arts and Technology)②教授社会学。

她共编著有四部重要学术著作:

《性别与学校教育:教室里的性别分工研究》(*Gender and Schooling:A Study of Sexual Division in the Classroom*,1981 年)。作者结合 11 年的中学教书经历,用女性主义视角研究教育领域的社会学问题。

《社会学引论》(*Introductory Sociology*,与 Tony Bilton 等合编,1982 年)

《女性与公众领域:社会学与政治学批评》(*Women and the Public Sphere:A Critique of Sociology and Politics*,与 Janet Siltanen 合编,1984 年)

《生育技术:性别、母道与医药》(*Reproductive Technologies:Gender,*

---

① 作者照片来自 http://www.halovine.com/scc6.html。

② 该学院于 1989 年同埃塞克斯高等教育学院(Essex Institute of Higher Education)合并为英吉利高等教育学院(Anglia Higher Education College),1992 年更名为英吉利理工大学(Anglia Polytechnic University)。

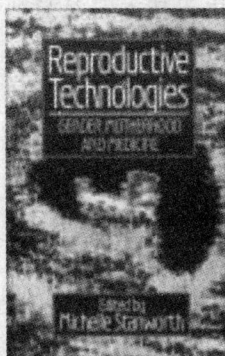

Motherhood, and Medicine, 1987 年）。生育技术已经深刻地影响了女性的生活,该书收入的 9 篇论文讨论在政治、经济、法律和社会背景下有关生育技术的争论,讨论不孕的本质、阻碍为女性提供健康关怀的障碍、技术与父母权利的问题、未出生胎儿的权利等问题。

本书选注的斯坦沃思所著"生育技术与母亲身份的解构"一文选自斯坦沃思编著的《生育技术:性别、母道与医药》,该书由剑桥 Polity Press 于 1987 年出版。

文章分为这样几部分:

引言。斯坦沃思首先把技术对人类生育繁殖过程的干预分为四种:控制生育、生育管理、育前监测、治疗不育①。其中最后一种技术最富有争议。女性主义者对于生育技术的使用及监控提出了尖锐的意见,她们不满足于把对于生育技术作用的评估交给所谓的"专家",因为许多专家本身就是极力倡导应用这些技术的人(第 13 页;第 341 页)。斯坦沃思指出,生育技术并非人们想象的那样能帮助女性决定做母亲的经历从而控制自己的生活,因为:其一,母亲经历还包含心理、社会以及智力上对孩子的关怀;其二,控制生育的现有技术仍然有缺陷;其三,女性对于生育技术的选择同女性的社会地位息息相关;其四,对于生理意义母亲的传统理念仍然很强烈;第五,控制怀孕和生育的技术把女性视为病人来处理(第 14 ~ 15 页;第 341 ~ 344 页)。因此,医学和技术的发展成为一柄双刃剑,一方面给予女性决定是否怀孕、何时怀孕的可能性,另一方面医疗机构对生育技术的控制也使得其他人能够在很大程度上控制女性的生活(第 15 ~ 16 页;第 344 页)。

第一部分,"母亲身份的解构"("The Deconstruction of Motherhood")。斯坦沃思认为,生育技术是一个工具,它把男人对生育力量的幻想变成了现实(第 16 页;第 347 页)。随着生育技术不断参与人们的生活,"母亲身份作为一个统一的生理过程将被彻底解构":将会出现提供卵子的卵巢母亲、孕育胚胎的

---

① Michelle Stanworth, "Reproductive Technologies and the Deconstruction of Motherhood," in Michelle Stanworth, ed., *Reproductive Technologies*: *Gender*, *Motherhood and Medicine* (Cambridge: Polity Press, 1987), pp. 10-11. 本节所引该文观点均出自此书,以下只在正文标明页码,分号后第二个页码为引文在本书的页码。

子宫母亲以及养育孩子的社会母亲（第16页；第345页）。由于技术的参与削减了生育的自然性特征，它将标志着母亲身份的被贬低化（第17页；第346页），从而使女性成为生育技术的普遍牺牲品和受害者（第18页；第347页）。

第二部分，"生育技术与基因父母身份"（"Reproductive Technologies and Genetic Parenthood"）。生育技术的介入引发了许多相关问题，其中较为重要的就是继承权的问题。生育技术满足了一些人生一个"自己的孩子"的愿望（第20页；第349~350页），但却使基因父母身份非法化，甚至打破传统意义上的所谓"生理的"概念（第21页；第351页）。斯坦沃思指出，血缘纽带在西方社会是非常重要的文化主题，家庭通常被视为一个生理单位，社会关系完全来自遗传基因关系（第22页；第352页）。生育技术显然改变了这些关系。

第三部分，"性、父母责任与家庭"（"Sexuality，Parenting and the Family"）。传统观点认为，性行为、父母责任和家庭是紧密联系在一起的三者关系，但生育技术使得父母的责任可以脱离性行为，父母责任也不一定局限在家庭内部（第23页）。这些问题的出现都源于生育技术不仅仅可以被异性婚姻的男女双方使用。

第四部分，"怀孕的状态"（"The Status of Pregnancy"）。在传统状态下，孕妇处于怀孕过程的中心，一些女性认为生孩子可以使她们的生活变得更加完整（第25页）。然而，试管婴儿的出现、人工受孕和代理母亲的技术改变了对于怀孕的传统概念（第26页），甚至有倾向把怀孕的成果——胎儿——看做高于母亲本身（第26~27页），结果，医生同胎儿的紧密联系给女性带来了威胁（第28页）。

第五部分，"新优生学"（"The New Eugenics"）。一些人错误地认为生育技术可以优生优育，事实上，英国从20世纪30年代开始临床上应用人工受精，到目前为止并没有看到优生的结果（第28~29页）。人们对DNA技术的认识告诉我们，有多达3 000种因素会影响基因的传递（第29页）。此外，把"适者生存"理论应用于人类社会也缺乏稳固的土壤（第29~30页），对"不适者"（unfit）的定义难免带有偏见和歧视，生物化学意义上的差别也有可能转变为判断人的价值观念的不同（第32页）。

结语。作者强调说，由于生育技术影响女性的身体、怀孕、生育以及生活本身，因此女性必须参与对生育技术的评价过程。但她也指出，对母亲身份的重视并不意味着把自然置于科技之上，并不意味着全盘接受自然怀孕的状态好、而人工技术不好的理念(第 34 页)。女性主义者关注的问题不应在技术本身,而应研究"我们是否能够创造适宜的政治、文化环境使这些技术能够被女性用来根据自己的需要决定生育经验"(第 35 页)。

　　这里选注的是该文的引言和第一、二部分。

Reproductive Technologies and the
Deconstruction of Motherhood

Technologies designed to intervene in the process of human reproduction fall, roughly speaking, into four groups. The first and most familiar group includes those concerned with fertility control— with preventing conception, frustrating implantation of an embryo, or terminating pregnancy. According to the General Household Survey (Office of Population Censuses and Statistics, 1985, p. 45) in Britain three women out of four aged between eighteen and forty-four use some form of contraception; just over 140,000 residents of England and Wales underwent an abortion in 1985 (WRRIC, June-July 1986). Many of the technologies of fertility control—diaphragms, intra-uterine devices, sterilization, abortion, even the newly visible condom—have been known in some form for centuries (McLaren, 1984, Chapter 3). Hormone-suppressing contraceptive drugs are one of the few genuine innovations in contraceptive technology this century (Gordon, 1977, Chapter 2). Since by the late 1970s the market for "the pill" in many Western countries was saturated, pharmaceutical companies now devote much of their research efforts to finding new ways of administering contraceptives that would open up expanding markets in the "Third World" (Bunkle, 1984).

A second group of reproductive technologies is concerned with the "management" of labour and childbirth. In the course of the past 150 years in Europe and America, childbirth changed from a home-based activity, undertaken primarily with the assistance of female healers and friends, to an activity defined as the province of medical professionals. The extent of the shift is illustrated by the rising proportion of British babies born in hospital—from 15 percent in 1927 to 99 percent in 1985 (see Chapter 2; Office of Population Censuses and Statistics, 1986b). In its wake, a range of technologies for monitoring and controlling the progress of labour and delivery—instruments to assist delivery, caesarian sections, ways of inducing labour, episiotomies, techniques for measuring foetal heart-rate and movement—have been applied on an increasingly routine basis; the caesarian section rate in the United States, for example, rose from 4.5 per hundred in 1965 to 19 per hundred in 1982 (Pfeufer Kahn, 1984, p. 15). In many Western countries, the potential for effective intervention in the management of labour and childbirth is approaching saturation point, not only because of the high proportion of birthing women who are already subject to these techniques, but also because of objections to "high-tech" deliveries from women themselves.

A current focus in terms of the development of reproductive technologies is upon extending obstetric services backwards into the antenatal period, through the use of more elaborate technologies and screening procedures for monitoring foetal development in the early stages of pregnancy (Farrant, 1985); at least one-third of all pregnant women in the United States now experience ultrasound (see Chapter 3). The focus is also upon perfecting new techniques for neonatal care; and upon research that might eventually enable the modification of inborn " defects" through human genetic engineering. In short, the third and one of the growth areas in reproductive technology is concerned with improving the health and the genetic characteristics of foetuses and of newborns—with the search for, as some have said, "the perfect child".

The fourth and perhaps most controversial group are the conceptive technologies, directed to the promotion of pregnancy through techniques for overcoming or bypassing infertility. Estimates for Britain suggest that 50,000 new cases of infertility present for treatment each year and the number of people requiring treatment at any one time may be as high as two million (see Chapter 9). Yet for much of this century, the treatment of infertility has been relatively static; apart from the clinical introduction of artificial insemination in the 1930s and the "fertility drugs" of the 1960s, no new technologies were introduced until in-vitro fertilization burst upon the scene in the late 1970s as a "miracle cure" (see Chapter 4). Most research in the area of infertility is now devoted to the refinement of in-vitro fertilization and to the development of new applications—through combination with, for example, egg donation, embryo donation, low-temperature storage of gametes and embryos, or surrogacy—rather than to alternative approaches to infertility. The conceptive technologies, often treated as if they were synonymous with "high-tech" medicine, in fact are immensely varied; they range from surrogacy or artificial insemination—both of which can be and are practised in ways that require no medical intervention at all—to in-vitro fertilization, which involves very sophisticated medical, surgical and laboratory procedures.

As the history of reproductive technologies is gradually being written, we have come to know more about the range of groups or institutions that have an interest in their development. Women themselves, as consumers of services concerned with reproductive care, have, to be sure, "demanded" techniques that would help them to control their fertility, their pregnancies, their experience of birth and the health of their children. Yet it is clear that there is no simple cause-and-effect relationship between the "demands" made by women and the "supply" of reproductive technologies. For one thing, the "demands" of those who can afford to pay are likely to be catered for far more assiduously than the "demands" of those with smaller resources; and the greater the proportion of total health costs that is met by individuals, the more powerfully such inequalities are likely to assert themselves. For another, part of the "demand" for reproductive technologies comes from state-subsidized programmes, and the objectives of the state in providing resources for the introduction of some technologies and withholding funding from others are not likely to reflect women's wishes in any straightforward way. The state responds to women's demands in the area of reproductive care selectively, in terms of its own priorities with respect to population policy, health expenditure and political pay-off. So, for example, in the context of rigorous insistence on reduction of public expenditure over the past decade, in-vitro fertilization programmes have received virtually no public funding in Britain, while the Department of Health and Social Security viewed benignly—in hopes of saving money on the care of handicapped children—the possibility of mass programmes of antenatal screening.

There are other reasons too, why the demands of women for technologies to aid in reproductive care are insufficient to explain the technologies currently on offer. What we "demand" (that is, what we are willing to tolerate) as consumers depends on the options available to us. Undoubtedly, the demand amongst heterosexual women who wished to avoid pregnancy for a 100 per cent reliable contraceptive technique that carried no risks to health or quality of life would be overwhelming; but in real life, women have to divide their "demands", more or less grudgingly between a range of less-than-satisfactory options. Even our notions of what "satisfactory" would be are shaped partly by our knowledge of existing or potential alternatives. If we come to believe that home births are dangerous (whether or not that belief is objectively "true") we are unlikely to be able to articulate clearly our dissatisfactions with hospital confinements.

Many of the groups most directly responsible for developing and promoting reproductive technologies have an agenda in which women's "demands" play only a small part. For obstetricians and gynaecologists, specific types of reproductive technologies may carry advantages quite separate from their impact on mothers and infants. Reproductive technologies often enhance the status of medical professionals and increase the funds they can command, by underpinning claims to specialized knowledge and by providing the basis for an extension of service. Such technologies may, in addition, help a profession in its attempts to dominate other competitors for control of an area of work; the application of new forms of technology has been one way that obstetricians have succeeded in reducing midwives to a subordinate status in the field of maternity services. Perhaps most significantly, new technologies help to establish those gynaecologists and obstetricians "know more" about pregnancy and about women's bodies than women do themselves. When the majority of the profession is male, it is perhaps not surprising that medical practitioners have been attracted to techniques that enable them to brush aside a woman's own felt experience of menstruation, pregnancy and birth.

Medical practitioners are themselves dependent upon the research and development activities of pharmaceutical and medical supply companies, and many of these corporations have a vast financial interest in the manufacture and promotion of technologies concerned with reproductive care. The buoyant market for infertility treatment has attracted considerable private finance for research and development, but even this is probably outstripped by investment in the realm of genetic engineering. Feminists have raised troubling questions about the accountability and public scrutiny of reproductive technologies, the development of which is motored by private investment (Rowland, 1985a, p. 541; Bunkle, 1984).

Precisely because of the different and sometimes conflicting interests at stake in the application of reproductive technologies, women have not been content to leave the evaluation of the impact of technology to "the experts", who are often the very people involved in their promotion. Instead, they have highlighted the ambivalent effects of reproductive technologies on the lives of women. Women in Western Europe and North America today, compared with their foremothers, have fewer pregnancies, bear fewer babies against their wishes, are less likely to die in childbirth and less often experience the death of their babies. This is no small matter—and it is due, in some part, to technologies for intervening in human reproduction. But the view that reproductive technologies have given women control over motherhood—and thereby over their own lives—simply will not do.

First, this view takes insufficient account of the impact of changing social definitions of motherhood. While women today spend less time in pregnancy and breast-feeding than in the recent past, the care of children has come to be defined in a far more rigorous way; mothering involves responsibility not only for the physical and emotional care of children, but for detailed attention to their psychological, social and intellectual development. Motherhood is seen, more than in the past, as a full-time occupation. Mothers may be expected now to lavish as much "care" on two children as they might previously have provided for six. In short, the reproductive technologies address themselves to only a small part of the experience of motherhood.

Secondly, reproductive decisions continue to be constrained by the shortcomings of existing means of fertility control. For example, the pill and the intra-uterine contraceptive device—heralded in the 1960s as instruments of women's liberation—appear now to carry worrying health risks and a range of distressing side-effects. Some contraceptive techniques, including some of the most reliable for preventing pregnancy, appear also to increase the risk of infertility, creating a catch-22 situation for women who wish to control the timing of child-bearing. The failure to develop safer and more acceptable means of birth control is not simply a technical problem; in part, it reflects the low priority given to women's health and a tendency to disregard symptoms and issues that women themselves think are important (Weideger, 1978; Pollock, 1984).

Thirdly, the way that access to means of fertility control is managed indicates how women's options regarding child-bearing are linked to their location in the social structure. In Britain, the recent Gillick case represented an attempt to restrict through the courts the access of younger women to contraceptive information and supplies. Controversial contraceptives such as the injectable long-acting Depo-Provera, though considered unsuitable for the majority of women in Britain, have been used extensively on their Asian and Black compatriots (Rakusen, 1981; Bunkle, 1984). Although the 1967 Abortion Act entitles British women to legal abortion on medical and social grounds, access to safe abortion in many parts of the country—as in the United States—depends on ability to pay; the bulk of legal abortions in Britain today are performed outside the National Healthy Service (WRRIC, June-July 1986). Infertility, and especially the infections that lead to tubal closure, are particular problems for Black women and women on low incomes in Britain and the United States, but these are precisely the women who have least access to new conceptive technologies like in-vitro fertilization (Wilkie, 1984; Behrman and Kistner, 1975)①.

Fourthly, the technical possibility of fertility control coexists with a powerful ideology of motherhood—the belief that motherhood is the natural, desired and ultimate goal of all "normal" women, and that women who deny their "maternal instincts" are selfish, peculiar or disturbed. At a conference in Oxford in 1987, Patrick Steptoe, the obstetrician who is credited with "creating" the first test-tube baby, declared: "It is a fact that there is a biological drive to reproduce. Women who deny this drive, or in whom it is frustrated, show disturbances in other ways." ② Research suggests that many members of the medical profession share this view (Barrett and Roberts, 1978).

While many women wish to have children, the views of medical personnel are not simply a reflection of that fact. The idea of maternal instinct is sometimes used to override women's expressed wishes with regard to child-bearing—discouraging young married women from sterilization or abortion, for example, while denying single women the chance to have a child (Macintyre, 1977; Veevers, 1980, Chapter 7). In other words, a belief in maternal instinct coexists with obstacles to autonomous motherhood - obstacles, that is, to motherhood for women who are not in a stable relationship to a man. According to ideologies of motherhood, all women *want* children; but single women, lesbian women (and disabled women) are often expected to forgo mothering "in the interest of the child".

Finally, technologies for "managing" pregnancy and childbirth are often embedded in a medical frame of reference that defines pregnant women as "patients", pregnancy as an illness and successful child-bearing in terms that de-emphasize the social and emotional dimensions. In some respects, reproductive technologies have made child-bearing safer for women and their infants, but they have also brought new dangers in their wake (see Chapter 2; Hubbard, 1984; Wertz, 1983). Apart from medical risks and benefits, as the process of pregnancy and childbirth has come under the control of medical professionals, the majority of whom are men, many women are left with a sense of being mere onlookers in the important process of giving birth.

Thus, medical and scientific advances in the sphere of reproduction—so often hailed as the liberators of twentieth-century women—have, in fact, been a double-edged sword. On the one hand, they have offered women a greater technical possibility to decide if, when and under what conditions to have children; on the other, the domination of so much reproductive technology by the medical profession and by the state has enabled others to have an even greater capacity to exert control over women's lives. Moreover, the "technical possibility" of choosing an oral contraceptive or in-vitro fertilization is only a small aspect of reproductive freedom (Petchesky, 1986). For some women, motherhood remains their only chance of creativity, while economic and social circumstances compel others to relinquish motherhood altogether.

The Deconstruction of Motherhood

Against the stark backcloth of the history of technologies for controlling fertility, pregnancy and birth, how are we to analyse the emergent technologies concerned with promoting conception and with eliminating "defects" in the unborn? One powerful theoretical approach sees in these new techniques a means for men to wrest "not only control of reproduction, but reproduction itself" from women (Raymond, 1985, p. 12). Following O'Brien (1983), it is suggested that men's alienation from reproduction— men's sense of disconnection from their seed during the process of conception, pregnancy and birth—has underpinned through the ages a relentless male desire to master nature, and to construct social institutions and cultural patterns that will not only subdue the waywardness of women but also give men an illusion of procreative continuity and power. New reproductive technologies are the vehicle that will turn men's illusions of reproductive power into a reality. By manipulating eggs and embryos, scientists will determine the sort of children who are born—will make themselves the fathers of humankind. By removing eggs and embryos from some women and implanting them in others, medical practitioners will gain unprecedented control over motherhood itself. Motherhood as a unified biological process will be effectively deconstructed: in place of "mother", there will be ovarian mothers who supply eggs, uterine mothers who give birth to children and, presumably, social mothers who raise them. Through the eventual development of artificial wombs, the capacity will arise to make biological motherhood redundant. Whether or not women are eliminated, or merely reduced to the level of "reproductive prostatutes", [3] the object and the effect of the emergent technologies is to deconstruct motherhood and to destroy the claim to reproduction that is the foundation of women's identity. [4]

The problem with this analysis is not that it is too radical, as some have claimed; rather, in seeking to protect women from the dangers of new technologies, it gives too much away. There is a tendency to echo the very views of scientific and medical practice, of women and of motherhood, which feminists have been seeking to transform. This analysis entails, in the first instance, an inflated view of science and medicine, the mirror image of that which scientists and medical practitioners often try themselves to promote. By emphasizing the continuities between technologies currently in clinical use, and those that exist merely in the fantasies of scientific commentators; by insisting that the practices involved in animal husbandry or in animal experimentation can unproblematically be transferred to human beings; by ignoring the ways in which women have resisted abuses of medical power and techniques they found unacceptable: by arguing this way, science and medicine have been portrayed as realms of boundless possibility, in the face of which mere human beings have no choices other than total rejection or capitulation. Any understanding of the constraints within which science and medicine operate, and of the way these can be shaped for the greater protection of women and men, is effectively erased.

Also integral to this approach is a view of women that comes uncomfortably close to that espoused by some members of the medical professions. Infertile women are too easily "blinded by science" (Hanmer, 1985, p. 104); they are manipulated into "full and total support of any technique which will produce those desired children" (Rowland, 1985b, p. 75); the choices they make and even their motivations to choose are controlled by men (Corea, 1985a, p. 3). In the case of doctors, it is the "maternal instinct" that allows women's own assessments of what they want from their bodies or their pregnancies to be overlooked; in this analysis, it is patriarchal and prenatal conditioning that makes infertile women (and, by implication, all women) incapable of rationally grounded and authentic choice. I argued above that the ideology of motherhood attempts to press women in the direction of child-bearing, and that in this sense women's motivations are socially shaped. But "shaped" is not the same as "determined"; and a rejection of child-bearing (for infertile women or fertile) is not necessarily a more authentic choice. The very existence of a range of sanctions and rewards designed to entice women into marriage and motherhood indicates, not that conformity is guaranteed, but that avoidance of motherhood (and autonomous motherhood) are genuine options, which efforts are made to contain. ⑤

Finally, this approach tends to suggest that anything "less" than a natural process, from conception through to birth, represents the degradation of motherhood itself. The motherhood that men are attempting to usurp becomes a motherhood that is biologically defined, and to which all women are assumed to have the same relationship. While it is the case that the lives of all women are shaped by their biological selves, and by their assumed or actual capacity to bear children, our bodies do not impose upon us a common experience of reproduction; on the contrary, our bodies stand as powerful reminders of the differentiating effects of age, health, disability, strength and fertility history. There is, moreover, little reason to assume that the biological potential to give birth has an identical meaning for women, regardless of their social circumstances or their wishes with regard to child-bearing. How can the experience of women who have chosen to remain childfree be fitted into a framework that sees the continuous biological process that culminates in birth as the core of our identity as women? How can we make sense from this perspective of women (such as those interviewed by Luker, 1984, pp. 168-169) who value children and child-bearing highly, but who experience pregnancy itself as merely an unpleasant reality *en route* to raising children? How can we explain the fact that fewer working-class women in Britain attend antenatal clinics, demand natural childbirth or breast-feed their infants? Luker's analysis (ibid.) suggests the possibility that while for many middle-class women pregnancy may be a scarce resource—time out from a hectic professional life to enjoy the sensations of being a woman—for a greater proportion of working-class women pregnancy may be more a taken-for-granted prelude to social motherhood, not an experience to be cherished in itself. Far too many women have experienced the type of reproductive care that is insensitive to their own wishes and desires; but shared reaction against unsatisfactory medical treatment should not be allowed to mask differences in women's own sense of what authentic motherhood might be. Women may legitimately, as Rayna Rapp said, "want other things from reproductive technology than merely to get it off our backs" (Rapp, 1985, p. 4).

Feminist critics of technologies have always and rightly insisted that technologies derive their meaning from the social and political context in which they emerge. But where the context that is invoked in connection with reproductive technologies is the universal victimization of women, then it is easy to underestimate the significance of political struggles concerning the future of reproduction which are currently being waged. I wish to argue in the following sections that reproductive technologies are controversial—not only amongst feminists, but among a wider public—because they crystallize issues at the heart of contemporary controversies over sexuality, parenthood, reproduction and the family; and that a concern for self-determination for women must engage, above all, with these struggles.

Reproductive Technologies and Genetic Parenthood

In the United States, a bioethicist warned the Ethics Advisory Board investigating in-vitro fertilization that this technique blurs the issue of genetic identity with potentially dire social consequences: "Clarity about who your parents are, clarity in the lines of generation, clarity about who is whose, are the indispensable foundations of a sound family life, itself the sound foundation of civilized community" (Leon Kass, cited in Grobstein, 1981, p. 65).

In Britain, the Warnock Committee devoted a large portion of its report to weighing up the legal rights of genetic parents over children born with the help of conceptive technologies, and to considering whether such children should have the right to know about, or to inherit estates or titles from, their genetic forbears (Warnock, 1985). The mass media, too, have found a lively source of controversial news stories in the question, not only of claims over children, but also over embryos: the fate of the "Rios twins"—two embryos stored at low temperature at Queen Victoria Hospital, Melbourne, after their parents had died in a plane crash—occupied Australian newspapers for a good two months (Albury, 1986).

The concern about inheritance, succession and rights in children by commissions appointed to inquire into reproductive technologies has been perceived sometimes as a side-issue, reflecting the preoccupation of the state with paternity and property. But it is much more than that. For reproductive technologies have become a battleground on which are being waged important campaigns about the significance of blood ties and of genetic parenthood.

These campaigns have their roots in current tensions of family life. Accelerating rates of divorce and remarriage in many western societies means that pressing questions about claims over children impinge directly on many people's lives. Between the late 1950s and early 1960s in Britain, the divorce rate increased fourfold; it trebled again between 1961 and 1971. Throughout the 1980s, for every three couples who married for the first time, two couples divorced (Central Statistical Office, 1986, pp. 37-41). A high and increasing proportion of divorced women and an even higher proportion of divorced men rapidly remarry, often establishing step-families or reconstituted families. Divorce does not signify in any clear way the "breakdown of the family", or of marriage as an institution. What it does signify, however, is a markedly greater uncertainty in the 1980s (compared with, say, the 1950s) about the ties that bind individual parents to individual children. Legal battles over custody and access are only part of the story: alongside these run uncounted numbers of households in which uncontested custody or access arrangements are nevertheless a source of anxiety, in which one parent or both have to be more self-conscious than before about the basis of their relationship with their child. And this experience is not confined to parents: other relatives—grandmothers and grandfathers, uncles and aunts—often discover in these circumstances that extra tact and effort is needed to sustain a relationship with children who are their kin. The concern about genetic parenthood that has greeted the arrival of new technologies— who will parent the offspring of surrogate mothers? —reflects these pre-existing tensions around claims on relationships to children. In the face of divorce, and rising rates of remarriage, the pressure to rethink the moral and legal basis of claims upon children is clearly intense.

Technologies such as in-vitro fertilization, egg donation, surrogacy and the like have crystallized these anxieties about relationships to children precisely because their relation to genetic parenthood is an ambivalent one. On the one hand, the conceptive technologies address in a powerful way people's desires, not merely to enjoy a life with children, but to have a child "of their own". Women whose oviducts have been damaged by pelvic inflammatory disease may, with in-vitro fertilization, give birth to a child conceived from their own egg and their partner's sperm. A women who is fertile, but who does not have a fertile male partner, may with artificial insemination, conceive and bear a child that is genetically her own. Through full surrogacy, women who are unable to bear children may yet raise a child conceived from their own egg and their partner's sperm. The market for conceptive technologies thrives on the yearning for genetic parenthood.

In the dominant culture of Western societies, the importance of blood ties is a powerful cultural theme. The family is often imagined as a biological unit, in which social relationships grow straightforwardly out of genetic ones, such that commitment to "the family" and to "blood ties" becomes inseparable in many people's minds; the overlapping responsibilities of mothers, fathers and children are filtered through a biological lens. The importance of blood ties is further underscored by scientific theories—from the very dubious accounts of intelligence as a largely genetic characteristic, to the equally contentious claims of biologically based prenatal bonding— which make it their business to explain human qualities and relationships in terms of biological inheritance. ⑥ Finally, the poignant publicity given in the past fifteen years to the search for genetic mothers and fathers by children born of artificial insemination by donor, or by adopted children, emphasizes the idea that genetic connection is an immutable and overriding element of identity. ⑦ Through these overlapping sets of ideas, blood ties have come to stand in our culture as a symbol of permanence in human relationships—and the more fragile and contingent other relationships seem to be, the more compelling that symbol's appeal:

When depressed about the fragility and transience of friendships, or the inconstancies of lovers, it was the myth of a child, a blood relation and what it could bring me, which seemed to me the only real guarantee against loneliness

and isolation, the only way of maintaining a connection to the rest of society.
(*Klepfisz, in Dowrick and Grundberg*, 1980, p. 18)

If the conceptive technologies thrive on these powerful cultural pressures towards having a child "of our own", it would not be true to say that they unambiguously strengthen the tendency to value genetic claims to relationships. For the same technologies that enable some infertile people to become genetic parents also place the whole notion of genetic parenthood in jeopardy. When embryologists and obstetricians are needed to bring about insemination and conception, genetic parenthood no longer seems a natural process, with all the positive connotations that "natural" carries in the area of reproduction. Moreover, practices such as artificial insemination by donor, or egg donation or (some forms of) surrogacy, pose a highly visible challenge to the notion that genetic parenthood guarantees familial relationship; a women who donates an egg to aid her sister's attempts to become pregnant may be the genetic mother, but she no longer appears as the "real" mother in any meaningful sense. Thus, reproductive technologies carry the threat (or the promise) of delegitimating genetic parenthood, and even of fracturing commonsense understandings of what "the biological" is.

If many official and media commentaries on reproductive technologies take the yearning for genetic parenthood for granted, feminist writers have posed the question differently. They have pointed out that an emphasis upon blood ties is not a given, but is historically and culturally specific (Edholm, 1982; and see Chapter 5); in other words, the significance accorded to genetic parenthood in establishing social relationships varies across time and from one culture or class to another. Within the American community known as the Flats, for example, family is as family does: a neighbour who stands by a woman and her children in hard times may be called "sister", while the genetic father of those children—if he chooses to distance himself from them will not be admitted to the status of kin (Stack, 1974).

Against the background of communities such as this, pertinent questions have been raised about the "obsessive" desire of infertile people for a child of their own. But—apart from the fact that there are compelling practical reasons why people, infertile or fertile, might seek genetic parenthood rather than, say, adoption ⑧—it is not the individual pursuit of genetic parenthood that is the most threatening aspect of new reproductive technologies. Rather, the real concern lies in the legal and political construction that may be placed on genetic ties.

Any attempt to rethink the legal and moral basis of claims to children must take into account the different relationship to parenthood of most women and men. While the promise of genetic parenthood is part of the appeal of the new conceptive technologies, this appeal may be to a degree gender-specific: it is stronger, I suspect, for men than for women. Some of the surveys conducted to assess public attitudes towards new technologies show that while people of both sexes are increasingly tolerant of the use of these techniques, women are more inclined towards adoption as a solution to involuntary childlessness than are men. This need not reflect an inherent male urge towards genetic paternity, as some would claim. Rather, the fact that women care for children in most households—and the very success of the women's movement in emphasizing that this care is not an effortless outpouring of maternal sentiment, but real labour that forges a strong relationship between women and their children—means that men are more likely than women to be anxious about the basis of relationships with children they intend to father.

Women's legal and moral claims to children rest on two bases: first, their day-to-day responsibility for the care of children, and secondly, the fact that children are born to them. The latter claim reflects not so much a mother's genetic input to the child as the commitment involved in pregnancy and birthing. Men cannot bear children, and current evidence on the division of labour in households shows clearly that few men are willing to take responsibility for their day-to-day care. Any trend towards enhancing the legal rights that flow from genetic parenthood, as opposed to real parental commitment, would work decisively to the detriment of women (see Chapter 5). Our concern must be to see that, in the search for a secure incontestable basis for claims to children, the anxieties that new reproductive technologies crystallize do not become the basis for giving even greater legal priority to genetic claims (see Chapter 6).

[……]

Notes:

① These examples are, of course, merely the tip of the iceberg. Campaigns against sterilization-abuse highlight many instances of coercive sterilization in the United States which tend to be concentrated among poor and ethnic minority women. Lower standards than those that apply in the West may govern the testing and marketing of contraceptive products in some Third World countries.

② Women, Reproduction and Technology Conference, organized by Robert King for the History Workshop Centre, Oxford, pp. 14-15 February 1987.

③ Andrea Dworkin (1983) sketched out the idea of the "reproductive brothel", as a metaphor for ways in which men attempt to exert standardized control over women's reproductive capacities. This notion has been applied to new reproductive technologies by several writers, including Ann Oakley in Chapter 2, or Gena Corea (1985a and b). For a critique of this analogy, see Rayna Rapp (1985) and Juliette Zipper and Selma Sevehuijsen in Chapter 6.

④ The writers who have been most influential in developing the approach to new technologies outlined in this paragraph include Gena Corea (1985a and 1985b); Renate Duelli Klein (1985); Jalna Hanmer (with Pat Allen 1980; 1981, 1985); Robyn Rowland (1984, 1985a and 1985b); Roberta Steinbacher (1983, and with Helen Holmes 1985) and Rita Arditti (et al., 1984; 1985).

⑤ In this context, it is interesting to note Jane Wilkie's (1984) argument that increases in infertility in the United States in recent years—which launch some women into a difficult search for motherhood against physiological odds—may be due in part precisely to the numbers of women who have been exercising new kinds of choices about their fertility. Pregnancies are more difficult to achieve for women in their late twenties and thirties, and the increasing number of women who have delayed child-bearing in order to pursue other avenues of identity is, Wilkie estimates, one of the major sources of fertility problems. The other major sources are chronic infections and the effects of infertility inducing contraceptive techniques.

⑥ Some writings on sociobiology take this furthest. In the claim that there is an innate urge to reproduce one's seed, an urge shared by tsetse flies and human beings, genetic transmission becomes not only a preference, but a species imperative. See the discussion in Fausto-Sterling (1985, Chapter 6) or Sayers (1982).

⑦ In some of the accounts of children seeking out genetic parents, the desire to maintain blood ties becomes not a contingent matter—dependent upon a child's upbringing and the circumstances of its separation from genetic parents—but an inevitable one. Polly Toynbee, for example, interviewed a large number of adopted children, some of whom were indifferent to their genetic origins; this she discounts as the repression of painful desires (Toynbee, quoted by Janet Watts, *The Observer* 21 July, 1985, p. 43).

⑧ Ways of establishing relationships with children other than by genetic parenthood are often subject to strict surveillance and regulation. Adoption agencies, for example, are (rightly) rigorous about who may parent: but their policies and criteria of assessment are framed against a conventional notion of parenting—and particularly, of motherhood—which will deter many would-be parents. Adoption agencies in Britain may refuse (and often do) single women or those aged over thirty; may refuse (and usually do) those who are not heterosexual, whether married or not; may refuse (and sometimes do) women who have jobs, women who have had psychiatric referrals, women with disabilities, women whose unconventional life-styles cast doubt—for the social workers at least—on their suitability as mothers. They are also likely to refuse, in spite of the long and uncertain waiting period for adoption, women who intend to continue trying to achieve a pregnancy. For many would-be parents, particularly those who want their relationship with a child to begin while it is still in infancy or toddlerhood, the conceptive technologies are not so much about genetic transmission as about having a child at all.

19 伊莲娜·瑞萍,"母道的未来:一些不切实际的幻想"
Elayne Rapping, "The Future of Motherhood: Some Unfashionably Visionary Thoughts"

伊莲娜·瑞萍(Elayne Rapping)①是一位著名的媒体评论家,文章散见在一些文化研究和大众传媒研究的杂志上。她目前在纽约州立大学布法罗分校(University at Buffalo, The State University of New York)艺术与科学学院美国学系任教授。她兴趣广泛,尤其关注性别、种族、民族和阶级如何在流行文化和媒体中得以再现,研究流行文化如何被制造和消费。

她的主要论著有:

《镜子世界》(Looking Glass World, 1987 年)

《本周电影:私人故事与公众事件》(*The Movie of the Week: Private Stories/Public Events*, 1992 年)。该书旨在帮助读者明晰电视电影运作的方式,参与公众事件,并做出判断。

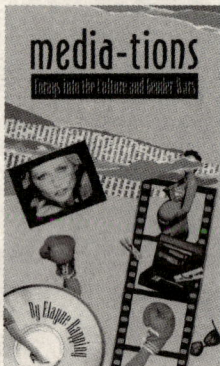

《媒体化:文化劫掠与性别战争》(*Media-tions: Forays into the Culture and Gender Wars*,1994 年)。瑞萍聚焦肥皂剧、音乐电视(MTV)等流行文化现象,探讨女性与媒体间的关系。

《复苏的文化:理解自助运动对女性生活的影响》(*The Culture of Recovery: Making Sense of the Self-Help Movement in Women's Lives*, 1996 年)。

---

① 访问 http://www.cas.buffalo.edu/depts/americanstudies/erapping.shtml。

《电视中的法律与正义》(*Law and Justice as Seen on TV*, 2003 年)。该书探讨同法律有关的电视节目中表现出的社会文化倾向。

本书选注的"母道的未来:一些不切实际的幻想"选自由汉森和菲利浦森编选的《女人、阶级和女性主义想象:社会主义-女性主义读本》(*Women, Class, and the Feminist Imagination: A Socialist-Feminist Reader*)一书,该书由坦普尔大学出版社于 1990 年出版。

该文分为这样几部分:

引言。作者首先指出,生育技术的发展促使我们对许多问题进行思考①:母道到底意味着什么? 家庭是什么? 性行为和生育的关系如何? 女性的科学成就与资本主义经济秩序的关系如何? 做女人意味着什么? 作者追溯了 20 世纪 60 年代以后女性主义发展的几部标志性著作——

舒拉米斯·菲尔斯通(Shulamith Firestone)②于 1970 年发表了《性别的辩证法》(*The Dialectics of Sex*):该书对母性的生理决定论提出质疑(第 538 页;第 361 页)。

玛吉·皮厄茜(Marge Piercy)③于 1976 年出版的未来小说《时间边缘的女人》(*Woman on the Edge of Time*):小说描写了一个理想的未来世界,所有的资源都被用来维系民主的、尊重生命的价值观念(第 538 页;第 361 页)。

佐伊·费尔巴恩(Zoe Fairbairn)④于 1979 年出版的反乌托邦小说《利益》(*Benefits*):该书描写的丑恶世界成为皮厄茜理想世界的对立面(第 538 页;第 361

---

① Elayne Rapping, "The Future of Motherhood: Some Unfashionably Visionary Thoughts", in Karen V. Hansen and Ilene J. Philipson, eds. *Women, Class, and the Feminist Imagination: A Socialist-Feminist Reader* (Philadelphia: Temple University Press, 1990), p.537. 本节所引该文观点均出自此处,以下只在正文标明页码,分号后第二个页码为引文在本书的页码。

② 舒拉米斯·菲尔斯通,美国极端女性主义的创始人之一。

③ 玛吉·皮厄茜,美国诗人、小说家、理论家。已出版诗集 17 部、小说 17 部以及数部散文集、回忆录。《时间边缘的女人》发表于 1976 年,是皮厄茜创作的一部科幻小说。小说描写一位被送入精神病院的母亲在精神被控制下几次访问未来世界,这是一个用去中心化的无政府主义思想组织的社会,人们对科技怀有积极的、环保主义的态度。孩子在人造子宫中孕育,每个孩子都有三个父母。小说中描写的理想社会折射出现实社会的弊端。访问 http://www.margepiercy.com。

④ 佐伊·费尔巴恩,英国小说家、女性主义者。

页)。同类反乌托邦小说还有玛格丽特·阿特伍德(Margaret Atwood)①的《女仆的故事》(*Handmaid's Tale*)。

苏·米勒(Sue Miller)②于 1985 年出版的小说《好母亲》(*The Good Mother*):该小说表现的思想代表了 20 世纪 80 年代(后)女性主义的主要观点和所处状态。瑞萍提醒我们,一味地强调对身体和子女的控制会导致生理特征决定的本质主义观点,因而也是危险的立场(第 539 页;第 363 页)。

安德瑞亚·多金(Andrea Dworkin)③于 80 年代发表的《右翼女性》(*Right-Wing Women*):多金尖锐地指出,男性科学家为进入子宫、获得权力不断进行实验,这使得母亲身份成为另一种滥用女性的表现(第 540 页;第 363 ~ 364 页)。

吉娜·克瑞亚(Gena Corea)④所著《母亲机器》(*The Mother Machine*):著作讨论了生育技术如何被用来剥削和压迫女性(第 540 页;第 364 页)。

在对这些著作进行分析后,瑞萍指出,应该承认,这些技术和实验的的确确在很大程度上继续对女性进行剥削,女性主义者无法对这一点视若无睹。但是,

---

① 玛格丽特·阿特伍德(1939 ~   ),加拿大小说家。访问 http://www.mscd.edu/~atwoodso 和 http://www.owtoad.com。

② 苏·米勒(1943 ~   ),美国小说家。代表作除《好母亲》外,还有《家庭照片》(*Family Pictures*)、《为了爱》(*For Love*)、《贵客》(*The Distinguished Guest*)和《我离开的时候》(*While I Was Gone*)。

③ 安德瑞亚·多金(1946 ~2005),美国作家、女性主义者。代表作《右翼女性》发表于 1983 年。其他代表作还有《我们的血液:关于性别政治的预言与观点》(*Our Blood: Prophecies and Discourses on Sexual Politics*,1974 年)、《仇恨女人》(*Woman Hating*,1974 年)、《性交》(*Intercourse*,1987 年)、《淫秽:男人占有女人》(*Pornography: Men Possessing Women*,1989 年)和《生命与死亡》(*Life and Death*,1997 年)。她还创作了小说《冰与火》(*Ice and Fire*,1986 年)。访问 http://www.nostatusquo.com/ACLU/dworkin/。

④ 吉娜·克瑞亚,美国作家、记者。代表著作有《隐形的流行病:女性与艾滋病的故事》(*The Invisible Epidemic: The Story of Women and AIDS*)、《母亲机器:从人工授精到人造子宫》(*The Mother Machine: Reproductive Technologies from Artificial Insemination to the Artificial Womb*)和《看不见的误操作:美国医学如何把女性视为病人和职业女性》(*The Hidden Malpractice: How American Medicine Treats Women As Patients and Professionals*)。访问 http://www.geryunant.com/Gena.htm。

她也认同雷纳·拉普(Rayna Rapp)①的观点,担心一味夸大这一点会使女性主义者丧失刚刚赢得的阵地:这一阵地认可女性同男性一样享有诸如科学、文化和养育等领域以及这些领域要求的职责(第 540 页;第 364~365 页)。

第一部分,"社会主义-女性主义的反响"("The Socialist-Feminist Response")。面对生育技术带来的社会变化,女性主义普遍反映出悲观倾向(第 541 页;第 365 页)。瑞萍以宝贝 M(Baby M)事件②为例讨论激进女性主义者和社会主义女性主义者如何如此强烈地坚持生理母亲对孩子拥有的权利以及母亲与孩子之间纽带的神圣性(第 541 页;第 366 页)。1988 年《女士》(*Ms.*)杂志五月号也开辟专刊讨论生育技术。其中的大部分文章几乎异口同声地维护生育权(pronatal)(第 541 页;第 366 页)。作者认为,女性主义者不得不紧紧抓住身体和亲生子女这两样尚可抓得住的东西来维护自己的权利。但同时她也指出,目前的这些理论都存在政治盲点和矛盾之处(第 542 页;第 366~367 页)。

第二部分,"去神秘化的母亲身份"("Motherhood Demystified")。作者指出,在现实生活中,许多女性生活在情感和物质缺乏的状态下(第 542 页;第 367 页),仍有一些年轻女性认为母爱是女性一生最大的自我实现(第 543 页;第 367 页)。由于女性经历千差万别,很难就生理母亲的权利和生育技术的关系作一个统一的解释。事实上,生育技术(包括计划生育)在使用上充满了矛盾和不平等。瑞萍对此提出两点意见:其一,单方面强调母亲的权利或结束对性的商品化都是不够的;其二,在技术如何才能融入我们对家庭、母亲的建构的问题上,还需考虑到技术对人类社会仍然有潜在的促进和改善作用(第 544 页;第 369 页)。

第三部分,"女性主义的未来"("A Feminist Future")。作者首先用精练的

---

① 雷纳·拉普,美国纽约大学人类学教授,女性主义理论家。瑞萍这里所引观点见拉普发表于 1988 年的文章《一个自己的子宫》("A Womb of One's Own")。访问 http://www.nyu.edu/gsas/dept/anthro/faculty/rapp.html。

② 这是关于生育技术的第一个涉及法律的案例。新泽西高等法院于 1988 年做出判决,孩子归生理父母斯特恩夫妇(William and Elizabeth Stern)抚养,通过人工授精为他们生孩子的代理母亲怀特海德(Mary Beth Whitehead)只享有探视权。访问 http://womenshistory.about.com/od/motherhood/a/baby_m.htm。

语言概括了女性主义的主要观点和立场,然后以《紫色》①为例阐明家庭关系、性行为、性关系、养育子女之间可以建立起一种和谐的联系,并建议我们应该"在建构一个真正友爱、民主、没有性别歧视、没有压迫的环境中思考如何广泛、廉价地运用生育技术为女性和儿童的利益服务"(第 546 页;第 372 页)。考虑到下一代年轻人将继承作者这一代人毕生为之奋斗的理想和信念,而在他们生活的世界,技术将比现在发挥更大的作用,而他们对此缺乏足够的准备,因此非常有必要让下一代了解母亲这一代人之所思、之所想、之所为(第 547 页;第 373 页)。

The Future of Motherhood
Some Unfashionably Visionary Thoughts

The brave new world of reproductive technology—contraceptive techniques, labor and childbirth "management," fetal monitoring, artificial insemination and surrogacy—more than any other social or scientific phenomenon I can think of forces feminists to confront central issues that have plagued us for twenty years. What is motherhood? What is a family? What is the relationship between sexuality and reproduction? What is the relationship of women to the scientific establishment and the capitalist economic order? And perhaps most difficult of all, what does it mean—really mean—to be a woman?

In the late 1960s and early 1970s, heady days for feminists and leftists, radical approaches to these matters were the order of the day. The very questioning of established thinking about motherhood and femininity was a radical and exhilarating act. For a generation raised on *Leave It to Beaver* and Freudian biological determinism, the realization that biology need not be destiny was liberating.

---

① 《紫色》(*The Color Purple*)是美国女黑人小说家艾丽丝·沃克(Alice Walker)的作品,发表于 1982 年。美国导演斯皮尔伯格(Steven Spielberg)根据该作品改编的电影曾提名多项奥斯卡奖和金球奖。

Things have changed since then, for reasons that are in some ways understandable and in others—to me at least—mysterious. In the heat and passion of feminist debate about reproductive technology one hears the rumblings of retreat from radical political visions to an at times alarmingly conservative view of the personal and political future of women, and of the relationships among women, men, children, and the larger community.

Before getting down to the nuts and bolts of the technical and political issues facing us today, it seems important to retrace the history of radical—and socialist-feminist thinking on these matters. It is in the imaginative literature that these feminist movements spawned—the novels we read and discuss with passion—that the convergence of the feelings and ideas that fuel our politics is often most clearly revealed. This seems particularly true in matters of motherhood.

In the groundbreaking 1970 political study *The Dialectics of Sex*, Shulamith Firestone, a radical feminist in those innocent days when left and radical feminists shared some crucial political visions, presented a theoretical and programmatic response to those who argued that women are biologically determined to be mothers: "the freeing of women from the tyranny of their reproductive biology ... and the diffusion of the child-bearing and childrearing role to the society as a whole" through the development of the very reproductive technologies that now seem, to many, anything but liberating. [1]

Some of Firestone's ideas were given imaginative life in left feminist Marge Piercy's 1976 futuristic novel *Woman on the Edge of Time*. In it Piercy describes in fascinating detail a future world in which all resources—technological and natural—are used to further such democratic, life-affirming values as pleasure, beauty, and individual development and expression in the context of full personal choice. Part of this vision, the most radical part, includes a fully delineated program for childbirth and parenting wholly separate from biological imperative and from the nuclear family. Each child, artificially produced in special reproductive nurseries, has three biological parents, none of whom are lovers. Men are as capable of nursing as women, and the choice to be or not be a parent is as accepted as the choice to be celibate or nonmonogamous. ②

Such feminist political utopias, whether fictional or theoretical, seem a quirky, aberrant glitch in today's dominant, and gloomier, approach to sexual and family matters. As early as 1979, British feminist Zoe Fairbairns's *Benefits* presented a very dystopian futuristic response to Piercy's idyllic vision. Fairbairns's future is one in which genetic engineering, in the hands of a mysoginist government, is the greatest weapon against feminism and the ultimate force for the enslavement of women. Socially and racially "fit" women are given rewards for returning to the traditional wife/mother role, while poor, black, and otherwise "unfit" women are deprived of their reproductive rights and forced to fill demeaning roles. Margaret Atwood's more recent *Handmaid's Tale* envisions a similarly bleak and terrifying future for women at the hands of an all-powerful reactionary government. ③

Sue Miller's 1985 book *The Good Mother*, about a single mother who loses custody of her daughter when her ex-husband charges her and her unconventional lover with "sexual irregularities," brings home— depressingly—how little progress women have actually made in our quest for sexual and political freedom. Divorced, impoverished, but happy for the first time in a fulfilling relationship with a man who loves her and her child, Anna Dunlap capitulates immediately to the obvious power of the male-dominated state once her lifestyle is challenged. Losing her beloved Molly, she embarks, like some latter-day Hester Prynne, on an apparent future of penance and personal misery. She breaks with her lover and moves to another city in order to have the few hours a week granted to her with her child ④.

Anna's plight is heartbreaking and tragic. The sensitive reader cannot judge her too harshly; after all, mother love is real, as is male power and sexual guilt. What's troubling about this novel is the way it poses its heroine's problems. While the first half of the book presents Anna's new and hopeful life from a perspective of optimism and spiritual growth, the second half-devoted to the custody case—switches perspectives in a way that is literarily brilliant but politically disturbing. The male power structure—represented by almost every man in the book—speaks, and Anna crumbles in total defeat. Sexual fulfillment and motherhood are seen—once more— as mutually exclusive, not because of Anna's own nature but because of the immovable force of patriarchal ideology. And when forced to choose, it is motherhood—even the disfigured form in which it is offered her—that she chooses. In the end, this one child is Anna's reason for being. She imagines no future life, no future children. More distressing, from my own perspective as a mother, she chooses to present herself to her growing daughter as a fallen woman, a loser, a victim. The real needs of a child must surely include the need to see one's mother as a model, a woman whose life is meaningful and dignified.

This novel (discussed in greater depth by Deborah Rosenfelt and Judith Stacey in the next chapter) is emblematic of the state of much feminist (or postfeminist) thought in the 1980s. In its sense of women's powerlessness against masculinist institutions, and in its reversion to an image of motherhood as the sole arena of female power, it mirrors the dominant feminist responses to the issues raised by the new reproductive technologies. Male power, in the realms of science, law, economics, and politics, is seen as absolute. Challenging that power is implicitly brushed aside by feminists in favor of a feverish focus on individual control of one's body and its offspring. Outside the context of a broader social vision, this narrow, single-minded focus too often leads not only to contradictory, even dangerous, political positions and alliances but to unconscious reversion to an essentialist view of femininity as defined by biology, by the ability to bear children.

With rare exceptions, feminist responses to the reproductive sciences have been grounded in totalizing visions of male power and female victimization. [5] Andrea Dworkin, in a 1980s version of radical feminism as dour as Firestone's was hopeful, sets the tone for this discourse in *Right-Wing Women*. "Motherhood is becoming a new branch of female prostitution with the help of scientists who want access to the womb for experimentation and for power. " She states in a chapter called "The Coming Gynocide. " ⑥

Gena Corea, another radical feminist who works with members of FINNRET, the Feminist International Network on the New Reproductive Technologies, paints a similarly harrowing and far more technically detailed picture in *The Mother Machine*. In chapters with titles such as "Cloning: The Patriarchal Urge to Recreate" and "Reproductive Control: The War against the Womb," she depicts a social and scientific world in which these techniques are used solely to exploit and oppress us. Jan Zimmerman's *Once upon a Future* is a similar but broader study of the science and technology, including the reproductive technologies, wholly controlled by men who intend, and successfully manage, to exploit and destroy women. *Test Tube Women*, an anthology of scholarly and personal essays, does include a few articles defending the use of reproductive technologies in individual cases. But like the others, it is primarily a critique of reproductive science as wholly oppressive. Most recently, *Made to Order: The Myth of Reproductive and Genetic Progress* echoes this common refrain. ⑦

I do not for a moment question the vital political truths these books present. Certainly women are being exploited by the scientific/medical profession. Certainly there are fascistic overtones to the current technologically based regimes that rate some women fit for motherhood on the basis of class, race, and marital status, while channeling others into "surrogacy" for their more fortunate sisters and depriving them of the right to reproduce and mother for themselves. A feminist would have to be a fool not to understand the class, race, and sex biases of capitalism. She or he would have to be worse than a fool not to see the importance of a feminist response to the situation. But what is the correct response? "Discourses of totalizing morality," says Rayna Rapp, astutely, in a review of some of these books, "persuade at a high price. When we accept them, we give up precious ground so recently won: on that ground science as well as nurturance, culture, not just nature, could be women's turf. " ⑧

It is that precious ground that I am concerned to reclaim, because once we give it up, we easily fall into thought and behavior that feeds into the worst right-wing agendas. As German writers Juliette Zipper and Selma Sevenhuisjen remind us, "the opponents of surrogacy in the Social Democratic Party in West Germany" fell into a program that "the right would, applaud: the ties between marriage, love, sexuality and reproduction may not be loosened; surrogacy must be prohibited and reproductive technology may not be applied outside of marriage". ⑨

The Socialist-Feminist Response

While the books referred to above primarily express radical-feminist thinking, socialist and other left feminists have more often than not concurred. The case of Baby M—in which the birth mother, Mary Beth Whitehead, reneged after being inseminated by William Stern and legally committed to giving him the child—brought the issues raised by reproductive technologies into the mainstream media in a most dramatic and sensational way. In the process it also forced feminists of all stripes to take positions. Many of these were particularly revealing of the widespread postfeminist sense of political pessimism about social change.

For example, 125 prominent feminists signed a statement supporting Whitehead's claim to her birth child. For the left feminists who took this position the primary issue was one of class. If Whitehead, a working-class housewife, was seen as less fit than the Sterns, who were both educated, wealthy professionals, then theoretically, millions of women could be deemed unfit and lose our children on the basis of our class standing.

On this level the argument is irrefutable. Poor women, black women, lesbians, and sexually unconventional women do in fact lose children all the time to those rare fathers who choose to sue for custody. But the Baby M case raised deeper issues for feminists. It demonstrated how socialist analysis of class and race bias can lead to a retreat from an equally crucial socialist-feminist tenet: that motherhood is socially, not biologically, constructed. Sympathy for Whitehead, the class underdog, led socialist feminists to not so logically agree with Whitehead's own political argument: that the child "belonged" to her as the birth mother. As a result, a number of feminists—liberal, radical, and socialist—were suddenly arguing as vehemently for the rights of the biological mother and the sanctity of the biological bond between mother and child as they had once argued for the right *not* to mother and the need for fathers to share equally in child rearing.

The May 1988 issue of *Ms.* magazine, devoted entirely to the matter of reproductive technologies, is telling. After presenting an overview of "the dilemmas posed by the new reproductive technologies," the bulk of the issue, the really hot articles, are almost uniformly "pronatal". Phyllis Chesler, in an excerpt from her book on the Baby M case, asks—as though no sane person could disagree—"How can we deny that women have a profound and everlasting bond with the children they've birthed; that this bond begins in utero?" A few pages later the mother of physician/novelist Perri Klass describes helping her liberated daughter deliver her firstborn as "a transcendent moment" shared with her daughter and son-in-law (white professionals with the time and money to "choose" the most intimate, natural setting for the occasion, one that was also safe, comfortable, and efficient). And Barbara Ehrenreich worries—as have so many feminists recently—that legitimizing "surrogacy," which defines the birth mother as something less than a "real" mother, "flagrantly trivializes the process of childbirth," reducing it to "womb rental" [10].

What all these pieces seem to me to have in common—and they are simply a representative sampling of feminist opinion on the matter—is an implicit and largely emotional sense that in a post-Reagan world where so much has been taken from us and so much that we dreamed of twenty years ago has not materialized, we must at all costs hang on to the two things we can still hope to own and control, our bodies and our biological offspring. And yet these articles are fraught with political blind spots and contradictions. Motherhood, after all, is not experienced by all women as an unmixed blessing. Nor do all women have the material advantages of many white feminists, which allow childbirth and parenting to be experienced in such neoromantic terms.

Motherhood Demystified

The truth is that most women today live lives characterized by emotional and material deprivation, compromise, and a healthy dose of spiritual and/or physical suffering. Among my own friends the issue of motherhood is often painful and usually at least difficult. Among those fortunate enough to have financial security and supportive mates—and, often, to have been lucky enough to conceive later in life than biology prefers—there are still the problems of child care, curtailment of social and political activity, and coping with a dangerous social environment. But more distressing are the problems of single women: those whose personal and economic positions prohibit them from having longed-for children; those who struggle to raise children alone, on inadequate incomes and with no help from ex-partners; and those who use reproductive technologies to become single mothers by choice at enormous economic and emotional sacrifice.

Among my own children's friends and acquaintances I see even greater misery and trouble looming. Teen pregnancy, especially among poor, black women, is widely known to be epidemic. What may be less well known is that many of these young women are among the brightest in their classes. Yet their futures—their potential for self-fulfillment, much less material security—are cut short because they believe, as do the writers in *Ms.* and Anna in *The Good Mother*, that biological mother love is at any cost the greatest, most meaningful fulfillment for a woman.

Finally, there are the women, whom I do not know personally, who do in fact choose to "rent their wombs" and their bodies to men because, in fact, it is the best option they see for surviving in this cruel, sexist society. What of their right to control their bodies? What of the realities of their situations? I am not suggesting that prostitution or surrogacy, as now practiced, are good things. I am suggesting that any socialist-feminist discussion of these matters must take into account the realities of capitalism for most women and the choices that exist.

From a broader, less personal perspective, the issues surrounding motherhood and reproduction appear even more politically difficult and confusing. Women's needs, desires, and situations do differ, after all. To assume that the fight for the "maternal rights" of the biological mother and against technical or commercial intrusion into this "natural" realm is the obviously correct feminist position is more than theoretically regressive. It is simplistic in its failure to confront political reality in its entirety. Looking more closely at the specific reproductive techniques available, we see a maze of political contradiction more mind-boggling than any survey of one's personal circle of friends could reveal.

The categories of reproductive technologies are varied, but each is fraught with its own apparently irreconcilable contradictions. Birth control itself is the most common and accepted of these techniques, yet its promise of sexual freedom to women has always been compromised by the social and economic context in which it was developed and distributed. Health risks, unequal access by poor and Third World women, and sterilization abuse of women who want to have more children than society wants them to have are well-known facts. Moreover, the possibility of fertility control is balanced by a strong ideological belief—widely held in the medical professions and society at large—that "motherhood is the natural, desired, and ultimate goal of all 'normal' women". Those who "deny their maternal instincts are selfish, peculiar and otherwise disturbed". ⑪ This thinking clearly influences political decisions to invest more in fertility research than in contraception. Still, who would do away with contraception because it is badly used by those in power?

The management of labor and childbirth and the monitoring of fetal development by the scientific community are also fraught with contradiction. Financially secure women have access to the best care and are in a position to make choices about continuing a pregnancy when the fetus is less than "perfect". On the one hand, such techniques can be a boon to the individual woman fortunate enough to have access to them. On the other, control of the birthing process, once in the hands of female midwives, is now taken from us. Moreover, the fascistic implications of a set of techniques and policies that allow for the production of "perfect" babies and the possibility of aborting the less than perfect is obvious. But again, what pregnant woman would wish away these methods?

In the realm of conceptive technologies—artificial insemination, *in vitro* fertilization and surrogacy—the political contradictions are most extreme. Poor women, single women who are not economically privileged, Third World women, lesbians and other sexual nonconformists do not have equal access to this technology. Surrogacy today is certainly an economically exploitative practice. Yet for individual lesbian, single, or infertile women, this technology can be a godsend.

In even so sketchy a survey, two things become obvious. First, single-issue fights for "maternal rights" or an end to the commercialization of sex and childbirth are inadequate, often wrongheaded and at cross-purposes with other feminist values. And second, the real issues we need to be addressing are the big ones that we started with: What is a mother? What is a family? What is the responsibility of the community to women and children? And how does technology fit into this picture? I believe these questions demand a return to visionary thinking and to a view of technology that sees it—despite what we know of the male power structure—as potentially progressive, liberatory, and positive in its promise of a better world, a better human family.

To begin rethinking our relationship to technology, we might reread Piercy's *Woman on the Edge of the Time* from the less idealistic perspective of late 1980s realities. While reading this we might want to remind ourselves how we have trapped ourselves, as Zipper and Sevenhuisjen suggest, "in an opposition between [views that stress total] oppression or liberation."

Technology inherently serves neither; "it is not technology itself that complicates theory and strategy" but "the *terms* in which technology and its social consequences are spoken about." [12] Free in her imagination, Marge Piercy envisioned a world—albeit a fantastic one—in which people do control technology and make it work for them. We may be far from the power to do so, but that is all the more reason to remind ourselves, in these hard times, of what we are ultimately fighting for, what kind of world we want our grandchildren and great-grandchildren to inhabit.

A Feminist Future

This brings me to the first matter, the questions about motherhood, family, and community as socialist feminists would like them to exist. As feminists, we began by challenging patriarchal notions of family and sexuality. In place of paternal ownership and control of women and children, we demanded individual freedom, shared child-care, and social responsibility for the human family. In place of blood ties and inherited property as the basis of the distribution of wealth, we demanded social ownership, control, and sharing of our common resources. In place of hierarchical structures, we demanded democratic institutions in which each of us had some power and importance. In place of a single norm for "proper womanhood," we demanded choice and a recognition of the vast differences not only in women's natures and desires but in the material and emotional situations of women of different backgrounds and lifestyles. And in place of the good girl/ bad girl dichotomy, we demanded the right to be fully integrated persons, capable of experiencing sexual freedom and intellectual fulfillment without losing our right to be—or not be—mothers.

As grandiose and unrealistic as all this may now seem, the fact is that we were right to make these demands. While some of us are shoring up our little havens in this heartless world and counting our blessings, most of us are in worse shape than we imagined twenty years ago. The feminization of poverty, rising divorce rates, sexual and physical abuse of women and children, illiteracy and alienation among youth, loneliness and isolation among the old and not-so-old—these are the realities of life today. We don't have the choice of returning to the family structure of the 1950s except in isolated, lucky cases. In fact, to be politically realistic is to face the fact that terms such as "family" and "mother" have lost their traditional meanings for most of us, and no amount of romanticizing the mysteries of pregnancy will change that. In the face of these truths, the need for imaginative, even visionary speculation seems obvious, if difficult to manage.

Difficult, but not impossible. If Marge Piercy seems bizarre and fantastic to today's young women, there is another literary tradition, that of black women novelists, which is easier for young readers to relate to and in its own way often as visionary in its view of family, motherhood, and community as the work of earlier white feminist writers. *The Color Purple* is Alice Walker's marvelous example. ⑬ In it, we see the most oppressed woman imaginable grow into a heroine of mythic proportions in the context of a radically progressive, supportive community. The novel, as fantastic in its way as *Woman on the Edge of Time*, pictures a community of black women that creates the kind of family and lives out the kind of sexual and emotional relationships earlier feminists envisioned. In a world in which white and male power can at any moment separate families, destroy people, and leave children motherless, Walker shows what family—certainly for blacks and increasingly for all of us—must become if love and community are to survive.

In *The Color Purple* children are raised by friends and relatives when parents disappear. Sexual relationships end abruptly, if not because of forced separation then because of the enormous strain under which relationships exist in a world of pain, trouble, and powerlessness. Sexual jealousy is overcome in the interest of sisterhood and community survival. Most marvelously, sex roles and heterosexual norms are turned on their head. Love between any two people is a blessing, albeit one that will almost inevitably be short-lived. Even men—those emotional laggards—are allowed to grow and change under the influence of these magical, majestic women.

This vision is very close to what 1960s feminists believed in. It's not surprising, however, that it is now black women who are the feminist visionaries of family and sexual matters, given the breakdown of the black community under the stress of capitalism. The role of women in preserving it—in lovingly raising whatever children need care, in constructing a new definition of family much more realistic than the one white society has tried to impose upon it—stands as a model to white socialist feminists. It is a model that is accepting of difference, accepting of the fragility of the biological "maternal bond," accepting of the need for radical alternatives in these nasty times.

To be sure, *The Color Purple* is economically and technologically anachronistic in its portrayal of a small family-based craft industry as the material basis for the extended family's survival. Which brings us back to the matter at hand—reproductive technologies. Rather than hanging on to our little bit of biological power to reproduce, we might consider the issues raised by reproductive technologies in the context of creating a truly loving, democratic, nonsexist, nonrepressive environment in which technologies are widely and inexpensively available and used in the interest of women and children themselves. It is only in that context that the contradictions raised by these technologies, as they affect different kinds of women, can be resolved. The idea of social responsibility for "family policy" is discussed ad nauseam, and to little effect, these days. A socialist-feminist agenda that transcends immediate special interests to raise larger questions of what a decent society would look like, and how it would distribute its economic and technical resources, is not unrealistic. It is the only realistic approach I can conceive of to the increasing impoverishment and deprivation of our lives and our political imaginations.

I am particularly concerned with the return of the visionary in political discourse because I have a grown daughter of my own and teach young women of her age every day. These daughters of the second wave are remarkable and irritating. They have a vast sense of their own personal potential, their own right to "have it all": meaningful love, important work, children, pleasure, and joy. But their sense of how to achieve these things is as narrow and socially constrained as their self-confidence and energy are vast. They understand Anna in *The Good Mother* perfectly. They accept the limits and contradictions other choices as given, and in their own lives they plan to avoid her tragedy by being smarter, more careful about their life choices. Implicitly, they have opted for less than sexual freedom, less than real freedom of any kind, less than what we, their biological and spiritual mothers, hoped to be able to offer them—although they cannot possibly know that that is what they are doing.

They can't know because they can't understand *Woman on the Edge of Time* any more than they could understand Shulamith Firestone, should I be foolhardy enough to assign it. Yet they will be inheriting the world we leave them and the values for which we fought. Most alarmingly, they will be inheriting a world in which technology is an ever greater part of their lives, while their control over that technology is virtually nonexistent. Surely they need to know that their biological and spiritual mothers thought, wrote, and even tried to do something about that state of affairs and that it is therefore possible, necessary, even imperative that they do the same.

Notes：

① Shulamith Firestone, *The Dialectic of Sex* (New York：Bantam, 1971), p.206.

② Marge Piercy, *Woman on the Edge of Time* (New York：Fawcett, 1976).

③ Zoe Fairbairns, *Benefits* (New York：Avon, 1979)；Margaret Atwood, *The Handmaid's Tale* (New York, Fawcett Crest, 1985).

④ Sue Miller, *The Good Mother* (New York：Dell, 1986).

⑤ The one thoughtful and politically balanced work is Michelle Stanworth, ed. *Reproductive Technologies： Gender, Motherhood, and Medicine* (Minneapolis：University of Minnesota Press, 1987).

⑥ Andrea Dworkin, *Right-Wing Women* (New York：Perigree, 1983), p. 180.

⑦ Gena Corea, *The Mother Machine： Reproductive Technologies from Artificial Insemination to Artificial Wombs* (New York：Harper &：Row, 1985)；

Jan Zimmerman, *Once upon a Future: The Woman's Guide to Tomorrows Technology* (New York: Pandora, 1986); Rita Arditti, Renate Duelli Klein, Shelley Minden, eds. , *Test-Tube Women: What Future for Motherhood?* (New York: Pandora, 1984); Patricia Spallone and Deborah Steinberg, eds. , *Made to Order: The Myth of Reproductive Progress* (New York: Pergamon 1987).

⑧ Rayna Rapp, "A Womb of One's Own," *Women's Review of Books*, April 1988, p. 10.

⑨ Juliette Zipper and Selma Sevenhuisjen, "Surrogacy: Feminist Notions of Motherhood Reconsidered," in Stanworth, *Reproductive Technologies*, p. 135.

⑩ Mary Thom, "Dilemmas of the New Birth Technologies"; Phyllis Chesler, "What Is a Mother?"; Sheila Solomon Klass, "A Transcendent Moment"; and Barbara Ehrenreich, "The Heart of the Matter," all in *Ms.*, May 1988, pp. 70-76, 38, 41, 20.

⑩ Barbara Stanworth, "Reproductive Technologies and the Deconstruction of Motherhood," in Stanworth, *Reproductive Technologies*, p. 15.

⑫ Zipper and Sevenhuisjen, "Surrogacy," p. 120.

⑬ Alice Walker, *The Color Purple* (New York: Pocket Books, 1985).

罗斯·布雷多蒂,"母亲、魔鬼与机器"
Rosi Braidotti, "Mothers, Monsters, and Machines"

20

布雷多蒂①是荷兰乌德勒支大学(Utrecht University)人文学院教授,荷兰妇女学研究中心主任,负责协调欧洲国家妇女研究的交流活动。1994～1995 年曾在普林斯顿大学任访问学者。她的主要研究领域包括:女性主义哲学、后结构主义和心理分析、女性主义思想史。她目前从多文化视角研究女性主义的后现代特征和"欧洲"的概念。

布雷多蒂出生在意大利,生长在澳大利亚,在巴黎接受教育,后来又到荷兰工作。她亲身经历的一种"游牧"生活使她的视角极富政治敏感性,她自称是后现代女性主义理论家,试图为当代女性建构一个多元化的主体模式。她的著作是用多种语言写成的,她本人曾戏称她的语言是意澳式的(Italo-Australian)、法英式的(Franglais)、纽约巴黎方言(New Yorkese Parisian Patois)或荷兰英语(Dutch-lish)②。布雷多蒂认为,女性主义是现代性的惟一话语。女性主义同机器、伦理、自然一样都是现代性过程中需要重建的他者,女性作为他者标志着边缘主体的兴起,因而是具有建设意义的。她提倡一种跨民

---

① 照片摄影 Linda Lopez McAlister,取自 http://bailiwick. lib. uiowa. edu/wstudies/Braidotti。

② 参见 Rosi Braidotti, "Nomadic Philosopher: A Conversation with Rosi Braidotti," Interviewed by Kathleen O'Grady, Netherlands, August 1995. Reprinted from *Women's Education des femmes*, Spring 1996 (12.1): pp. 35-39. 引自 http://bailiwick. lib. uiowa. edu/wstudies/Braidotti, n. p. 。

族、跨学科的方法作为控制哲学规范的策略,在全球经济、技术革命以及多元文化、社会和理论文化现实的大背景下,如何把女性主体同对"人"的重新定义结合起来,这毫无疑问是政治性的话题①。

布雷多蒂的代表著作有:

《游牧主体:当代女性主义理论中的赋形与性别差异》(*Nomadic Subjects: Embodiment and Sexual Difference in Contemporary Feminist Theory*,1994年)

《不和谐模式:当代哲学中的女性研究》(*Patterns of Dissonance: A Study of Women in Contemporary Philosophy*,1991年)

《变形:建构关于正在形成的唯物主义理论》(*Metamorphoses: Toward a Materialistic Theory of Becoming*,2002年)

布雷多蒂还同 Nina Lykke 主编《魔鬼、女神和机器人之间》(*Between Monsters, Goddesses and Cyborgs*,1996年),同 Sabine Hausler, Ewa Pluta 和 Saskia Wieringa 合著《女性、环境与可持续发展》(*Women, the Environment and Sustainable Development: Towards a Theoretical Synthesis*)。

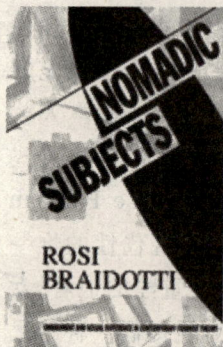

"母亲、魔鬼与机器"选自1994年出版的《游牧主体》一书。该书共分15章,此篇为第三章。布雷多蒂在该书中提倡一种新式的哲学思维,这一思维包括了女性主义的视角,而在此之前的严肃理论完全是男性霸权的模式。布雷多蒂探索的问题包括:西方的认识论同妇女问题的关系、女性主义与生物医学伦理问题、欧洲女性主义、美国的女性主义理论同欧洲妇女运动的关系等。可以看出,布雷多蒂在努力把女性主义纳入主流的哲学话语②。

该文章聚焦母亲、魔鬼和机器这三个概念间的四个连接点,讨论了母亲在文化上的负面象征意义以及科技使男性有能力生育之后对

---

① 参见 Rosi Braidotti, "Nomadic Philosopher: A Conversation with Rosi Braidotti," Interviewed by Kathleen O'Grady. Netherlands, August 1995. Reprinted from *Women's Education des femmes*. Spring 1996 (12.1): pp. 35-39. 引自 http://bailiwick. lib. uiowa. edu/wstudies/Braidotti, n. p.

② http://www. columbia. edu/cu/cup/catalog/data/023108/0231082355. HTM, n. p.

女性生活的影响。文章共分 6 个部分：

第一部分，"问题的提出"（Figuring Out）。作者首先告诉我们她的意图旨在摒弃阳具中心的模式，通过运用男人的话语温柔而坚定地表达女性的沉默①。在作者看来，这种"游牧"风格的模式最适合女性寻求表现的努力。它不是二元的、对立的思维方式，而是"把话语视为一种积极的、多重的权力关系网络"（第60 页；第 380 页）。作者进而对母亲、魔鬼和机器这三个术语做了详细解释。"母亲"指的是"女人的母性功能"（第 61 页；第 381 页），女性主义通过批评作为权力体制的性别（gender）因而把性别差异的纬度引入实践。"机器"指的是"广义上的科学的、政治的、零散的技术领域"（第 61 页；第 382 页）。"魔鬼"则一方面指天生生理肌体有缺陷的人，另一方面也指既令人恐怖又令人艳羡的东西（第 61~62 页；第 382 页）。由于魔鬼象征与人类基本形态不同的身体差异，因此是异形的、异常的（第 62 页；第 383 页）。对于母亲、机器和魔鬼之间主题联系的研究表明，当代生物技术通过把生育变成一件高科技的活动而置换了母亲的位置（第 63 页；第 384 页）。

第二部分，"连接点 1：作为魔鬼的女性/母亲"（Conjunction 1：Woman/Mother as Monster）。作者首先指出，把母亲视同魔鬼可以追溯到亚里士多德，并从此成为西方科学话语中的常态，由此产生对女性身体的恐惧（第 63~64 页；第 384 页）。在哲学话语中，"'她'永远同邪恶的、无秩序的、亚人类的、难看的现象相联系。似乎'她'身体内部有某种东西使她成为人类的敌人，成为文明的外来者，成为'他者'"（第 64 页；第 387 页）。女性因此成为差异的象征符号，女性身体同魔鬼一样可以独特地把神奇和恐怖融为一体（第 65 页；第 387 页）。布雷多蒂继而分析了弗洛伊德心理分析学说对女性身体的看法以及弗洛伊德之后的法国女性主义思想家（克里斯蒂娃、伊里加蕾等）对弗氏理论的批判。由于阳具中心理论曲解了女性性征，因此女性性征就同魔鬼性同形了：

女性/母亲由于其过度的特征具魔鬼性：她可以超越既定规范，跨越界限。

---

① Rosi Braidotti，"Mothers, Monsters, and Machines," in Katie Conboy, Nadia Medina, and Sarah Standbury, eds. , *Writing on the Body：Female Embodiment and Feminist Theory*（New York：Columbia University Press, 1997），p. 60. 本书所引该文观点均出自此处，以下只在正文标明页码，分号后第二个页码为引文在本书的页码。

女性/母亲又由于其缺乏的特征而具魔鬼性:她不具备男性主体的实质统一体。更为重要的是,由于认同女性的一切,女性/母亲通过被置换而具有魔鬼性:作为区域间东西的符号,作为无法确定的、模糊不清的、混合的东西的符号,女性/母亲被迫处于一个象征为"非"的持续过程中。(第66～67页;第388～389页)

"女人"于是成为被分配的对象,没有自我定义的权利。"女人"成为确保规范正常性的异形(第67页;第389页)。

第三部分,"连接点2:畸形学与女性"(Conjunction 2:Teratology and the Feminine)。畸形学的发展历史清晰地表明身体以及女性身体如何在西方科学话语中被概念化(第67页)。布雷多蒂告诉我们,在畸形学发展史的第一阶段,希腊和罗马人认为魔鬼是一个"种族",把魔鬼视为上帝施怒的结果(第68页)。到了16、17世纪,魔鬼仍然具有古代的那种"稀罕"、"神奇"的意义,畸形人甚至享有一定特权(第68页)。在医学处于前科学时代的时候,人们错误地认为有许多因素会影响生育,如天气、受孕的时间、妇女的想象等(第68～69页)。

第四部分,"连接点3:男人生育的幻想"(Conjunction 3:The Fantasy of Male-Born Children)。关于男人生育的幻想源自炼金术士制造侏儒的实践(第70～71页)。到了19世纪,这一实践开始借助解剖学和生物医学的技术。虽然器官移植和尸体解剖仍然在法律的监督下进行,但为科学目的而进行的身体试验已经被普遍认可了(第72页)。布雷多蒂指出,求知欲是所有思维和概念化形式的母体(matrix),"知识是了解欲望的一种欲望"(第73页)。而这种欲望的根本是人类的偷窥欲(scopophilic drive)和虐待欲(sadistic drive)。从心理分析角度看,西方现代科学提出了这样一个假设:身体是可以被观看和观察的对象。这一假设支持了现代理性的发展(第73页)。虽然(科学)哲学家对科学话语和技术能力做了大量理性的论述,但许多问题仍有待回答(第74页)。

第五部分,"连接点4:畸形人的时代"(Conjunction 4:The Age of Freaks)。"魔鬼"一词的拉丁语词源显示,这种扭曲的人一直都是展示的对象,供公众观看(第74页;第389页)。这种展示一方面带有种族偏见或东方主义的歧视,另一方面却也让医学获益(第74～75页;第389页)。现在,这种畸形人更多地表现为科幻电影中的机器人(androids)、半机械人(cyborgs)、仿生人(bionic women and men)。在布雷多蒂看来,我们这个时代正同时经历着科学话语正式化和消除魔鬼的过程,这表明把魔鬼视为既恐怖又艳羡的传统已经被置换(第75页;第390页)。布雷多蒂甚至总结说,从某种意义上讲,当代流行文化本身就是关于畸形人的文化(第75页;第390页)。更引人注目的是,对于畸形人的商品化过程恰恰促使这些畸形人群组织起来争取一种新的尊严和更为广泛意义的社会和政治权力(第76页;第391页)。

第六部分,"过渡时期:为了游牧主义"(In Transit; or, for Nomadism)。在讨论母亲、魔鬼和机器之间的关系时,女性主义的立场是跨学科的。这意味着女性主义理论家只能处于"过渡时期",永远在运动、置换/换位(dis-placing),永远在寻找新的方式。而布雷多蒂提出的"游牧"方式似乎正符合这一处于变化中的状态(第76页;第391页)。不仅如此,"在后现代困境中,古典模式的理性已经不再能够表现人类理性的整体或者过于具有人类特征(all-too-human)的思维活动"(第76~77页;第392页)。布雷多蒂辩解说,这并不意味着她主张非理性,她试图"重新定义人们认可的人类主体相对于差异的结构和目的"(第77页;第392页)。她总结说:"我们生活的世界是男性占统治地位的……最好的选择就是建构一种'游牧'式的女性主义风格,允许女性重新思考她们在后工业、后形而上学的世界里所处的地位,不带丝毫的怀旧情绪、痴心妄想甚或虚假的多愁善感"(第77页;第393页)。

这里选取的是该文的第一、二、五、六部分。

Mothers, Monsters, and Machines

Figuring Out

I would like to approach the sequence "mothers, monsters, and machines" both thematically and methodologically, so as to work out possible connections between these terms. Because women, the biological sciences, and technology are conceptually interrelated, there can not be only one correct connection but, rather, many, heterogeneous and potentially contradictory ones.

The quest for multiple connections—or conjunctions—can also be rendered methodologically in terms of Donna Haraway's "figurations."①

The term refers to ways of expressing feminist forms of knowledge that are not caught in a mimetic relationship to dominant scientific discourse. This is a way of marking my own difference: as an intellectual woman who has acquired and earned the right to speak publicly in an academic context, I have also inherited a tradition of female silence. Centuries of exclusion of women from the exercise of discursive power are ringing through my words. In speaking the language of man, I also intend to let the silence of woman echo gently but firmly; I shall not conform to the phallogocentric mode. ② I want to question the status of feminist theory in terms not only of the conceptual tools and the gender-specific perceptions that govern the production of feminist research but also of the form our perceptions take.

The "nomadic" style is the best suited to the quest for feminist figurations, in the sense of adequate representations of female experience as that which cannot easily be fitted within the parameters of phallogocentric language.

The configuration of ideas I am trying to set up: mothers, monsters, machines, is therefore a case study—not only in terms of its propositional content but also in defining my place of enunciation and, therefore, my relationship to the readers who are my partners in this discursive game. It is a new figuration of feminist subjectivity.

Quoting Deleuze, ③ I would like to define this relationship as "rhizomatic"; that is to say not only cerebral, but related to experience, which implies a strengthened connection between thought and life, a renewed proximity of the thinking process to existential reality. ④ In my thinking, "rhizomatic" thinking leads to what I call a "nomadic" style.

Moreover, a "nomadic" connection is not a dualistic or oppositional way of thinking ⑤ but rather one that views discourse as a positive, multilayered network of power relations. ⑥

Let me develop the terms of my nomadic network by reference to Foucauldian critiques of the power of discourse: he argues that the production of scientific knowledge works as a complex, interrelated network of truth, power, and desire, centered on the subject as a bodily entity. In a double movement that I find most politically useful, Foucault highlights both the normative foundations of theoretical reason and also the rational model of power. "Power" thus becomes the name for a complex set of interconnections, between the spaces where truth and knowledge are produced and the systems of control and domination. I shall unwrap my three interrelated notions in the light of this definition of power.

Last, but not least, this style implies the simultaneous dislocation not only of my place of enunciation as a feminist intellectual but also accordingly of the position of my readers. As my interlocutors I am constructing those readers to be "not just" traditional intellectuals and academics but also active, interested, and concerned participants in a project of research and experimentation for new ways of thinking about human subjectivity in general and female subjectivity in particular. I mean to appeal therefore not only to a requirement for passionless truth but also to a passionate engagement in the recognition of the theoretical and discursive implications of sexual difference. In this choice of a theoretical style that leaves ample room for the exploration of subjectivity, I am following the lead of Donna Haraway, whose plea for "passionate detachment" in theory making I fully share. ⑦

Let us now turn to the thematic or propositional content of my constellation of ideas: mothers, monsters and machines.

For the sake of clarity, let me define them: "mothers" refers to the maternal function of women. By WOMEN I mean not only the biocultural entities thus represented, as the empirical subjects of sociopolitical realities, but also a discursive field: feminist theory. The kind of feminism I want to defend rests on the presence and the experience of real-life women whose political consciousness is bent on changing the institution of power in our society.

Feminist theory is a two-layered project involving the critique of existing definitions, representations as well as the elaboration of alternative theories about women. Feminism is the movement that brings into practice the dimension of sexual difference through the critique of gender as a power institution. Feminism is the question; the affirmation of sexual difference is the answer.

This point is particularly important in the light of modernity's imperative to think differently about our historical condition. The central question seems to be here: how can we *affirm* the positivity of female subjectivity at a time in history when our acquired perceptions of "the subject" are being radically questioned? How can we reconcile the recognition of the problematic nature of the notion and the construction of the subject with the political necessity to posit female subjectivity?

By *MACHINES* I mean the scientific, political, and discursive field of technology in the broadest sense of the term. Ever since Heidegger the philosophy of modernity has been trying to come to terms with technological reason. The Frankfurt School refers to it as "instrumental reason": one that places the end of its endeavors well above the means and suspends all judgment on its inner logic. In my work, as I mentioned in the previous chapter, I approach the technology issue from within the French tradition, following the materialism of Bachelard, Canguilhem, and Foucault.

By *MONSTERS* I mean a third kind of discourse: the history and philosophy of the biological sciences, and their relation to difference and to different bodies. Monsters are human beings who are born with congenital malformations of their bodily organism. They also represent the in between, the mixed, the ambivalent as implied in the ancient Greek root of the word "monsters," *teras*, which means both horrible and wonderful, object of aberration and adoration. Since the nineteenth century, following the classification system of monstrosity by Geoffroy Saint-Hilaire, bodily malformations have been defined in terms of "excess," "lack," or "displacement of organs." ⑧ Before any such scientific classification was reached, however, natural philosophy had struggled to come to terms with these objects of abjection. The constitution of teratology as a science offers a paradigmatic example of the ways in which scientific rationality dealt with differences of the bodily kind.

The discourse on monsters as a case study highlights a question that seems to me very important for feminist theory: the status of difference within rational thought. Following the analysis of the philosophical ratio suggested by Derrida ⑨ and other contemporary French philosophers, it can be argued that Western thought has a logic of binary oppositions that treats difference as that which is other-than the accepted norm. The question then becomes: can we free difference from these normative connotations? Can we learn to think differently about difference? ⑩

The monster is the bodily incarnation of difference from the basic human norm; it is a deviant, an a-nomaly; it is abnormal. As Georges Canguilhem points out, the very notion of the human body rests upon an image that is intrinsically prescriptive: a normally formed human being is the zero-degree of monstrosity. Given the special status of the monster, what light does he throw on the structures of scientific discourse? How was the difference of/in the monster perceived within this discourse?

When set alongside each other, mothers/monsters/machines may seem puzzling. There is no apparent connection among these three terms and yet the link soon becomes obvious if I add that recent developments in the field of biotechnology, particularly artificial procreation, have extended the power of science over the maternal body of women. The possibility of mechanizing the maternal function is by now well within our reach; the manipulation of life through different combinations of genetic engineering has allowed for the creation of new artificial monsters in the high-tech labs of our biochemists. There is therefore a political urgency about the future of women in the new reproductive technology debate, which gives a polemical force to my constellation of ideas—mothers, monsters, and machines.

The legal, economic, and political repercussions of the new reproductive technologies are far-reaching. The recent stand taken by the Roman Catholic Church and by innumerable "bioethics committees" all across Western Europe against experimentation and genetic manipulations may appear fair enough. They all invariably shift the debate, however, far from the power of science over the women's body in favor of placing increasing emphasis on the rights of the fetus or of embryos. This emphasis is played against the rights of the mother—and therefore of the woman—and we have been witnessing systematic slippages between the discourse against genetic manipulations and the rhetoric of the antiabortion campaigners. No area of contemporary technological development is more crucial to the construction of gender than the new reproductive technologies. The central thematic link I want to explore between mothers, monsters, and machines is therefore my argument that contemporary biotechnology displaces women by making procreation a high-tech affair.

Conjunction 1: Woman/Mother as Monster

As part of the discursive game of nomadic networking I am attempting here, let us start by associating two of these terms: let us superimpose the image of the woman/mother onto that of the monstrous body. In other words, let us take the case study of monsters, deviants, or anomalous entities as being paradigmatic of how differences are dealt with within scientific rationality. Why this association of femininity with monstrosity?

The association of women with monsters goes as far back as Aristotle who, in *The Generation of Animals*, posits the human norm in terms of bodily organization based on a male model. Thus, in reproduction, when everything goes according to the norm a boy is produced; the female only happens when something goes wrong or fails to occur in the reproductive process. The female is therefore an anomaly, a variation on the main theme of man-kind: The emphasis Aristotle places on the masculinity of the human norm is also reflected in his theory of conception: he argues that the principle of life is carried exclusively by the sperm, the female genital apparatus providing only the passive receptacle for human life. The sperm-centered nature of this early theory of procreation is thus connected to a massive masculine bias in the general Aristotelian theory of subjectivity. For

Aristotle, not surprisingly, women are not endowed with a rational soul. ⑪

The *topos* of women as a sign of abnormality, and therefore of difference as a mark of inferiority, remained a constant in Western scientific discourse. This association has produced, among other things, a style of misogynist literature with which anyone who has read *Gulliver's Travels* must be familiar: the horror of the female body. The interconnection of women as monsters with the literary text is particularly significant and rich in the genre of satire. In a sense, the satirical text is implicitly monstrous, it is a deviant, an aberration in itself. Eminently transgressive, it can afford to express a degree of misogyny that might shock in other literary genres.

Outside the literary tradition, however, the association of femininity with monstrosity points to a system of pejoration that is implicit in the binary logic of oppositions that characterizes the phallogocentric discursive order. The monstrous as the negative pole, the pole of pejoration, is structurally analogous to the feminine as that which is other than the established norm, whatever the norm may be. The actual prepositional content of the terms of opposition is less significant for me than its logic. Within this dualistic system, monsters are, just like bodily female subjects, a figure of devalued difference; as such, it provides the fuel for the production of normative discourse. If the position of women and monsters as logical operators in discursive production is comparable within the dualistic logic, it follows that the misogyny of discourse is not an irrational exception but rather a tightly constructed system that requires difference as pejoration in order to erect the positivity of the norm. In this respect, misogyny is not a hazard but rather the structural necessity of a system that can only represent "otherness" as negativity.

The theme of woman as devalued difference remained a constant in Western thought; in philosophy especially, "she" is forever associated to unholy, disorderly, subhuman, and unsightly phenomena. It is as if "she" carried within herself something that makes her prone to being an enemy of mankind, an outsider in her civilization, an "other." It is important to stress the light that psychoanalytic theory has cast upon this hatred for the feminine and the traditional patriarchal association of women with monstrosity.

The woman's body can change shape in pregnancy and childbearing; it is therefore capable of defeating the notion of fixed *bodily form*, of visible, recognizable, clear, and distinct shapes as that which marks the contour of the body. She is morphologically dubious. The fact that the female body can change shape so drastically is troublesome in the eyes of the logocentric economy within which to see is the primary act of knowledge and *the gaze* the basis of all epistemic awareness. ⑫ The fact that the male sexual organ does, of course, change shape in the limited time span of the erection and that this operation—however precarious—is not exactly unrelated to the changes of shape undergone by the female body during pregnancy constitutes, in psychoanalytic theory, one of the fundamental axes of fantasy about sexual difference.

The appearance of symmetry in the way the two sexes work in reproduction merely brings out, however, the separateness and the specificity of each sexual organization. What looks to the naked eye like a comparable pattern: erection/pregnancy, betrays the ineluctable difference. As psychoanalysis successfully demonstrates, reproduction does not encompass the whole of human sexuality and for this reason alone anatomy is *not* destiny. Moreover, this partial analogy also leads to a sense of (false) anatomical complementarity between the sexes that contrast with the complexity of the psychic representations of sexual difference. This double recognition of both proximity and separation is the breeding ground for the rich and varied network of misunderstandings, identifications, interconnections, and mutual demands that are what sexual human relationships are all about.

Precisely this paradoxical mixture of "the same and yet other" between the sexes generates a drive to denigrate woman in so far as she is "other-than" the male norm. In this respect hatred for the feminine constitutes the phallogocentric economy by inducing in both sexes the desire to achieve order, by means of a one-way pattern for both. As long as the law of the One is operative, so will be the denigration of the feminine, and of women with it. ⑬

Woman as a sign of difference is monstrous. If we define the monster as a bodily entity that is anomalous and deviant vis-à-vis the norm, then we can argue that the female body shares with the monster the privilege of bringing out a unique blend of *fascination and horror*. This logic of attraction and repulsion is extremely significant; psychoanalytic theory takes it as the fundamental structure of the mechanism of desire and, as such, of the constitution of the neurotic symptom: the spasm of the hysteric turns to nausea, displacing itself from its object.

Julia Kristeva, drawing extensively on the research of Mary Douglas, connects this mixture ⑭ to the maternal body as the site of the origin of life and consequently also of the insertion into mortality and death. We are all of woman born, and the mother's body as the threshold of existence is both sacred and soiled, holy and hellish; it is attractive and repulsive, all-powerful and therefore impossible to live with. Kristeva speaks of it in terms of "abjection"; the abject arises in that gray, in between area of the mixed, the ambiguous. The monstrous or deviant is a figure of abjection in so far as it trespasses and transgresses the barriers between recognizable norms or definitions.

Significantly, the abject approximates the sacred because it appears to contain within itself a constitutive ambivalence where life and death are reconciled. Kristeva emphasizes the dual function of the maternal site as both life- and death-giver, as object of worship and of terror. The notion of the sacred is generated precisely by this blend of fascination and horror, which prompts an intense play of the imaginary, of fantasies and often nightmares about the ever-shifting boundaries between life and death, night and day, masculine and feminine, active and passive, and so forth.

In a remarkable essay about the head of the Medusa, Freud connected this logic of attraction and repulsion to the sight of female genitalia; because there is *nothing to see* in that dark and mysterious region, the imagination goes haywire. Short of losing his head, the male gazer is certainly struck by castration anxiety. For fear of losing the thread of his thought, Freud then turns his distress into the most overdetermined of all questions: "what does woman want?"

A post-Freudian reading of this text permits us to see how the question about female desire emerges out of male anxiety about the representation of sexual difference. In a more Lacanian vein, Kristeva adds an important insight: the female sex as the site of origin also inspires awe because of the psychic and cultural imperative to separate from the mother and accept the Law of the Father. The incest taboo, the fundamental law of our social system, builds on the mixture of fascination and horror that characterizes the feminine/maternal object of abjection. As the site of primary repression, and therefore that which escapes from representation, the mother's body becomes a turbulent area of psychic life.

Obviously, this analysis merely describes the mechanisms at work in our cultural system; no absolute necessity surrounds the symbolic absence of Woman. On the contrary, feminists have been working precisely to put into images that which escapes phallogocentric modes of representation. Thus, in her critique of psychoanalysis, Luce Irigaray points out that the dark continent of all dark continents is the mother-daughter relationship. She also suggests that, instead of this logic of attraction and repulsion, sexual difference may be thought out in terms of recognition and wonder. The latter is one of the fundamental passions in Descartes' treatise about human affectivity: he values it as the foremost of human passions, that which makes everything else possible. Why Western culture did not adopt this way of conceptualizing and experiencing difference and opted instead for difference as a sign of negativity remains a critical question for me.

It is because of this phallogocentric perversion that femininity and monstrosity can be seen as isomorphic. Woman/mother is monstrous by excess; she transcends established norms and transgresses boundaries. She is monstrous by lack: woman/mother does not possess the substantive unity of the masculine subject. Most important, through her identification with the feminine she is monstrous by displacement: as sign of the in between areas, of the indefinite, the ambiguous, the mixed, woman/mother is subjected to a constant process of metaphorization as "other-than."

In the binary structure of the logocentric system, "woman," as the eternal pole of opposition, the "other," can be assigned to the most varied and often contradictory terms. The only constant remains her "becoming-metaphor" whether of the sacred or the profane, of heaven or hell, of life or death. "Woman" is that which is assigned and has no power of self-definition. "Woman" is the anomaly that confirms the positivity of the norm.

[……]

Conjunction 4: The Age of Freaks

As the Latin etymology of the term *monstrum* points out, malformed human beings have always been the object of display, subjected to the public gaze. In his classic study, *Freaks*, Leslie Fiedler ⑮ analyses the exploitation of monsters for purposes of entertainment. From the county fairs, right across rural Europe to the Coney Island sideshows, freaks have always been entertaining.

Both Fiedler and Bogdan ⑯ stress two interrelated aspects of the display of freaks since the turn of the century. The first is that their exhibition displays racist and orientalist undertones: abnormally formed people were exhibited alongside tribal people of normal stature and bodily configuration, as well as exotic animals.

Second, the medical profession benefited considerably by examining these human exhibits. Although the freak is presented as belonging to the realm of zoology or anthropology, doctors and physicians examined them regularly and wrote scientific reports about them.

Significantly, totalitarian regimes such as Hitler's Germany or the Stalinist Soviet Union prohibited the exhibition of freaks as being degenerate specimens of the human species. They also dealt with them in their campaigns for eugenics and race or ethnic hygiene, by preventing them from breeding.

Fiedler sees a connection between the twentieth-century medicalization of monsters, the scientific appropriation of their generative secrets, and an increased commodification of the monster as freak, that is, the object of display.

Contemporary culture deals with anomalies by a fascination for the freaky. The film *Freaks* by Tod Browning (1932) warns us that monsters are an endangered species. Since the sixties a whole youth culture has developed around freaks, with special emphasis on genetic mutation as a sign of nonconformism and social rebellion. Whole popular culture genres such as science fiction, horror, rock'n'roll comics, and cyberpunk are about mutants.

Today, the freaks are science fiction androids, cyborgs, bionic women and men, comparable to the grotesque of former times; the whole rock'n'roll scene is a huge theater of the grotesque, combining freaks, androgynes, satanies, ugliness, and insanity, as well as violence.

In other words, in the early part of our century we watch the simultaneous formalization of a scientific discourse about monsters and their elimination as a problem. This process, which falls under the rationalist aggression of scientific discourse, also operates a shift at the level of representation, and of the cultural imaginary. The dimension of the "fantastic," that mixture of aberration and adoration, loathing and attraction, which for centuries has escorted the existence of strange and difficult bodies, is now displaced. The "becoming freaks" of monsters both deflates the fantastic projections that have surrounded them and expands them to a wider cultural field. The whole of contemporary popular culture is about freaks, just as the last of the physical freaks have disappeared. The last metaphorical shift in the status of monsters—their becoming freaks—coincides with their elimination.

In order not to be too pessimistic about this aspect of the problem, however, I wish to point out that the age of the commodification of freaks is also the period that has resulted in another significant shift: abnormally formed people have organized themselves in the handicapped political movement, thereby claiming not only a renewed sense of dignity but also wider social and political rights. ⑰

In Transit; or, for Nomadism

Mothers, monsters, and machines. What is the connection, then? What con/dis-junctions can we make in telling the tale of feminism, science, and technology? How do feminist fabulations or figurations help in figuring out alternative paradigms? To what extent do they speak the language of sexual difference? Where do we situate ourselves in order to create links, construct theories, elaborate hypotheses? Which way do we look to try and see the possible impact modern science will have on the status of women? How do we assess the status of difference as an ontological category at the end of the twentieth century? How do we think about all this?

The term "trandisciplinary" can describe one position taken by feminists. Passing in between different discursive fields, and through diverse spheres of intellectual discourse. The feminist theoretician today can only be "in transit," moving on, passing through, creating connections where things were previously dis-connected or seemed un-related, where there seemed to be "nothing to see." In transit, moving, dis-placing—this is the grain of hysteria without which there is no theorization at all. ⑱ In a feminist context it also implies the effort to move on to the invention of new ways of relating, of building footbridges between notions. The epistemic nomadism I am advocating can only work, in fact, if it is properly situated, securely anchored in the "in between" zones.

I am assuming here a definition of "rigor" away from the linear Aristotelian logic that dominated it for so long. It seems to me that the rigor feminists are after is of a different kind—it is the rigor of a project that emphasizes the necessary interconnection-connections between the theoretical and the political, which insists on putting real-life experience first and foremost as a criterion for the validation of truth. It is the rigor of passionate investment in a project and in the quest of the discursive means to realize it.

In this respect feminism acts as a reminder that in the postmodern predicament, rationality in its classical mode can no longer be taken as rep resenting the totality of human reason or even of the all-too-human activity of thinking.

By criticizing the single-mindedness and the masculine bias of rationality I do not intend to fall into the opposite and plead for easy ready-made irrationalism. Patriarchal thought has for too long confined women in the irrational for me to claim such a non-quality. What we need instead is a redefinition of what we have learned to recognize as being the structure and the aims of human subjectivity in its relationship to difference, to the "other."

In claiming that feminists are attempting to redefine the very meaning of thought, I am also suggesting that in time the rules of the discursive game will have to change. Academics will have to agree that thinking adequately about our historical condition implies the transcendence of disciplinary boundaries and intellectual categories.

More important, for feminist epistemologists, the task of thinking adequately about the historical conditions that affect the medicalization of the maternal function forces upon us the need to reconsider the inextricable interconnection of the bodily with the technological. The shifts that have taken place in the perception and the representation of the embodied subject, in fact, make it imperative to think the unity of body and machine, flesh and metal. Although many factors point to the danger of commodification of the body that such a mixture makes possible, and although this process of commodification conceals racist and sexist dangers that must not be underestimated, this is not the whole story. There is also a positive side to the new interconnection of mothers, monsters, and machines, and this has to do with the loss of any essentialized definition of womanhood—or indeed even of motherhood. In the age of biotechnological power motherhood is split open into a variety of possible physiological, cultural, and social functions. If this were the best of all possible worlds, one could celebrate the decline of one consensual way of experiencing motherhood as a sign of increased freedom for women. Our world being as male-dominated as it is, however, the best option is to construct a *nomadic* style of feminism that will allow women to rethink their position in a postindustrial, post-metaphysical world, without nostalgia, paranoia, or false sentimentalism. The relevance and political urgency of the configuration "mothers, monsters and machines" makes it all the more urgent for the feminist nomadic thinkers of the world to connect and to negotiate new boundaries for female identity in a world where power over the body has reached an implosive peak.

I wish to thank Margaret R. Higonnet, of the Center for European Studies at Harvard, and Sissel Lie, of the Women's Research Center at Tronheim, Norway, for their helpful comments on an earlier draft of this paper.

Notes:

① Donna Haraway, " 'Gender' for a Marxist Dictionary: The Sexual Politics of a Word," in *Simians*, *Cyborgs*, *and Women*, pp. 127-148 (London: Free Association Books, 1991).

② For an enlightening and strategic usage of the notion of "mimesis," see Luce Irigaray, *Ce sexe qui n'en est pas un* (Paris: Minuit, 1977).

③ To refer to the concept elaborated by the French philosopher of difference, see Gilles Deleuze in collaboration with Felix Guattari, *Rhizome* (Paris: Minuit, 1976).

④ The notion of "experience" has been the object of intense debates in feminist theory. See for example, Teresa de Lauretis, *Alice Doesn't* (Bloomington: Indiana University Press, 1984); Sandra Harding, *The*

Science Question in Feminism (London: Open University, 1986), and *Feminism and Methodology* (London: Open University, 1987); Joan Scott, "Experience," in Joan Scott and Judith Butler, eds. , *Feminists Theorize the Political* (London and New York: Routledge, 1992), pp. 22-40.

⑤ Genevieve Lloyd, *The Man of Reason* (London: Methuen, 1985).

⑥ Cf. Michel Foucault, *L'ordre du discours* (Paris: Gallimard, 1971); *Surveiller et punir* (Paris: Gallimard, 1975); " Les intellectuels et le pouvoir," *L'Arc*, no. 49 (1972).

⑦ This expression, originally coined by Laura Mulvey in film criticism, has been taken up and developed by Donna Haraway in a stunning exploration of this intellectual mode; see "Situated Knowledges: The Science Question in Feminism and the Privilege of Partial Perspective," and "A Cyborg Manifesto: Science, Technology, and Socialist-Feminism in the Late Twentieth Century," in *Simians, Cyborgs, and Women*, pp. 183-202 and 127-148.

⑧ I explored this notion of monstrosity at some length in a seminar held jointly with Marie-Jo Dhavernas at the College International de Philosophic in Paris in 1984-1985. The report of the sessions was published in *Cahier du College International de Philosophie*, no. 1 (1985): pp. 42-45.

⑨ See Jacques Derrida, *L'ecriture et la différence* (Paris: Seuil, 1967); *Marges de la philosophie* (Paris: Minuit, 1972); *La carte postale* (Paris: Flammarion, 1980).

⑩ On this point, see Alice Jardine, *Gynesis: Configurations of Woman in Modernity*, (Ithaca: Cornell University Press, 1984).

⑪ For a feminist critique of Aristotle, see Sandra Harding and Maryl Hintikka, eds. , *Discovering Reality* (Boston: Reidel, 1983).

⑫ The most enlightening philosophical analysis of the scopophilic mode of scientific knowledge is Michel Foucault's *Naissance de la clinique* (Paris: Gallimard, 1963).

⑬ This is the fundamental starting point for the work of feminist philosopher of sexual difference Luce Irigaray; see, for instance *L'éthique de la différence sexuelle* (Paris: Minuit, 1984).

⑭ Julia Kristeva, *Pouvoirs de l' horreur* (Paris: Seuil, 1980).

⑮ Leslie Fiedler, *Freaks* (New York: Simon & Schuster, 1978).

⑯ Robert Bogdan, *Freak Show* (Chicago and London: University of Chicago Press, 1988).

⑰ David Hevey, ed., *The Creatures Time Forgot: Photography and Disability Imagery* (London and New York: Routledge, 1992).

⑱ As Monique David-Menard argues in *L' Hystérique entre Freud et Lacan* (Paris: Ed. Universitaire, 1983).

未尽的话
Afterword

　　母亲身份是女性身份既独特又极端的表现形式,母亲身份在女性追求性别平等的过程中到底发挥着什么样的作用,这里还有几个问题需要我们思考:

　　第一,关于女性话语。法国女性主义理论家大多关注女性话语的建立,认为女性只有通过女性话语才能表达女性经验。伊莲娜·西克苏提倡女性书写(l' écriture feminine),主张女性用自己的声音充分表达思想。她认为,母亲的声音为女性书写提供了"永不枯竭的奶浆"。她还断定说,"在她体内总会有一点儿健康的母亲的奶汁残留下来,她用白色的墨水书写"①。伊里加蕾也呼吁在父权文化中建立母女关系这个在父权文化中缺失的支柱②,她认为,父权体制的问题以及社会不平等的原因最终可以归结为"女性繁衍的线索已经被中断"③。为重新建立基本的社会公正和正常的母女关系,"女性必须相互间作为母亲般用母爱去爱,同时也作为女儿般用亲情去爱"④。伊里加蕾甚至还提出了一些具体的建议帮助女性建立相互之间的亲密关系⑤。伊里加蕾没有区分两代女性,她把她们视为复数的"我们"。这样做的目的是把母亲和女儿归为一类,这是不同于男性的一类,是分享许多相似之处的一类,她们应该共同努力建设一个没有

---

　　① Hélène Cixous and Catherine Clément, *The Newly Born Woman*, trans. Betsy Wing (Minneapolis, MN: University of Minnesota Press, 1986), p.94.

　　② Luce Irigaray, *Thinking the Difference*, trans. Karin Montin (London: The Athlone Press, 1994), p.112.

　　③ Ibid., p.106.

　　④ Luce Irigaray, *An Ethics of Sexual Difference*, trans. Carolyn Burke and Gillian C. Gill (London: The Athlone Press, 1993), p.105.

　　⑤ 参见 Luce Irigaray, *Je, Tu, Nous: Toward a Culture of Difference*, trans. Alison Martin (New York: Routledge, 1993), pp.47-50.

男性参与和干涉的未来。她还提倡建立一种不把女性鄙视为第二性的中性语言。但是语言的建立可并不是一件容易的事。在理论上讲,建立一种完全不同于男性话语的女性话语体系是不可能的,克里斯蒂娃就曾经对此提出质疑①。罗伯特·德·博格兰德也对这样一个中性话语的可行性表示怀疑:"如果话语的偏见这么深,我们怎么能希望找到一种适合我们批评的中性的话语呢?"②女性生长在男性文化中,这一文化既然以性别偏见为特征,女性又怎能在这一背景下建构一个性别平等的文化呢? 女性要颠覆现有的男性话语体系就必须依赖解构的方法,而解构本身也面临许多固有的问题。在后现代环境下,意义的产生是一个重复的过程,作者在这一过程中已经消失。"作者的死亡带来意义的死亡,意义的死亡带来真理的丧失"③。这样看来,寻找绝对真理已经成为不可能。

第二,关于解构后的母亲身份。全球化带来的经济、政治、文化、观念的多元化倾向在社会生活中也有反映和表现,科学技术从根本上改变了传统的劳动分工,女性完全可以与男性一样从事同样的工作。在计算机面前,性别差异带来的影响已经降低到很小,越来越多的青年女性视网络为可以充分享受自由和平等的空间。随着社会分工的改变,家庭结构和模式也发生了改变。单亲家庭出现,一些人结婚但选择不生育,还有一些人同居生子但不结婚,甚至还出现了同性婚姻以及同性恋家长④。克隆技术、冷冻技术、DNA 和基因技术为人类提供了许多控制和监测生育的可能性:促进妊娠药片、繁殖药物、试管婴儿、体内植芯片、人工授精、体外受精、胎儿监测、变性手术、人造子宫等技术彻底改变了传统的生理母亲的概念。甚至还有科学家一直在尝试让男人怀孕。这些技术伴随着一系列道德、伦理、心理、社会和政治的问题。此外,生育技术的应用本身存在不平衡和不平等,并不是每一位希望生育技术改变生活的人都能够平等地享用。生育技术在开发和使用上仍然存在缺陷,女性在有可能享受技术带来的好处的同时,

---

① Julia Kristeva, "Women's Time," trans. Alice Jardine and Harry Blake, *The Kristeva Reader*, ed. Toril Moi (New York: Columbia University Press, 1986), p.200.

② Robert de Beaugrande, "In Search of Feminist Discourse: The 'Difficult' Case of Luce Irigaray," *College English* 50.3 (March 1988): p.253.

③ Lynne Huffer, *Maternal Pasts, Feminist Futures: Nostalgia, Ethics, and the Question of Difference* (Stanford, CA: Stanford University Press, 1998), p.55.

④ Juliet Mitchell, "Feminism and Psychoanalysis at the Millennium," *Women: a Cultural Review* 10.2 (Summer 1999): p.191.

其生活也被技术进一步控制。首先,生育技术更多地表现为男性运用科学技术对生育过程进行控制,在此过程中,女性被视为病人,成为生育技术的受害者,女性的身体被当做实验的对象。女性主义理论家瑞萍就曾指出,"女性正在被科学/医学技术所剥削"①。伊里加蕾也曾说,"那些认为自己已经从父权体制中被根本解放的女性,重又使自己的命运从身体到精神屈服于这个叫做人工生育的技术上"②。其次,试管婴儿的出现、人工受孕和代理母亲的技术改变了对于怀孕的传统概念,技术的结果——胎儿——被看做高于母亲本身,这置换了女性的存在。再次,随着生育技术不断参与人们的生活,母亲身份将被彻底解构,将会出现提供卵子的卵巢母亲、孕育胚胎的子宫母亲以及养育孩子的社会母亲。由于技术的参与削减了生育的自然性特征,这使得母亲身份被贬低化③。生育技术毫无疑问是"一柄双刃剑"④,面对它给我们的生活带来的诸多奇迹,我们不能持盲目乐观的态度。

第三,母亲身份与女性主体。女性在母亲身份上是否能够获得一定的自主性从而确立其主体性呢?克里斯蒂娃清楚地指出女性面临的窘境:要么她认同母亲,这意味着她将像母亲一样继续保持沉默,并继续母亲在父权体制下担负的母性角色;要么她认同父亲,这意味着她将从父亲的"象征秩序"中寻找身份。"父亲的女儿?还是母亲的女儿?"⑤——这两种选择相互矛盾,母亲的声音是对父权体制的颠覆,但从男性的角度来看,这呼唤是"疯狂的",违背社会秩序,会危及社会安全和稳定。女儿在成长过程中寻找身份的时候,很可能会追随父亲的脚步,因为母亲自己也缺少独立的身份,因而无法为女儿提供样板。伊里加

---

① Elayne Rapping, "The Future of Motherhood: Some Unfashionably Visionary Thoughts," *Women, Class and the Feminist Imagination: A Socialist-Feminist Reader*, eds. Karen V. Hansen and Ilene J. Philipson (Philadelphia: Temple University Press, 1990), pp. 539-540.

② Luce Irigaray, *Je, Tu, Nous: Toward a Culture of Difference*, trans. Alison Martin (New York: Routledge, 1993), p. 135.

③ Michelle Stanworth, "Reproductive Technologies and the Deconstruction of Motherhood," *Reproductive Technologies: Gender, Motherhood and Medicine*, ed. Michelle Stanworth (Cambridge: Polity Press, 1987), pp. 16-17.

④ Ibid., 16.

⑤ Julia Kristeva, "About Chinese Women," trans. Seán Hand, *The Kristeva Reader*, ed. Toril Moi (New York: Columbia University Press, 1986), p. 151.

蕾认识到,女儿要成为女性时一定要打破母女纽带①。但如果是这样,女儿同父亲的联系就会得到加强,而同母亲的联系就会相应减弱。女儿怎能一边保持同母亲的纽带联系另一边又依照父亲的榜样寻求独立的身份呢?如果母女纽带变得脆弱,女性世系又怎能得到保证和维系呢?南茜·乔德罗从社会-文化以及心理分析的角度出发指出母亲身份是世世代代再生的,女性建立女性身份似乎比男性建立男性身份要容易得多,因为女孩"成长过程中具有一种同母亲的连续性和相似性,具有一种同世界的相关联系",而男孩却必须"否定内心同女性的认同,否定他们体验到的女性经历"②。但是,女孩成长时却被灌输了这样一种观点,即女性在父权社会是被贬值的。乔德罗还提醒我们说,如果女性继续把自己局限在父权体制赋予的母亲角色中,她们就会"继续养育出其性别身份依赖于贬低女性气质的儿子,无论是内心还是外部;她们也会继续养育出必须接受这样一个处于被贬低的社会地位的女儿,她们将屈从地生育更多延续贬低女性的体制的男性"③。

女性主义理论家认为弗氏学说是在参照男性性征的前提下定义女性性征的,她们明确地指出母亲在男性话语中所占据的边缘化地位。母亲缺乏象征权力和话语的阳具,因此被排斥在男性秩序之外。她被客体化为他者,满足男性需要和欲望的同时自己的需要却被他人的利益所湮没。母亲角色是父权体制强加在女性身上的社会角色,这一角色基于男性的价值观念,因而自然成为束缚女性寻找个体性的羁绊,成为一个摧毁女性自我的机构和体制。在传统观念中,女性一直为自己的母亲身份感到自豪,因为母性代表生命的起源,因此女性似乎拥有一种男性不具有的力量。"在动物物种中,雌性也许有优越性,这仅仅由于她身体具备的生育能力"④。然而,正是生育能力标志着女性/母亲的客体化地位,也正因为女性拥有生育能力才使得男性世系得以延续。因此,"在父权体制下,母

①　Luce Irigaray, *An Ethics of Sexual Difference*, trans. Carolyn Burke and Gillian C. Gill (London: The Athlone Press, 1993), p.108.

②　Nancy Chodorow, *Feminism and Psychoanalytic Theory* (New Haven, CT: Yale University Press, 1989), pp.109-110.

③　Ibid., p.44.

④　Juliet Mitchell, *Psychoanalysis and Feminism: A Radical Reassessment of Freudian Psychoanalysis* (London: Penguin Books, 1974), p.307.

亲不是坚强有力的,而是软弱无力的"①。伊里加蕾也注意到母亲角色对女性的约束,她主张"只有当她们[女性]找到身为女性而不是母亲的价值的时候",她们才能享有同男性平等的权利。"这意味着对几个世纪以来形成的社会－文化价值进行重新思考并彻底改变"②。如果女性能够找到身为女性的价值,这意味着女性不再利用自己生育能力的优势,她们就能够建立一整套同男性价值观念相匹配的女性价值观念。只有当她们成功地做到了这一点的时候,她们才能够理论化女性主体性并因此建构女性身份。

不管女性主义理论家最终能否完美地回答这些问题,我们都应该重新思考母亲身份给女性经验带来的影响,思考现代技术给传统母亲身份带来的冲击,思考女性主体性的真正内涵。我们要牢记伊里加蕾的提醒:

> 我们一定不能再次谋杀母亲了,她已经为我们文化的起源牺牲过一次了。我们必须赋予她以新的生命,赋予母亲以新生命,赋予我们内心的母亲和我们之间的母亲以新生命。我们必须阻止她的欲望被父亲律法所消灭。我们必须给她追求快乐的权利,享受愉悦[*jouissance*]的权利,拥有激情的权利,我们必须恢复她讲话的权利,甚至间或哭泣和愤怒的权利。③

---

① Nancy Chodorow, *Feminism and Psychoanalytic Theory* (New Haven, CT: Yale University Press, 1989), p. 83.

② Luce Irigaray, "Equal or Different?" trans. David Macey, *The Irigaray Reader*, ed. Margaret Whitford (Cambridge, Mass.: Blackwell Publishers, 1991), p. 31.

③ Luce Irigaray, "The Bodily Encounter with the Mother," trans. David Macey, *The Irigaray Reader*, ed. Margaret Whitford (Cambridge, Mass.: Blackwell Publishers, 1991), p. 43.

参考文献
Bibliography

Botticelli, Sandro. "The Birth of Venus." http://www. webtheo. com.

Braidotti, Rosi. "Mothers, Monsters, and Machines." In *Writing on the Body: Female Embodiment and Feminist Theory*. Eds. Katie Conboy, Nadia Medina, and Sarah Standbury. New York: Columbia University Press, 1997. 59-79.

—. "Nomadic Philosopher: A Conversation with Rosi Braidotti." Interviewed by Kathleen O'Grady. Netherlands, August 1995. *Women's Education des femmes*. Spring 1996 (12.1): 35-39.

Briganti, Chiara, and Robert Con Davis. "Luce Irigaray". http://www. press. jhu. edu/books/hopkins_guide_to_literary_theory/ luce_irigaray. html.

Chodorow, Nancy. *Feminism and Psychoanalytic Theory*. New Haven: Yale University Press, 1989.

—. *The Reproduction of Mothering: Psychoanalysis and the Sociology of Gender*. Berkeley: University of California Press, 1978.

Cixous, Hélène. "*Guardian of Language*: An Interview with Hélène Cixous." Interviewed by Kathleen O'Grady. Trans., Eric Prenowitz. http://bailiwick. lib. uiowa. edu/wstudies/cixous.

—. "The Laugh of the Medusa." Trans. Keith Cohen and Paula Cohen. *Signs: Journal of Women in Culture and Society* 1. 4 (Summer 1976): 875-893.

—, and Catherine Clément. *The Newly Born Woman*. Trans. Betsy Wing. Minneapolis, MN: University of Minnesota Press, 1986.

Clarke, Richard L. W. "Luce Irigaray." http://humanities. uwichill. edu. bb/ RLWClarke/PhilWeb/Feminist/Contemporary/Continental/(Post-) Structura- lisms/Deconstruction/Irigaray/Irigaray. htm.

de Beaugrande, Robert. "In Search of Feminist Discourse: The ' Difficult' Case of Luce Irigaray. " *College English* 50. 3 (March 1988): 253-272.

de Beauvoir, Simone. "Interview with Simone de Beauvoir". Interviewed by John Gerassi. *Society* (Jan. -Feb. , 1976), qtd from http://www. marxists. org/reference/subject/philosophy/works/fr/debeauvoir-1976. htm.

—. *The Second Sex*. Trans. H. M. Parshley. Alfred A. Knopf, Inc. , 1952.

Dinnerstein, Dorothy. *The Mermaid and the Minotaur: Sexual Arrangements and Human Malaise*. New York: Harper & Row, Publishers, 1976.

Donchin, Anne. "The Future of Mothering: Reproductive Technology and Feminist Theory". *Hypatia* 1. 2 (Fall 1986): 121-137.

Ehrensaft, Diane. "When Women and Men Mother. " In *Women, Class, and the Feminist Imagination: A Socialist-Feminist Reader*. Eds. Karen V. Hansen and Ilene J. Philipson. Philadelphia: Temple University Press, 1990. 399-430.

Ferguson, Ann. "Motherhood and Sexuality: Some Feminist Questions. " *Hypatia: A Journal of Feminist Philosophy* 1. 2 (Fall 1986): 3-22.

Flax, Jane. *Disputed Subjects: Essays on Psychoanalysis, Politics, and Philosophy*. New York: Routledge, 1993.

Freud, Sigmund. *Totem and Taboo*. Trans. James Strachey. London: Routledge &. Kegan Paul, 1950.

Gilbert, Sandra M. "Introduction. " In *The Newly Born Woman*. Hélène Cixous and Catherine Clement. Trans. Betsy Wing. Minneapolis: University of Minnesota Press, 1986.

Hirsch, Marianne. "Mothers and Daughters". *Signs: Journal of Women in Culture and Society* 7. 1 (1981): 200-222.

Holland, Bridget. "Luce Irigaray: A Biography". http://www. cddc. vt. edu/ feminism/irigaray. html.

http://aurora. wells. edu/ ~ lpurdy.

http://bailiwick. lib. uiowa. edu/wstudies/Braidotti.

http://dsc. discovery. com/convergence/nefertiti/nefertiti. html.

http://epc. buffalo. edu/authors/brossard.

http://feministstudies. org.

http://homepage. mac. com/cparada/GML/Minotaur. html.

http://ms. cc. sunysb. edu/ ~ hvolat/kristeva/kristeva. htm.

http://muse. jhu. edu/journals/hyp.

http://olincenter. uchicago. edu/kass_cv. html.

http://religion. ciweb. org/biobox_hibri. html.

http://shc. stanford. edu/shc/1996-1997/96-97events/suleiman. html.

http://signehammer. com.

http://somaweb. org.

http://w3. liberalarts. iupui. edu/faculty/fgMain. asp? action = view&Faculty-
    Number = 60.

http://womenshistory. about. com/od/motherhood/a/baby_m. htm.

http://www. akhet. co. uk/nefertit. htm.

http://www. alteich. com/links/kass. htm.

http://www. amazon. com/gp/product/1572304502/104-6855247-8176717? v
    = glance&n = 283155&tagActionCode = infoline-20.

http://www. amazon. de/exec/obidos/ASIN/0029094402/ref% 3Dnosim/ase-
    arch/028-6862001-3070907.

http://www. arlindo-correia. com/021003. html.

http://www. cas. buffalo. edu/depts/americanstudies/erapping. shtml.

http://www. columbia. edu/cu/cup/catalog/data/023108/0231082355. HTM.

http://www. cyberpsych. org/homophobia/noframes/chodorow. htm.

http://www. dartmouth. edu/ ~ jewish/faculty/hirsch. html.

http://www. egs. edu/resources/cixous. html.

http://www. egs. edu/resources/deleuze. html.

http://www. fas. harvard. edu/ ~ rll/people/faculty/suleiman. html.

http://www. geryunant. com/Gena. htm.

http://www. halovine. com/scc6. html.

http://www. hup. harvard. edu/reviews/SULSUB_R. html.

http://www. journals. uchicago. edu/Signs/home. html.

http://www. kent. ac. uk/sspssr/staff/sayers. htm.

http://www. kirjasto. sci. fi/rbarthes. htm.

http://www. lillyendowment. org.

http://www. loggia. com/myth/medusa. html.

http://www. margepiercy. com.

http://www. mermaid. net.

http://www. meta-library. net/bio/annas-body. html.

http://www. mscd. edu/ ~ atwoodso.

http://www. nancyfriday. com.

http://www. nostatusquo. com/ACLU/dworkin/.

http://www. nyu. edu/gsas/dept/anthro/faculty/rapp. html.

http://www. owtoad. com.

http://www. pshares. org/Authors/authorDetails. cfm? prmAuthorID = 208.

http://www. sonoma. edu/users/d/daniels/exphil/Simone _ de _ Beauvoir. html.

http://www. sps. cam. ac. uk/stafflist/jmitchell. html.

http://www. sps. cam. ac. uk/stafflist/jmitchell_profile. html.

http://www. studiocleo. com/librarie/blanchot/indexFl. htm.

http://www. sup. org/cgi-bin/search/getmoreinfo. cgi? bookid = 3025 + 3026 &q = paral.

http://www. theory. org. uk/ctr-fouc. htm.

http://www. uic. edu/orgs/cwluherstory/CWLUMemoir/Arcanatalk. html.

http://www. umass. edu/philosophy/faculty/ferguson. htm.

http://www. unex. berkeley. edu/dept/bhs/instructors. html.

http://www. usc. edu/isd/archives/womens_salons/photos/dinnerstein. html.

http://www. uwm. edu/ ~jg.

http://www. webster. edu/ ~ woolflm/chodorow. html.

http://www. webster. edu/ ~ woolflm/women. html.

http://www. writersontheedge. org/arcana. html.

http://www-scf. usc. edu/ ~ cipolla/virtour6. htm.

Huffer, Lynne. *Maternal Pasts, Feminist Futures: Nostalgia, Ethics, and the Question of Difference*. Stanford, CA: Stanford University Press, 1998.

Irigaray, Luce. " Je—Luce Irigaray': A Meeting with Luce Irigaray." Interviewed by Elizabeth Hirsh and Gary A. Olson. Trans. , Elizabeth Hirsh and Gaëton Brulotte. *Hypatia* 10. 2 (Spring 1995): 93-114.

—. "And the One Doesn't Stir without the Other". Trans. Hélène Vivienne Wenzel. *Signs: Journal of Women in Culture and Society* 7. 1 (1981): 60-67.

—. "Equal or Different?" Trans. David Macey. In *The Irigaray Reader*. Ed. Margaret Whitford. Cambridge, Mass.: Blackwell Publishers, 1991. 30-33.

—. "The Bodily Encounter with the Mother." Trans. David Macey. In *The Irigaray Reader*. Ed. Margaret Whitford. Cambridge, Mass.: Blackwell Publishers, 1991. 34-46.

—. "Women-Mothers, the Silent Substratum of the Social Order." Trans. David Macey. In *The Irigaray Reader*. Ed. Margaret Whitford. Cambridge, Mass.: Blackwell Publishers, 1991. 47-52.

—. *An Ethics of Sexual Difference*. Trans. Carolyn Burke and Gillian C. Gill. London: The Athlone Press, 1993.

—. *Je, Tu, Nous: Toward a Culture of Difference*. Trans. Alison Martin. New York: Routledge, 1993.

—. *Thinking the Difference: Toward a Peaceful Revolution*. Trans. Karin Montin. London: The Athlone Press, 1994.

Jacobus, Mary. "Freud's Mnemonic: Women, Screen Memories, and Feminist Nostalgia." In *Women and Memory*. Eds. Margaret A. Lourie, Domna C. Stanton, and Martha Vicinus. *Michigan Quarterly Review* 8 (1987): 117-139.

Jasken, Julie. http://www. engl. niu. edu/wac/cixous_intro. html.

Klages, Mary. http://www. colorado. edu/English/ENGL2012Klages/cixous. html.

Kristeva, Julia. "About Chinese Women." Trans. Séan Hand. In *The Kristeva Reader*. Ed. Toril Moi. New York: Columbia University Press, 1986. 139-159.

—. "Women's Time." Trans. Alice Jardine and Harry Blake. In *The Kristeva Reader*. Ed. Toril Moi. New York: Columbia University Press, 1986. 188-213.

Le Van, Alicia. http://www. perseus. tufts. edu/classes/finALp. html.

Lechte, John. "Luce Irigaray". http://www. envf. port. ac. uk/illustration/images/vlsh/psycholo/irigaray. htm.

Leighton, Frederic. "The Return of Persephone." http://www. loggia. com/art/19th/leighton16. html.

Lindemans, Micha F. http://www. pantheon. org/articles/m/minotaur. html.

Mitchell, Juliet. "Feminism and Psychoanalysis at the Millennium." *Women: A Cultural Review* 10. 2 (Summer 1999):185-191.

—. *Psychoanalysis and Feminism: A Radical Reassessment of Freudian Psychoanalysis*. London: Penguin Books, 1974.

Moi, Toril. *What Is a Woman? And Other Essays*. New York: Oxford University Press, 1999.

Myers, Ellen. "Forerunner of New Age Madness: A Critique of Norman O. Brown". http://www. creationism. org/csshs/v13n1p07. htm.

O' Leary, Stephen. http://www. amazon. com/gp/cdp/member-reviews/A2LM0I6AJ00Y25/ref = cm_cr_auth/104-9915692-6092755.

Oliver, Kelly. "Julia Kristeva." http://www. cddc. vt. edu/feminism/Kristeva. html.

—. "Julia Kristeva." http://www. press. jhu. edu/books/hopkins_guide_to_literary_theory/julia_kristeva. html.

Parrine, Mary Jane. "Hélène Cixous." http://prelectur. stanford. edu/lecturers/cixous.

Pope, Deborah. "Adrienne Rich". *The Oxford Companion to Women's*

Writing in the United States. Oxford University Press, 1995; http://www. english. uiuc. edu/maps/poets/m_r/rich/bio. htm.

Rapping, Elayne. "The Future of Motherhood: Some Unfashionably Visionary Thoughts". In *Women, Class, and the Feminist Imagination: A Socialist-Feminist Reader.* Eds. Karen V. Hansen and Ilene J. Philipson. Philadelphia: Temple University Press, 1990. 537-548.

Rhode, Deborah L. *Theoretical Perspectives on Sexual Difference.* Binghampton: Vail-Ballou Press, 1990.

Rich, Adrienne. "The Possibilities of an Engaged Art: An Interview with Adrienne Rich." Interviewed by Ruth E. C. Prince. http://www. english. uiuc. edu/maps/poets/m_r/rich/onlineints. htm.

—. *Of Woman Born: Motherhood as Experience and Institution.* New York: W. W. Norton & Company Inc. , 1976.

Sato, Kumiko. http://www. personal. psu. edu/staff/k/x/kxs334/academic/theory/chodorow_mothering. html.

Schmitz, Christopher. http://www. amazon. com/gp/cdp/member-reviews/A3CM1CDUSWYDIO/104-9915692-6092755?%5Fencoding = UTF8&display = public&page =4.

Schor, Naomi. "Previous Engagements: The Receptions of Irigaray." In *Engaging with Irigaray: Feminist Philosophy and Modern European Thought.* Eds. Carolyn Burke, Naomi Schor and Margaret Whitford. New York: Columbia University Press, 1994. 3-14.

Simons, Margaret A. "Is *The Second Sex* Beauvoir's Application of Sartrean Existentialism?" http://www. bu. edu/wcp/Papers/Gend/GendSimo. htm.

Spivak, Gayatri Chakravorty. "French Feminism in an International Frame." *Yale French Studies* 62 (1981):154-185.

Stamm, Alice. http://www. dearest. com/transcripts/friday720. htm.

Stanton, Domna C. "Difference on Trial: A Critique of the Maternal Metaphor in Cixous, Irigaray and Kristeva." In *The Poetics of Gender.* Ed. Nancy K. Miller. New York: Columbia University Press, 1986. 157-

182.

Stanworth, Michelle. "Reproductive Technologies and the Deconstruction of Motherhood." In *Reproductive Technologies*: *Gender*, *Motherhood and Medicine*. Ed. Michelle Stanworth. Cambridge: Polity Press, 1987. 10-35.

Suleiman, Susan Rubin. "Writing and Motherhood." In *The (M)other Tongue*: *Essays in Feminist Psychoanalytic Interpretation*. Eds. Shirley Garner, Claire Kahane, and Madelon Sprengnether. Ithaca, NY: Cornell University Press, 1985. 352-377.

Wenzel, Hélène Vivienne. "Introduction to Luce Irigaray's 'And the One Doesn't Stir without the Other'". *Signs*: *Journal of Women in Culture and Society* 7.1 (1981):56-59.

陈欢著."正本清源"女性"圣经".《中华读书报》2004 年 8 月 4 日第 3 版.

刘岩著. 西方现代戏剧中的母亲身份研究. 中国书籍出版社,2004

鲁刚,郑述谱编译. 希腊罗马神话词典. 中国社会科学出版社,1984

萨莉·J·肖尔茨著. 龚晓京译. 波伏娃. 中华书局,汤姆森学习出版集团, 2002

吴康如著.《第二性》写作动机与出版始末.荒林主编《两性视野》.知识出版社, 2003 年. 第 92～100 页.

母亲身份与女性身份研究阅读书目
Further Readings in Motherhood
and Female Identity

Appignanesi, Lisa. *Simone de Beauvoir*. Penguin Books, 1988.

Arcana, Judith. *Our Mothers' Daughters*. Berkeley: Shameless Hussy Press, 1979.

Assiter, Alison. *Enlightened Women: Modernist Feminism in a Postmodern Age*. New York: Routledge, 1996.

Bair, Deirdre. *Simone de Beauvoir: A Biography*. New York: Touchstone, 1991.

Baruch, Elaine H., and Lucienne J. Serrano, eds. *Women Analyze Women in France, England and the United States*. New York: New York Univ. Press, 1988.

Bauer, Nancy. *Simone de Beauvoir, Philosophy, and Feminism*. New York: Columbia University Press, 2001.

Benjamin, Jessica. *The Bonds of Love: Psychoanalysis, Feminism, and the Problem of Domination*. New York: Pantheon Books, 1988.

Bennett, Joy, and Gabriella Hochmann. *Simone de Beauvoir: An Annotated Bibliography*. Garland Pub, 1989.

Benvenuto, Bice, and Roger Kennedy. *The Works of Jacques Lacan: An Introduction*. New York: St. Martin's Press, 1986.

Brenkman, John. *Straight Male Modern: A Cultural Critique of Psychoanalysis*. New York: Routledge, 1993.

Brennan, Teresa, ed. *Between Feminism and Psychoanalysis*. Routledge, 1989.

Burke, Carolyn. "Irigaray through the Looking Glass." *Feminist Studies* 7 (Summer 1981).

—, Naomi Schor, and Margaret Whitford, ed. *Engaging with Irigaray*. Columbia University Press, 1994.

Butler, Judith. *Gender Trouble: Feminism and the Subversion of Identity*. New York: Routledge, 1990.

—. "The Body Politics of Julia Kristeva." *Hypatia* 3 (1989).

Caws, Mary Ann. "Tel Quel: Text and Revolution." *Diacritics* 3.1 (1973): 2-8.

Chodorow, Nancy. *Feminism and Psychoanalytic Theory*. New Haven, CT: Yale University Press, 1989.

—. *The Power of Feelings: Personal Meaning in Psychoanalysis, Gender, and Culture*. New Haven, CT: Yale University Press, 1999.

—. *The Reproduction of Mothering: Psychoanalysis and the Sociology of Gender*. Berkeley, CA: University of California Press, 1978.

Cixous, Hélène. "Aller à la mer." Trans. Barbara Kerslake. *Modern Drama* 27 (1984): 546-548.

—. "Castration or Decapitation?" Trans. Annette Kuhn. *Signs: Journal of Women in Culture and Society* 7.1 (1981):41-55.

—. *Coming to Writing and Other Essays*. Trans. Sarah Cornell, et al. Ed. Deborah Jenson. Cambridge, Mass.: Harvard University Press, 1991.

—. "The Laugh of Medusa". Trans. Keith Cohen and Paula Cohen. *Signs: Journal of Women in Culture and Society* 1.4 (Summer 1976): 875-893.

—, and Catherine Clement. *The Newly Born Woman*. Trans. Betsy Wing. Minneapolis: University of Minnesota Press, 1986.

Clark, Suzanne and Kathleen Hulley. "An Interview with Julia Kristeva: Cultural Strangeness and the Subject in Crisis." *Discourse: A Review of the Liberal Arts* 13.1 (Fall-Winter, 1990-1991):149-180.

Conboy, Katie, Nadir Medina, and Sarah Standbury, eds. *Writing on the Body: Female Embodiment and Feminist Theory*. New York: Columbia

University Press, 1997.

Crownfield, David R., ed. *Body/Text in Julia Kristeva: Religion, Women and Psychoanalysis*. Albany, NY: State University of New York Press, 1992.

de Beaugrande, Robert. "In Search of Feminist Discourse: The 'Difficult' Case of Luce Irigaray." *College English* 50.3 (March 1988): 253-272.

de Beauvoir, Simone. *The Second Sex*. Trans. H. M. Parshley. Harmondsworth: Penguin Books Ltd., 1972.

De Nooy, Julia. *Derrida, Kristeva, and the Dividing Line: An Articulation of Two Theories of Difference*. New York: Garland Pub., 1998.

Dew, Chris. *From One Chora to Another: Kristeva, Chora, Abjection*. Clayton: Monash University, 1996.

Dinnerstein, Dorothy. *The Mermaid and the Minotaur*. New York: Harper & Row, 1976.

Diquinzio, Patrice. *The Impossibility of Motherhood: Feminism, Individualism, and the Problem of Mothering*. Routledge, 1999.

Doane, Janice L., and Devon Hodges. *From Klein to Kristeva: Psychoanalytic Feminism*. Ann Arbor, MI: University of Michigan Press, 1992.

Elliott, Anthony. *Social Theory and Psychoanalysis in Transition: Self and Society from Freud to Kristeva*. Oxford: Basil Blackwell, 1992.

—, and Stephen Frosh. *Psychoanalysis in Contexts: Paths Between Theory and Modern Culture*. New York: Routledge, 1995.

Evans, Mary. *Simone de Beauvoir, a Feminist Mandarin*. New York: Routledge, 1985.

Ferguson, Ann. "Sex War: The Debate between Radical and Libertarian Feminists." *Signs: Journal of Women in Culture and Society* 19.1 (Autumn 1984): 106-112.

Finzi, Silvia. *Mothering: Toward a New Psychoanalytic Construction*. Trans. Katherine Jason. Guilford Press, 1995.

Firestone, Shulamith. *The Dialectic of Sex: The Case for Feminist*

Revolution. Farrar Straus & Giroux, 1970.

Flax, Jane. *Disputed Subjects: Essays on Psychoanalysis, Politics, and Philosophy*. New York: Routledge, 1993.

—. "The Conflict between Nurturance and Autonomy in Mother-daughter Relationships and Within Feminism." *Feminist Studies* 2 (1978): 171-189.

—. *Thinking Fragments: Psychoanalysis, Feminism, and Postmodernism in the Contemporary West*. Berkeley, CA: The University of California Press, 1991.

Fletcher, John, and Andrew Benjamin, eds. *Abjection, Melancholia, and Love: The Work of Julia Kristeva*. London and New York: Routledge, 1990.

Freud, Sigmund. *The Standard Edition of the Complete Psychological Works of Sigmund Freud*. Trans. James Strachey. London: The Hogarth Press, 1964.

—. *Totem and Taboo*. Trans. James Strachey. London: Routledge &. Kegan Paul, 1950.

Friday, Nancy. *My Mother/My Self: The Daughter's Search for Identity*. New York: Dell, 1977.

Fuss, Diana. *Essentially Speaking: Feminism, Nature, and Difference*. New York: Routledge, 1989.

Galligan, Carol. *In a Different Voice: Psychological Theory and Women's Development*. Cambridge, Mass. : Harvard University Press, 1982.

Gallop, Jane. *Feminism and Psychoanalysis: The Daughter's Seduction*. London: The Macmillan Press Ltd, 1982.

—. *Reading Lacan*. Ithaca, N.Y. : Cornell University Press, 1985.

Garry, Ann, and Marilyn Pearsall, eds. *Women, Knowledge and Reality*. Routledge, 1996.

Gilbert, Sandra M. "Introduction." *The Newly Born Woman*. Hélène Cixous and Catherine Clement. Trans. Betsy Wing. Minneapolis: University of Minnesota Press, 1986.

Glenn, Evelyn Nakano, Grace Chang, and Linda Rennie Forcey, eds. *Mothering: Ideology, Experience, and Agency*. Routledge, 1993.

Gross, Elizabeth A. *Irigaray and the Divine*. Local Consumption Occasional Papers (Monograph No. 9), 1986.

—. *Jacques Lacan: A Feminist Introduction*. Routledge, 1990.

—. *Sexual Subversions: Three French Feminists*. Boston: Unwin Hyman, 1985.

—. *Space, Time, and Perversion: Essays on the Politics of Bodies*. New York: Routledge, 1995.

Hansen, Karen V., and Ilene J. Philipson, eds. *Women, Class and the Feminist Imagination: A Socialist-Feminist Reader*. Philadelphia: Temple University Press, 1990.

Heath, Jane. *Simone de Beauvoir*. Prentice Hall, 1989.

Huffer, Lynne. *Maternal Pasts, Feminist Futures: Nostalgia, Ethics, and the Question of Difference*. Stanford, CA: Stanford University Press, 1998.

Humm, Maggie, ed. *Feminisms: A Reader*. New York: Harvester Wheatsheaf, 1992.

Huntington, Patricia. *Ecstatic Subjects, Utopia and Recognition: Kristeva, Heidegger, Irigaray*. Albany, NY: State University of New York Press, 1998.

Irigaray, Luce. "And the One Doesn't Stir without the Other." Trans. Hélène Vivienne Wenzel. *Signs: Journal of Women in Culture and Society* 7.1 (1981): 60-67.

—. *An Ethics of Sexual Difference*. Trans. Carolyn Burke and Gillian C. Gill. London: The Athlone Press, 1993.

—. *Elemental Passions*. Trans. Joanne Collie and Judith Still. New York: Routledge, 1992.

—. *I Love to You: Sketch for a Felicity Within History*. Trans. Alison Martin. New York: Routledge, 1996.

—. "Is the Subject of Science Sexed?" Trans. Edith Oberle. *Cultural*

Critique (Fall 1985): 73-88.

—. "Is the Subject of Science Sexes?" Trans. Carol M. Bove. *Hypatia* 2 (Fall 1987): 65-87.

—. "Je—Luce Irigaray': A Meeting with Luce Irigaray." Interview with Elizabeth Hirsh and Gary A. Olson. Trans. Elizabeth Hirsh and Gaëton Brulotte. *Hypatia* 10.2 (Spring 1995): 93-114.

—. *Je, Tu, Nous: Toward a Culture of Difference.* Trans. Alison Martin. New York: Routledge, 1993.

—. *Marine Lover: Of Friedrich Nietzsche.* Trans. Gillian C. Gill. New York: Columbia University Press, 1991.

—. "Questions to Emmanuel Levinas on the Divinity of Love." Trans. Margaret Whitford. In *Re-Reading Levinas.* Ed. Robert Bernasconi and Simon Critchley. Bloomington: Indiana Univ. Press, 1991.

—. *Sexes and Genealogies.* Trans. Gillian C. Gill. New York: Columbia University Press, 1993.

—. "Sorcerer Love: A Reading of Plato's 'Symposium: Diotima's Speech'." *Hypatia* 5 (Winter 1989): 32-44.

—. *Speculum of the Other Woman.* Trans. Gillian C. Gill. Ithaca, N.Y.: Cornell University Press, 1985.

—. "The Question of the Other." *Yale French Studies* 87 (1995).

—. "Thinking Life as Reason: An Interview with Stephen Pluhacek and Heidi Bostic." *Man and World* 29 (1996): 343-360.

—. *Thinking the Difference.* Trans. Karin Montin. London: The Athlone Press, 1994.

—. *This Sex Which Is Not One.* Trans. Catherine Porter and Carolyn Burke. Ithaca, N.Y.: Cornell University Press, 1985.

—. *To Be Two.* Trans. Monique M. Rhodes and Marco F. Cocito-Monoc. London: The Athlone Press, 2000.

—. "Women, the Sacred, and Money." *Paragraph: A Journal of Modern Critical Theory* 8 (Oct 1986): 6-17.

—. "Women's Exile." Trans. Couze Venn. *Ideology and Consciousness* 1

(1977):62-76.

Ives, Kelly. *Cixous, Irigaray, Kristeva: The Jouissance of French Feminism*. Kidderminster: Crescent Moon, 1996.

Jardine, Alice. *Gynesis: Configurations of Woman and Modernity*. Cornell University Press, 1986.

Jones, Ann Rosalind. "Julia Kristeva on Femininity: The Limits of a Semiotic Politics." *Feminist Review* 18 (1984).

Kristeva, Julia. *Black Sun: Depression and Melancholy*. Trans. Leon Roudiez. New York: Columbia University Press, 1989.

—. *Desire in Language: A Semiotic Approach to Literature and Art*. Ed. Leon Roudiez. Trans. Thomas Gora, Alice Jardine, Leon Roudiez. New York: Columbia University Press, 1980.

—. *In the Beginning Was Love: Psychoanalysis and Faith*. Trans. Arthur Goldhammer. New York: Columbia University Press, 1987.

—. *Powers of Horror: An Essay on Abjection*. Trans. Leon Roudiez. New York: Columbia University Press, 1982.

—. *Revolution in Poetic Language*. Trans. Margaret Waller. New York: Columbia University Press, 1984.

Lacan, Jacques. *Écrits: A Selection*. Trans. Alan Sheridan. New York: W. W. Norton & Company Inc. , 1977.

—. *The Four Fundamental Concepts of Psycho-analysis*. Trans. Alan Sheridan. New York: W. W. Norton & Company Inc. , 1978.

Lechte, John. *Julia Kristeva*. London and New York: Routledge, 1990.

—, and Mary Zournazi, ed. *After the Revolution: On Kristeva*. Sydney, Australia: Artspace, 1998.

Marks, Elaine, and Isabelle de Courtivron, eds. *New French Feminisms*. New York: Harvester Wheatsheaf, 1981.

Miller, N. K. , ed. *The Poetics of Gender*. New York: Columbia University Press, 1986.

Mitchell, Juliet. "Feminism and Psychoanalysis at the Millennium." *Women: A Cultural Review* 10. 2 (Summer 1999): 185-191.

—. *Psychoanalysis and Feminism: A Radical Reassessment of Freudian Psychoanalysis*. London: Penguin Books, 1974.

—, and Jacqueline Rose, eds. *Feminine Sexuality: Jacques Lacan and the école freudienne*. Trans. Jacqueline Rose. London: The Macmillan Press Ltd, 1982.

Moi, Toril, ed. *The Kristeva Reader*. New York: Columbia University Press, 1986.

—. *Sexual/Textual Politics: Feminist Literary Theory*. New York: Methuen & Co. Ltd., 1985.

—. *Simone de Beauvoir: The Making of an Intellectual Woman*. Cambridge, Mass.: Blackwell Publishers, 1994.

—. *What Is a Woman? And Other Essays*. New York: Oxford University Press, 1999.

Mortley, Raoul, ed. *French Philosophers in Conversation*. London: Routledge, 1991.

Mothers and Mothering: An Annotated Feminist Bibliography. Garland Pub, 1991.

Ohmann, Richard. "In Lieu of a New Rhetoric." *Professing the New Rhetorics: A Sourcebook*. Ed. Theresa Enos and Stuart C. Brown. Englewood Cliffs, N. J.: A Blair Press Book, 1994.

Okely, Judith. *Simone de Beauvoir*. Pantheon, 1986.

Oliver, Kelly, ed. *The Portable Kristeva*. New York, Columbia University Press, 1997.

—. *Ethics, Politics and Difference in Julia Kristeva's Writing*. New York: Routledge, 1993.

—. "Julia Kristeva's Feminist Revolutions," *Hypatia* 8.3 (Summer 1993): 94-114.

—. *Reading Kristeva, Unraveling the Double-bind*. Bloomington: Indiana University Press, 1983.

Orr, Catherine M. "Charting the Currents of the Third Wave." *Hypatia* 12.3 (Summer 1997): 29-45.

Pateman, Carole, and Elizabeth Gross, eds. *Feminist Challenges: Social and Political Theory*. Allen & Unwin, 1986.

Payne, Michael. *Reading Theory: An Introduction to Lacan, Derrida, and Kristeva*. Boston: Blackwell Publishers, 1993.

Plaza, Monique. "'Phallomorphic Power' and the Psychology of 'Woman.'" *Ideology and Consciousness* 4 (1978).

Reddy, Maureen T. , et al, eds. *Mother Journeys: Feminists Writing About Mothering*. Spinsters Ink, 1994.

Reineke, Martha J. *Sacrificed Lives: Kristeva on Women and Violence*. Bloomington: Indiana University Press, 1997.

Rhode, Deborah. *Theoretical Perspectives on Sexual Difference*. New Haven and London: Yale University Press, 1990.

Rich, Adrienne. *Of Woman Born: Motherhood as Experience and Institution*. New York: W. W. Norton & Company Inc. , 1976.

Rossi, Alice. "A Biosocial Perspective on Parenting." *Daedalus* 106. 2 (1977): 1-31.

—. "Considering 'A Biosocial Perspective on Parenting': Reply by Alice Rossi." *Signs* 4 (1979): 712-717.

—. "Materialism, Sexuality and the New Feminism." *Contemporary Sexual Behavior*. Eds. Joseph Zubin and John Money. Baltimore: John Hopkins University Press, 1973.

Rubin, Gayle. "The Traffic in Women: Notes on the 'Political Economy' of Sex." In *Toward an Anthropology of Women*. Ed. Rayna R. Reiter. New York: Monthly Review Press, 1975. 157-210.

Schor, Naomi and Elizabeth Weed, eds. *The Essential Difference*. Bloomington: Indiana Univ. Press, 1991.

Schwartzer, Alice. *After the Second Sex*. Pantheon, 1984.

Sellers, Susan, ed. *The Hélène Cixous Reader*. London: Routledge, 1994.

—, ed. *Writing Differences: Readings from the Seminar of Hélène Cixous*. New York, NY: St. Martin's Press, Inc. , 1988.

—. *Hélène Cixous: Authorship, Autobiography and Love*. Oxford: Polity

Press, 1996.

Shiach, Morag. *Hélène Cixous: A Politics of Writing.* London: Routledge, 1991.

Silverman, Kaja. *The Acoustic Mirror: The Female Voice in Psychoanalysis and Cinema.* Bloomington: Indiana University Press, 1988.

Simons, Margaret A. *Beauvoir and the Second Sex: Feminism, Race, and the Origins of Existentialism.* Lanham, Maryland: Rowman & Littlefield Publishers, 1999.

Smith, Anna. *Julia Kristeva: Readings of Exile and Estrangement.* New York: St. Martin's Press, 1996.

Smith, Anne-Marie. *Julia Kristeva: Speaking the Unspeakable.* London: Pluto Press, 1998.

Smith, Joseph H., and Afaf M. Mahfouz, eds. *Psychoanalysis, Feminism, and the Future of Gender.* Baltimore: The John Hopkins University Press, 1994.

Spivak, Gayatri Chakravorty. *Outside in the Teaching Machine.* New York: Routledge, 1993.

Sprengnether, Madelon. *The Spectral Mother: Freud, Feminism, and Psychoanalysis.* Ithaca, N. Y.: Cornell University Press, 1990.

Stanworth, Michelle, ed. *Reproduction Technologies: Gender, Motherhood and Medicine.* Cambridge: Polity Press, 1987.

Storey, John. *An Introduction to Cultural Theory and Popular Culture.* Athens: The University of Georgia Press, 1998.

Trebilcot, Joyce, ed. *Mothering: Essays in Feminist Theory.* Rowman & Littlefield, 1984.

van Mens-Veerhulst, Janneke, and Karlein Schreurs. *Daughtering and Mothering: Female Subjectivity Reanalysed.* Routledge, 1993.

Vasseleu, Cathryn. *Textures of Light: Vision and Touch in Irigaray, Levinas and Merleau-Ponty.* Routledge, 1998.

Whitford, Margaret, ed. *The Irigaray Reader.* Cambridge: Basil Blackwell, 1991.

—. "Irigaray's Body Symbolic." *Hypatia* 6. 3 (Fall 1991): 97-110.

—. *Luce Irigaray: Philosophy in the Feminine*. Routledge, 1991.

Whitmarsh, Anne. *Simone de Beauvoir and the Limits of Commitment*. New York: Cambridge University Press, 1981.

Winnicott, D. W. *Playing and Reality*. London: Tavistock Publications, 1971.

Xu, Ping. "Irigaray's Mimicry and the Problem of Essentialism." *Hypatia* 10. 4 (Fall 1995): 76-89.

Young-Bruehl, Elisabeth, ed. *Freud on Women: A Reader*. New York: W. W. Norton & Company, 1990.

Ziarek, Ewa. "At the Limits of Discourse: Heterogeneity, Alterity, and the Maternal Body in Kristeva's Thought." *Hypatia*7 (1992).

Acknowledgements

The editors and publishers of the book would like to thank the following for permission to reprint their materials:

"Mother," from *The Second Sex* by Simone De Beauvoir, translated by H. M. Parshley, copyright 1952 and renewed 1980 by Alfred A. Knopf, a division of Random House, Inc. Used by permission of Alfred A. Knopf, a division of Random House, Inc.

"The 'Sacred Calling'," by Adrienne Rich, from *Of Woman Born*: Motherhood as Experience and Institution. Copyright © 1986, 1976 by W. W. Norton & Company, Inc. Used by permission of the author and W. W. Norton & Company, Inc.

"The Domestication of Motherhood," by Adrienne Rich, from *Of Woman Born*: Motherhood as Experience and Institution. Copyright © 1986, 1976 by W. W. Norton & Company, Inc. Used by permission of the author and W. W. Norton & Company, Inc.

"The Fantasy of the Perfect Mother", by Nancy Chodorow and Susan Contratto, from *Feminism and Psychoanalytic Theory*. Copyright © 1989 by Yale University Press. Reprinted by permission from the publisher.

"About Chinese Women," by Julia Kristerva, from *The Kristeva Reader*, by

Toril Moi. Copyright © 1986 Columbia University Press. Reprinted with permission of the publisher.

"The Laugh of the Medusa," by Hélène Cixous, translated by Keith Cohen and Paula Cohen, from *Signs*: *Journal of Women in Culture and Society* 1976, vol. 1, no. 4. Copyright © 1976 by The University of Chicago. Reprinted with permission of the publisher.

"And the One Doesn't Stir without the Other," by Luce Irigaray, translated by Hélène Vivienne Wenzel, from *Signs*: *Journal of Women in Culture and Society* 1981, vol. 7, no. 1. Copyright © 1981 by The University of Chicago. Reprinted with permission of the publisher.

"Mothers and Daughters," by Marianne Hirsch, from *Signs*: *Journal of Women in Culture and Society* 1981, vol. 7, no. 1. Copyright © 1981 by The University of Chicago. Reprinted with permission of the publisher.

"Motherhood and Sexuality," by Ann Ferguson, from *Hypatia*: *A Journal of Feminist Philosophy* 1986, vol. 1, no. 2. Copyright © 1986 by Indiana University Press. Reprinted with permission of the publisher.

"The Future of Mothering: Reproductive Technology and Feminist Theory," by Anne Donchin, from *Hypatia*: *A Journal of Feminist Philosophy* 1986, vol. 1, no. 2. copyright © 1986 by Indiana University Press. Reprinted with permission of the publisher.

"Mothers, Monsters, and Machines," by Rosi Braidotti, from *Nomadic Subjects*, by Rosi Braidotti. Copyright © 1994 Columbia University Press. Reprinted with permission of the publisher.

After painstaking effort, we still cannot contact the copyright holders of other essays in the book.

编 后 记

　　《女性身份研究读本》和《母亲身份研究读本》是体例相同、内容相关的两部介绍西方女性身份理论代表观点的著作。

　　编写这两部书的缘起可以追溯到 2003 年。那时我刚刚从香港中文大学完成博士学位的研究来到坐落在白云山下的广东外语外贸大学任教，校园的宁静美丽让我可以继续潜心读书。虽说秀丽的南方不像北方那样四季分明，但在背依白云山、面傍云溪河的广外，怒放的木棉、淡雅的紫荆、沁肺的桂花香，还有坚韧的白千层，同样给生活在这里的每一个有心人带来不同的风景。所有这一切让初来南方的我对生活充满了新的憧憬和期盼。

　　在指导硕士研究生完成学业和撰写毕业论文的过程中，我发现国内直接引进的国外关于性别研究的成果不多，学生苦于很难寻找到比较新的国外文献，研究偶而陷入困境。我于是想到应该在总结自己研究经验的基础上把西方的最新研究成果介绍给更多的国内学者，并逐渐梳理出西方女性身份理论发展的主要脉络。

　　我在 2004 年秋季设计了两本书的基本框架：

　　《女性身份研究读本》一书选取的 20 篇理论文章被划分在三个大的部分："精神分析理论体系中的性别身份"，"女性主义框架中的性别身份"和"多元文化语境下的性别身份"。文章的时间跨度从弗洛伊德的"处女的禁忌"（1918 年）到朱丽叶·米切尔的"千禧之际的女性主义与精神分析"（1999 年），长达 80 余年，基本涵盖了 20 世纪西方关于女性身份问题的主要思想观点。书中选取的理论文章带有鲜明的时代特征。在以弗洛伊德为代表的精神分析理论中，女性的身份参照男性身份定义和描述。西方女性主义的主要代表人物对此进行了批判，并试图创造性地定义女性身份。而在多元文化语境下，女性身份则具有了多重的、流动的特征。读者可以从我们选取的著作中清晰地看到西方女性身份研究领域主要思想的流变。

《母亲身份研究读本》一书选取的 20 篇理论文章也被划分在三个大的部分："自然召唤与家庭化——西方文明中的母性传统"，"边缘、消音与癫狂——女性主义框架中的母亲"和"科技、解构与后现代——后现代语境下的母亲身份"。从波伏娃的"母亲"（1949 年）到布雷多蒂的"母亲、魔鬼与机器"（1994 年），文章时间跨度近半个世纪。同样，读者也可以看到在对待母亲身份问题上西方主要观点的演变过程。在传统父权体制下，母亲身份被视为女性的天职，是一种自然召唤。许多女性主义理论家都注意到母亲身份在父权体制下被边缘、母亲话语被消音的现实。而在后现代语境下，随着人们围绕生育技术展开的试验，母亲的身份被解构。女性由于具有生育能力的身体而不断被塑造成与魔鬼同形的怪物，这仿佛继续着母亲在西方文明中承载的象征意义。

我从 2006 年秋季开始联系文章版权事宜。出于对知识产权的尊重，也考虑到国内学者做研究时引用的方便，我们非常努力争取联系上所有的版权拥有者。这一过程因为有了互联网而变得快捷，其中有几篇文章获得出版社或杂志社授权免费使用，但遗憾的是，至今仍然未能同个别出版社或作者取得联系，我们已在书中作了说明。

广外文印中心的周丹、杨焕英、刘春明、巫彩霞几位老师协助我们把全部理论文章扫描并转变为电子文本，我指导的几名博士、硕士研究生参与了文章的校对工作。《女性身份研究读本》所选文章的校对工作由邱小轻、詹俊峰和梁婷婷承担，《母亲身份研究读本》所选文章的校对工作由洪文慧、颜婷和吴桐承担。这几位年轻人先后交叉校对了两遍，每人至少细读了 10 到 12 篇文章。虽然他们个人的研究兴趣并不都集中在性别问题，但我相信，这样的基础性工作让他们经历了一部书的诞生过程，品味其中的甘苦，培养他们的学术研究意识和严谨的学术规范，为他们未来的学术道路开创了良好的开端。

这两部书的出版得到武汉大学出版社外语事业部谢群英女士的大力支持。在此之前我们有过很好的合作，她帮助我院策划出版了"新视角文学与文化系列教材"，目前已正式出版 5 本，另有 5 本也将于今年陆续出版。更重要的是彼此间的信任。谢女士和她的同事具有敏感的编辑眼光和专业的出版经验，这使得出版过程务实而高效。

我和我的同事希望这两部书能够为从事性别研究、女性主义研究的国内各高等院校或研究机构的教师、学者、研究人员、硕士和博士研究生以及社会各界对性别问题感兴趣的人士提供一些引导。由于所选理论文章时间跨度大，一些文章内容新，加上国内介绍很少，一些理论术语的译法有待规范，所以在书中我们只能使用目前较为合理的译法。同时，西方关于女性身份的研究著作和文章浩如烟海，我们的选取虽然有一定的标准，但一定有挂一漏万之嫌。由于我们对西方哲学思想的背景了解得还不够透彻，导读可能有一些未尽如人意之处，还请读者、同行、专家谅解并提出宝贵的意见。在引介西方最新文学文化批评理论方面，国内学者尚需续续努力。

　　在书稿付梓之际，我谨代表两部书的编者对所有帮助过我们的朋友表示衷心的谢意！

刘　岩

2007 年 6 月于广外